Catholic Christianity

A Guide to the Way, the Truth, and the Life

Richard Chilson

Paulist Press ◊ New York ◊ New Jersey

Index prepared by Dolores Deikmann.

IMPRIMATUR
John S. Cummins,
Bishop of Oakland

Date: June 15, 1987

The Imprimatur is an official declaration that a book or pamphlet is free of doctrinal or moral error. No implication is contained therein that those who have granted the Imprimatur agree with the contents, opinions or statements expressed.

Library of Congress Cataloging-in-Publication Data

Chilson, Richard.
    Catholic Christianity.

    Includes bibliographies and index.
    1. Catholic Church—Doctrines.   I. Title.
BX1751.2.C455   1987   282   87-7028
ISBN 0-8091-2878-0 (pbk.)

Published by Paulist Press
997 Macarthur Boulevard
Mahwah, New Jersey 07430

Printed and bound in the
United States of America

◇

Contents

INTRODUCTION

THE WAY

THE TRUTH

THE LIFE

EPILOGUE

◇

Appreciations

I want to thank all those who read this manuscript and offered their suggestions. Among them are Jean Marie Hiesberger, Robert Hamma, Richard Gula, Lawrence Cunningham, Thomas Hart, Bobette Adcock, Pheme Perkins.

And my Paulist brothers—Kevin Lynch who asked for it in the first place, George Fitzgerald, Thomaso Kane, John E. Lynch, Bob O'Donnell, Ken McGuire, Dick Sparks, Larry Boadt.

Pentecost 1986

IN THANKSGIVING FOR
GOOD POPE JOHN
WHO OPENED THE WINDOWS

INTRODUCTION

◊   **A Guide to Christianity**

◇

1. A Guide to Christianity

The Purpose of This Book
The Structure of This Book
A Guide to References

Christianity is the religion which proclaims the good news of Jesus Christ. It encompasses a multitude of communities called churches in various shades of agreement concerning details. However the common foundation is Jesus—his life and teachings, his death and resurrection.

Among these churches, one claims an authoritative position centering upon the Bishop of Rome: a sign of unity from earliest days. This guide introduces the Roman Catholic expression of Christianity. Although much is held in common, in the few places (often crucial) where various churches disagree, this guide presents the Roman Catholic viewpoint.

The essence of Christianity, detailed throughout this book, can be summarized by four passages from Scripture. Jesus calls people to "repent and believe in the gospel" (Mk 1:14). St. Peter confesses that this Jesus is "the Christ, the son of the living God" (Mt 16:16). St. John says, "God so loved the world that he gave his only Son, that whoever believes in him should not perish but have eternal life" (Jn 3:16). And St. Paul speaks of Christian life as putting on Christ: "it is no longer I who live but Christ who lives in me" (Gal 3:20). In a sense this entire book is merely a commentary upon these four sentences.

The Purpose of This Book

This is a reference book. It refers to something outside itself—the Christian religion. It is a road map to the territory. The map is not the territory; the map only charts the territory, pointing out its features.

By necessity this book is a map which charts the language of Christianity. Language is the primary bearer of meaning. This guide introduces the world of Catholic Christian language: the vocabulary of the faith. It shows the relationships between different words, ideas and concepts.

Since Christianity is centered upon God's word addressed to humankind, the language is drawn into the sacred. So, secondly, the book refers frequently to *the* book—the Bible—the most authoritative presentation of our faith.

The book refers to other books as well. It is merely an introduction, a *vade mecum* to use the old Latin. To go deeper into certain matters you will be referred to other books. But words do not exhaust our faith. They point to other symbols in which faith is contained and passed on—ritual, art, community, charity. These symbols also speak for Jesus, the Word.

Since language is so important, it must be precise and clear. When treating matters common to Christians (meaning here those churches adhering to the ancient creeds[1]) it uses the word Christian. Referring to matters common among Catholics (including Roman Catholic, Orthodox, Anglo-Catholic and Catholic members of other churches) it uses the designation Catholic. Matters exclusive to the Roman Catholic Church are so identified.

---

1. Truth 53

The Structure of This Book

This guide is a presentation of the good news. How does this Gospel take shape in the Roman Catholic Church? A church is made up of people—thus the faith is an organism rather than a philosophy: a living whole developing and changing while remaining true to its essence. Organisms because of their vitality are difficult to study. Thus, the lived reality of Roman Catholic Christianity, not some description of it, is our true focus.

Some structure is necessary to sort out the various elements. This guide uses traditional Christian structures to explore the religion. The book's shape is not arbitrary but determined by tradition.

The overall structure derives from John the Evangelist in whose Gospel Jesus declares himself to be the Way, the Truth and the Life.[2] These categories provide a rounded picture of the Christian religion.

THE WAY

Christianity was originally known as THE WAY since the earliest disciples followed Jesus as a spiritual teacher. The condition for becoming a Christian is not primarily to acknowledge certain truths but rather to convert—to change one's way of life in accordance with Jesus' Way. Thus much of Christianity concerns the Way of conversion which Jesus reveals. This Way in all its varied dimensions is the subject for the first part.

This Way is first discovered through becoming a Christian. One learns from Jesus by following him. The Way to Jesus is also the Way of Jesus. **The Way to Christianity** introduces this process.

THE TRUTH

Conversion is not without a content. Jesus reveals and fulfills a vision which Christians regard as THE TRUTH. This Truth is found in the Christian Scriptures, creeds, and commandments of life. The second part presents these teachings as well as the rituals by which Christians continue the process of conversion, conforming more to the image of Christ. The following introduction presents a summary of the good news in **The Truth of the Gospel.**

---

2. Jn 14:6

THE LIFE

Finally Christianity presents a new life to those who hear and turn toward its message. THE LIFE is explored in the final part. What is Christian existence like? For what purpose does the Christian live and act? What qualities define Christian existence? What is life like in the Christian Church and world? How is the Christian's life illuminated and penetrated by the kingdom of God? **The Life of Catholic Practice** introduces the fundamentals of Christian life as followed by Catholics.

Obviously this categorization should not be taken rigorously. The Way, the Truth and the Life are not three separate realities, but aspects and viewpoints into the one reality. The heart of Christianity lies in the Trinity—that God is one and yet manifested in three persons. So here these three dimensions flow into, support and complement each other. Thus in reading this book it will be necessary to jump from one place to another at times to gain the full picture.

This is not a book to read from cover to cover. Some parts are more important than others. What you read depends on what you know and what you want to find out. If you know nothing about Christianity you will want to begin with the basics. In the Way to Christ[3] you will be referred to appropriate material for each of the stages of becoming a Christian.

If you are knowledgeable about Christianity, but wish to investigate its specifically Catholic expression, you will be drawn to areas where Catholicism is different from Protestantism such as the understanding of Church and sacrament. If you are a Catholic returning to the Church after a period away and seeking a renewed understanding of the faith, your reading might be guided by the changes you notice from what you experienced of the Church before. If you are a Catholic Christian seeking a deeper understanding of the fundamentals of the faith, you probably have some idea of what you wish to learn and where you would like to begin.

There are basically three levels of importance. First are the primary traditions of Christianity: Scripture,[4] the liturgy,[5] the Lord's Prayer,[6] the Creed,[7] the ten commandments,[8] the sacraments,[9] and the

---

3. Intro 4ff
4. Way 2–7; Truth 2–20
5. Way 8–35
6. Way 50
7. Truth 25–44
8. Truth 45–56
9. Truth 74–84

PRIMARY TRADITIONS*

A Christian should be familiar with and able to grow and pray with the Scriptures and the liturgy, including the sacraments.

SCRIPTURE (Way 3–7, Truth 2–20)
LITURGY (Way 8–35)
THE SACRAMENTS (Truth 74–84)

A Christian should know from memory the Creed and Lord's Prayer as well as be knowledgeable concerning the commandments and the beatitudes.

THE CREED (Truth 25–44)
THE COMMANDMENTS (Truth 45–56)
THE LORD'S PRAYER (Way 50)
THE BEATITUDES (Life 47)

Within the text, material relating to Primary Traditions is highlighted in grey.

Secondary Traditions

Church precepts (Intro 15–21)
The works of mercy (Way 37–39)
The seven sins and virtues (Truth 57–73)
The twenty-third psalm (Life 1)
Gifts and fruits of the Holy Spirit (Life 4–5)
Catholic social teaching (Life 44)

A Christian is also familiar with the ideas of *covenant* (Way 1) and *revelation* (Truth 1) as well as the process of *moral decision making* (Way 41–45), *conversion* (Way 46–49) and the ways of *prayer* (Life 6–9).

Other Traditions

The twelve steps (Life 3)
Catholic culture (Life 13)
Church government, sociology and history (Life 15–37)
Daily prayer of the Church and other popular prayers (Life 38–43)
Saints (Life 46)

beatitudes.[10] Knowledge of these is necessary to be considered a literate Christian.

The secondary level consist of those elements which explain these primary traditions. Finally, there are the "trivia," a host of people, places and things which make up the world of Roman Catholicism. Knowledge of trivia is not essential, but it is often fun and may be part of your attraction to Catholicism.

There are a number of places where one may begin. If you have made contact with a Catholic community and are attending the inquiry sessions or catechumenate, this book provides background on various topics: customs, traditions, teachings, beliefs. If you are still on your own, your curiosity might lead you to skip around to acquaint yourself with the shape of Catholicism.

10. Life 47

A Guide to References

This guide is set up in three parts—The Way, The Truth, The Life. Each part is referred to in making references to other places in the text. And each part is further broken down into consecutively numbered sections. The numbers are found in all tables of contents and outlines, both at the beginning of the book and before each chapter. They are also found in the notes.

These notes refer to other sections which deepen or explain terms and concepts: "Truth 3" refers to the third section of The Truth. Appropriate scriptural passages are also indicated in the text.[11] Other reference aids are found under a number of different headings in the text.

TO PREPARE—indicates introductory or background material for the present section.

TO DEEPEN—suggests questions to stimulate thought and discussion, ways to enter into Christian experience, relevant Catholic prayers, and books which explore the topic further.

TO CONTINUE—indicates other sections of the book which continue and deepen the current topics.

TO DEEPEN—

Further Reading:

Here are some other books that also explore Catholic Christianity:

Hanson, James E. *If I'm a Christian, Why Be a Catholic? The Biblical Roots of Catholic Faith*. Paulist Press, 1984.

Lewis, C. S. *Mere Christianity*. Macmillan, 1964. A favorite modern classic. Lewis argues for the common sense of Christianity.

Kohmescher, Matthew F. *Catholicism Today: A Survey of Catholic Belief and Practice*. Paulist Press, 1980.

Wilhelm, Anthony. *Christ Among Us*. A Modern Presentation of the Catholic Faith for Adults. Harper & Row, 1985.

Winter, Betty and Art. *Stories of Prayer—Interviews with Leading Catholics on their Experience of God*. Sheed and Ward. 1985.

TO CONTINUE—

Intro 2—presents the call of God and the invitation of the Church to explore the new life and happiness Jesus provides.

---

11. Way 7

◇

2. The Call

The Christian experience begins with a call. Jesus' first words in Mark's Gospel are a call to "Repent and believe in the gospel."[1] And immediately he calls two particular men, Simon and Andrew: "Follow me and I will make you become fishers of men."[2]

No one is born a Christian; one becomes Christian in response to God's invitation. God desires to enter into relationship with us.

True, from our perspective it may appear we have initiated our approach to Christianity through an interest in this religion. Perhaps we hope it may enrich our life. Nevertheless, such an interest is itself sparked by an original call from God. Christianity claims to present the truth about ourselves, our world and God. And the first truth is that God desires to draw close to us, revealing himself.

---

1. Mk 1:15b
2. Mk 1:17

11

Jesus throughout his ministry invited people to follow him. He asks the rich young man to sell his possessions, give the money to the poor, and to follow him.[3] He invites the weary and heavy laden to take up his easy yoke.[4] An attraction to Jesus and his message is already a response to his invitation to come and see what he is about.[5]

Being called might seem mysterious. But consider some of the ways this call might be perceived. Certainly few people hear it as a straight-out voice as in the story of St. Paul's conversion.[6] God calls us in a number of ways, but for most the call is subtle, arising out of life's circumstances.

An Old Testament story tells of God calling the young boy Samuel in his sleep.[7] At first Samuel thinks his teacher Eli is calling. But finally Eli, awakened three times by Samuel asking what he wants, recognizes the call as from God. Sometimes it takes time for the call to be recognized.

Perhaps that call arises out of our life. Do we feel called to a different way of living than we have experienced so far? Do we experience an inner longing for a spiritual reality?

Some experience the call of the Christ. They are attracted by the idea of the Christ—that God has come to show us the way. Christ calls us to walk in the light. Do you see your life so far as a darkness which has been or might be illumined by the light of God?

Christ is also called the Word.[8] He embodies the meaning of life. Is your call one toward richer and deeper meaning? Today America is in a spiritual awakening; many are drawn to the spiritual life. They seek a way to a better and richer life. Some have already sought this life through spiritual paths such as Alcoholics Anonymous or the various psychological or Eastern spiritual disciplines. Then at some point, realizing that Christianity embodies the traditional path for the West, they turn to explore Christianity.

Christians treasure God's Word to humanity in our Scriptures. They reveal a God who, throughout human history, has entered into relationship with men and women. Exposed to Scripture God's call soon invites us to a deeper and richer life in fellowship. These Scriptures are the product of the Christian community. They guide and direct the Church. And they speak of God's invitation to become part of

---

3. Mt 19:16–30; Mk 10:17–31; Lk 18:18–30
4. Mt 11:30
5. Jn 1:39
6. Acts 9:1–22
7. 1 Sam 3
8. Jn 1:1; Intro 3

the Christian community. Since our culture was molded by the Judeo-Christian tradition, we have likely encountered the call of God through Scripture or its many cultural offshoots from books and films to popular song.

God's call may come through another human being. Many approach Christianity and the Church initially through a Christian friend or relative. Learning about Christianity helps us understand our friend. Perhaps we admire this person's values and lifestyle. These things invite us to approach the source of these values.

Events or turns of life may extend God's call. At times of change or illness people experience a need to re-examine their life, questioning whether there might be a meaning that at present eludes them. Perhaps they seek happiness, or a purpose for living. Here life itself mediates God's call.

Then the Church itself calls people. The Christian Church exists not for itself but for the world. In the world it bears witness to the truth of God. And as part of its witness it invites everyone who will to come and experience Christian life.

Reading this book, you are responding to God's call to meet Jesus and his community. Even your curiosity is an aspect of that call, for who gave such a gift if not the God who created you? But Christianity is not a book but a community of faith. Only that community can communicate Christ fully. So if you have not already done so, the Church invites you to contact a Roman Catholic community. There you may explore what the call of God means for you specifically.

TO DEEPEN—

Do you think you have heard the call of God in your own life?

How has it been manifested?

Can you say what drew you to this book?

What do you hope you might find through exploring Catholic Christianity?

Further Reading:

Krailsheimer, A. J. *Conversion.* SCM Press, 1980. Examines the lives of a number of converts exploring the nature of conversion.

Augustine. *Confessions.* Andrews & McMeel, 1969. A classic that really begins the genre of autobiography. St. Augustine converted in the fourth century and became one of the greatest theologians and saints.

Day, Dorothy. *The Long Loneliness.* Harper & Row, 1981. A modern classic of a woman's journey from communism to Catholicism and the founding of the Catholic Worker.

Merton, Thomas. *The Seven Storey Mountain.* Harcourt Brace Jovanovich, 1978. A best seller in the 1950's of a young man's conversion from libertinism to Catholicism and into the contemplative life of the Trappists.

TO CONTINUE—

Intro 3—the Gospel truth provides a summary of the good news—what Christianity believes.

Intro 4—introduces the catechumenate—the structure which introduces a person into the Christian faith.

Intro 5—describes the minimal practices which all Catholics follow.

3. The Gospel Truth—John's Prologue

In the beginning was the Word,
and the Word was with God,
and the Word was God.
He was in the beginning with God;
all things were made through him,
and without him was not anything made that was made.
In him was life,
and the life was the light of men.
The light shines in the darkness,
and the darkness has not overcome it.

There was a man sent from God, whose name was John. He
came for testimony, to bear witness to the light, that all might
believe through him. He was not the light, but came to bear
witness to the light.

The true light that enlightens every man
was coming into the world.
He was in the world,
and the world was made through him,
yet the world knew him not.
He came to his own,
and his own people received him not.
But to all who received him,
who believed in his name,
he gave power to become children of God;
who were born,
not of blood
nor of the will of the flesh
nor of the will of man,
but of God.
And the Word became flesh and dwelt among us,
full of grace and truth;
we have beheld his glory,
glory as of the only Son from the Father.
And from his fullness have we all received,
grace upon grace.

For the law was given through Moses;
grace and truth came through Jesus Christ.

No one has ever seen God;
the only Son, who is in the bosom of the Father,
he has made him known.[1]

Christianity proclaims the good news of Jesus Christ, the Gospel.
The Fourth Gospel—John—opens with a prologue introducing Jesus,
his invitation and message. For many years the Roman Church read this
passage to conclude every Mass.

Reading this passage, St. Augustine asked,

Who can fathom this? Who can imagine it? Who can conceive
it? Who can contemplate it? Who can worthily meditate on it?
No one! "The Word was made flesh and dwelt among us." He
calls you to be a worker in his vineyard, "The Word was made
flesh." He himself calls you. The Word will be your glory, the
Lord will be your reward.[2]

In the beginning was the Word,
and the Word was with God,
and the Word was God.

Christianity claims that God has expressed himself to humanity.
The search for meaning constitutes our humanity. Humans are beings
who seek meaning in life. We want to know why we are here, what we
are to do, where we are headed. We are the animals who ask questions.

The meaning of existence is found with God. The Word is with God
and is God. So if we would find meaning to our existence we must seek
God.

He was in the beginning with God;
all things were made through him,
and without him was not anything made that was made.

The Word is the origin of all existence—it was in the beginning.
And everything that exists was brought into existence through this
Word and thus owes its existence, its form and its true meaning to this
Word that is God.

Existence does not simply happen. Existence is created. What exists owes its being to God who creates through the Word. Sharing the

---

1. Jn 1:1–18
2. Sermon, Guelf, IX

imprint of the Word creation is essentially meaningful. Existence, life and history, whether of the universe, the planet, humanity or the individual, is not a chance occurrence but charged with meaning and purpose.

> In him was life,
> and the life was the light of men.
> The light shines in the darkness,
> and the darkness has not overcome it.

In the created order the Word manifests primarily as life. What is alive exists and is given life by the Word of God. Life itself has real meaning. And in humanity the primary image of life is light. What in us is light is the focus for meaning, for the Word, for God. And is not this light primarily consciousness—the ability to form words, to find meaning, to reason, to discern order?

But the light shines in the darkness. So in addition to order and meaning, there is darkness—unknowing, chaos, absence of meaning. Indeed this darkness threatens the light. There is opposition to God, rejection of God and of the light. Humanity is in darkness. But the light shines into that darkness. There is a possibility of illumination. We might through God's gift come to live in the light.

> There was a man sent from God, whose name was John. He came for testimony, to bear witness to the light, that all might believe through him. He was not the light, but came to bear witness to the light.

Throughout human history this light has been perceived by people. And God has sent people to witness to the profound meaning of existence. The man John spoken of here appears on the scene shortly before Jesus and prepares the way for Jesus.

John is the greatest of a whole succession of witnesses to the light. That lineage of witnesses encompasses the tradition of Israel. In addition others witnessed to the light in the other spiritual traditions. These witnesses, having seen the light, are sent by God to proclaim and reveal what they have seen—how they have penetrated more deeply into the meaning of existence.

But none of these people are themselves the Word. They are ordinary people, although enlightened, who share their experience with the light. And their witness now points toward the real light.

There have been similar witnesses in your own life to the light of

Christianity. Perhaps it is primarily because of these witnesses that you have come to this point of wishing to explore Christianity. How have these witnesses pointed to the light for you?

> The true light that enlightens every man
> was coming into the world.

But now the light itself comes into the world. What is at the very center of creation, what has shaped the creation, the image in which all is made, is now itself present in the world. There is no longer any need to grasp in the darkness for glimmers of the light. The light itself comes into the world so that it may be seen and illuminate this creation, bringing forth its deepest meaning.

> He was in the world,
> and the world was made through him,
> yet the world knew him not.
> He came to his own,
> and his own people received him not.

Yet when the light came into the world, it was met not with acknowledgement but refusal. The very image in which all things were made was not recognized by its creation. The people who had been prepared to receive the light refused it. The darkness is powerful. Something in humanity loves the darkness, even preferring it to the light. And part of entering into Christianity implies a coming to know our darkness and to overcome its resistance to the light. The coming of the light results in crisis and opposition. Becoming a Christian means allowing oneself and one's ideals, values and actions to be brought into the light to be seen for what they truly are: revealed in the presence of the light and understood in relation to it.

> But to all who received him,
> who believed in his name,
> he gave power to become children of God;
> who were born,
> not of blood
> nor of the will of the flesh
> nor of the will of man,
> but of God.

However, not everyone rejects the light. And for those who receive the light, life is changed. Central to Christianity is transformation
or conversion. Those who receive the light become children of God—
children of the Word. Their lives are lifted into a new dimension.
Whereas ordinarily human life is born of flesh and blood, of the desires
of the flesh, of the will of human beings, this new life in becoming children of God results from God's actions rather than from humanity's will.

> And the Word became flesh and dwelt among us,
> full of grace and truth;
> we have beheld his glory,
> glory as of the only Son from the Father.

The light comes into this world as a human being: Jesus of Nazareth. It is by believing in his name that people become children of God.
Jesus lives among us manifesting the light in a human way. In his life
grace and truth shine out as "glory"—a scriptural term referring to that
aspect of God revealed to us. Glory is related to light—it is the radiance
of light.

> And from his fullness have we all received,
> grace upon grace.
> For the law was given through Moses;
> grace and truth came through Jesus Christ.
> No one has ever seen God;
> the only Son, who is in the bosom of the Father,
> he has made him known.

From Jesus flows God's grace: God's favor toward us, God's love,
illuminating us and our world. The world is charged with the grace of
God. But that grace flows out from Jesus. In the tradition of Israel, the
greatest gift was the law of God which was given to Moses. The law
established a covenant—formed a relationship between God and the
people of Israel—which issued in blessings. But now John points out
that a greater gift comes through Jesus—God's grace and truth.

Jesus makes known the very heart of God, since he comes from the
bosom of the Father. This heart of God reveals the meaning of existence. And it transforms our life with blessings and grace.

TO DEEPEN—

In your own words, what is the good news of Christianity?
Why is Jesus at the center of Christianity?
What questions do you have about the teaching of Christianity?
What attracts you about the Gospel?
What about the Gospel causes you difficulty?

At this point, to go deeper into the good news, read one of the Gospels. Mark's is the shortest of the four and can be read in a couple of hours. He will give flesh and detail to this introduction.

Further Reading:

Frankl, Viktor. *Man's Search for Meaning.* Pocket Books, 1977. A psychiatrist's explanation of the central importance of meaning to human life.
Chilson, Richard. *The Way to Christianity—In Search of Spiritual Growth.* Winston Press, 1979. Explorations of basic scriptural stories so that a person may grow into the Christian experience. Can be used throughout this book to enter into the Christian vision.

TO CONTINUE—

Intro 4—shows how a person can approach Christianity and become initiated into it.
Truth 1—introduces the concept of revelation—what God has revealed in our tradition.

4. The Way to Christ—
The Catechumenate

Christians view life and faith as a journey. Christian faith involves a process of conversion. Coming to understand this process initiates a person into the Christian lifestyle. The journey by which people come to Christianity is the same by which Christians continue converting at ever deeper levels.

Those who have decided to begin their journey toward Christianity are called catechumens. Catechumens learn a foundation for all Christian life. The catechumenate, an order within the Church,[1] introduces people to Catholic Christianity. It existed in the early Christian Church but died out around the sixth century as adult converts decreased and children became the main source of new Christians. It has been restored by the Second Vatican Council.

The catechumenate divides the spiritual journey into stages by which the person progresses toward full initiation. These stages are inquiry, the catechumenate itself, enlightenment and purification, and mystagogy. The language derives from Latin and will be explained as each stage is explored.

5. THE STAGE OF INQUIRY

The journey begins with the period of inquiry: an opportunity to become acquainted with Christianity. Take the image of journey and apply it to your life. What is the shape of your life's journey? How does it help to see life in this way? What story does your life tell? How have you come to this point of considering Christianity?

The inquiry group offers an opportunity to consider your life in this light and to begin sharing your journey with others. Considering your life from this vantage point, whether you have understood it so or not, you have already been on a journey that has brought you to this place. People and events have led you here. Just what has led to this moment when you want to know more about Jesus and his community? How does it help to see life as a pilgrimage? And what does it tell you about Christianity already to understand that pilgrimage lies at the very heart of that faith?

Inquiry also introduces Jesus and Christianity. So the inquiry period explores Christianity and Catholicism in its broad outlines. Since

---

1. Life 17

there are many Christian denominations it is important to know how the Catholic understanding of Christianity relates to other traditions and ways. People have many conceptions of Catholicism. Inquiry provides an opportunity to ask questions and to have areas of Catholicism clarified so that you can decide whether you wish to pursue this way.

But Christianity and especially Catholicism is not a philosophy but a faith lived in community. And you will want to become acquainted with this flesh and blood community that you have approached. Inquiry introduces various Catholics to speak about their faith and to show how they live their faith. For if you decide to pursue your exploration you will learn Christianity from this particular group. Thus here at the outset you want to know something about this group and its members. Is this the kind of community that I would like to be a part of?

TO DEEPEN—

If you haven't yet approached a Catholic community, why not do so now? There is no commitment involved; it could simply be a way of continuing to explore Christianity which you are doing in part by reading this book.

What has been your own journey to this point in your life? Take some time to consider the major stepping-stones of your life. Write them down. "First, I was born . . . then . . . "

What questions do you have about Catholic Christianity? What appeals to you at this point about Catholicism? What are your fears? What obstacles do you feel would prevent you from accepting Jesus or the Catholic Church?

TO CONTINUE—

Sections appropriate to this stage:

All of the Introduction

Introductions to the Three Parts:
  The Covenant (Way 1)
  Revelation (Truth 1)
  Life in the Spirit (Life 1)

If you have questions about certain aspects of Catholic Christianity, look them up in the Index.

6. THE CATECHUMENATE

Should you decide to continue, the Church invites you to embark on a faith journey. This beginning is celebrated in the rite of becoming a catechumen. At the entrance to the church you will be greeted and asked what you want of our community. In saying you want to know Jesus, the Church will receive you as a member so that you may accompany us on our journey and learn the Christian Way, Truth and Life by experience.

This ceremony marks the actual beginning of the Christian journey. You become a catechumen—a special group within the community. Catechumens explore the faith with us as together we journey through time. Hopefully as time goes on you will come to see your life and search as a pilgrimage.

And the catechumen's journey follows a particular route. The Church signs you with the cross.[2] And the catechumenate journey enriches your understanding of this cross—the central symbol of our faith. What does it mean? What is it for a Christian? Appreciating more deeply the cross, you understand Jesus and his vision.

To aid your exploration the community provides a sponsor—a Christian who will become a friend, perhaps attending church with you, praying, and sharing faith. The sponsor is a role model of how a Christian lives, someone who cares about you and your growing faith.

Signed with the cross the new catechumens enter the church to join those gathered for worship.[3] There one comes to know, love and serve God. We give thanks to God for the goodness and beauty of all creation. And through hearing the Scriptures we learn what God reveals.

Having listened to the word of God and responded to it, the new catechumens are given a Bible. They are charged to learn the word of God in these Scriptures. This word will reveal the truth and show us how to live and grow in wisdom.

Catechumens, like other Christians, walk between the word and the cross. These symbols enrich Christian life. And in coming to know the word and the cross catechumens experience Christian life and begin to adopt the vision of Jesus.

Now the catechumens are sent forth from the assembly to explore this word. Catechumens are Christians in formation who through study, prayer, community, service, and experience in the Church are moving toward full commitment to Jesus Christ.

---

2. Way 8
3. Way 19

7. The Structures of the Catechumenate

The catechumenate path is shaped by the Way of Jesus. He teaches the meaning of life and how to grow in wisdom. The Church provides guidance to walk this Way. Of course each journey is different and unique, but there is a certain overall shape, and the catechumenate itself guides the journey.

Catechumens join the faithful at the table of the Lord's word[4] where we praise God and give thanks, and are nourished by God's word in Scripture. They may join in other celebrations[5]—for they are members of the Church now with a special place in all its liturgies except the sacraments. They develop a knowledge and appreciation for the Church's worship[6]—forms of prayer,[7] the liturgical year,[8] the importance of celebration in Christian life.[9]

Catholics keep feast days and festivals:[10] holy times and days when we worship together. Most important is Sunday, the day of the Lord devoted to worship and rest.[11]

Catechumens learn how Catholicism sanctifies the times of the year and the day.[12] They observe customs and keep feasts. In celebrating, praying and playing together, community evolves which sustains and gives life meaning.

At different times the Church prays over the catechumens, asking that God deepen their conversion. It prays that they may come to see our life more clearly, turning from those things which are not life-giving toward God and God's love. The primary concern both of the catechumenate and of Christian life is a deeper and deeper turning toward God and God's kingdom.

The Christian is first of all converted to Christ. He or she has abandoned the visions and values of the world in favor of the kingdom of God. The heart of conversion is a surrender and trust in the risen Lord. All the activities of the catechumenate foster this awakening. The Church's prayers provide God's grace to foster awareness and move toward the kingdom of God.

With various blessings the Church shows catechumens God's love

---

4. Way 21
5. Life 38, 41–42
6. Way 8ff
7. Life 7ff
8. Way 28ff
9. Way 10ff
10. Intro 17
11. Intro 16
12. Life 40

and the Church's care.[13] The blessings open them to the gifts God showers upon his people.

Anointings throughout the catechumenate prepare for initiation. Signs of God's love and concern, they heal faults, strengthen faith, and prepare catechumens to respond to God's call to baptism.

8. Contents of the Catechumenate

Reading and Praying the Scriptures

The catechumenate provides ample opportunity to explore the faith. They study the Scriptures as unfolded in the liturgy.[14] They learn how to read and pray with Scripture.[15] The word of God challenges, heals and transforms.

Christian Teachings

They study Jesus and his message in depth. They receive the key stories of the Christian faith,[16] both those concerning Jesus and the early Christians as well as those of Israel without which Jesus cannot be understood. They study the Church's teachings—the important doctrines of the faith[17]—as well as ethics,[18] customs[19] and Church organization.[20] The history of the Church[21] and the Catholic Church's relations to other Christian Churches and other religions[22] might also be covered.

Experiencing the Christian life

These teachings aid conversion to Christ. Catechumens explore the Christian lifestyle—its values, how Christians make decisions, what they consider important for full human life, their commitment to the ideals of love, fellowship, and service. They do this both through direct experience and through study and discussion with catechists and sponsors.

---

13. Way 13
14. Way 3ff
15. Way 6
16. Truth 3ff
17. Truth 21ff
18. Truth 45ff, 58ff
19. Life 40ff
20. Life 16ff
21. Life 29ff
22. Life 27–28

With this formal instruction, there is opportunity to relate this knowledge to their own life and experience. Christianity is not a concept so much as a way of living.

Fostering Conversion

Christianity calls to conversion, so the means by which such transformation is fostered and nurtured must be communicated. Catechumens are taught how to pray.[23] The development of prayer life, both publicly, with fellow catechumens and the larger community, and privately, is crucial. Catechumens learn to share their prayer journey with others and seek help with important decisions in life through prayer and community.

Service

Christian life expresses itself in action—a life in service of others for the kingdom of God.[24] The Christian lives for others as Jesus did. In serving, Christians come to know and join in God's work.

The catechumenate introduces the outreach and ministries of the parish. Catechumens choose a way of service to others.[25] This ministry provides first-hand experience of Christian living. In service Jesus' teachings come alive, prayer nurtures and sustains the ministry, and catechumens experience Christian community with their fellow ministers and begin to understand how the kingdom of God works through human gifts and talents.

All this activity acquaints catechumens with the local Christian community. Through the sponsors, Sunday worship, ministry with other Christians, and the catechumenate itself, community blossoms.

9. Time of Catechumenate

There is no definite time period for the catechumenate. One remains a catechumen as long as it takes to come to know the Christian message and community and decide whether God is calling to full initiation. It may be nine months, a year, even more. Indeed the Church encourages people to take their time and suggests two years.

The length of catechumenate depends upon a number of factors. First there is the question of education. Do the catechumens have a

---

23. Way 50
24. Way 36, 51
25. Life 18

fundamental grasp of Christianity? Do they have sufficient experience of the teachings and practices to continue to grow in Christ once fully initiated? Are they integrated into the community?

But more important is the person's relationship to Jesus. Is he or she ready to accept Jesus as Lord? To die to one's self so that Christ might live in one? Is life moving away from dominance by worldly values toward God's kingdom?

Do you feel at home in your new community? Have you found here sources of nourishment, support and challenge? Does the Christian life of service and love appeal to you and enrich your living? Arriving at a positive response in agreement with one's sponsor, catechists and the parish staff, at the beginning of the next Lent the catechumen is enrolled among the elect.

TO DEEPEN—

Sections appropriate to the catechumenate:
    The Way of Scripture (Way 2–7)
    The Way of Worship (Way 8–35)
    The Way of Mission (Way 36–40)
    The Way of Christian Life (Way 40–51)
    The Truth of Scripture (Truth 2–20)
    The Truth of the Tradition (Truth 21–56)
    The Truth of the Christian Path (Truth 57–65)
    Foundations of Christian Living (Life 3)
    Prayer Life (Life 6–8)
    The Structure and Organization of the Church (Life 15–22)
    The Worship Life of the Church (Life 38–42)
    The Life of the Church in the World (Life 44–45)
    The Beatitudes (Life 47)

If you are a catechumen approaching the time of Lent, ask yourself the above questions. You might talk about them with your sponsor, with your catechist and the other catechumens. What draws you toward baptism? What stands in your way? How do you experience God's call to baptism or membership in the Catholic Church?

10. ELECTION AND ENLIGHTENMENT

Lent[26] inaugurates the period of enlightenment. Studies are over for now. During Lent the elect pray together, fast, perform a Lenten practice and explore the symbols of Christianity.

---

26. Way 32

11. Rites of the Period of Enlightenment and Purification

Rite of Enrollment or Election

On the First Sunday of Lent, those elected gather first with the parish members who rejoice in the election to take place later at the cathedral. Those who are called go forward after the homily, and all pray for them as they take this final step toward baptism and reception.

In the afternoon all go to the cathedral where with catechumens from all over the diocese they are enrolled as called to baptism and reception. The bishop hears the godparents' and catechists' testimony that these catechumens are ready for the Easter sacraments. In the name of the Church he acknowledges their call and receives them. Enrolling them as the elect he bids them this Lent through prayer and fasting to prepare themselves for baptism and full reception. The candidates for membership in the Roman Catholic Church are welcomed by the bishop marking their rite of entry into the Lenten season.

Scrutinies

The community of the elect continue to meet on the Sundays of Lent. The scrutinies are celebrated on the Third, Fourth and Fifth Sundays during the liturgy of the word.

> The scrutinies are intended to purify the catechumens' minds and hearts, to strengthen them against temptation, to purify their intentions, and to make firm their decision so that they remain more closely united with Christ and make progress in their efforts to love God more deeply.[27]

The scrutinies relate to the Johannine Gospels proclaimed on these Sundays. They weave prayers for the elect from the Gospel themes. John sees two alignments—the way of Satan and the way of Christ, darkness and light, the world or the kingdom.

Lenten prayer, fasting and penance reveal sin and enable the elect to move from their hold into the freedom of the kingdom. The scrutinies reveal the bonds of the world, and through prayer God gradually frees the elect from worldly ways of thinking and living so that they may adopt the vision and life of the kingdom. We pray that the elect may find what they thirst for, that their eyes may be opened and that they may be raised as was Lazarus into the light of God. The scrutinies foster

---

27. Rite of Christian Initiation of Adults #154

conversion—turning the elect away from what is dead and dark in their lives toward the light of Christ. Thus the scrutinies focus the entire work of Lent—dying to one's self to be raised up in Christ.

Presentations

During Lent as well the Christian community presents the elect with its treasured gifts—the Creed[28] and the Lord's Prayer.[29] The elect have studied the Creed and prayed the Prayer, but now they are given them as their special inheritance to guide their Christian life.

12. Lenten Observance for the Elect

The key images of Lent are the action of dying and rising. Lenten fasting, practice and prayer centered this action in our own life.[30] Dying to ourselves we come alive and rise to richer life in Christ.

After the first week the patterns of Lent establish themselves. Daily prayer nourishes the journey. Sometimes it becomes an oasis from daily routine—a way of making each day special. Penance is at times difficult. Failure occurs—but even failure shows that conversion cannot be done alone and leads the elect to rely upon God and the community.

The Sunday Gospels focus upon the key Christian symbols which blossom in the sacraments. Through prayer and rituals they explore these symbols of water, fire, oil, bread and wine as preparation for the Easter sacraments.

The elect meet in community for prayer, sharing and strengthening. As always they do not make the journey alone but in company. In the rigors of Lenten practice the community provides support, encouragement and strength to die to self in order to be raised in the Lord.

TO DEEPEN—

Sections appropriate to Election:
 Lenten Season (Way 32)
 The Way of Conversion (Way 47–49)
 The Way of Prayer (Way 50)
 The Path of Illumination (Truth 66–73)

---

28. Truth 25
29. Way 50
30. Life 40

13. INITIATION

Easter[31] is the climax of the catechumenate. At the Vigil service the elect are baptized, confirmed, received into the Church and join in the Eucharist.[32] After the service of readings, the priest calls the elect forward to be baptized. Together they affirm the Creed they have come to honor and believe. Then stepping into the pool they are immersed in the water. Going under the water is a death; there is real surrender. As they emerge from the water the faithful burst into shouts of affirmation! Changed and clothed, the new Christians receive a lighted candle and a white garment as signs of their new life. Then they are confirmed and charged to witness their faith. Then all together celebrate the Easter Eucharist.

14. MYSTAGOGIA

During the Easter season the neophytes (new Christians) continue to meet. Attention focuses upon their experience of Easter: what happened and what is happening now. They speak of the great sacraments and explore their beginning life as fully initiated Christians. The catechist explains how Christians have traditionally understood and named this experience. They examine the sacraments as well as Christian life, looking ahead to how they will join in the ongoing life of the community and give expression to their mission. This period is called mystagogy. This word literally means "learning the mysteries." The mysteries referred to are the sacraments and the new experience of Christian life.

They continue to pray with one another throughout this joyous Easter season and perhaps celebrate a special liturgy with the bishop. They are introduced and welcomed to the different parish groups and activities. On Pentecost they mark the end of the catechumenate and the continuation of their pilgrimage as fully initiated Christians. As fully initiated Christians, they too now share the responsibility to spread the Gospel.

---

31. Way 33
32. Truth 75

TO DEEPEN—

Sections appropriate to this stage:
  The Pasch (Way 33)
  Easter Season (Way 34)
  The Way of Mission (Way 36–39)
  The Way of Action (Way 51)
  The Sacraments (Truth 74–84)
  The Gifts and Fruits of the Spirit (Life 4–5)
  The Beatitudes (Life 47)
  The Kingdom in the World (Life 48–50)

Further Reading:

Upton, Julia. *Journey into Mystery—A Companion to the R.C.I.A.* Paulist Press, 1986. Guides a person on the catechumenate journey toward faith.

Duggan, Robert, ed. *Conversion and the Catechumenate.* Paulist Press, 1984. More a book about the catechumenate than one to use for the journey itself.

TO CONTINUE—

Intro 15—introduces the minimum practices which all Catholics observe.

Way 1—introduces the Christian covenant—the relationship established between God and humanity in Jesus Christ.

15. Catholic Life—The Church's Precepts

Christians live in a covenant with God.[1] Being part of this covenant involves certain obligations and duties. Catholic tradition offers certain precepts: basic practices necessary for active membership in the Church.

16. KEEPING THE LORD'S DAY

First and foremost, a Catholic attends the celebration of the Eucharist[2] each Sunday. Sunday commemorates the feast of Easter.[3] It is also the Christian expression of the sabbath.[4] It was transferred from Saturday to Sunday in the light of the resurrection memorial. Christians keep Sunday as a day of rest and relaxation, celebration and thanksgiving. And the Christian gives thanks primarily through the Eucharist.

17. CELEBRATING THE MAJOR FEASTS

In addition to Sundays each country keeps a number of feast days; Catholics attend Mass on that day. In the United States these holy days of obligation are:

Immaculate Conception[5]—December 8
Christmas[6]—December 25
Octave of Christmas[7]—January 1
Ascension[8]—the Thursday forty days after Easter
Assumption of Mary[9]—August 15
All Saints[10]—November 1

18. KEEPING THE TIMES OF FAST AND ABSTINENCE

Catholics are obliged within certain ages to keep the Church's regulations concerning fast and abstinence.[11] Abstinence means refraining

---

1. Way 1
2. Truth 78
3. Way 33
4. Truth 49
5. Life 39
6. Way 30
7. Way 30
8. Way 34
9. Life 39
10. Life 39
11. Way 49

from meat. All over the age of fourteen are bound by the laws of abstinence which apply on Ash Wednesday and Good Friday.[12]

A bishop may decide that Catholics in his diocese should abstain on the Fridays of Lent; check for the local custom. Finally the American bishops have recommended the practice of Friday abstinence as a sign of commitment to the struggle for peace. This is not binding but a suggestion as a sign of solidarity.

Fasting is the primary means by which Christians in solidarity do penance and seek to reform their lives. The regulations on fasting apply to all between the ages of twenty-one and fifty-nine. Days of obligatory fast are Ash Wednesday and Good Friday. On a fast day one may have one full meal and two other meals which taken together do not exceed the main meal, and there is no eating between meals.

19. REGULATIONS REGARDING THE RECEPTION OF SACRAMENTS

The Catholic has the obligation to move toward *full initiation* in the Church. Thus a catechumen fulfills this obligation by moving through the stages of the catechumenate[13] toward full Initiation at the Easter Vigil. A Catholic baptized as an infant approaches Holy Communion at the proper time (five to seven years old), and receives confirmation at the appropriate time (varies among dioceses).

In addition to attending Mass, the Catholic is obligated to receive **Holy Communion**[14] at least once a year during the Easter Season (from Ash Wednesday through Trinity Sunday). And if in serious sin, one receives the sacrament of penance before receiving Communion. The precept defines the minimum of acceptable practice—not the norm.

Today a Catholic in good standing will receive the Eucharist frequently—at least weekly on Sunday. Also, except under special circumstances or on the feasts of Easter and Christmas, one only receives the Eucharist once a day.

Catholics keep a short fast before receiving Communion. The regulations prohibit food or drink (other than water or medicine) for at least one hour before Communion out of reverence for the sacrament.

The good Catholic will also celebrate the **sacrament of penance**[15] as part of one's spiritual life. One is obliged to receive the sacrament

---

12. Way 32
13. Intro 4ff
14. Truth 78
15. Truth 80

when in serious sin.[16] But the Church encourages regular reception to heal sin and promote growth in the Spirit.

The Catholic is encouraged to receive the sacrament of the **anointing of the Sick**[17] whenever serious illness strikes. One may receive the sacrament as preparation for a major operation. The person should not be at the point of death before the priest is called; the sacrament is for healing. If the person is near death, the last rites[18] are celebrated.

Finally a Catholic is obliged to observe the Church's laws and customs regarding **sacrament of matrimony.**[19] Thus one should consult a pastor in preparing for marriage. The Church prohibits marriage within certain degrees of kinship. And the partners should be capable of entering into the sacrament and free to do so.

20. SUPPORT OF THE LOCAL COMMUNITY

Catholics have an obligation to support the local parish community. This includes monetary support for the Church's programs, ministries, salaries, parish expenses and charities. But support also includes a willingness to be involved in the ministries of the parish. The Church is not an other—a group of professionals—but all of its members sharing ministry and service.

The Catholic also has a general obligation to be of service. Jesus showed the importance of service and of developing human community.[20] A Christian life without some service dimension is deficient. This service need not be Church work. It is any service to others which shows forth the selfless love revealed as the essence of God by Jesus.

21. MAINTAINING A LIFE OF PRAYER

A Christian's life is nourished by prayer and practice. This may take a variety of forms from grace at meals to a time each day for prolonged meditation, prayer or Scripture. Without prayer our life is not nourished; we do not provide God the opportunity to reveal himself in the depths of our being so that we may be converted.

---

16. Way 45
17. Truth 81
18. Truth 81
19. Truth 83
20. Mt 23:11

TO DEEPEN—

From this description of Catholic practice, what picture of Christian life can you imagine?

What would it be like to belong to this group and live this way?

How might your life be changed?

How might it remain the same?

What values underlie these practices?

What do these values tell you about Christianity?

Further Reading:

Kenny, John. *Now That You Are a Catholic.* Paulist Press, Revised 1986. A practical book for the beginning Catholic. Includes prayers, practices, customs, etc.

Haughton, Rosemary. *The Catholic Thing.* Templegate, 1980. An exciting description of just what makes Catholicism what it is. Examines people, art, poetry, theology.

TO CONTINUE—

Way 1—introduces the covenant which gives shape to Christian life.

Life 1—gives a further introduction to the shape of Christian existence.

THE WAY

◇ **The Covenant**
◇ **The Way of Scripture**
◇ **The Way of Worship**
◇ **The Way of Mission**
◇ **The Way of Christian Life**

◇

1. The Covenant

God has created special communities by means of covenants. A covenant is a special kind of relationship which is basic to the Judaeo-Christian tradition. These covenants extend back beyond the old covenant which founded the Hebrew people in the time of Moses[1] and forward to the new covenant established with all humanity in Jesus Christ.[2]

Covenants—a basis for government and community in the ancient world—were contracts established between the ruler and those ruled. A covenant is not an agreement among equals. One party to the covenant is superior to the other. The superior party initiates and extends the covenant to the other.

God has in various times initiated covenants with humanity bringing the two parties into relationship. God initiates the covenant by revealing himself in some way. Thus there is a revelation—a content underlying the covenant.[3]

God then calls the group to enter into a covenant relationship with him. This relationship involves certain promises and extends blessings to the group. Those covenanted agree to certain responsibilities flowing from that covenant. If the commitments are carried out, life is blessed. Sins against the covenant result in curses.

The covenant brings the group into a definite relationship with God. God becomes Lord—the ultimate authority. While much of the Judaeo-Christian tradition focuses upon liberation, it is liberation of a special kind. Thus, as covenanted people, Christians are not free to do as they will. Rather they attempt to do God's will. In this way they are liberated from those powers which rule them in their own self-interest to become subject to God who governs toward their ultimate good.

In Jesus Christ all are invited to enter into a special relationship to God. God offers knowledge of himself and his purpose. God promises to care for and to support the covenant community. Life in covenant is one of blessings and grace. The community observes the covenant's injunctions in regard to ways of living, thinking and acting.

---

1. Ex 20
2. 1 Cor 11:25
3. Truth 1

Through exploring the Christian faith and coming to know the Catholic community a person decides whether to enter into that covenant. Following Jesus' words in John's Gospel (Jn 14:5), this book explores the way of life demanded by the covenant in the first part, the Way. The revelation by God of himself and his purpose is known as the Truth and explored in the second part. And in the final part the Life of the covenant community is explored.

This first part presents the working out of covenant living—how does the community follow the way of Jesus? "The Way of the Christian Covenant" presents the means by which the community is nourished and transformed through relationship to God in Jesus Christ.

"The Way of Christian Life" shows how this covenant shapes Christian life through behavior and spirituality. For although a community, Christians are also individuals who along with their brothers and sisters journey toward wholeness aided by God's favor and blessings.

TO DEEPEN—

What do you see as advantages of living in a covenant relationship?

What do you foresee as disadvantages of such a relationship? Christians consider marriage as a covenant between the two people. How does this shed light on the nature of covenant?

Further Reading:

Guinan, Michael, *Covenant in the Old Testament*. Franciscan Herald Press, 1975.

TO CONTINUE—

The following section considers in more detail the actual shape of the Christian covenant.

2. The Way of the Christian Covenant

A Christian has entered into the covenant established with all humanity by God in Jesus Christ. This covenant promises the gift of eternal life. In return it imposes certain duties upon its members.

> And behold, a lawyer stood up to put (Jesus) to the test, saying, "Teacher, what shall I do to inherit eternal life?" (Jesus) said to him, "What is written in the law? How do you read?" And he answered, "You shall love the Lord your God with all your heart, and with all your soul, and with all your strength, and with all your mind; and your neighbor as yourself." And he said to him, "You have answered right; do this, and you will live."[1]

The first phrase of Jesus' answer is the "Shema," a prayer recited daily by Jews, and a creed[2] as well: "Hear, O Israel: The Lord our God is one Lord, and you shall love the Lord your God with all your heart, and with all your soul, and with all your might."[3] The second phrase also comes from Israel's law: "You shall not take vengeance or bear any grudge against the sons of your own people, but you shall love your neighbor as yourself: I am the Lord."[4]

Jesus does not bring a new law; his teaching is unique in joining together these two phrases from the law, making them equal. Although these commands are often considered in a moral context, and indeed ground Christian understanding of the law,[5] they first and foremost define the Christian way of life.

Our first duty, then, is to come to know the Lord, our God. "The Lord our God is one." Catechumens are given the Scriptures and signed with the cross to guide them toward full initiation. These Scriptures and the cross are key tools for conversion to the vision of Jesus Christ.

God is revealed authoritatively in the Scriptures. But how can the Scriptures aid conversion and nourish faith? How are they to be read? **The Way of Scripture** shows how the Christian community relates to Scripture.

---

1. Lk 10:25–28
2. Truth 23
3. Dt 6:4–5
4. Lev 19:18
5. Truth 24

Jesus tells us to love God with all our mind and heart and strength. Christians fulfill this commandment primarily through their worship. The sign of the cross, which begins all Catholic prayer, initiates the catechumen into the community's worship. **The Way of Worship** introduces Catholic liturgical life and shows how participation in divine worship fosters conversion.

Finally, Jesus calls the Christian to love one's neighbor as one's self. The Christian and the Christian Church live for others. Through service the catechumen experiences Christian life in its fullness. The ways in which Christianity demonstrates love of neighbor are introduced in **The Way of Mission.**

TO DEEPEN—

How might a life which follows these commands be different from an ordinary life? What values might be different?

What actions might be different?

◇

3. *The Way of Scripture*

The Church has always venerated the divine Scriptures as it venerated the body of the Lord, insofar as it never ceases, particularly in the sacred liturgy, to partake of the bread of life and to offer it to the faithful from the one table of the word of God and the body of Christ. It has always regarded, and continues to regard the Scriptures, taken together with sacred tradition, as the supreme rule of its faith. For, since they are inspired by God and committed to writing once and for all time, they make the voice of the Holy Spirit sound again and again in the words of the prophets and apostles. It follows that all the preaching of the Church, as indeed the entire Christian religion, should be nourished and ruled by sacred Scripture. In the sacred books the Father who is in heaven comes lovingly to meet his children, and talks with them. And such is the force and power of the word of God that it can serve the Church as its support and vigor, and the children of the Church as strength for their faith, food for the soul, and a pure and lasting fount of spiritual life. Scripture verifies in the most perfect way the words: "The word of God is living and active,"[6] and "is able to build you up and to give you the inheritance among all those who are sanctified"[7] (Vatican II, *Constitution on Divine Revelation* 21).

6. Heb 4:12
7. Acts 20:32; cf. 1 Th 2:13.

4. Introduction to the Bible

THE STRUCTURE OF THE BIBLE

The word "Bible" comes from the Greek for a collection of books. And it is indeed such, containing traditions which span more than a millennium. The Christian Bible is divided into two Testaments or covenants. The Hebrew Scriptures[8]—those Scriptures referring to Israel—make up almost two-thirds of the Bible. The New Testament includes those books which refer to Jesus and his work.

The Hebrew Scriptures comprise various categories of literature. Most important is the law or Torah—the first five books, also known as the Pentateuch (Greek for five books). Following these, the historical books detail the sacred history of Israel. Books called "the writings" in Jesus' day are scattered among the historical books as well as grouped after them. Finally the books of the prophets complete the library.

The New Testament begins with the four Gospels—the Christian equivalent of the Torah. Next the Acts of the Apostles by Luke describes the origin and growth of Christianity, under the Spirit's guidance. Then follow the letters of Paul and others.

And finally Revelation—an apocalyptic[9] book—concludes the New Testament.

TO DEEPEN—

What does the term "Bible" mean?

What are the major divisions in the Christian Bible?

Take a copy of the Bible and find the different books indicated above.

Further Reading:

Hann, Robert R. *The Bible: An Owner's Manual.* Paulist Press, 1983.
Lohfink, Gerhard. *The Bible: Now I Get It!* Doubleday, 1979.

---

8. Throughout this guide this term replaces the more traditional "Old Testament." It includes all the pre-Christian Scriptures, some of which have not survived in Hebrew or were written in other languages.

9. Truth 13, 20

THE BOOKS OF CATHOLIC SCRIPTURE

HEBREW SCRIPTURES
(39 books in Hebrew/Protestant Bibles; 46 in Catholic Bibles)

PENTATEUCH:　　GENESIS (Gen)
("TORAH")　　　　EXODUS (Ex)
　　　　　　　　LEVITICUS (Lv)
　　　　　　　　NUMBERS (Num)
　　　　　　　　DEUTERONOMY (Dt)

HISTORICAL
BOOKS:

"Deuteronomic History"	⎧ JOSHUA (Jos) ⎨ JUDGES (Jgs) ⎪ 1 & 2 SAMUEL (Sam) ⎩ 1 & 2 KINGS (Kgs)	In Greek Bible = 1 & 2 In Greek Bible = 3 & 4 Kings
"Chronicler's History"	⎧ 1 & 2 CHRONICLES (Chr) ⎨ EZRA (Ezr) ⎩ NEHEMIAH (Neh)	In Greek Bible = "Paralipomenon"
	RUTH (Ru) ESTHER (Est) LAMENTATIONS (Lam)	
Apocrypha/ Deuterocanon*	⎧ JUDITH (Jdt) ⎨ TOBIT (Tob) ⎨ BARUCH (Bar) ⎩ 1 & 2 MACCABEES (Macc)	Only included in the Greek Septuagint and part of the Catholic Bible

WISDOM
WRITINGS:

	JOB (Job) PSALMS (Ps) PROVERBS (Prv) ECCLESIASTES (Eccl) SONG OF SONGS (Song)	 = "Qoheleth" = "Canticle of Canticles"
Apocrypha/ Deuterocanon*	⎧ ECCLESIASTICUS (Sir) ⎨ WISDOM OF SOLOMON (Wis)	= "Sirach" or "Jesus ben Sira"

PROPHETS:

Major Prophets:	ISAIAH (Is) JEREMIAH (Jer) EZEKIEL (Ez) (DANIEL) (Dan)	 In Hebrew, Daniel is not a prophet

Minor Prophets: ("The Twelve")	HOSEA (Hos) JOEL (Jl) AMOS (Am) OBADIAH (Ob) JONAH (Jon) MICAH (Mic)	NAHUM (Nah) HABAKKUK (Hab) ZEPHANIAH (Zeph) HAGGAI (Hag) ZECHARIAH (Zec) MALACHI (Mal)

*Books that are underlined are found only in Catholic Bibles

THE NEW TESTAMENT		
GOSPEL	MATTHEW (Mt) MARK (Mk) LUKE (Lk) JOHN (Jn)	
ACTS	Acts of the Apostles (Acts)	
PAULINE **EPISTLES**	ROMANS (Rom) 1 CORINTHIANS (1 Cor) 2 CORINTHIANS (2 Cor) GALATIANS (Gal) 1 THESSALONIANS (1 Th) 2 THESSALONIANS (2 Th)	
	EPHESIANS (Eph) PHILIPPIANS (Phil) COLOSSIANS (Col) PHILEMON (Phlm)	CAPTIVITY EPISTLES
	1 TIMOTHY (1 Tim) 2 TIMOTHY (2 Tim) TITUS (Tit)	PASTORAL EPISTLES
APOSTOLIC **LETTERS**	HEBREWS (Heb) JAMES (Jas) 1 PETER (1 Pet) 2 PETER (2 Pet) 1 JOHN (1 Jn) 2 JOHN (2 Jn) 3 JOHN (3 Jn) JUDE (Jude)	CATHOLIC EPISTLES
APOCALYPTIC	REVELATION (Rev)	= Apocalypse

5. Interpretation of Scripture

The Scriptures are read within the understanding of the Catholic community—in the context of the Church whose treasure they are. The Church does not lay down many rules of interpretation and a breadth of interpretation is possible on many texts.

Furthermore a scriptural text has more than one level of meaning known as the senses of Scripture. An examination of the most prominent senses shows how Scripture is understood and studied in the Church.

THE LITERAL SENSE

The literal sense is most important and accounts for most contemporary Scripture study. It is not the same as a literal reading of the text. Rather it ascertains what the original author meant to communicate. Pope Pius XII in the encyclical *Divino Afflante Spiritu* which inaugurated modern Catholic Scripture scholarship wrote:

> What the literal sense of a passage is, is not always as obvious in the speeches and writings of the ancient authors of the East as it is in the works of our own time. For what they wished to express is not to be determined by the rules of grammar and philology alone nor solely by the context; the interpreter must, as it were, go back wholly in spirit to those remote centuries of the East and with the aid of history, archeology, ethnology, and other sciences accurately determine what modes of writing, so to speak, the authors of that ancient period would be likely to use and in fact did use.[1]

It would be wrong to interpret what the original author intended to be a fiction as though it were history as in the Book of Daniel. Nor should one expect to find the author of the creation story[2] using or rejecting a theory of evolution which only appeared in the modern age.

Scripture scholarship has developed a number of tools which aid in determining the literal sense of Scripture. Following are some of these types of biblical criticism. First **literary criticism** deals with the words, images and symbols. What characters appear in the text? What is their relationship to one another? It also considers the thought expressed. It determines the literary form which the author used to ex-

---

1. Ench bibl 558–560
2. Gen 1:1—2:4a

press his message. And it asks how that form contributes to expressing the content. It also focuses upon the specific words in the text. Where else do these words appear and what is their meaning? What does the word mean in the current context? Finally, the text is considered in terms of other texts. What is their relationship to one another? What do they have in common? How do they differ?

Textual criticism considers variant readings in the ancient manuscripts. Which is the most authentic of the variants? It then might extend to evaluating translations of the Scriptures. What philosophy did the translators use in making their decisions? Has anything been lost in the translation?

Source criticism looks for the source of the text. For example, the Gospels are composed of different stories passed down in the Christian communities. Those stories may change and develop as they are passed along. What did the source say? How has the present scriptural author used the source?

Redaction criticism focuses upon the final text. It seeks to discover the unique views or unusual emphases which the author placed upon his sources. It asks what were the author's life situation and theological outlook.

Form criticism studies the literary form of the text. And it shows what this literary form tells about the history of the community which gave birth to the text. **Historical criticism** asks what really happened. And finally **hermeneutics** determines what the text says, as well as what we bring to the text and what the text means today.

THE SPIRITUAL SENSE

The spiritual sense provides the Christian with a focus by which one reads the Scriptures—the figure of Christ. We recognize the life and work of Christ prefigured in the Hebrew Scriptures. Indeed the Christian Scriptures might be understood as primarily a key by which to read and understand Israel's experience of God. The image of shepherd in the 23rd Psalm is recognized by the Christian to speak of Jesus our shepherd.[3] This sense appears in the Christian Scriptures where Christ is spoken of as the Passover lamb.[4] St. Paul speaks of this sense when he says:

Yes, to this day whenever Moses is read a veil lies over their minds; but when a man turns to the Lord the veil is removed.

---

3. Life 1
4. 1 Pet 1:19

Now the Lord is the Spirit, and where the Spirit of the Lord is, there is freedom. And we all, with unveiled face, beholding the glory of the Lord, are being changed into his likeness from one degree of glory to another; for this comes from the Lord who is the Spirit.[5]

Pope Pius XII explains the spiritual sense as follows:

The exegete, just as he must search out and expound the literal meaning of the words intended and expressed by the sacred writer, must also seek the spiritual sense, provided it is clearly intended by God. . . . Now our divine Savior himself points out to us and teaches us this same sense in the holy Gospel; the apostles also . . . profess it in their spoken and written words; the unchanging tradition of the Church approves it; and finally the most ancient usage of the liturgy proclaims it . . . [6]

The qualification "provided it is clearly intended by God" is crucial. It is possible and was the case that practically every incident and figure of the Hebrew Scriptures was seen as a type of Christ and clearly that often stretched the meaning. This fuller sense must be kept within the Church's tradition.

This scriptural sense is especially used by the Church Fathers in their scriptural exposition and theology. It also sometimes provides the basis for selecting the first reading and Gospel texts of the Sunday and feastday liturgies. Often the first reading foreshadows an event or theme which finds its fullness in the Gospel.[7]

OTHER SENSES

A third, **consequent sense** expands beyond the previous two senses. Scripture interpretation need not be tied exclusively to the literal or even spiritual senses. It is valid to develop the author's thought, understand what is said in the light of current theories and understanding, and translate scriptural ideas into current modes of thought and speech. This is often done in homilies[8] and in some theology.

---

5. 2 Cor 3:15-18
6. Pius XII, Divino Afflante Spiritu
7. Way 22
8. Way 22

However the consequent sense should not be cut off from and certainly not opposed to the literal sense. There should be some connection. After all if the consequent sense is not a sound development it can hardly be a valid meaning of Scripture.

An example of consequent sense can be found in modern theology's attempts to understand the Adam and Eve story[9] (which teaches original sin)[10] in terms of modern concepts and science. How, for example, might original sin be understood in the context of an evolutionary theory of human development?

Finally one must point out another sense of Scripture if only to reveal its inadequacy. The **accommodated sense** results when a passage of Scripture is applied to modern situations almost at random with little regard for the literal meaning. Thus the phrase "Many are called but few are chosen" might be applied to modern politics. This is obviously not within the bounds of valid interpretation.

However accommodation can become a means of entering into Scripture by the Christian. In approaching Scripture Christians seek meaning and guidance for their lives. Thus it is beneficial to enter into scriptural stories seeking meaning for our life. In such a case the Scripture may be accommodated to the person. This is permissible provided one does not go on to assert that the accommodation—what he or she discovered—is as valid or significant as the literal, spiritual or even consequential meaning.

TO DEEPEN—

Which sense of Scripture is most important and the focus of most current Scripture scholarship?

Does the literal sense mean that a Catholic must take everything in Scripture literally?

What are some critical tools which scholars use to study the Scriptures?

What does the spiritual sense of Scripture mean? Where is it sometimes encountered by Catholics today?

Further Reading:

Fuller, Reginald, and Wright, G. Ernest. *Book of the Acts of God: An Introduction to the Bible.* Doubleday, 1957.

---

9. Gen 2:4b—3:24
10. Truth 57

Hagen, Kenneth, Harrington, Daniel, Osborne, Grant, Burgess, Joseph. *The Bible in the Churches. How Different Christians Interpret the Scriptures.* Paulist Press, 1985.

Kelly, George A. *The Church's Problem with Bible Scholars.* Franciscan Herald, 1985.

Kelsey, Morton. *Myth, History, Faith.* Paulist Press, 1974.

Marrow, Stanley. *Words of Jesus in Our Gospels. A Catholic Response to Fundamentalism.* Paulist Press, 1979.

Stacy, David. *Interpreting the Bible.* Seabury, 1977

6. Working with Scripture

How can Scripture become a tool for the spiritual journey? Although biblical scholarship is vast, the Christian need not master that field to read the Scriptures as a guide to life.

First, Christian life is an ongoing conversion to Jesus Christ. Scripture fosters **conversion.** It holds up a mirror showing our true selves. It addresses God's word to our human condition, calling us to abandon old ways to embrace a new life in Jesus Christ.

Two groups of guiding questions help Scripture foster continuing conversion. First, what does this scriptural passage promise you? What does it offer of life, meaning, fulfillment, happiness? What does it reveal of ultimate reality?

Second, what does this revelation demand? What is the price of this good news? How are you challenged to change opinions, values, behavior, lifestyle?

For example, Jesus forgives a person's sins, releasing that person from sin's bondage. He or she is reincorporated into the human community. Perhaps he or she is also healed of illness. Thus the Scripture promises all of these things and more.

But this forgiveness has a price. Perhaps it is becoming forgiving in turn. Or it demands changing one's actions or lifestyle—living without that sin in the future. Or you must trust Jesus' power to heal. Perhaps the price is forsaking accustomed beliefs.

The Christian further reads Scripture for **instruction.** Scripture is God's revelation addressed to humanity. The contents of that message are the Scriptures. The Christian pursues the wisdom of Scripture within the context of the Church's liturgy. The Bible does not invite cover to cover reading. Some texts are more important than others. Some are best read in the context of others. The Church's liturgy gathers scriptural themes[11] in such a way that one is led into the message.

Of course one's study of the Scriptures for wisdom should be guided by Scripture scholarship.[12] The literal meaning is not always on the surface. Scholarship helps understand the text's intentions, as well as the author's ideas and viewpoints.[13]

The Christian also approaches the Scriptures as a means for **prayer.** The Book of Psalms is the Christian prayerbook. And many other scriptural passages give word to the deepest thoughts we wish to

---

11. Way 22
12. Life 13
13. Truth 2ff

address or hear from God. Scripture words and phrases are ideal for meditation.[14] Contemplation allows the Christian to enter into the various scriptural scenes.

Whether or not a Christian uses the Scriptures for prayer, whenever approaching Scripture the Christian's attitude should be prayerful—open to God. Scripture is a means of dialogue with God. Traditionally Catholics have used a short prayer before reading Scripture.

TO DEEPEN—

How should the reading of Scripture differ from reading another book or magazine?

How do the Scriptures help the average Christian?

Look at next Sunday's Scriptures. How do they instruct you? Use them for prayer this week. How do they help your conversion?

Further Reading:

Gallagher, Maureen, Wagner, Clare. *Praying with Scripture*. Paulist Press, 1984.
McKenzie, John. *How Relevant Is the Bible?* Thomas More, 1981.

Prayer:

O God, who instructed the hearts of the faithful by the light of the Holy Spirit, grant us the same Spirit so that we may have a right judgment in all things and ever rejoice in his consolation. Amen.

---

14. Life 7

7. Basic Considerations

VERSIONS

Significant variations exist among Christians concerning the canon[15] of Scripture. At first there was no definite list of scriptural books. A number of books in Hebrew were sacred to Israel. At the time of Christ, the most popular version was a Greek translation—the **Septuagint.** This actually became the official Christian version of Israel's Scriptures. St. Jerome made the authoritative translation of the Scriptures into Latin—the **Vulgate.** The Council of Trent chose this version—with Jerome's listing of books—as the correct canon. Protestants in choosing their canon went back to the Hebrew Scriptures, accepting only those books extant in Hebrew.

Catholics include a number of books[16] considered apocrypha (not Scripture) by Protestants. Catholics name these "deutero-canonical"— they are part of the canon.[17] The Orthodox Church includes books not included in Catholic or Protestant Bibles. The Catholic apocrypha includes these plus other books not considered Scripture but helpful and instructive.

All Churches agree upon the contents of the New Testament. Minor variations occur in the numbering of certain chapters and verses, and in older Bibles some of the books' names differ.[18]

A Catholic version will usually be identified as such. The Catholic version is substantially the same as the two Testaments plus the (Protestant) apocrypha.

TRANSLATIONS

The second consideration regards the translation. The Scriptures were originally written in Hebrew (Hebrew Scriptures), Aramaic (certain parts of the Hebrew Scriptures) and Greek (New Testament). Thus any English edition is a translation. A wealth of translations are available today. Some are Catholic in sponsorship, some Protestant, some ecumenical,[19] some the work of one or two scholars. Below is a list of the most common translations available today with a short description.

---

15. Truth 3
16. Truth 4
17. Truth 3
18. Most prominent is the Old Catholic numbering of the Psalms. Modern translations usually follow the Hebrew numbering. Psalm references necessitate knowing which version one is using as well as the reference's version.
19. Life 27

The traditional English edition, the **King James Bible,** was produced for Protestants under the patronage of King James I of England. It is noted for its beauty of language and profoundly influenced English language and style. The **Revised Standard Version** is a modernization in the light of scholarship while keeping as much as possible the original style. Thus it combines tradition with accuracy.

Catholic-sponsored modern translations include the **New American Bible** which combines scholarship with a modern American style. The **Jerusalem Bible** is an English translation from the original tongues. But in questions of interpretation it follows the work of the French scholars who produced this modern edition. A second edition has improved the overall quality of this translation.

The **New English Bible** is an ecumenical Protestant effort by the Churches of Great Britain—an English equivalent of the New American Bible (although its style is more elegant). **Today's English Version** (also known as **The Good News for Modern Man**) by the American Bible Society provides a clear, modern translation. In aiming for simplicity and clarity it sacrifices literary style.

Finally there are a number of paraphrases. These are not translations but interpretations of the text. Thus they reflect a certain bias. However they can be helpful in wrestling with a text as long as it is borne in mind that this is indeed an interpretation. **The Living Bible** falls into this category, as does the beautiful paraphrase of the New Testament by J. B. Phillips.

SCRIPTURAL REFERENCES

A scriptural reference consists of three parts: a name and two sets of numbers. The name or abbreviation refers to the book where the passage is located. First determine the appropriate book referred to. In the case of abbreviations a table will usually be found at the front of the Bible.[20] Books existing in a number of volumes are prefaced with a numeral. Thus 1 Cor refers to the First Letter of Paul to the Corinthians.

The following numeral locates the book's chapter. Following a colon another numeral or series refers to the numbered chapter verses. Thus Is 52:3–5 refers to the Book of Isaiah, the 52nd chapter, verses 3–5. These chapter and verse numbers were added by later scribes.

---

20. Way 4

TO DEEPEN—

How do Catholic and Protestant versions of the Bible differ?

Look up a certain verse such as Jn 3:16 in a number of different translations. What are the differences? What are the similarities?

Look up the following Scripture references:

Jn 3:16
Mt 6:9–13
2 Sam. 1:17–27
Ps 100
1 Cor 13

Further Reading:

Here are some tools for Scripture study:

Achtemeier, Paul J., ed., *Harper's Bible Dictionary*. Harper and Row, 1985.

Brown, Raymond; Fitzmyer, Joseph; Murphy, Roland, eds. *Jerome Biblical Commentary*. Prentice-Hall, 1968. The standard one-volume Catholic commentary.

Cambridge Bible Commentaries. Cambridge University Press. Separate paperback commentaries for each book based on the New English Bible.

Cruden, *Concordance of the Bible*. Zondervan, 1976. Enables you to find a scriptural reference by means of a key word in the quotation.

Funk, Robert. *New Gospel Parallels*. Fortress, 1986. Sets out the passages of the gospels which present similar material side by side for comparison.

Hughes & Travis. *Harper's Introduction to the Bible*. Harper & Row, 1982.

May, Herbert & Hunt, G. H. *The Oxford Bible Atlas*. Oxford University Press, 1974.

McKenzie, John. *Dictionary of the Bible*. Macmillan, 1965.

Rouet, Albert. *A Short Dictionary of the New Testament*. Paulist Press, 1982.

TO CONTINUE—

If you want to continue to explore the contents of the Scriptures go to Truth 2ff.

The core of Christian belief is found in the Gospels—Truth 15ff.

You might want to continue into Way 8 and discover how Scripture is integrated into Christian worship.

Life 7 provides traditional ways of praying with Scripture.

Life 2 shows an example of how Christians have seen Christ in the Hebrew Scriptures.

$\Diamond$

8. The Way of Worship

The Way of the Cross

Catechumens are signed with the cross to guide their journey toward full faith. Tertullian[1] says: "At every forward step and movement, at every going in and out, when we put on our clothes and shoes—in all the ordinary actions of everyday life, we trace the sign of the cross." Exploring this sign's meaning leads into Catholic worship.

A Roman Catholic makes the sign of the cross by joining together the first two fingertips and the thumb of the right hand, then touching forehead, sternum, then left and right shoulders. The words "In the name of the Father, and of the Son, and of the Holy Spirit" accompany the gesture. Dip the fingers first in holy water when available.

Confessing the Cross as the Means of Our Salvation

The sign first acknowledges Jesus' cross as the instrument of our salvation. Jesus' sacrificial death on the cross effects the salvation of the world. The cross makes us whole.

Catholics enter into the cross through the liturgy and worship of the Church since this is Jesus' prayer and work. The liturgy applies the salvation won by Jesus to the contemporary community.

Jesus' cross also symbolizes the personal work of conversion and transformation. Christian life is a practice of dying to oneself to be brought to full life in Jesus Christ.[2] Thus the sign of the cross (especially with the use of holy water) is a renewal of our baptism.

Confession of the Holy Trinity

The words profess the Holy Trinity[3] and thus the shape of Christian prayer. There is only one God. But there are three persons: Father, Son and Holy Spirit.

Christian prayer has a particular shape. The Christian does not pray to God as though God were out there—a separate being. Christian prayer is addressed to the Father—the source of Godhead. But it is given shape and utterance by the Son. Thus Christian prayer is through the Son. All Christian prayer is taken up in the prayer of Jesus, the path to the Father. But prayer arises not from what is not God, but from

---

1. Life 30
2. Rom 6:1–14
3. Truth 27

God's self—the Holy Spirit—the breath of God within which sustains existence itself. Thus prayer is in the Holy Spirit.

In the liturgy Christ is seldom the direct object of prayer. The liturgy itself is Christ's prayer—offering himself and the world to the Father. And similarly Christians do not address a God far off or totally other. Prayer is grounded in the Spirit of God who groans and yearns for unity.[4] The Spirit bears us home along the Way of Christ to the Father.

Blessing of Spiritual Centers

The sign of the cross blesses and unites our spiritual centers. The mind is likened to the Father, the source of all wisdom. We ask that our thoughts be purified so that we might comprehend and cling to the Truth.

The body is blessed in the name of the Son. God does not save from embodiment, but through the body. God does not scorn or shrink from our flesh.[5] Indeed it becomes the very means of salvation. Thus we ask that flesh become a means to wholeness. May our will be aligned with the will of God as was the will of Jesus in whose name we stand before God and whose prayer we make our own.[6]

Finally we cross our heart, the seat of love. The Holy Spirit is the love between Father and Son. As love unites Father and Son, so love unites our minds and bodies. Love unites the many in the one Christ. Sin fragments humanity from oneself and others. God makes us whole—mind, body and spirit. God makes us one in the body of Christ united in the Holy Spirit and presented to the Father through the obedience of the Son.

TO DEEPEN—

How does the sign of the cross symbolically express Christian faith?

Practice making the sign of the cross whenever you begin to pray.

Make the sign of the cross using the holy water whenever you enter the church.

---

4. Rom 8:22
5. Life 48
6. Way 50

Further Reading:

Benson, George. *The Cross: Its History and Symbolism.* Hacker, 1976.
Irwin, Kevin W. *Liturgy, Prayer and Spirituality.* Paulist Press, 1984.
Weatherhead, Leslie. *The Meaning of the Cross.* Abingdon, 1982.

Prayer—The Doxology

Glory to the Father, and to the Son, and to the Holy Spirit, as it was in the
beginning, is now, and will be forever. Amen.

TO CONTINUE—

A practical guide through the Sunday liturgy is found in Way 19ff.
Way 18ff explains the meaning of liturgy.
If a major season is underway Way 28ff introduces the Christian year.

9. The Way of the Liturgy

The Church derives its life and sustenance from the Lord's paschal mystery—Jesus' living, dying and rising. That sacrifice establishes the new covenant with humanity. And people enter into that covenant by participating in Jesus' saving action liturgically. This worship is the center of the Church's life. This public liturgy is distinct from the prayer life and devotions of the Christian.[1] The liturgy informs and inspires all other Christian prayer.

The contents of the covenant are the revelation of God.[2] Those contents flow as two streams—Scripture and tradition. Tradition is the entire handing down of the Christian faith—the process by which the Church transmits the word of God.

---

1. Life 6
2. Truth 1ff

10. The Meaning of Christian Liturgy

Tradition is encountered primarily in the Church's worship. Liturgy is not arbitrary but structured according to Christ's prayer and life into which the community enters to be converted to the kingdom of God.[3] The word "liturgy" means work of the people. Through the liturgy, the people of God offer praise and thanksgiving to a saving God. The liturgy encompasses the Eucharist,[4] the sacraments[5] and the Liturgy of the Hours, often called "the Office."[6]

The roots of Christian worship are in Israel. That worship is passed on as one of the Church's most precious treasures. Participation in the liturgy immerses us in the tradition and passes it to succeeding generations.

But just what is liturgy? How do Christians understand it? How can one enter into the celebration? The Second Vatican Council defined liturgy in the document responsible for the sweeping reforms of Catholic worship begun in the 1960's and continuing today—namely, the Constitution on the Sacred Liturgy, from which the following excerpts, from the Introduction and paragraphs 7–10, are especially relevant.

---

3. Truth 16
4. Way 19ff
5. Truth 74ff
6. Life 38

The Purpose of the Liturgy

For it is the liturgy through which, especially in the divine sacrifice of the Eucharist, "the work of our redemption is accomplished," and it is through the liturgy, especially, that the faithful are enabled to express in their lives and manifest to others the mystery of Christ and the real nature of the true Church. . . .

The liturgy daily builds up those who are in the Church, making of them a holy temple of the Lord, a dwelling-place for God in the Spirit, to the mature measure of the fullness of Christ. At the same time it marvelously increases their power to preach Christ and thus show forth the Church, a sign lifted up among the nations, to those who are outside, a sign under which the scattered children of God may be gathered together until there is one fold and one shepherd.

The Presence of Christ in the Liturgy

To accomplish so great a work Christ is always present in his Church, especially in liturgical celebrations. He is present in the Sacrifice of the Mass not only in the person of his ministry, "the same now offering, through the ministry of priests, who formerly offered himself on the cross," but especially in the eucharistic species. By his power he is present in the sacraments so that when anybody baptizes it is really Christ himself who baptizes. He is present in his word since it is he himself who speaks when the Holy Scriptures are read in the Church. Lastly, he is present when the Church prays and sings, for he has promised, "Where two or three are gathered together in my name there am I in the midst of them."[7]

The Action of the Church in the Liturgy

The liturgy, then is rightly seen as an exercise of the priestly office of Jesus Christ; it involves the presentation of humanity's sanctification under the guise of signs perceptible by the

7. Mt 18:20

senses and its accomplishment in ways appropriate to each of these signs. In it full public worship is performed by the mystical body of Jesus Christ, that is, by the head and his members.

From this it follows that every liturgical celebration, because it is an action of Christ the priest and of his body, which is the Church, is a sacred action surpassing all others. No other action of the Church can equal its efficacy by the same title and to the same degree.

The Liturgy and the Mission of the Church

The sacred liturgy does not exhaust the entire activity of the Church. Before (people) can come to the liturgy they must be called to faith and to conversion. . . .

Nevertheless the liturgy is the summit toward which the activity of the Church is directed; it is also the fount from which all its power flows. For the goal of apostolic endeavor is that all who are made sons and daughters of God by faith and baptism should come together to praise God in the midst of his Church, to take part in the sacrifice and to eat the Lord's supper.

The liturgy, in its turn, moves the faithful filled with "the paschal sacraments" to be "one in holiness"; it prays that "they hold fast in their lives to what they have grasped by their faith." The renewal in the Eucharist of the covenant between the Lord and humanity draws the faithful and sets them aflame with Christ's insistent love. From the liturgy, therefore, and especially from the Eucharist, grace is poured forth upon us as from a fountain, and the sanctification of (humanity) in Christ and the glorification of God to which all other activities of the Church are directed, as toward their end, are achieved with maximum effectiveness.

11. The Actions of the Liturgy

Liturgy involves ritual words, action, symbols and gesture. As ritual, it is sacred drama that a person enters to grow in faith and to be transformed into the image of Jesus Christ. Ritual uses the full array of symbolic and non-verbal communication to convey the drama of worship. Ritual uses symbols, gestures, ritual objects, and music to involve the community in the sacred action.[8]

A ritual, of course, also involves words. Christian ritual never divorces words from the action. The words give concrete expression to the ritual action. Actually, the words make the actions specifically Christian—baptism is not simply a bath, but a death and resurrection in Jesus Christ. The words reveal that meaning.

Ritual's essence is action, a sacred drama entered into so that a person may grow in faith and be transformed. To enter into the liturgy we perform the actions of the rite. Certain key actions are important to understand for meaningful participation. These actions are found in the sacraments of the Church as well as other prayers and celebrations. They embody essential revealed truths. Participation in these actions applies Jesus' message to our concrete life. Our life changes, transformed into the likeness of Christ.

Liturgy moves between two poles reflecting the covenant which it serves. First, God calls us to the covenant and worship. Thus liturgy embodies God's call. In the liturgy then God blesses his people, reconciles them, heals them and sends them forth to mission.

The second movement of liturgy is our response to God. By entering into the covenant we praise God. We give thanks for blessings. We confess our sins and we offer our lives to God.

GOD'S CALL

12. Conversion

God calls first for conversion to the new life offered in Jesus. Christian living involves many small conversions adding up to a turning from darkness toward the light of Christ.

Three things are necessary for conversion. First is self-knowledge. We must know who we are and what we have made of ourselves and

---

8. Truth 74ff

our world. The liturgy and in particular the Scriptures guide this process.

But the truth of who we are only begins conversion. Who might we become? Indeed, who are we already in the grace of Christ? A better possibility exists for ourselves and our world: the kingdom of God. This kingdom is experienced through Jesus' words and liturgical actions: forgiveness, healing, nourishment, blessing.

With this twofold knowledge and God's grace—the third component—the person responds and experiences transformation: turning from sin toward grace, from death to life, from sickness to health, from the world to the kingdom. Conversion permeates the entire liturgy.

13. Blessing

God created all that is and considers it good.[9] He creates through his word sent forth in glory. Creation is not an event far off in the mists of time but ongoing.

Blessing grounds Christian faith. God rejoices in creation, blessing it abundantly. Blessing expresses God's love for creatures. It establishes God's relationship to us. God's blessing reveals himself and his goodness to creation. God draws creatures into relationship. Blessed by God we turn in love to our fellows and the entire creation in blessing. This act of blessing unites and lifts us to God.

Blessings promise favors, fruitful lands, healthy children, wholesome living. Blessing Israel, God tells her what that blessing will bring. When God blesses us it is in promise of a full life and happiness.

Christian liturgy is filled with blessing. It confers God's love and favor. It enables us to see the wonder of creation and to rejoice with God in it. We are graced, moving out of sin and selfishness to embrace the kingdom of God. God's blessing promises a radiant future. God's people look forward to the kingdom's coming in glory, when all God's promises, heard from the prophets and Jesus, will be ours. The action of blessing keeps these promises in mind, and spurs Christians to continue Jesus' mission on behalf of the kingdom.

Blessing reveals God's love and constant care. Each blessing proclaims that love anew. And transformed by Christ Christians become vehicles of blessing. As blessing abounds the creation turns from the darkness of sin and selfishness to the light of love and eternal life.

---

9. Truth 28

14. Healing

Healing prepares us for mission. God does not simply heal inner, spiritual hurts; grace aids the healing of body and society. God's grace always works toward healing. Participation in the liturgy involves bringing God one's brokenness, asking to be healed. This healing is not magic and certainly does not replace medicine or hygiene. Grace works through these processes. And healing, as Jesus constantly reminds those who are healed, comes not solely from God's power but depends upon faith: trust in God's power to transform. Participation in the liturgy strengthens that trust essential to our and the world's healing.

15. Mission

Every liturgy concludes by sending us forth to be for the world what we have experienced in this liturgy: a sign of God's grace and kingdom. Christians are not distinguished by the grace of God's salvation. In Jesus Christ the entire creation is already reconciled. Christians have responded to Jesus' call, thus allowing God's grace to reconcile here and now so that the kingdom's presence might be manifested. Transformed, Christians in turn become signs of the kingdom's presence to others.

So, having together celebrated what God has accomplished in Jesus Christ, they are sent to show forth that good news in daily living. Not all are called to be missionaries preaching the good news, but all are witnesses through example to the joy, blessing, healing, and reconciliation they have found. Those fed with the body of Christ become bread for their nourishment are now sent to become in turn bread for the world.[10]

Only in sharing faith does it grow in power to transform not only us but the very world we live in. If we try to keep our faith, preserving it in purity lest it be tarnished, it withers and dies. Only in giving it away, in sharing joy with others, does faith blossom.

OUR RESPONSE

16. Praise

Christians gather to praise God and the wonders of creation. Prayers which give glory to God are known as **doxologies**.[11]

---

10. Way 36
11. Way 8

A Christian is basically joyful, rejoicing in the beauty of creation. But such an attitude is not necessarily easy or even natural. People can become bogged down and dejected by life's difficulties or evil encountered. But difficulties do not lead Christians to abandon their vision. At base the world is good and elicits hope rather than despair.

Christians gather together to affirm one another in this vision. They join together in adoration of the beauty, truth, and goodness of life whose source is God.

Praise is expressed through song in Christian liturgy. Song raises the heart, rallies the emotions. Singing and the gift of melody can change one's outlook.

17. Confession

Humanity is not today as originally created, but fallen into sin.[12] Sin must be reconciled in confession so that we may become whole. Although central to the sacrament of penance,[13] confession extends far beyond. It is the first step on the Christian path not only at the beginning, but at every beginning: the beginning of the catechumen's journey, the beginning of the liturgy, the beginning of each prayer.[14]

Confession occurs often during Christian liturgies, and, although assuming different shapes, the action remains the same. First, Christians look into their hearts to discover where they have sinned, where they have fallen short of the Gospel's demands, how they have failed to recognize and to serve the Christ. An examination of conscience, the usual format, is a detailed and prolonged process as in the sacrament of penance. A briefer formula simply acknowledges sin as in the Lord's Prayer: "Forgive us our trespasses. . . . "[15]

Acknowledgement of sin is never met with condemnation as might be expected. Instead in response we hear God's word of forgiveness and reconciliation. This forgiveness restores our relationship with God. God's grace raises us from our fall and continues the kingdomward journey.

Whereas in the world failure or sin leads to disgrace, humiliation, rejection, God meets sin with an outstretched hand. Confession is never easy. It goes against the world's grain; we dare see ourselves in the Gospel's light with all faults exposed. Seeing ourselves as we truly

---

12. Truth 57
13. Truth 80
14. Life 3
15. Way 50

are, we are not left to despair but instead given the power to move out of this misery into the happiness extended by Jesus as a present possibility.

Confession more than other liturgical actions necessitates bringing our life to mind in the action. Mere recitation of sins does nothing to help. Without such self-knowledge we cannot move beyond sin to become a new people. Confession has the power to change that which, alone, we are powerless to effect.

18. Thanksgiving

At first glance thanksgiving might seem the same as praise. But Christians praise God for his act of creation. They give thanks for the saving works of Jesus Christ. The Greek-derived word "Eucharist" means thanksgiving. It has come to denote the entire action of the liturgy because the earliest Christian liturgies begin immediately with thanks to God for our redemption in Christ.

The biblical words describing the Eucharist, appearing in the various Gospel eucharistic stories, define the action. The components are: taking, thanksgiving, breaking and sharing which together form the Christian act of thanksgiving.

The miracle of the loaves and fishes[16] demonstrates the power of this action. While common sense says that supplies are scarce, Jesus shows that if we are open to God and trust, we will be given what we need.

The disciples complain that there is no food and that the hungry crowd may grow violent. Jesus asks them to bring what they have to him. He receives the loaves and fish. Similarly we first become aware of what God has given. The gifts begin with life itself and the continuing gift of breath. Too often people ignore what has been given. Instead they believe that they have somehow created themselves or brought themselves to this present state. A Christian realizes that all life is truly a gift beyond compare that must be consciously accepted to enter fully into one's inheritance. So thanksgiving begins by acknowledging gifts received from God.

Jesus then gives thanks for the loaves and fish. He doesn't make demands on God, asking for a miracle. He simply, honestly and wholeheartedly gives thanks. This act of pure thanksgiving effects what happens next.

Jesus breaks up the food to distribute. This breaking is sometimes

---

16. Mt 14:13–21; Mk 5:30–44; Lk 9:10–17

spoken of as sacrifice. A sacrifice is a joyful surrender to God. Christians are called to imitate Jesus, making their very lives a sacrifice. Jesus cautions us not to be concerned to save our life.[17] "Lose your life for my sake." The Christian pours himself or herself out in a joyous sacrifice for our brothers and sisters. Besides this ultimate sacrifice, many small sacrifices are made daily. Had we the courage to risk them, they might reveal the fruits of sacrifice not as death and annihilation as is feared, but life and abundance.

Jesus shares the broken bread and fish with the people. And Christians sacrifice to share life and wealth with others. The crumbs gathered afterward filled twelve baskets. And when Christians sacrifice they believe that they are not depleted or short-changed, but instead life becomes full, rich, and abundant.

The eucharistic action and other thankful actions throughout the liturgy allow Christians to practice thanksgiving. Bringing to mind what they have received, with Jesus they give thanks to God. And since they give thanks in Jesus he purifies our action, transforming it into his perfect sacrifice. Strengthened in belief they go forth and enact what was practiced in the liturgy.

TO DEEPEN—

How have you experienced these actions in your life?

Attend a Christian liturgy and notice when and how these actions occur.

What do these actions tell you about Christianity's view of life?

Further Reading:

Bernier, Paul, ed. *Bread Broken and Shared.* Ave Maria Press, 1981.

Bouyer, Louis. *Liturgical Piety.* University of Notre Dame, 1965.

Cuming, Geoffrey. *To Give Thanks and Remember.* Grove Press, 1981.

Jean-Mesmy, Claude. *Living the Liturgy.* Alba, 1966.

Mitchel, Leonel. *The Meaning of Ritual.* Paulist Press, 1974.

Ramshaw-Schmidt, Gail. *Christ in Sacred Speech: The Meaning of Liturgical Language.* Fortress, 1986.

Searle, Mark. *Liturgy Made Simple.* Liturgical Press, 1981.

White, James F. *Introduction to Christian Worship.* Abington, 1980.

---

17. Mt 16:25

19. The Shape of the Liturgy

TO PREPARE—

Attending a Sunday Eucharist provides a reference for the following material.

Catholic liturgy takes two basic forms. The sacramental liturgy is most familiar since it includes the Eucharist celebrated on Sundays as well as daily. The second form is the daily prayer of the Church,[1] not as well known because it has largely been supplanted by daily Mass. But it is prayed by those in religious life,[2] all priests, and some lay people. The Second Vatican Council encouraged its restoration to parish life.

Since the Church's worship centers upon the Mass, our exploration is based upon it. Indeed the other sacraments[3] are often celebrated within it.

Prior to the Second Vatican Council the liturgy was rigidly uniform. Mass in Hong Kong was little different from Mass in New York. The Council reformed the liturgy in accordance with the early Church and allowed it to be celebrated in the language of the local congregation, calling for further modifications based upon local usage and custom. Gone are the days of absolute identity. However the essential structures and movements remain the same and clearly recognized from one community to another.

The celebration of the sacraments includes two basic components: the word and then the sacrament. These complement each another— the word gives concreteness to the sacramental celebration, grounding it in the experience of Jesus, and the sacrament gives depth and resonance to the Word, applying God's grace to this moment and these people.

Ministries

Celebration of the Eucharist involves a number of ministries and ministers who enable the people to perform the liturgy. The clerical ministers are those in holy orders.[4] The priest presides over the liturgy, and thus is called the presider. He may be assisted by a deacon who

---

1. Life 38
2. Life 11
3. Truth 74ff
4. Truth 84

proclaims the Gospel, delivers the homily and helps with other parts of the rite.

Acolytes assist the ministers by holding candles, bringing the gifts to the altar and helping with Communion. Lectors read the first and second readings. Lay ministers of the Eucharist help distribute Communion.

A minister of music and the choir provide music and lead the congregation in song. Artistic ministries oversee the decoration of the church. Banners proclaim seasonal themes and feasts. Altar and lectern decorations, hangings, flowers, and incense all contribute to the liturgy of thanksgiving. These arts are not simply icing to the liturgy. They are integral to our celebration. Music raises the heart to God. Pictures bring to mind the great events of our salvation. Dance gives bodily expression to thanksgiving. And the shape of the church itself determines how a congregation feels about itself and how it worships. A ministry of hospitality has grown up in many places that provides coffee and donuts afterward. Again, this is not merely nice, but rather an expression and way of celebrating our communion in Christ.

The fine arts are rightly classed among the noblest activities of humanity's genius; this is especially true of religious art and of its highest manifestation, sacred art. Of their nature the arts are directed toward expressing in some way the infinite beauty of God in works made by human hands. Their dedication to the increase of God's praise and of his glory is more complete, the more exclusively they are devoted to turning people's minds devoutly toward God.[5]

All these ministries exist not to celebrate the liturgy, but rather to assist God's people in their thanksgiving. The people are not bystanders or secondary. Their praise and thanksgiving form the content of Christ's praise to the Father.

20. Introductory Rites

Liturgy begins with a hymn or psalm as the ministers process toward the sanctuary. The song introduces the theme, feast or season.

---

5. Constitution on the Sacred Liturgy, n. 122

Singing lifts prayer to a higher level—involving us more in the act of praise. St. Benedict[6] encouraged his monks to sing the psalms, "He who sings prays twice." On Sundays, feast days and special occasions the procession may include colorful banners and the processional cross.

The ministers approach the altar and kiss it in reverence. This entire procession is a means of focusing and calling the people to prayer. We have a sense of being gathered before the altar to begin the celebration. The presider leads the people in the sign of the cross.[7]

The **greeting** follows as the presider proclaims the Lord's presence in the community. The people respond, acknowledging that presence of Christ that creates community.

All Christian worship celebrates Jesus' conquest of sin and death, reconciling us to God. "Coming together as God's family, with confidence let us ask the Father's forgiveness, for he is full of mercy and compassion."

On certain occasions holy water is sprinkled, recalling baptism. An ancient litany from the Greek Church praises God's mercy and compassion which we see in God's actions toward us. A longer formula, sometimes used, stresses penitence. Confession and reconciliation is a constant motif[8]—Jesus heals and forgives so that we may enter into community with one another and God.

The **Gloria** or hymn of praise is appropriate to major celebrations (Sundays and major feast days). Its opening words are drawn from the angels' song to the shepherds.[9] Originally it was used only during the Christmas celebrations. The rest is of unknown origin from the fourth century or before. During Advent or Lent its absence expresses the penitential dimension of these seasons.

The **opening prayer** concludes the introductory rites. This entire rite has been a call to prayer. Now the presider invites the people to pray. Silence allows all to address the Lord. Then the celebrant gathers the prayer in a summation, bringing it to the Lord.

Amen, a biblical affirmation, means "So be it." It concludes every Christian prayer and is one of the most common liturgical responses. It is an expression of ratification, consent and acceptance: the people make the Church's words their own.

---

6. Life 30
7. Way 8
8. Way 17
9. Lk 2:14

21. LITURGY OF THE WORD

This liturgy forms part of every sacramental celebration. It instructs catechumens in the faith and nourishes their journey toward full initiation.[10] This liturgy is most fully developed in the Eucharist. Other celebrations may modify it but essentials remain the same.

In the liturgy of the word Christians come together to thank God for God's gifts. Listening to God's word they grow in faith, more conformed to the mind of Christ. They praise God for his goodness and glory. Liturgy celebrates the wonders of creation and gives thanks for the reality of redemption.

22. Service of Readings

Having gathered, sung God's praises and opened our hearts in prayer we are prepared to celebrate God's presence in Scripture. This service is not primarily instruction, although that is certainly present. It is a celebration not of what God has said, but of God today speaking to us.

> When the Scriptures are read in the Church, God himself speaks to his people, and it is Christ, present in his word, who proclaims the Gospel.
>
> The readings should be listened to with respect; they are a principal element of the liturgy. In the biblical readings God's word is addressed to all people of every era and is understandable in itself, but a homily, as a living explanation of the word, increases its effectiveness and is an integral part of the service.[11]

The lectionary contains the Scripture readings for every official liturgy. Scripture is the living word of God addressed not only to the people of its day but to every succeeding generation. We listen to the Scriptures to hear what God is saying to us today. We listen to deepen our faith and appreciation of Jesus. And in responding to what we have heard we affirm our faith.

---

10. Intro 6ff
11. General Introduction of the Roman Missal, n. 9

First Reading: Hebrew Scriptures

The first reading is mostly chosen from the Hebrew Scriptures; during liturgical seasons the Book of Acts might be read. This reading usually harmonizes with the Gospel. It might present a story upon which the Gospel for the day is based, or amplify a Gospel theme. It reveals the continuity between Israel and Jesus who comes not to replace but to fulfill Israel.[12]

Responsorial Psalm

The psalm reflects themes in the readings. The psalm consists of an antiphon (a repeated verse) sung by the people alternating with psalm verses by the choir. It is a vehicle of prayer and praise—an atmosphere of prayer within which the readings occur. The psalm is a corporate proclamation of the word. The people take the word of the Lord for the day, make it their own and proclaim it prayerfully.

Second Reading: Christian Scriptures

The second reading, commonly called the Epistle, is usually from a letter,[13] although Revelation or Acts may also be read. While addressed to particular situations in the early Church, their message transcends the centuries to motivate contemporary Christians and deepen our appreciation of the mystery of Christ. These readings operate on a cycle independent of the Gospel, so that, outside of special times and feasts, selected passages of the letter are read in order each week.

Gospel Acclamation: Alleluia

"Alleluia" is a Latin echo of the Hebrew acclamation "Praise God." It has become a key word in Christian worship. Here it heralds the Gospel.

In a solemn celebration the deacon goes to the altar where the Gospel is enthroned. He lifts the book and, accompanied by servers with incense and candles (symbols of Christ's light), processes with the Gospels held high while choir and community acclaim the good news with "Alleluia," alternating with verses appropriate to today's Gospel. Christians acclaim the most wonderful deed of God among humankind, Jesus Christ, here made visible in the book containing his words.

---

12. Mt 5:17–20
13. Truth 14

The Alleluia is not sung during Lent. It is replaced by a verse echoing the day's Gospel theme. During Easter and Pentecost, a poetic introduction called a sequence prepares the community for its proclamation.

Gospel

The Gospel[14] is the climax of the liturgy of the word. Catholics believe that in the proclamation of the Gospel Christ is truly present to the community. For this reason they stand to witness to Christ's resurrection which allows him to be present to his people.

As the deacon or priest introduces the Gospel all sign themselves with the cross traced on their foreheads, lips and hearts. Doing so asks Christ to come into our minds and hearts so that we may in turn proclaim him with our lips.

Hearing the Gospel proclaimed, Catholics identify with the first community who heard these words. And the living word addresses our situation today as it did the original gathering.

On concluding, the minister proclaims, "This is the gospel of the Lord." He means not the book, but the Gospel, the good news itself. Catholics affirm faith by responding, "Praise to you, Lord Jesus Christ."

Homily [Sermon]

Christians believe that "faith comes through preaching."[15] This idea is rooted in Jewish belief that the creative power of God's word transforms human life.

The Scriptures are not always easy to understand and apply to present life. For this reason the homily breaks open the Scriptures, showing how the word of God addresses us today. What import does the Gospel have for our lives today, for the world we live in, for issues in the community forum?

Profession of Faith [Creed]

The creed[16] is a written profession summarizing the community's search for an ever deepening understanding of Jesus and his message. The Nicene-Constantinople Creed is most often used at mass, although the Apostles' Creed may be used at some liturgies.

Originally the creed's primary place was the Easter liturgy where

---

14. Truth 15
15. Rom 3:13–15
16. Truth 23

those to be baptized were asked to profess their faith.[17] The Apostles' Creed still occurs in all baptismal liturgies, but the Nicene Creed is now recited on Sundays and major feasts as well. The creed affirms continuity with the entire Christian tradition.

General Intercessions [Prayers of the Faithful]

A restoration introduced by the Second Vatican Council, the prayers of the faithful until that time were limited to the liturgy for Good Friday. But these prayers had been part of the early Christian celebrations.

The people petition God for the needs of the Church, society, the parish, people in need, the sick and suffering, and those who have died. They direct our faith which has been deepened through prayer and listening to God's word to specific situations today. These conclude the liturgy of the word.

23. LITURGY OF THE EUCHARIST

While the liturgy of the word focused upon the table of the Lord's word—the lectern—the eucharistic liturgy centers upon the altar— both a place of sacrifice as well as the table from which we are fed. These themes of sacrifice and meal dominate.

24. Preparation of the Altar and the Gifts

This rite has undergone great change and development and is celebrated in various ways today. The fullness of the rite is described here. A much simpler action is also possible.

The gifts of bread and wine are placed at the back of the church before the service. The people then join in giving their monetary offerings in support of the ministries of the community. This collection is a real expression of religious commitment.

Afterward, in procession, people bring the bread and wine forward with the people's offerings. The priest receives them in the community's name. "The rite of carrying up the gifts continues the spiritual value and meaning of the ancient custom when the people brought bread and wine for the liturgy from their homes."[18]

Taking is the first of the eucharistic actions. While the Western

---

17. Way 33
18. General Instruction of the Roman Missal, n. 49

Church in the past emphasized the bread and wine which are transformed, originally the Hebrew context stressed the actions themselves.
Thus the Eucharist is often referred to in Scripture not in terms of the
bread and wine but as actions of taking, blessing, breaking and sharing.[19] The early Church commonly referred to the Eucharist as the
"breaking of the bread."[20]

When he has received the gifts the priest prepares them, reciting
prayers patterned on the ancient Jewish Kiddush of the Passover[21]
meal: "Blessed art thou, O Lord our God, Creator of the fruit of the
earth. The earth is the Lord's and the fullness thereof."

The priest then adds a drop of water to the wine—a custom deriving from the ancient Greeks who diluted their wine and considered
those who drank their wine straight to be barbarians. Medieval Christians considered it symbolic of the union of Christ's humanity and divinity, or of Christ with his Church.

The priest washes his hands as did the Jewish leader before the
ritual meal. This action has also taken on symbolic significance. The
priest prays, "Lord, wash away my iniquity, cleanse me from my
sins."[22]

Now the presider invites the people to prayer; they respond. The
rite concludes with a short prayer over the gifts.

25. Eucharistic Prayer

Now at the very heart of the Eucharist, this prayer in some aspects
antedates Christianity itself. Its model is derived from the Jewish Berakah or blessing prayer. Berakah prayer generally praises and blesses
God for all the wonderful gifts of creation.

It begins with the **preface.** A dialogue between presider and people invites all to lift their hearts to the Lord in praise. The celebrant
gives thanks to God in imagery appropriate to the day or season.

The prayer of the angels,[23] the **Holy, Holy, Holy** is sung or recited
by the people. It is an acclamation, praising and giving thanks to God
for God's glory.

Now in a longer prayer of thanksgiving, the priest on behalf of all
gives thanks to God for Christ. He asks the Father to send the Holy

---

19. Mt 26:26
20. Acts 2:42, 44–46; 7:11; 20:7
21. Truth 8
22. Ps 51:2
23. Is 6:3

Spirit upon the gifts of bread and wine transforming them into Christ's body and blood. This invocation is known as the **epiclesis**.

The **institution narrative** recalls the Last Supper when Jesus took bread and wine, commanding his followers to remember him when in the future they broke bread. These words, in essence, go back to Jesus himself. Even Paul[24] quotes these words as tradition.[25]

The institution narrative leads the people to acclaim their faith in one of four different acclamations. The people are not simple observers but active participants in the mystery being celebrated.

Remembrance of the saving acts of Jesus follows. This section is known as the **anamnesis**. Remembrance is a much stronger action in Jesus' day than in our culture. To remember something meant to enter into it and bring its power into the present. Thus in remembering, Jesus' sacrifice becomes present and can be entered into just as the first disciples did. Jesus nourishes through the gift of himself in the form of bread and wine. The Church in celebrating the Eucharist is fulfilling Jesus' command to keep his memorial. It does this by recalling especially his passion, resurrection and ascension.

In this memorial, the Church joins in Christ's self-offering to the Father in the Holy Spirit. It calls the faithful not only to offer the spotless victim but also to learn to offer themselves. In doing so they are drawn into ever more perfect union, through Christ the Mediator, with the Father and with each other, so that at last God may be all in all.

We then again invoke the Holy Spirit in the **epiclesis** to bless the Church and unite it. As in the first epiclesis we prayed that the Holy Spirit come upon the gifts, now we pray that the Holy Spirit unite the Church that shares in the gifts and make it holy in conformity with its Lord.

The **intercessions** make it clear that the Eucharist is celebrated in communion with the entire Church in heaven and on earth. The offering is made for the Church in all its members, living and dead, who are called to share in salvation. We remember the saints[26] as well as our brothers and sisters who have died and our friends in need.

The great prayer concludes with a **doxology**. The people confirm this entire prayer with a final "Amen." Although most of the words in the eucharistic prayer are spoken by the priest, he acts in the name of the assembly. So the people's acclamations throughout, in the Holy, Holy, Holy, the eucharistic acclamation, and this final Amen affirm the

---

24. 1 Cor 11:23ff
25. Truth 21
26. Life 46

priest's words and join all in the one prayer of the Church to the Father in Jesus Christ through the Holy Spirit.

There are different forms for the eucharistic prayer as well as ninety-one different prefaces. These allow for a variety of celebrations from the everyday liturgy to special feasts and themes (such as reconciliation) as well as three sets of prayers for children.

26. Communion Rite

Communion expresses unity in the body of Christ. Through communion Christians are united with God in Christ and through Christ with one another. The various elements of the communion rite emphasize and create this unity.

The **Lord's Prayer**[27] opens this rite in the words and according to the model of Jesus. After the prayer the priest's short prayer continues its spirit. This is followed by a doxology not originally part of the Lord's Prayer but added by a scribe. Stemming originally from the liturgy, in the past Protestants preserved it while Catholics preferred the shorter original. The Second Vatican Council restored it: after all it is a prayer that all Christians share.

The **sign of peace,** while another recent restoration, goes back to the earliest Christian usage. Justin Martyr asked the people to "greet each other with a kiss" after finishing the prayers. This kiss of peace is the result of God's reconciliation which begins among Christians and then flows into the world at large.

The **breaking of the bread** is the third great action of the Eucharist. To the early Christians, sharing in one loaf was a symbol of unity, solidarity and family; sliced bread or individual hosts (special eucharistic wafers) lose this significance.

As grain, once scattered on the hillsides,
Was in this broken bread made one,
So from all land thy Church be gathered
Into thy kingdom by thy Son.[28]

During this action the people sing a litany acknowledging Jesus as the Lamb of God pointed to by John the Baptist[29] and that the bread we share is indeed that same Christ.

---

27. Way 50
28. The Didache
29. Jn 1:36–37

Now the priest holds up the host and cup, inviting us to come forward to receive. The people respond with the words of the Roman centurion to Jesus.[30] Then they journey toward the altar to receive **Communion**; this procession reflects the journey toward God. And made with friends in community it is one more sign of unity flowing from the Eucharist. The psalm sung also creates that unity.

Cyril of Jerusalem explains the fitting reception of the Eucharist:

> When you approach do not come with your hands outstretched or with your fingers open but make your left hand a throne for your right one, which is to receive the King. With the hand hollowed receive the Body of Christ and answer Amen. . . . Consume it, making sure that not a particle is wasted, for that would be like losing one of your limbs. Tell me, if you were given some gold dust, would you not hold it very carefully for fear of letting any of it fall and losing it? How much more careful, then, you should be not to let fall even a crumb of something more precious than gold or jewels! After receiving the body of Christ, approach the chalice of his blood; do not stretch out your hands, but bow in an attitude of adoration and reverence, and say, "Amen."

After receiving Communion all return to their seats and spend the time in prayer. The priest then draws the prayers together in the **prayer after Communion.**

27. Concluding Rites

These rites now focus upon the sending forth of the community. No sacrament exists as an end in itself. Christians are transformed and nourished in the sacraments to in turn become sacraments to the world.

The priest gives a **final blessing.** As at the beginning all trace the sign of the cross. The **dismissal** sends us forth to in turn become bread for the world. The word "Mass" comes from the ancient Latin dismissal, "Ite, missa est." ("Go, it is sent.")

TO DEEPEN—

Attend Mass and identify each of its parts.

How does the shape of the liturgy proclaim and pass on the good news?

---

30. Mt 8:8; Lk 7:6

Listen to a recording of a musical setting of the Mass texts. The most imposing are the B Minor Mass of Bach and the Missa Solemnis of Beethoven. Other composers include Haydn, Mozart, Schubert, and Vaughan Williams. How does the musical setting deepen your understanding of these sacred texts?

Further Reading:

Fitzgerald, George. *Handbook of the Mass.* Paulist Press, 1982.
St. Joseph's Daily Missal. Catholic Book Publishing Company. Provides texts
  and readings for each day's Mass.

TO CONTINUE—

*The other sacraments are described in Truth 74ff but this material is appropriate
  for the Easter season after Initiation.*

*If presently in a major liturgical season it may be explored in Way 28ff as well
  as Life 40.*

28. The Liturgical Year

Some acquaintance with the Gospel story as found in Truth 15ff is helpful.

Dominical Cycle

> Holy Mother Church believes that it is for her to celebrate the saving work of her divine Spouse in a sacred commemoration on certain days throughout the course of the year. Once each week, on the day which she has called the Lord's Day, she keeps the memory of the Lord's resurrection. She also celebrates it once every year, together with his blessed passion, at Easter, that most solemn of all feasts.
>
> In the course of the year, moreover, she unfolds the whole mystery of Christ from the incarnation and nativity to the ascension, to Pentecost and the expectation of the blessed hope of the coming of the Lord.
>
> Thus recalling the mysteries of the redemption, she opens up to the faithful the riches of her Lord's powers and merits, so that these are in some way made present for all time; the faithful lay hold of them and are filled with saving grace. (Constitution on the Divine Liturgy, par 102)

The Church runs on a yearly calendar sanctifying the times and seasons. This calendar in its totality can seem a confusing mix because there are different cycles of varying importance; when these are placed together it is hard to see any pattern. But each cycle considered separately and in order of importance clearly reveals the overall shape of the year. This section considers only the major dominical (the Lord's) cycle which includes the greatest Christian feasts and seasons.

The Church year spans four special seasons: Advent and Christmas, Lent and Eastertime. These occupy less then twenty weeks of the year. The remainder is considered Ordinary Time.

Finding the Correct Point in the Cycle

The following chart will help locate the current time of year. Starting and ending times are sometimes ambiguous (indicated by a ?). Then the liturgical colors of the vestments and altar cloths reveal the season.

The liturgical colors have a basic significance. **White** and **gold** are used with major feasts of the Lord. **Green** is used on Sundays and week-days during Ordinary Time. **Purple** signifies either penance for Lent or expectation for Advent. **Red** is used for martyrs and the Holy Spirit.

Last of November?—December 24—Advent
Purple indicates Advent. The first Sunday of December is always in Advent.

December 25—January 6—Christmas season

January 7—Mid February (or into early March)?—Ordinary Time
Green indicates Ordinary Time.

Late February?—Mid April?—Lent
Color will be purple.

March?—April?—THE PASCH
Color on Easter will be gold or white.

Late March?—Early June? (time varies)—Eastertime
Colors will be gold, white, or red.

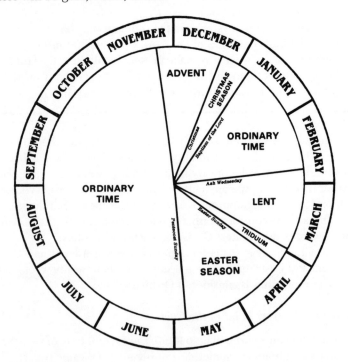

Late May?—Late November?—Ordinary Time
Green indicates Ordinary time. In May and early June gold or red indicates it is still Eastertime. At other times various colors may be seen
  but the Church is still in Ordinary Time.

The time varies for some of these seasons because the greatest
Christian feast—Easter—is determined by a lunar rather than the ordinary solar calendar. Thus it shifts from year to year along with those
feasts and seasons dependent upon it.

29. ADVENT SEASON

Advent inaugurates the Christian year. It is a season of preparation
for the parousia or the coming of Christ in glory. This time of joyful
expectation leads to Christmas, when Christians celebrate Jesus' first
appearance among us, God in human flesh.

Since the Christian year is a cycle, Advent is both the beginning
and the end. It continues looking forward to the second coming of
Christ at the end of history (the themes of November in Ordinary
Time), and at the same time it celebrates the coming of Christ at Christmas through the words of the prophets. It is a season of waiting and
watching.

Advent begins on the Sunday closest to the feast of St. Andrew the
Apostle (November 30)—the last Sunday of November or the first of
December. It comprises four Sundays approximating four weeks.

The liturgical color is purple. On the Third Sunday pink may signal
the rejoicing that the Savior is near. The pre-Vatican II liturgy called
this Sunday "Gaudete," from the Latin entrance psalm,[1] and rejoicing
is still heard in the first and second readings for this week.

The readings are from the prophets who foresaw the birth of the
Messiah, particularly the first part of Isaiah. The Gospels move in a sequence from the apocalyptic theme of the First Sunday, continuing the
themes of the end of Ordinary Time, to the preaching of John the Baptist on the Second Sunday and Third Sundays. The Fourth Sunday re-
counts events leading to Jesus' birth.

TO CONTINUE—

The stories of Advent are discussed in the Gospel preludes (Truth 16).
Advent customs are discussed in Life 40.

---

1. Way 20

30. CHRISTMAS SEASON

This season begins December 25 with Christmas—the celebration of the incarnation.[2] The season continues till the baptism of the Lord. This season celebrates the birth of Christ and his manifestation in grace and glory.

Many believe that **Christmas** is not Jesus' birthday. Indeed his birth date is unknown. In the third century Christmas developed to replace the pagan Saturnalia celebrating the winter solstice.[3] Here is Catholicism at its best—adapting all things to Christ. As Jesus fulfilled the Jewish law and ideals, so Christians saw him bringing to completion the pagan religion.

Christmas is the third important feast of Christendom, although in the culture at large it seems pre-eminent. But it ranks behind Easter and Pentecost. It is a holy day of obligation for Catholics in the United States.[4]

The colors of the Christmas season are white. But special feasts may have their appropriate colors such as red for martyrdom on St. Stephen's feast day and the Holy Innocents.

The name is a contraction for Christ's Mass—for the feast, like all Christian feasts, is celebrated primarily with a Eucharist. Christmas has three different Masses—at midnight, at dawn, and during the day. In addition it has a vigil as all the greatest feasts do—Christmas Eve, December 24th.

Seasonal themes come from the infancy Gospels[5] and the prologue to John.[6] The First Readings are primarily from Isaiah. The epistle fits the overall theme.

As with other major feasts, Christmas has an octave—a second celebration eight days later—the Feast of the **Solemnity of Mary**, the Mother of God (January 1) commemorating Mary's role as mother of the Savior. This day has other themes—New Year's Day and a day to pray for world peace. This too is a holy day of obligation for Catholics in the United States.[7]

The Feast of the **Epiphany** (January 6 or in the United States the nearest Sunday to January 6) is the traditional feast of Twelfth Night—the twelfth day of Christmas. Epiphany, a Greek word, means "mani-

---

2. Truth 30
3. Life 39
4. Intro 17
5. Mt 1—2; Lk 1:5—2:52
6. Jn 1:1–18
7. Intro 17

festation" or "showing forth." The feast commemorates the shining forth of Christ's light into the world.

Actually the feast commemorates three different epiphanies: the coming of the magi,[8] the baptism of Jesus when the dove made manifest God's beloved Son,[9] and Jesus' first miracle at the marriage in Cana when the disciples witnessed his glory.[10]

But the magi have taken primary place in Christian hearts. And in Europe this day is the real celebration of Christmas with the giving of gifts to celebrate the adoration of the magi. The other two manifestations are now commemorated on the following Sundays.[11]

Since Christmas is really a twelve day feast it is filled with different feast days—some of the most important in the Sanctoral Cycle.[12]

St. Stephen (December 26) is given the place of honor right after Christmas as the first Christian martyr.[13]

St. John the Evangelist (December 27) occupies the next day as the beloved disciple[14] and because his is the great Gospel of the Incarnation when the Word became flesh.[15]

The **Holy Innocents** (December 28) were slaughtered by King Herod who attempted to preserve his throne by killing the King of the Jews who would supplant him (namely Jesus).[16]

The **Holy Family** occurs on the Sunday between Christmas and New Year's. Catholics celebrate the family (Mary, Joseph and Jesus) into which Jesus was born and in which he was nourished, growing in wisdom and grace.

The Christmas feast officially ends on the Sunday after Epiphany which is the Feast of the **Baptism of the Lord**. (This replaces the First Sunday of the Year in the cycle of Ordinary Time.)[17]

TO CONTINUE—

The Christmas Scriptures are discussed in the Gospel preludes (Truth 16).
Christmas customs are discussed in Life 40.

---

8. Mt 2:1–12
9. Lk 3:21–22
10. Jn 2:1–11
11. Way 31
12. Life 39
13. Acts 6:1—8:1
14. Jn 13:23
15. Jn 1:14
16. Mt 2:16–18
17. Way 31

31. ORDINARY TIME I

During this time the Church reads through one of the Gospels (Matthew [Cycle A], Mark [Cycle B] or Luke [Cycle C]) pretty much in sequence, meditating upon and celebrating the words and actions of Jesus. This **three-year cycle** determines the particular readings for each Sunday and major feast. Most of the time the Gospel proclaimed at the Sunday Eucharist reveals the proper cycle. Cycle C is read in years divisible by three such as 1989, 1992, etc. John's Gospel is reserved for the seasons of Lent and Easter. And since Mark's Gospel is shortest, parts of John are read during Ordinary Time of Cycle B.

This first segment of Ordinary Time occurs between the end of the Christmas season (mid-January) and the beginning of Lent. Anywhere from five to eight Sundays comprise this sequence, numbered simply as First, Second, Twenty-third, etc. Sunday of the Year.

The First Sunday of Ordinary Time (the Sunday after Epiphany) celebrates the **Baptism of the Lord.** The Second Sunday Gospel is always from John and commemorates the events leading up to (Cycle A: Jn 1:29–34; Cycle B: Jn 1:35–42) as well as the first miracle at Cana of Galilee (Jn 2:1–12)—the traditional third epiphany.

Beginning with the Third Sunday the Gospel of the year is begun, omitting the infancy narratives, the preaching of John the Baptist, Jesus' baptism and the temptation in the wilderness covered in the Advent-Christmas season or in Lent (Mt 1—2; Mk 1:1–13; Lk 1:5—3:22).[18] During Ordinary Time only first-class solemnities falling on Sunday replace the Ordinary Sunday.

The Third Sunday tells of the beginning of Jesus' ministry. Succeeding Sundays in A come from the Sermon on the Mount (Mt 5—7), Jesus' miracles in B, and the beginning ministry in C. Each instance simply follows the account of that year's Gospel.

A number of feast days within the Church calendar do not necessarily fall upon Sunday. This discussion is restricted to mentioning the various feasts of the Lord which fall during the year. The early part of the year has two feasts not mentioned thus far.

Feast of the Presentation[19]—February 2

Annunciation of our Lord[20]—March 25; this feast usually falls during Lent. If it falls during Holy Week it is postponed.

---

18. Way 22
19. Lk 2:22–40
20. Lk 1:26–38

TO CONTINUE—

The characteristics of the different Gospels are discussed in Truth 15.

32. LENTEN SEASON

"Lent" derives from the Anglo-Saxon "Lencten" meaning "spring." Although occurring in springtime, Lent is hardly the Christian festival of spring; that is Easter. Lent has developed as a time of preparation for Easter—a spiritual spring-cleaning preparing to celebrate Jesus' victory over sin and death.

Lent's overarching image is Jesus' temptation in the wilderness.[21] Lent comprises the period of forty days (do not count Sundays) before Easter.[22] Lent ends on Holy Thursday with the celebration of the liturgy of the Lord's Supper. The number forty symbolizes completeness in the biblical tradition—the period of a generation. Jesus spent forty days being tested in the wilderness.[23] And his temptations are modeled upon Israel's forty year wilderness sojourn after having entered into the covenant on Mount Sinai.[24]

Over the centuries the common Christian practice and understanding of Lent has changed much. Lent first (in a much shorter form) was the time for the elect to prepare for baptism. It then became a time of penitence for all the faithful. The eclipse of the catechumenate in the fourth century left Lent simply as a penitential season.

The Second Vatican Council reformed Lent so that its true purpose might once more be understood.

The season of Lent has a twofold character: primarily by recalling or preparing for baptism and by penance, it disposes the faithful, who more diligently hear the word of God and devote themselves to prayer, to celebrate the paschal mystery.[25]

---

21. Mt 4:1–11; Mk 1:12–13; Lk 4:1–13
22. Way 33
23. Truth 19
24. Truth 8
25. Constitution on the Sacred Liturgy, n.109

At Easter new people are baptized into the Christian community which powerfully makes present the death and resurrection of Jesus. So Lent first of all prepares **the elect** for their initiation. The Sunday Scriptures of Cycle A, appropriate for the elect, center around baptismal themes.[26]

But Lent is not only for the elect. At Easter all Christians recall their baptism and celebrate God's redeeming love which leads out of darkness into Christ's kingdom. So all join the elect on their pilgrimage of prayer and penance so that at Easter, witnessing their baptism, the faithful might find a deeper appreciation and understanding of their own. For although this sacrament is given only once it does not cease working once the action is over. Throughout life we continue to explore what God has accomplished in this mystery. And as we open more to our Father we allow him to lead us further into the new life.

The second character of Lent is penitential. As the Second Vatican Council explained,

By penance, (Lent) . . . disposes the faithful, who more diligently hear the word of God and devote themselves to prayer, to celebrate the paschal mystery.[27]

The readings from Cycles B and C stress penitence appropriate for this season. The faithful join with the elect in the practice of penance. Catechumens who are not yet elect fast and undertake a Lenten practice which continues their work of conversion and preparation for full initiation.

The liturgical color is purple for penitence. Certain feast days occurring during Lent have their appropriate color. Sometimes on the Fourth Sunday pink is used as in Advent to signify that Lent is drawing to a close. In the old liturgy this Sunday was known as "Laetare" Sunday from the entrance psalm which means "Be glad."

All the Gospels present the story of Jesus' temptation on the First Sunday of Lent. And the transfiguration[28] on the Second Sunday glimpses the glory of Christ to be revealed at Easter. For the final three Sundays Cycle A centers upon baptismal themes from John's Gospel.

---

26. Intro 10ff
27. Constitution on the Sacred Liturgy, n.109; Way 48
28. Mt 17:1–8; Mk 9:2–8; Lk 9:28–36

These are dialogues between Jesus and the Samaritan woman,[29] the man born blind,[30] and Mary and Martha, the sisters of Lazarus.[31] These readings focus upon the journey of the elect and are used each year at the Mass where the elect are present. Cycle B also draws from John, emphasizing both rebirth and repentance. Cycle C continues from Luke and repentance dominates.

The Hebrew Scripture readings throughout the five weeks of Lent proper present a summary of salvation history[32] moving from the beginnings through Abraham, Moses, Joshua and the period of monarchy, and culminating in the prophets. The second readings echo the dominant Lenten themes.

There are six Sundays of Lent. The first five are simply numbered; the last is **Passion Sunday** (Palm Sunday in the old terminology) and begins with a celebration of Jesus' triumphal entry into Jerusalem.[33] Usually this celebration involves a blessing and distribution of palm branches outside the church, and then a procession into the church. The color is red—the color of triumph as well as martyrdom. The Gospel is the passion narrative of that year's Gospel.[34] (John is read on Good Friday.) Thus Passion Sunday inaugurates Holy Week.

TO CONTINUE—

The history of salvation in Israel which forms the sequence of Lenten First Readings is discussed in Truth 4–12. The temptation and transfiguration are discussed in Truth 18.

33. THE PASCH

The pasch is the greatest Christian feast comprising a period of three days from Thursday evening through Sunday night. It is not three separate feasts but one spanning the passion and resurrection of Jesus Christ.

The date of Easter, the climax of the pasch, is reckoned as the first Sunday after the first full moon of the spring equinox (March 21–22). Naturally this date determines as well the interruption of Ordinary

29. Jn 4:1–42
30. Jn 9:1–41
31. Jn 11:1–57
32. Truth 2ff
33. Mt 21:1–11; Mk 11:1–10 (or as an alternate Jn 12:12–16); Lk 19:28–40
34. Mt 26:14—27:66; Mk 14:1—15:47; Lk 22:14—23:56

Time, the beginning of Lent and the end of the Easter season. Being the oldest Christian feast it is determined according to the lunar calendar of Israel rather than the later solar calendar of Rome (the basis of modern calendars).

Easter is the Christian fulfillment of the great Israelite feast of Passover[35] which commemorates the liberation of the slaves from Egypt and specifically the passing over of the hand of the Lord when the Egyptian firstborn were slain[36] as well as the passing over the Red Sea into freedom.[37]

The new feast does not replace but fulfills the older one. While in Passover Israel celebrates her liberation and deliverance from slavery, the Christian sees this liberation now extended even to sin and death itself. The older theme is taken up and woven into a richer and fuller fabric.

Holy Thursday

In the morning the bishop traditionally celebrates the **chrism Mass** with his priests. The sacred chrism used to anoint and confirm the elect and all baptized and confirmed throughout the year, as well as the oil for anointing the sick and the oil of catechumens, is blessed. Then the priests receive part to take back to the local parishes for use during the next year. The priests also renew their ordination promises with the bishop. This celebration is often anticipated for convenience.

The principal liturgy begins at sundown with the **liturgy of the Lord's supper.** The order of Mass is as usual until after the Gospel[38] when the celebrant imitates Jesus' action of washing his disciples' feet. Usually the celebrant washes the feet of certain members of the parish community. Sometimes this ritual is omitted.

The liturgy then continues through the eucharistic commemoration and Communion. After Communion the remaining bread which is reserved for the next day is taken in solemn procession to the altar of repose—another altar in the church, usually decorated with flowers. All sing the great hymn "Pange Lingua Gloriosa" during the procession.

When the procession is completed and all have spent a short time in adoration, the service ends with the stripping of the altar and church. The church is left bare, all cloths and banners being removed. The tab-

---

35. Ex 12:1–28
36. Ex 11:1–10; 12:29–32
37. Ex 13:17—14:22
38. Jn 13:1–15

ernacle door is left open, the tabernacle empty. The service ends in silence. The church may remain open until midnight for prayer and vigil, recalling how Jesus asked the disciples to keep watch with him in the Garden of Gethsemane.[39]

Good Friday

Often churches commemorate the three hours of Jesus' suffering on the cross with a special service focusing on the stations of the cross[40] or the seven last words. But this is a devotional service and not the official liturgy.

The solemnity of the Lord's passion takes place either in the afternoon or evening. It is not a Eucharist: Good Friday and Holy Saturday are the only days the Eucharist is not celebrated. The liturgy of the word includes the passion according to John and an extended prayer of the faithful. John's Gospel stresses the glorification of Jesus and the triumph achieved through his cross. Thus Good Friday does not separate the movements of the pasch. In Jesus' death is seen his victory.

Then the cross is unveiled for veneration. A Communion ritual concludes the service using the bread consecrated on Holy Thursday. The stark simplicity accords with the day, but this is not simply a remembering of Jesus' passion and death. In its celebration the Church keeps in mind the entire course of our saving action. And Christians venerating the cross do so not to remember the torture Jesus suffered but to acknowledge the cross as the instrument of our salvation. This is the holy cross of triumph.

Holy Saturday

This is a day of quiet and waiting. In the morning many churches celebrate the final preparations for baptism with the elect or the Liturgy of the Hours. Mass is not celebrated until the vigil.

Easter Vigil

This is the principal celebration of the Christian year. A vigil is a service in which Christians keep watch. Late Saturday night they gather to bless the new fire in front of the church. The fire symbolizes the light of Christ which penetrates the darkness. The fire lights the

---

39. Mt 26:30–56
40. Life 42

Easter candle which throughout the Easter season remains as a symbol of the risen Christ. The lit candle is carried through the congregation and all light their candles from it. The deacon then chants the ancient song to the light, the Exultet (which means "rejoice"). It speaks of the symbolism of the candle and recalls the history of salvation.

The service then turns to the vigil proper—the reading of several Scriptures concerning the history of God's dealings with Israel. This service ends with Paul's witness to the resurrection.[41]

The elect are called forward to profess the faith. Then they go down into the pool for baptism. Coming forth they are greeted by the community and given a white garment and candle as signs of their new life. With the candidates (those already baptized) they are confirmed. Then the faithful renew baptismal promises and are signed with baptismal water.

Then all celebrate the Easter Eucharist. With much song, rejoicing and even dancing the celebration makes present once again the triumph of Jesus over death and our membership in his kingdom signified by the Eucharist.

TO CONTINUE—

The passion narratives are discussed in Truth 19. The Easter Gospels are discussed in Truth 20.

34. EASTER SEASON

Easter continues Sunday morning with other parish Eucharists. The fifty days of Easter form one solemn feast which St. Athanasius called the Great Sunday. The days of Easter week proclaim the accounts of the Lord who rose early in the morning, and the early preaching of disciple witnesses to the resurrection. The next Sunday is called the Second Sunday of Easter. The liturgical colors throughout the Easter season are gold or white. The church remains decorated throughout the season.

During Eastertime the new Christians and Catholics explore the mysteries of Christian life particularly as unfolded in the sacraments. The readings are the resurrection narratives, passages from John's Gospel, and sometimes from the history of the early community in Acts.

The **ascension**[42] of Jesus occurs forty days after Easter on Thursday

---

41. Rom 6:3–11
42. Acts 1:6–11

of the Sixth Week. This feast does not appear until the fourth century when it was introduced to celebrate the Lukan story.[43]

The nine days between the Feasts of the Ascension and Pentecost are considered as time the disciples spent in prayer and quiet. Jesus had departed, and the Holy Spirit had not yet descended. This period of time, called a novena,[44] has come to designate special times of prayer covering nine days and often associated with a special feast day.

Fifty days from Easter the Feast of **Pentecost** celebrates the Holy Spirit's descent upon the disciples: the Church is born.[45] Pentecost is the second solemn feast of the Christian year: Easter is first, Christmas third.

In the chronology of these feasts the original schema is based more upon a replacement of Israel's feasts than history. Pentecost originally celebrated the first harvest as well as the giving of the law on Mount Sinai.[46] The Feast of the Ascension is traced by some scholars to an Israelite enthronement festival celebrating God's rulership. The liturgical chronology follows principally the Gospel of Luke-Acts. John differs as usual: the entire action of resurrection-ascension-pentecost takes place on Easter Sunday.

TO CONTINUE—

The Acts of the Apostles are discussed in Truth 14.

35. ORDINARY TIME II

The rest of the year is again Ordinary Time. But as in January, feasts supplant the first Sunday. **Trinity Sunday** follows Pentecost, celebrating the Trinity[47] which is unique to Christianity and its understanding of God. The United States moved **Corpus Christi** (the feast of the eucharistic body of Christ composed by Thomas Aquinas) to the Sunday after Trinity Sunday. This feast's original date is Thursday of this week looking back to Holy Thursday's institution of the Eucharist but now is celebrated with Easter splendor apart from the solemnity of Holy Week.

The Church now returns to the weekly cycle of readings begun be-

---

43. Truth 21
44. Life 7
45. Acts 2:1–47
46. Ex 19:1–25
47. Truth 27

fore Lent. Depending upon the number of weeks in the year, that reading is begun where it left off or a week is omitted. (The feasts of the two previous weeks replace their respective Sundays and readings of Ordinary Time.) The Gospel themes throughout the summer flow sequentially from the Gospels themselves (omitting stories and themes touched in the various seasons). The general theme is the teaching and ministry of Jesus.

As the year draws to a close in November the readings assume an apocalyptic tone, looking forward to the consummation of this age and the coming of the kingdom in glory. This theme reaches its climax on the last Sunday of the Church year.

Christ the King is a relatively new feast. Instituted originally by Pope Pius XII on the last Sunday of October as a counterpart to Reformation Sunday, the Second Vatican Council moved it to the last Sunday of the Church year—more appropriately looking forward to the coming of Christ's kingdom in glory. And today Catholics commemorate the reformation along with Protestants, seeking ways to restore unity.

Finally certain feasts of the Lord fall during this period of Ordinary Time. These are:

Sacred Heart[48]—Friday of the Second Week after Pentecost
Transfiguration[49]—August 6

TO DEEPEN—

How does this cycle present the entire Gospel to Christians?
How do the Church's seasons reflect the tone of the actual seasons?

Further Reading:

Adam, Adolf. *The Church Year: Its History and Meaning After the Reform of the Liturgy.* Pueblo Publishing, 1981.
Bradner, John. *Symbols of Church Seasons and Days.* Morehouse. 1977.
Buckland, Patricia. *Advent to Pentecost—A History of the Church Year.* Morehouse. 1979.
Daniélou, Jean. *The Bible and the Liturgy.* University of Notre Dame, 1966.

---

48. Life 7
49. Mt 17:1–8; Truth 18

TO CONTINUE—

The other liturgical cycles are found in Life 40.
The Church's daily prayer is found in Life 38.
Liturgical objects and furnishing are found in Life 43.
The overall story of Christianity is discussed in Truth 15ff.

◇

36. The Way of Mission

37. **The Works of the Spirit**
38. **Corporal Works of Mercy**
    Feed the Hungry
    Give Drink to the Thirsty
    Clothe the Naked
    Shelter the Homeless
    Visit the Sick
    Ransom the Captive
    Bury the Dead
39. **Spiritual Works of Mercy**
    Instruct the Ignorant
    Counsel the Doubtful
    Admonish the Sinner
    Bear Wrongs Patiently
    Forgive Offenses
    Comfort the Afflicted
    Pray for the Living and the Dead

Every sacrament concludes by sending Christians into the world. One's sending is given in baptism and confirmation. The catechumen is a disciple becoming acquainted with Jesus and being taught by him. But once their training is done the disciples are made apostles—sent on a mission which continues today in the Church as the body of Christ.

The Church was founded to spread the kingdom of Christ over all the earth for the glory of God the Father, to make all people partakers in redemption and salvation, and through them to establish the right relationship of the entire world to Christ. Every activity of the mystical body with this in view goes by the name of "apostolate"; the Church exercises it through all its members, though in various ways. In fact, the Christian vocation is, of its nature, a vocation to the apostolate as well. In the organism of a living body no member plays a purely passive part, sharing in the life of the body it shares at the same time in its activity. The same is true for the body of Christ, the Church: "The whole body achieves full growth in dependence on the full functioning of each part."[1] Between the members of this body there exists, further, such a unity and solidarity that a member who does not work at the growth of the body to the extent of his possibilities must be considered useless both to the Church and to himself.

In the Church there is diversity of ministry but unity of mission. . . . From the fact of their union with Christ the head flows the laypersons' right and duty to be apostles. Inserted as they are in the mystical body of Christ by baptism and strengthened by the power of the Holy Spirit in confirmation, it is by the Lord himself that they are assigned to the apostolate.[2]

---

1. Eph 4:16
2. Decree on the Apostolate of Lay People, nn.2–3

37. The Works of the Spirit

Christian initiation confers the gifts of the Holy Spirit not for our own sake, but so that we might be about the Spirit's work—building up the kingdom. Christian life is essentially love and service to God and others. How that service is made concrete is detailed by the works of mercy.

The term "mercy," although traditional, needs explanation. A better term might be compassion since mercy has been denigrated by our culture. Mercy is identified with pity. But it is not so.

Compassion shares in the suffering of others. The compassionate person suffers with others, shares in their pain, and so comes to feel with them. Pity is a superior or proud emotion coming from a standpoint above those suffering. But compassion does not look down but puts one at the sufferer's side.

And being at someone's side as a Christian does not end the matter. Grieving with the other over suffering forms only part of compassion. Compassion is also active, working with the other to move through suffering toward liberation. Jesus' compassion leads him to lay down his life for us. Similarly our compassion stirs us to work for the world's transformation.

38. Corporal Works of Mercy

Traditionally Christians have listed the works of compassion in two sevenfold lists. The first lists corporal works—actions in the world, actions of movement and body. Their source is Matthew's Gospel[3]—they are conditions for being allied with the kingdom.

Nourished in the Eucharist, Christians are sent into the world where first we work to insure that all creatures receive the minimum conditions for life and livelihood. Spiritual life is not independent of bodily life, the former grows out of and rests upon the latter.

The first corporal works of mercy, **feeding the hungry, giving drink to the thirsty, clothing the naked, sheltering the homeless,** are basic works of charity needing no explanation. They are done both by individuals and institutions. On the institutional level this work is accomplished by organizations such as the St. Vincent de Paul Society.[4] Organizations and individuals working outside the Church or in other religions also perform these actions. We share in that work through monetary contributions and if possible join in some way ourselves. We cannot remain Christian and deny our link with all our brothers and sisters or our duty to ensure their well-being.

The next work of mercy is **visiting the sick.** Sickness removes a person from normal life and society; it is alienating. But Christians do not believe that worth is dependent upon accomplishments. Sickness does not sever the person from the Christian community but becomes a potentially sacred experience. Visits keep the person in touch with the larger community, assuring our prayers and concern. And the visit itself may promote healing.

The Christian has a calling to **ransom the captive,** a rather romantic sounding phrase far from modern life. Yet consider some modern forms of captivity, addiction, poverty, imprisonment, and economic, political, psychological and religious oppression. Christians, cooperating with the Holy Spirit, join in the work of freeing those who are captive. God wills the full liberation of all. This happens partly through our own ministry to the captive.

To **bury the dead** may be expanded to include acknowledgment of all family obligations. True, family obligations sometimes blind us to the Spirit's call, and Jesus tells a would-be follower to let the dead bury the dead.[5] But here he counsels just the opposite. So while Christians ac-

---

3. Mt 25:34–36
4. Life 45
5. Mt 8:22; Lk 9:60

knowledge their first obligation to follow the Spirit, usually this obligation begins at home.

Mission sometimes conjures visions of strange lands and peoples. But mission first brings compassion into one's present life. Thus the first objects of our compassion should be our own flesh and blood. Only from them does the mission extend outward into the larger community.

Burying the dead takes on a broader aspect today with life significantly extended. Old people are sometimes left to fend for themselves. They are treated as though already dead. How might these older people be brought again into the human circle, given a role integral to our society, rather than cast away as used and now useless?

39. Spiritual Works of Mercy

The spiritual works of mercy look beyond the material to encompass intellect and spirit. They spell out ways to serve in this dimension of being.

The first work is to **instruct the ignorant.** In the narrow context we make it our duty to reveal the Gospel to those who do not yet know it. The Gospel provides new insight into life and so liberates from the many bonds. Christian mission proclaims that liberating knowledge. Although not forcing our knowledge upon others, we should be willing when asked to share our faith.

This work also involves general education. Ignorance is the root of much misery. The Church joins with other groups to educate people so that they may share in building the kingdom. These works should not be interpreted in a religiously narrow way. Education is part of our spiritual nature—our minds are meant to explore and understand God's creation.

We are called to **counsel the doubtful.** Christians acknowledge our link with all in one human family. We are part of the human community. We want to be available for one another in times of crisis. Sometimes the most valuable gift is a willingness to listen to another's problems. We need not be professional counselors. An open ear and a compassionate heart are often all that people need to air their difficulties and be renewed in hope. Again the Church provides services for carrying out this work such as pastoral care, counseling services, family clinics, and support groups.

The Christian **admonishes the sinner.** Now this can be taken in the wrong spirit. It is all too easy to cast stones at others from a supposedly superior position. The Christian through revelation has come to see the truth. But this vision is not private. When society or others tend toward sinful and hurtful actions, Christians should speak out to raise consciousness.

Through its teachings the Church also raises consciousness among people at large—pointing out our true nature as children of God and warning of ideas and actions which threaten our happiness. At times in the past this teaching office seemed excessively scolding and condemning; today the Church sees itself as a help to the world in the journey toward God's kingdom. But whatever the teaching, the Church and the Christian condemn the sin, not the sinner, toward whom the only acceptable attitude is compassion.

We **bear wrongs patiently.** Life is not smooth. Things do not always go our way. In a sinful world, we ourselves contribute to the mass of sin and wrong. And inevitably we will find ourselves wronged and sinned against. Human nature responds by lashing out. Our justice rises on a cloud of anger. But this merely adds to the hurts and wrongs. The Christian is called to have faith and trust in God. We are not passive to wrongs suffered, but patiently go with the ebb and flow of life.

We grow in the mind of Christ that prays for his persecutors, because in truth they do not know what they are doing.[6] How much evil and sin are committed by ignorance? Christians are called to illumine what is now done in darkness. We should not add to the darkness. Trusting in God we allow wrongs to pass unavenged as we await God's kingdom.[7]

Forgiving offenses continues the previous thought, helping us to move out of sin into the freedom of God's children. Our forgiveness of offenders enables God to break sinful patterns and liberate the world.

The Christian is sent to **comfort the afflicted.** Jesus showed compassion for those who in one way or another are afflicted. Alienated from society, they are told that they are not wanted or needed. Healing begins when our compassion reaches out with a hand of comfort and love.

The opposite is also a Christian trait, to **afflict the comforted.** Jesus had little consolation for the oppressors of his day, and the Christian community should with courage as well as compassion carry on that prophetic work.

Finally Christians, realizing our solidarity in the society of God's creation, build communion by **praying for the living and dead.** We bring our cares and concerns to the Lord, having faith that God will respond. And Christian care extends beyond ourselves, our family and local community to encompass the entire world and even those who are gone. In Christ we are made one. There are no boundaries to our compassion.

Wherever compassion is found the Christian recognizes the kingdom breaking through. We live in the hope that God's kingdom is indeed coming and that the creation is being renewed. We join others in cooperating with the new creation here and now. So even our present dark and troubled world is pierced by the Gospel light which reveals God's love.

Perhaps the most beautiful thing about the teaching of Jesus and of Christianity is its commonness. This teaching does not demand that we leave the world behind, or undertake an extraordinary way of life, or be especially talented. It is a way for the ordinary person in daily life,

---

6. Lk 23:34
7. Truth 74

practiced in the common life of marriage and family, of living in community, of one's emotions and dreams. Jesus' teaching reveals such a life not as "common" but extraordinary in its glory. Jesus chose fishermen, prostitutes, and tax collectors as disciples. He continues to call ordinary folk to his extraordinary mission.

TO DEEPEN—

How might you put into practice some of these works in your life?

How has your service to others illumined the teaching of Jesus for you?

In what ways do you see the Church carrying out these works of compassion?

In what ways does your local parish exercise its mission to the community and the world?

Further Reading:

Greenleaf, Robert K. *Servant Leadership: A Journey into the Nature of Legitimate Power and Greatness.* Paulist Press, 1977.

Kelsey, Morton. *Caring—How Can We Love One Another?* Paulist Press, 1981.

Martin, John B. & Catherine. *Works of Mercy.* Paulist Press, 1980.

Pennington, Basil. *In Peter's Footsteps—Learning To Be a Disciple.* Doubleday, 1985.

TO CONTINUE—

The Way of Action (Way 51) gives further discussion to what a Christian is to do.

Life in the Spirit is further explored in Life 4–5 by means of the gifts and fruits of the Spirit.

Catholic social teaching is presented in Life 44–45.

◇

40. The Way of Christian Life

One's Christianity is molded within the Christian tradition.[1] But the Christian is an individual, and Jesus addresses the person's need for transformation. How does Jesus' teaching affect a person's behavior? How does a Christian make a decision, tell right from wrong? The Way of Morality explores these questions.

However, Jesus is not primarily concerned with morality—that has already been established in his Jewish tradition. Jesus is concerned with the spiritual life—the life of perfection. Jesus calls to transformation so that we may cease living as prisoners of this human world and experience the true freedom of God's beloved children. The Way of the Spirit explores this conversion. Christian existence is founded upon a relationship in prayer with God revealed in the prayer Jesus teaches his disciples. And finally the teachings of Jesus result in action in the world. This action's shape is determined by commands that Jesus left to his disciples.

---

1. Way 2ff

41. The Way of Morality

The Christian has responded to Jesus' call to enter into relationship with God.[2] The shape of Christian life then is determined by growth and transformation in the Holy Spirit. This relationship is in service of the kingdom of God to which Jesus directed his attention and to which the Christian also gives his or her life. Our covenant like all relationships implies a dynamism.[3]

Covenant living demands that one live according to certain truths. A special kind of life is envisioned in the Christian covenant (which includes and brings to perfection the previous covenants).[4] If one enters into this covenant, certain ways of behavior and values are adopted as one's own. This section concerns the ways in which one keeps the covenant rather than the contents.[5]

Upon entering the covenant a Christian is opened to the Spirit's transforming power which recreates and perfects the person. Thus the foundation for all Christian action cannot be a law or prescription of any kind, but instead is the Holy Spirit who informs all Christian action. The Holy Spirit enables the Christian to be converted and transformed into the wholeness of God's kingdom.

Fidelity characterizes the living relationship of God and God's people. So faithfulness lies at the core of Christian behavior. Nevertheless principles and precepts help discern the overall shape of Christian behavior—or this covenantal fidelity.

The art of ethics is discerning the proper and harmonious way of living. The moral law of the Judaeo-Christian tradition shares much in common with other non-religious approaches to the moral life. For example, the early Christians found the Greek and Roman philosophical tradition on the virtues helpful in explaining Christian moral life.[6] Insight into what constitutes good behavior is no secret or the result of some exclusive revelation.

What distinguishes the Christian from the non-Christian is not in the area of moral versus immoral but in the experience of God and the Christian's cooperation with the Holy Spirit in ongoing conversion. Of course this cooperation might lead to action in worldly eyes above and beyond the call of morality, like laying down one's life for the sake of one's neighbor.

---

2. Intro 2
3. Way 2
4. Way 36ff
5. Truth 45–73
6. Truth 67–70

42. Concerns of Morality

Moral Standards

The Christian Way is a spiritual path of conversion. Morality is concerned with the way we travel along that path. Jesus calls us not only to embrace the law in its outward form as law-abiding people might, but actually to become the law inwardly and outwardly. That is, we are to live by the spirit of the law and to embody its values. To live this way we need to be clear about the way we make decisions and live them out.

Morality raises at once a profound question concerning human existence. Morality implies a purpose, a meaning to life. There is a certain way to live: not all actions are alike. Some are good, others not so good or downright evil. So any morality must address the primary question: Why are we here? What is human life all about? What is its purpose? Only then is one ready to hear how to live in order to fulfill this purpose.

Thomas Aquinas[7] defines morality as that way of acting which leads to ultimate happiness. He follows Jesus' teaching of the beatitudes—keys to real, lasting blessedness. Naturally there are different kinds of happiness, and much of what passes for happiness has little depth. The happiness that Jesus and Thomas have in mind is deep-blessedness: a life sustained by God's blessings.

Christian ethics is oriented toward ultimate happiness. Of course the happiness sought is more than one's individual happiness which might be gained through our neighbor's misery. The happiness sought is that of the entire harmonious creation, and thus at times individual happiness must be sacrificed for the greater good.

But of what immediate benefit is morality? It helps create a climate of fair play and harmony between individuals as well as harmony within the individual. Morality is at the very foundation of all society, enabling community. It sets down conditions for fruitful and productive cooperation. Thus morality is not only ideal—toward ultimate happiness—but practical—the present harmonious functioning of human society.

Interior Values

At this point one might think that if all simply followed the laws, things would be fine, and the kingdom might appear. Such thinking misses morality's deeper concerns. True morality linked to a spiritual path does not strive for conformity of action to laws. Indeed the rule-

---

7. Life 33

keeper may be further from the kingdom than the person following no rules. For although on the surface particular actions are important—society is impossible without respect for life and property—this is not the final extent of morality. The outward action alone is not sufficient. Jesus is concerned with the quality and motivation of action as much as with the action itself.

Refraining from killing may make human society possible, but Jesus asks, what about inner thoughts? What about the murder committed in the heart? Is not this also important? And this raises morality to an entirely new level, beyond the establishment of a human society and toward the kingdom where inner and outer are united.

Such underlying concerns need to be considered in embarking upon Christian morality. While minimal moral standards are crucial for society's healthy functioning, Christians realize that God does not merely judge actions outwardly, but values the interior as well.

Not all people are created equal in talents, gifts or brains. What is easy for one may be very difficult if not impossible for another. While it may be quite easy for one person to stay sober, maintaining a healthy relation to alcohol, the alcoholic finds this a daily and lifelong struggle. Should these people be judged simply on the basis of accomplishment? Christianity believes that people are evaluated according to what has been done with what was given. How are we going to create a beautiful life for God out of the raw material—genes, environment, family, material resources—which grace us. From the one to whom much is given, much will be expected.[8]

Quality of action is important in terms of the spiritual path. Each perceives the other's path as easier or better. But we are responsible not for the other's path, or for the way things might have or should have been, but rather for what our own life reveals and provides and what we in turn with the help of God make out of it. Christian living is not simply following rules and doing good, but creating out of our lives something beautiful for God.

TO DEEPEN—

What part does the covenant play in a Christian's moral life?

What distinguishes Christian morality from non-Christian morality?

Why is morality important for the Christian?

What is the relation of morality to law for a Christian?

8. Lk 12:48

Further Reading:

Gaffney, James. *Newness of Life.* Paulist Press, 1979.

Gallagher, John. *The Basis for Christian Ethics.* Paulist Press, 1985.

Gula, Richard M. *What Are They Saying About Moral Norms?* Paulist Press, 1982.

Hanigan, James B. *As I Have Loved You: The Challenge of Christian Ethics.* Paulist Press, 1986.

May, William E. ed. *Principles of Catholic Moral Life.* Franciscan Herald, 1981.

McDonagh, Enda. *Doing the Truth: The Quest for Moral Theology.* University of Notre Dame, 1979.

O'Connell, Timothy. *Principles for a Catholic Morality.* Seabury, 1978.

Varga, Andrew C. *On Being Human: Principles of Ethics.* Paulist Press, 1978.

43. Conscience

Definition

The key to any moral decision lies with the individual's conscience, the voice of the reasoning heart. We exercise our conscience by sorting through various moral teachings in order to arrive at a judgment of what we must do concerning the problem at hand. At root, conscience is deciding what "I" must do after making a sincere effort to discover what is right. Our conscience is the primary means by which the Holy Spirit guides us. Because conscience is so allied with the Holy Spirit, it is the most sacred sanctuary within the human person. To violate conscience is to sin.

Formation of Conscience: Biological Factors

Conscience is not simply a given of human nature but is formed throughout childhood by genes, nurture and environment. First it is determined by genetic heritage which enables us to perceive situations and act in accord with perception. And genetic traits are different. Biological organisms differ as well. Some are able to think better than others, some better able to feel, some better able to act.

Nurture and Environment

Secondly conscience is formed by upbringing and environment. The values of parents, society, school, and Church are presented to children who by and large adopt and own them. But these values are not simply poured into the empty container of conscience. They are appropriated according to one's pre-disposed makeup. Some accept everything handed down. Some rebel and reject what is given.

The Christian Moral Tradition

Since we are part of the Christian community, we are shaped by its values. Growing up in a Christian household we receive these values along with the others that our parents and society pass on. Becoming Christian later in life, initiation involves learning the Christian moral tradition and assimilating it into one's conscience.

The Christian moral tradition[9] embodies over two thousand years of wisdom and experience. Catholics find that tradition given concrete expression in the magisterial teaching.[10] The Catholic conscience is shaped by the Church. Church teaching is given the presumption of truth. But although it embodies the objective moral law it is not a standard to be blindly followed.

The Christian in Community

In addition to these values given by nature and society, a person forms conscience through the activities of prayer, the practice of virtue, a growing sensitivity to the Holy Spirit, discussion and advice from one's pastor and other Christians, as well as reading and information-gathering on specific issues. Conscience is a part of our person which develops, stagnates, or degenerates on the basis of overall behavior. Sin blunts and virtue sharpens it. We are accountable for what we have done with what we have been given.

While genes, environment and the Christian teaching help form a person's conscience, the actual activity of conscience helps the person create his or her life by making concrete moral decisions regarding specific situations. What story is our life telling? And what part do we play in creating and shaping that story? Conscience lies at the heart of this process which itself is the working out of our salvation.

Inviolability of Conscience

If after prayer and study the person is unable to accept the formulation of a value or the application of a teaching because it seems wrong, then the person is obliged to follow conscience over against the

---

9. Truth 24
10. Truth 24

teaching. Fidelity to conscience links Christians with all humanity in the search for truth.

This teaching is older than Vatican II: Thomas Aquinas taught that when one has come to the conviction that a particular aspect of a teaching is wrong, one must follow conscience. Although this teaching has been present throughout Christian history, at times it has not been stressed sufficiently in deference to obedience and submission.

The substance of what is taught must be distinguished from the formulations used to communicate it. Catholics believe that God will not allow the Church to err concerning the substance of the faith.[11] However a specific formulation may not be the best possible. Today there is dissent over how the Church handles divorce and remarriage. However no one challenges the teaching that marriage is meant to be permanent.

There is also a hierarchy of truths within the Church: some teachings are more fundamental than others. It is one thing to challenge the Church's policy of celibacy for the clergy, another to question the restriction of holy orders to males, and yet another to deny that there exists an ordained ministry within the Church. The first challenges merely a Church law, the second questions the way that the Church understands tradition, the third denies tradition itself.

Dissent from Church teaching should never be undertaken lightly or without sufficient prayer and consideration. For we risk today an individualism with no patience for values that seem to go against the self. In this direction lies a selfish coddling and nourishing of the ego which leads away from wholeness.

In any argument each extreme leads toward a distortion of the truth. And if Christians or the Church in the past erred on the side of obedience and authority, how will this age be judged by the future if it considers only the individual self and neglects the good of the whole?

If qualms of conscience affect more than a few teachings and values, one needs to consider one's relation to the Christian community and its vision anew. This is a sinful and broken world. We ourselves are not whole. Through ignorance, greed and hatred people do things which in their hearts they know are wrong.

A standard, shining the light of truth into our lives, is needed. The Church's teaching—coming from Israel's heritage and Jesus—provides such a light. If we allow ourselves to be seen in the light of this goodness we will view ourselves and our actions with more honesty than is human custom. And this insight leads not to despair, but, experiencing God's

---

11. Truth 22ff

forgiveness, we begin anew. And our actions, far from leading to death, now lead toward life and happiness.

TO DEEPEN—

What is conscience? Why is it important?

What factors help create a Christian's conscience?

When should a Christian go against his or her conscience?

What role should the Church play in forming a Christian's conscience?

Further Reading:

Fowler, James. *Becoming Adult, Becoming Christian.* Harper & Row, 1984.

Fowler, James & Keen, Sam, eds. *Life-Maps: Conversations on the Journey of Faith.* Word Books, 1978.

Hall, Brian P. *Development of Consciousness—A Confluent Theory of Values.* Paulist Press, 1976.

Shea, John. *Stories of Faith.* Thomas More, 1980.

Sobosan, Jeffrey. *Guilt and the Christian.* Thomas More, 1982.

44. The Moral Decision

Having seen how conscience is formed, we turn to the decision-making process. Just how does a Christian go about making a decision on a course of action?

First there is the Christian moral tradition.[12] What has the tradition said on the question? But the moral tradition is not simply taken at face value. Sometimes since it spans many cultures and centuries it is difficult to understand. Situations and cultures change. A law meant for a particular situation may not have the same intent when applied to a different structure.

Here determining the inner meaning of the law, or what is most reasonable in this situation of conflict is important. This is known as exercising the virtue of *epikeia*. Without this principle the law would ignore the truth that people and situations are not absolute but concrete.

The major problem in decision-making arises from applying abstract moral principles (fairly easy to arrive at and understand) to concrete existential situations (which do not lend themselves to such

---

12. Truth 24, 45ff, 58–73

clarity). Here responsibility is called for. How do we live so that these abstract principles enable us to create a moral life? Through these daily decisions we create our life.

Much of the Catholic moral tradition attempts to think out the implications of the teaching for concrete situations. This moral theology has created a vast reservoir to aid the Christian with decisions. Current Catholic moral thinking stresses that in any action which results in both good and bad consequences it is not morally justifiable to achieve a few trivial good effects at the cost of grave evil.

But in the end our decisions embody our responsibility to create a life in harmony with Jesus' vision of the kingdom even though we live in a world deeply at variance with such a vision. Here is our challenge and our mission.

A Model For Decision-Making

So let us consider a model for decision-making. There are four factors to consider: first, the person doing the action, second, the beliefs influencing his or her behavior, third, ethical norms supplied by the Church, and, finally, an understanding of the situation itself.

The first and most important factor is the human person doing the action. That action will be influenced by our self-awareness, integrity, education, and other factors that contribute to our moral sense.

Second, we bring certain beliefs to our decision-making. Some of these come from our religious tradition, others come from our society and culture. There are different value systems in any culture. For example, being a member of the white middle class in America will provide a different set of values than being a member of the white lower class. For Christians, Scripture further influences our values since it provides images and orientations for the moral life.

Third, the norms of Church teaching influence a Catholic's behavior. Our moral tradition provides guidelines and principles which help to decide an issue. This provides the wisdom necessary to evaluate the situation and decide.

Finally knowledge of factors and influences at work in the concrete instance are crucial. Disciplines from psychology to history can help here. What concrete factors must be taken account of in our decision? As a symbol consider the New York *Times* (or your other favorite source of information), although here too the symbol includes far more than its narrow meaning: embracing the wealth of human knowledge and understanding which can be brought to bear. For example in approaching an election one would want to know who the candidates are and what they stand for and believe in. All the wisdom in the world will not help if one is ignorant of specifics.

Making a Prayerful Decision

In making such a decision the Christian prays, asking God for guidance in this decision. Such guidance presupposes that we have done our homework on the tradition and the situation. The decision must be informed, not simply "inspired." Prayer is no substitute for knowledge. But neither is knowledge self-sufficient. Situations are always morally ambiguous. Action is risk, but a risk that tries to do the will of God rather than self-interest.

True prayer rarely results in a clear voice for action. Indeed Catholics are suspicious with reason of "private revelations." Prayer provides a means and aid in doing the right thing. It is not an abdication of responsibility and reason nor simply a pious gesture. The mystery of prayer reveals our path toward wholeness and the kingdom even though "through a glass darkly."[13]

But we do not pray alone. Christian community plays a key role in forming moral decisions for its members. From the community we received the tradition's wisdom. But the concrete community provides other means to aid decision-making. We may discuss our problem with other Christians or a pastor trained both in the tradition and in counseling. Such discussion may naturally lead into prayer together. And the community supports the action. So in a decision we find ourselves armed with the tradition in one hand, the situation in the other, on our knees in prayer with our community.

Obviously most choices in life are limited, clear-cut issues easily responded to in everyday living. But enough issues become important signposts determining the overall shape of life as well as the society in which one lives.

These key issues challenge response in such a way that the kingdom of God might shine out from our action and enable others to see a life richer and more blessed than so far experienced. Christian moral life is the arena in which we mold and make flesh the wholeness which Jesus gives us as promise as well as the place where we witness through our actions and our living to the kingdom's reality as the yeast leavening the world.

---

13. 1 Cor 13:12

TO DEEPEN—

What factors operate in determining the morality of an act for a Christian?

How does a Christian go about making a moral decision?

What part can the Christian community play in helping a person make moral decisions?

Further Reading:

Stevens, Edward. *Making Moral Decisions.* Paulist Press, 1981.

45. Sin and Forgiveness

Humanity is deformed by original sin.[14] This is a state of being rather than an action. Original sin signifies a tendency toward sinful actions when left to one's own devices. We have a propensity toward evil in spite of the fact that we are created good.

Original sin is the ground out of which actual sin arises. Christians primarily regard sin as infidelity toward the covenant we have entered into with God.[15] Sin also injures the social fabric—either between the person doing the wrong and the person wronged, or between the sinner and society itself.

Although sin is a fundamental Christian teaching and reality, the emphasis is rather upon God's forgiveness. Christianity uncovers the sinful nature of much human conduct not to plunge us into despair but to offer God's reconciliation to move out of sin into the kingdom.

Given the ideal of the kingdom of God, much of human activity is sinful. Catholic tradition calls this common sinfulness venial sin. It is reconciled within the Christian community primarily through the Eucharist.[16]

Mortal Sin

In addition to this general sinfulness common to all and adding to our confusion and misery, other actions, regarded as grave transgressions of morality, are called mortal sins because they kill the spirit. To be considered a mortal sin three conditions must be met.

---

14. Truth 57
15. Way 2
16. Truth 78

Catholicism believes that true mortal sin involves some rejection of God. Modern moral theology speaks of a fundamental option—the basic commitment we make to orient our lives either toward self-centeredness or other-directedness. Christians try to act in accordance with the will of God as it is revealed in regard to human actions through the commandments and the moral teaching of the Church.[17] But a person may commit an action regarded as serious moral wrongdoing, but in so acting the person does not intend to reject God. To the extent that this is so, the seriousness of the action is not a mortal sin.

For example, homosexual acts are against Church teaching. But to what extent does a homosexual person mean to reject God or God's will when driven to engage in homosexual acts? The act may be objectively wrong, yet the person may not have severed his or her relationship to God in so acting. To that extent the person is not cut off from God.

Pastorally such persons may be counseled so that they may be able to acknowledge the truth of Catholic teaching and embrace that truth to the extent they are able. Catholicism has ethical rules, but in discerning specific actions Christ's compassion and reconciliation take precedence over any legalism.

The person must know that the action is seriously sinful. Ignorant actions, causing serious problems and harm, are not regarded as mortally sinful for that person. Furthermore, if the person knows that this action is considered sinful by the Christian tradition, and yet cannot see it as sinful in conscience, sinfulness is diminished. An action may be morally wrong and yet, because of ignorance, not be a sin.

The action must be freely done. If one is compelled by force to commit a sin, one's sinfulness is diminished to the extent that conditions take away from one's freedom. Thus to steal a loaf of bread might be gravely sinful for a person who could afford to buy it, but not as sinful for a starving person with no money. The objective act is wrong in each case, but the second situation is not really the act of a free agent.

Finally the action must have serious matter—it must be objectively and seriously wrong. Believing it sinful to step on the crack in a sidewalk does not make such action sinful since no objective evil is involved.

TO DEEPEN—

What is the difference between original and mortal sin?

What factors must be present for a sin to be mortal?

---

17. Truth 45–70, Life 44

Further Reading:

Menninger, Carl. *Whatever Became of Sin?* Bantam Books, 1978.
Gaffney, James. *Sin Reconsidered.* Paulist Press, 1983.

TO CONTINUE—

The contents of Christian moral teaching are presented in Truth 45–73 and in Life 44.

The moral life unfolds into the spiritual life presented in Way 46ff.

The forgiveness of sins is further explored in Truth 43, 76, 80.

The Christian view of the human condition is found in Truth 57.

46. The Way of the Spirit

We have now reached the peak of the Christian Way. The Scriptures reveal God's call to follow Jesus: they present Jesus' teaching. Morality is the foundation upon which the spiritual life builds. The Liturgy provides the grace and blessing necessary for conversion. But what are Christians called to become?

What does conversion mean in the context of Jesus' teaching? What does it involve? What do Christians convert from and to? Then, since the life of Jesus' followers is nourished by prayer, how does Jesus understand prayer? What is the shape and content of our Christian prayer? Finally, what life results from following this Way?

47. THE WAY OF CONVERSION

TO PREPARE—

Some acquaintance with the Gospel (Truth 15ff) is helpful, especially the material on the kingdom of God (Truth 17).

Jesus' message is basically, "Repent and believe in the kingdom of God." The kingdom is breaking into the world. This kingdom brings a new vision, new values, a new way of living, and will eventually replace the present way of the world.

This is God's kingdom, dependent on God's action for its coming. Human effort cannot bring it about. But we have a part. Its coming depends upon our cooperation with God. We are called to continue Jesus' ministry which announced the kingdom and revealed its presence.

The kingdom is built upon God's grace, favor and blessings. Grace makes us workers for the kingdom and sustains our efforts in the face of failure and rejection. Awareness of grace keeps us from thinking that this kingdom depends upon us or that our concerns and values match those of the kingdom.

In spite of grace people remain sinful and limited. Much of the world and its values cling to Christians although they seek to follow Jesus. We easily perceive our wants as what is necessary for the kingdom. Yet in truth we are but servants.[1] Only God can bring that kingdom. And God ultimately works in his own way. God uses our limited and

---

1. Lk 17:10

half-converted state. But we should not project our sinfulness, pride, or trust in worldly power into that kingdom.

The kingdom is a society. Made up of creatures, a society reflects the nature of its members. Presently various societies reflect fallen humanity. But the kingdom of God is composed of a new humanity—redeemed and recreated. Inasmuch as a person is transformed, so much does that person show forth the glimmerings of the Kingdom even in the midst of this world.

And what is this new person like? Jesus calls us to become perfect like our heavenly Father.[2] But ordinary notions of perfection differ from Jesus' concept. A closer word is "wholeness."

We are fragmented people hiding our imperfections from ourselves and others. We also try to make ourselves perfect by stressing our virtues and repressing our faults. But perfection cannot be attained in this way. Indeed such attempts usually increase sin. For we are cutting off a part of ourselves in hope of finding perfection. Of course we do not look at it like this. It takes a spiritual teacher like Jesus to reveal our error.

For Jesus, wholeness does not come from developing only a part of ourselves. It comes from a total acceptance—the parts we like, the parts we cannot stand. The path to the kingdom lies first of all in this acceptance, which does not come easily. Only then can we discover our true nature, becoming whole as God wills us.

Radical transformation is necessary for citizenship in the kingdom. It goes to the root of the problem, to the very core of our human nature. It is not an easy change. It cannot be done under our own power. Jesus is calling us to become something new, something unheard of in this world.

48. The Nature of Penance

Jesus reveals a new way of living and seeing life through parables and signs. Instead of continuing to live as we have learned to do, he invites us to share the vision appropriate to the kingdom. Christians move from present ties to worldly thought and action into a life inspired by God and his kingdom. Christians give up a way of living that puts our own will first; with Jesus we now want to pray, "Thy will be done."[3]

But such a switch in allegiance is not easy. We are stuck in our old ways. Deciding to act differently will not make it so. Such ingrained

2. Mt 5:48
3. Way 50

habits are hard to change; indeed they are hard to recognize as habits rather than simply the way things are. What makes us believe that our will, so used to its own way, will gladly surrender its powers to another, even God?

Jesus is clear about the cost of discipleship: "If any man would come after me, let him deny himself and take up his cross and follow me."[4] To follow Jesus means renouncing that part of us that takes center stage. Only through this denial can we become selfless. And only by being selfless is there be room for the Father and his kingdom.

Self Denial

For Christians self-denial is a means of discipline—a method for learning how to live selflessly. We do not hate the flesh; how can we hate that which God became? We do not despise ourselves. Through self-denial we tame our self, realign our priorities, and find the true happiness Jesus promised.

We are fragmented people. There is an ego—an "I"—which likes to think it is in charge, even that it is all of us. But there is more to us than the ego. For example there are denied parts of our being. Often we project these qualities onto other people. But this projection does little real good.

The way to health lies through a greater integration of our total self. Coming to acknowledge our darker side, we need to reconcile ourselves with it and the other parts of ourselves. Only such reconciliation brings true peace and happiness.

Self-denial creates conflict which in turn highlights our shadow. We come to see in ourselves those qualities we project onto others. And once we come to see these split-off fragments we can move with God's help toward integration.

In addition our self-denial brings to our attention the plight of our brothers and sisters throughout the world who daily are denied even the necessities of life. These too are potential members of God's kingdom. Indeed through their poverty they are already God's chosen people. God joins their struggle with injustice.[5] God's kingdom belongs first to those whom the world rejects.

Through penance Christians share in their situation. We come to feel solidarity with the poor and oppressed. Penance raises conscious-

---

4. Mt 16:24b
5. Mt 5:3

ness and creates compassion. And that compassion joins us with the poor in their struggle so that they too may share even now in the bounties of our Father's world.

Much oppression is caused by our own blindness. Penance reveals the extent to which we and our nation create oppression. Repentant, we might move to break the oppression at its source and make reparation to those who have suffered for so long. We follow Jesus in the hope of entering his kingdom. But how can that kingdom where all shall live in wholeness come about as long as even Christians work against it by denying the benefits of God's goodness to sisters and brothers who share this earth?

Repentance

Consider the words used by Christians to speak of penance: conversion, metanoia and repentance. Each has a different focus. Conversion or turning toward God is really a matter of the heart. Metanoia refers more to the mind—change your mind, change your accustomed ways of thinking. And repentance refers to our body or will—what we do, how we act.

The will reveals best the results of penance. Often repentance is considered as being sorry. We have done something wrong; having hurt someone, we feel sorrow for what we have done and try to rectify the wrong. But this is not the most profound meaning. Repentance does not simply bandage the wounds we have caused. For what would really be accomplished? Yes, it is valuable in the current situation. But will such repentance help us refrain from hurting someone in the future? Will it enable us to live more by the vision of God's kingdom? Hardly.

The difference between the way we live and perceive things and the kingdom way of seeing is great indeed. More than sorrow is needed to move us from our current vision into that of the kingdom. Our attitudes and thoughts brought us into that sinful action in the first place: these we must repent. The real problem is not the hateful words spoken in anger, but the fears and insecurities which lead to hateful words.

True repentance moves behind sins to the sinful condition itself. What makes us hurt people? What prevents us from forgiving others? Why are we afraid to love? We move to the heart of the matter; we discover our integrated self as it was and as it still is in the mind of God. For if we can discover who we truly are, then we shall naturally act in accord with our true nature. Then it won't be a problem of avoiding sin—by nature we shall act in a wholesome and healthy way.

Conversion

The second word for penance—conversion—leads into the heart. St. Paul says that we know what is right and what is wrong, but that does not help.[6] We cannot prevent ourselves from doing what is wrong and failing to do the good. Knowledge does not help. There is but one way out of this prison: Jesus Christ who, while we were still in sin, died for us to bring us out of sin into our Father's love.[7]

In the heart love conquers all. Certainly if we were able to turn our heart toward God we would find a way out of our prison. In Jesus God has already extended his love even to the point of dying for us. All is already reconciled in him. Nothing remains to be set right. We need only recognize this great love and allow it to renew us. When we allow God to love us we find ourselves recreated. In Jesus God has taken upon himself our likeness out of love.[8] When we acknowledge his love we take on the image of God which is Jesus, once more resembling the original creation.

Conversion has always been just this call to a real change of heart. The prophets called Israel to conversion:[9] not your sacrifices, rituals or other religious practices do I desire. Rather let your heart be turned toward me. Open your heart to the poor in the land so that you cease your exploitation and oppression. Let me replace your hearts of stone with hearts of flesh.

Similarly in our own conversion external actions are not the core of the matter. Externals are only important if in harmony with our internal life. If not, we are mere hypocrites, confessing one thing but living another.

How might this conversion occur? Begin by listening to what God has already accomplished for us in his love. We are being wooed by Jesus. God wishes to be with us, to heal, to forgive, to love, to raise us from death into life. As we open to God's plan we fall in love—first with God, then with ourselves, healing the divisions within, then with all creation.

And things begin to happen when we fall in love. The world changes. You are no longer the same. You see through your beloved's eyes. You want to be like your beloved. You want to join in union. Nor is this hard or difficult. Desiring it, you cannot be content until everything is shared.

---

6. Rom 7:19
7. Eph 2:4–7
8. Jn 3:16
9. Am 5:21–24

Metanoia

Our worldly attitudes separate us from union with God. When Jesus announces that he must go to Jerusalem, there to be handed over and killed, Simon Peter protests that he should do no such thing. Jesus' reply seems harsh, "Get behind me, Satan! You see not as God sees but as the world sees."[10]

The word "Satan" might give pause. Jesus is not really calling Peter the devil as that word is popularly understand. That would be strange indeed since Jesus has just put Peter in authority over the Church. Here Satan represents that part of the world in antagonism to God. The world is not evil, for it is God's creation and by nature good. But the world is out of joint.

Worldly values are not those of the kingdom. Satan relies upon force rather than love. Satan counsels retaliation rather than forgiveness. Satan believes in "me first" rather than in charity. Satan believes in saving your own skin rather than the world. Humanity shares these values; Jesus rebukes this spirit. "Peter, you are thinking and seeing as the spirit of this world has taught you. Do not cling to these ideas. Instead see life as it truly is when seen in the light of my Father's kingdom."

To leave behind the tyranny of Satan we must change our vision, outlook, attitudes, and grounding beliefs. Metanoia means to change one's mind. Our basic belief structures create and foment all the sinful acts which pollute our world. If we can move out of these beliefs, putting in their place the kingdom values, we will find our life and our world changing.

Just what are these basic beliefs? Begin with something as fundamental to human existence as fear and worry. Everyone is caught in webs of anxiety. Consider how much time you devote to these "realities." Yet the Scriptures tell us to fear not.[11]

Yes, fear has value. In a dangerous situation fear alerts us to the danger and hopefully marshals our resources to deal with the problem. But fear and worry consume much more of our time than just such emergency situations. Fear is generalized and tinges all of our living. Indeed as Jesus points out, our worry can prevent us from living altogether. So Jesus encourages us not to worry.[12] What does all this worry gain us? Nothing. So do not worry about what tomorrow may bring. Each day has enough troubles of its own.

---

10. Mt 16:23 (my own translation)
11. Mt 10:31; Lk 12:7
12. Mt 6:25ff

Much easier said than done—this dropping of worry and other worldly beliefs. When we explore the extent of worry in our own life we find just how deeply ingrained, how much a part of us, how terribly natural it has become. Trying to let go of these habits we find them to be even more deeply embedded. They have become so natural that we are blind to their importance and presence. Only when we begin to examine and work with them do we realize how extensive their hold.

We were, to use modern language, brainwashed into these beliefs and attitudes. But the situation is more serious still. There is a part of us—indeed it would like us to regard it as the whole of us—which is quite committed to keeping us stuck in the world's ways—in the ideology of Satan. We can call this part of us by various names: some call it the ego. It uses fear and worry to keep itself in power. It claims to love but really only seeks control and possession of the beloved. When wronged, it seeks vengeance and shuns forgiveness. It stands between our enslavement to Satan and our liberation as God's children.

TO DEEPEN—

Why is conversion necessary?

What does self-acceptance have to do with conversion?

What does self-denial have to do with conversion?

What is the purpose of repentance?

What are some ways in which a person might go about repentance?

Further Reading:

Conn, Walter. *Conversion: Perspectives on Personal and Social Transformation*. Alba, 1978.

Griffen, Emily. *Turning—Reflections on the Experience of Conversion*. Doubleday, 1980.

Haughton, Rosemary. *The Transformation of Man*. Templegate, 1980.

49. Ascetical Practices

Christians at various times choose an ascetical practice which converts them more to Jesus' vision. During Lent the entire Christian community does penance.[13] And at times our life needs these practices in

---

13. Life 40

order to be purified and make progress on the Christian Way. Jesus used and advocated three basic practices to further conversion: fasting, prayer vigil, and almsgiving.

Fasting

Fasting is a practically universal ascetical practice. We fast to purify our bodies and spirit. It raises consciousness. It provides the time and motivation for prayer. It reveals the games of ego and draws us into a confrontation with our ego.

Fasting should also raise our consciousness concerning food not only in our own life but in our world. Fasting is a natural way from time to time to purify the body and restore appetite. If we have become addicted to junk foods a short fast restores our original taste and appetite. Then when we begin to eat again we can be conscious of what we eat and make decisions to change our diet.

Fasting makes us aware of our world and the scarcity which still afflicts most peoples. Fasting shares the hunger of our brothers and sisters. We share, if only temporarily, in their constant plight. Hopefully as our fast raises the issue to consciousness we will keep them in mind and work toward a more equitable distribution of the world's resources. Christian fasting always includes this social dimension. Jesus teaches us to pray to God for our daily bread.[14]

The primary story of Jesus' fasting occurs during his temptation in the wilderness.[15] In his hunger Satan comes to him and asks him to turn the stones into bread. Jesus responds that it is not by bread alone that we live, but rather by the word of God. Jesus' fast becomes a model. We attempt to recognize the voices as those of world and ego. And we come to realize that we are truly sustained in this life not simply by food and drink but by God.

Prayer Vigil

Jesus at various points withdraws from the public arena to pray.[16] He spends the night before his arrest in such prayer.[17] Christians too are a people of prayer. But Jesus often prayed through the night, and so the vigil becomes another means of asceticism.

Sleep is a favorite New Testament metaphor for the human con-

---

14. Mt 6:11
15. Mt 4:1–11
16. Mt 14:20
17. Mt 26:36

dition.[18] We are naturally asleep. And Jesus wakes us up to the life missed because of slumber. Paul quotes a Christian hymn, challenging people to "Wake up."[19]

Now although sleep and waking are metaphors, they are not just colorful images. These metaphors are in themselves related to the spiritual sleep and wakefulness which are Jesus' concern. The prayer vigil, by creating a special situation through lack of sleep, becomes a means whereby the person can break through ordinary consciousness to be touched and transformed by God.

As fasting takes away food, vigil deprives us of sleep, another assumed human necessity. Keeping vigil, we perceive how reliant we must be upon God to get us through. Our vulnerability opens us to the Spirit. We might come to see our life in new ways, perceiving things more in the light of Jesus' vision.

Vigils still form a part of Catholic practice in certain communities. Before major feasts or events, groups gather to keep vigil. In doing so they are practicing at a basic level the command to be vigilant and watchful.

Almsgiving

Almsgiving is easily recognized as an ancient Christian practice. But often today it is considered only charity. However, these spiritual disciplines aid us in our growing consciousness. Just as fasting raises consciousness around food, and vigil around sleep, so almsgiving concerns the place of money in our lives.

Money can very easily become our God. Indeed Jesus says that we can not serve the two masters of God and mammon.[20] It isn't that money in itself is evil—it is morally neutral. But our concern for it, our overvaluing of it, turns us from our true course toward the kingdom and binds us to worldly values.

Almsgiving loosens money's hold upon us. We give it away to the poor. In so doing we take money less seriously. We also help our brothers and sisters and acknowledge our tie to them. And if our giving seriously dents our budget we, as in fasting and vigil, are thrown upon the Lord to sustain us.

The practice of almsgiving finds a place in each Catholic's life. During Lent many give up meals, using that money to feed the hungry. Our

---

18. 1 Th 5:6
19. Eph 5:14
20. Mt 6:24

almsgiving as well supports the many charities. It is a recognition that our common human bond goes deeper than our commitment to money.

Other Practices

Other practices common among Christians have evolved from these original practices. From the practice of vigil we might turn to a consideration of how a Christian prays.[21] Along with the practice of fasting Catholics also abstain from meat on certain days.[22] And as an amplification of almsgiving Christian practice includes service[23] as a way of entering into the mystery of the kingdom and of being its herald.[24] Finally during the season of Lent Christians undertake some special Lenten practice which raises consciousness and converts us ever more deeply to the Gospel.[25]

While at times[26] Catholics abstain in solidarity, many during Lent (or at other times) abstain from various things. Like fasting, abstinence places an obstacle that raises consciousness around an issue. Some abstain from cigarettes or other habits. Abstention allows us to see how the habit dominates our life and provides the leverage to choose what part (if any) we would like this habit to occupy.

Abstention raises consciousness by taking something that has become customary and changing its place in our life. Encountering habitual situations we are forced by our abstention to use our will power to deny ourselves our usual customs. Hopefully in learning to live without we learn to rely upon the Lord's assistance. In our abstention we should try to succeed not through our own will power but relying upon God. Only in this way are we freed from the world and converted more toward the kingdom way.

The kingdom reveals all as brothers and sisters in the Lord, and we join in God's compassion for the poor. True happiness comes from **service** of others rather than being served. This is radically different from worldly thought.

TO DEEPEN—

Experiment with one of the ascetical practices of Jesus and observe how it works.

---

21. Way 50
22. Intro 18
23. Way 36ff, 51
24. Truth 17
25. Life 40
26. Intro 18

What is the difference between repentance and reconciliation?

How does fasting differ from abstinence?

What are the Catholic regulations on fast and abstinence? (Intro 18)

How might a Christian go about "dying to one's self"?

Further Reading:

Ryan, Thomas. *Fasting Rediscovered.* Paulist Press, 1981.

TO CONTINUE—

Lent as the time when the Church practices repentance is found in Way 32.

Conversion and penance as the basis of daily Christian existence is discussed in Life 3.

The highest expression of the means of passing into the kingdom are the beatitudes discussed in Life 47.

50. THE WAY OF PRAYER—THE LORD'S PRAYER

Our Father, who art in heaven,
hallowed be thy name.
Thy kingdom come.
Thy will be done on earth as it is in heaven.
Give us this day our daily bread,
and forgive us our trespasses
as we forgive those who trespass against us,
and lead us not into temptation,
but deliver us from evil.

TO PREPARE—

Some knowledge of the Christian covenant is necessary—Way 2ff
This section is best read after some acquaintance with material toward the beginning of both the Way and the Truth—including Scripture (Way 3ff, Truth 2ff), the Gospel (Truth 15ff), and the Creed (Truth 25ff).

Now according to the Church's tradition, after giving you the Creed we next go on to teach you the prayer our Savior gave us. This too must be learned by heart and recited next week; and this too must be repeated continually by all who embrace the Christian faith.

There is a text of scripture that says that all who call on the name of the Lord shall be saved.[1] But, as St. Paul says, how can people call on the name of the Lord unless they believe in him? And how can they believe in him if they have never heard of him?[2] This passage of scripture explains why we do not teach you the Lord's Prayer until you have learned the Creed. We give you the Creed first so that you will know what to believe, and then the Prayer so that you will know who it is you are praying to and what to ask him for. Then you will be praying in faith, and your prayer will be heard.[3]

Asked how to pray Jesus teaches his disciples the Lord's Prayer— the most Christian basic prayer. More than simply a prayer, it describes the shape of a Christian's prayer life.

Obviously today knowledge of this prayer extends far beyond the boundaries of Christianity. It may be the world's most popular prayer. To cite only one example of its use outside the Church, it concludes each Alcoholics Anonymous meeting.

Yet there is still reason for the Church to present this prayer to those about to be baptized. For in spite of its universality this prayer binds Christians to Jesus. We pray through Jesus to the Father; in this prayer Jesus literally becomes our word. And through baptism we enjoy a special relationship with God through Jesus Christ. We are heirs of Christ and thus daughters and sons of God.

This section concerns the way of praying rather than types of prayer.[4] The way of praying lies at the foundation of all true Christian prayer. Only when initiated into this basic prayer life can we effectively determine which spiritual practices to make our own.

How simple this prayer is, without a superfluous word! Jesus warned us not to imagine that the longer and more eloquent our prayer the more likely it would be to be answered. Some people, by their verbosity, give the impression of wanting to make sure God knows all the facts and arguments of the case.

---

1. Jl 2:32
2. Rom 10:13–15
3. Augustine, Sermon 56
4. Life 6ff

But our Lord told his disciples: "Your Father knows all your needs before you ask him,"[5] Don't be longwinded with the Lord; he knows all about it beforehand.

Why pray at all then, we might ask? If God knows what we need, will he not give us the things he knows to be necessary without our troubling to ask?

Yes, God does know the things we need, and he does want to give them to us. But he wishes us to pray for them because he wants us to appreciate his gifts and earnestly desire them; otherwise we should be like spoiled children who do not know how to value the good things they take for granted. Our desire for God's gifts is itself his gift; in fact the prayer Jesus taught us is simply the expression of the desire he has put into our hearts.

Every prayer you need to make is included in this short formula. Any request that cannot be reduced to one of the petitions of the Lord's Prayer ought not to be made at all.

Let us go through it now in detail.[6]

Our Father, who art in heaven

First, notice the overall similarity of this prayer to both the ten commandments—the foundation of Israel's life—and the summary of the law which Jesus gave to love God and neighbor. The first four petitions center upon God just as do the first commandments. Then the focus in both shifts to our neighbor. The priority in both cases, and with both traditions, therefore is God. We can only do right by our neighbor or in the world if we are in proper relationship to God.

Jesus is hardly unique in Israel in calling God "Father." But he does provide a new dimension to this word by using "Abba,"[7] which is close to, "Dearest Father." Today the Fatherhood of God (and the brotherhood of man) have become clichés in a post-Christian culture.

But a deeper dimension of the Christian's relationship to God through Jesus should be remembered. Jesus says; "All things have been delivered to me by my Father; and no one knows the Son except the Father, and no one knows the Father except the Son and anyone to whom the Son chooses to reveal him."[8] Jesus not only gives God a

5. Mt 6:8
6. Augustine, Sermon 56
7. Mk 14:36
8. Mt 11:27

name, but establishes a relationship between God and his disciples. Through baptism we are joined in Jesus Christ, so that his relationship to God becomes our inheritance.

The image of Father has become dominant in the minds of certain Christians. But it is not the only image that the Christian Scriptures use to speak of God. Nor should the secular understanding of fatherhood—namely patriarchal dominance—simply be applied to God. Indeed Jesus seems to do away with patriarchy altogether: "And call no man your father on earth, for you have one Father, who is in heaven."[9] If Christians apply the word "father" to any human being, it should be to the extent to which that person imitates God, rather than applying to God cultural attributes of males.

Later Christians such as Juliana of Norwich address God as Mother as well. God's personhood does not imply that God has a sex, but that God is approachable. In our prayer we are encouraged to address God as we would our parents—in reverence and love, confident that they in turn love and care for us. Being God of all creation, God is said to be in the heavens—over all that is. In praying to God we address the very source of creation. We pray to the power that brought into being everything that is and that sustains everything in being from moment to moment.[10]

Jesus makes the distinction between "my Father" and "our Father." This is not a prayer for an individual, although individuals certainly use it, but the prayer of Jesus' community. We know God because of Jesus. And joined to Jesus as brothers and sisters God is *our* Father. Christianity is based upon a covenant relationship—God and the Church.[11] It is not primarily an individual religion, although it has become such in the minds of many.

That "our Father" is "in heaven" means that God is not to be restricted to any place or time. God is both immanent—here among us especially in Jesus—as well as transcendent—all creation can not contain him. There is no other power equal to God—no rival—although humanity erects many idols or false gods.

Hallowed be thy name

The first commandment reveals God to Israel,[12] and the first petition reveals the Father to Christians. So the second commandment

9. Mt 23:9
10. Truth 28
11. Way 1
12. Truth 47

parallels this second petition. "Do not take God's name in vain," echoes Jesus' phrase "Hallowed be thy name."

"To hallow" is to sanctify—to be mindful of God's glory. Throughout the Scriptures God manifests God's glory. It appears as a pillar of cloud and fire to guide the Israelites.[13] It leaves the temple before the destruction of Jerusalem by Babylon.[14] It overshadows Mary to conceive Jesus,[15] and it appears again in Jesus' transfiguration.[16]

Although Jesus brings us into intimacy with God, he does not put aside the transcendence and the awe which is a universal experience of the divine. When Moses encounters God in the burning bush he is told to put aside his sandals because he is on holy ground.[17] God is holy by the transcendence of his nature which contrasts with everything created. We may see signs of God in the storm, the sunset and other aspects of creation, but God is not limited or caught by any of God's creation.

Our worship of God begins always by hallowing God's name: giving praise and reverence and thanksgiving to God. Included in this phrase is the preparation that is needed for prayer. Although we might pray at all times or in all situations, there is still a need to enter into prayer. We need to call God to mind and to turn ourselves toward God as we begin our prayer.

God's holiness is also a judgment. God judges and bends all that does not conform to his demands.[18] Thus all sin profanes God's holy name. This petition does not only speak of our immediate preparation for prayer—getting oneself into the proper frame of mind. It speaks of our whole life. How does our way of living sanctify the name of God?

Jesus tells us to hallow God's *name*. Names have lost their original power in our culture, but it was not always thus. In scriptural times, as people were nearer to the dawn of language, the power of the word was still felt. To know someone's name gave one power over that person. The name was not simply a label, but somehow revealed the essence of what was named. Israel dared not even call God by his name. The name YHWH—the tetragram—was written in the Scriptures, but it was not pronounced. Instead the euphemism "Adonai" or "Lord" was used. And by writing the vowels of Adonai under the consonants of YHWH

---

13. Ex 16:10
14. Ez 10–11
15. Lk 1:35
16. Lk 9:28–36
17. Ex 2:5–6
18. Is 6:3–5

(since Hebrew originally only wrote the consonants), the rabbis gave rise to the word "Jehovah."

Jesus himself provided another name for God—Abba. And Christians believe that since Jesus himself is God, that name now takes pride of place. The Jesus prayer of the Eastern Church sanctifies all of life through taking the divine name of Jesus into the heart.

Thy kingdom come

Christians dedicate their lives to the coming of God's kingdom which offers a new vision based upon new values which Jesus introduces.[19] Longing for the kingdom forms part of our prayer life. But we are called to do more—to give our lives to the kingdom, to become transformed in Christ so that the reality of the kingdom shines in our life to be seen there by others. Ongoing conversion is necessary so that God's reign might shine forth through the Church into the world.

Thy will be done on earth as it is in heaven

Christians align themselves with God's kingdom. We have given our lives over to the Lord. We try no longer to live out our own will but instead to come to know God's will and to live in harmony with it. This is not easily accomplished.

To obey God's will means to enter into God's action. In purity of spirit Christians welcome God's gifts and make them fruitful. Yet as we attempt to do God's will we become mindful of the distance that separates us from God. We pray that we may enter more deeply into the mystery of salvation, following God's will freely and without compunction. So we become instruments through whom God might reveal God's glory in Jesus to others.

Knowing God's will involves discernment. Jesus teaches us to ask for what we need.[20] But our prayer must also end as his did: "But not my will but yours be done."[21]

Bringing our needs to the Lord and seeking his will is a daily practice that transforms life. We learn to look honestly at our life, free from the confusions ordinarily thrown up to keep us in the dark. We become more conscious. We really examine what we need. Bringing this need to God, we put ourselves on the line. Do we trust God to answer us? Do we dare surrender control to rest in God's will?

---

19. Truth 16
20. Mt 7:7
21. Mt 26:39

Give us this day our daily bread

Now the prayer turns toward ourselves and our world. Food supplied by God formed part of Israel's messianic hope. Jesus speaks of the reign of God in images of a great banquet. He feeds five thousand people out of compassion. And in John's Gospel he identifies himself with this bread.[22]

Jesus teaches us to ask our Father for what we need. The phrase puts the matter clearly; we ask for daily bread, mundane yet necessary. We look to God to sustain us ultimately. This petition goes hand in hand with the previous phrase: in bringing our needs to God we also surrender to God's will rather than clinging to our own.

This phrase refers to three daily needs. First, we have obvious need of sustenance. God supplied the Israelites with manna in the desert. The phrase speaks of "daily bread," and the Israelites were told to gather only the manna which they needed for that day. In this way they learned how to rely upon God to sustain them.

The earliest Christians were very aware of the importance of bread in their lives. It forms the staple of many people's diets. And they realized that God's kingdom is manifested through the abundance of bread. Thus they prayed to God for daily bread, and they in turn shared their bread with others as a sign of the kingdom's presence in them. Christians take responsibility for feeding the hungry. It appears as table ministry in Acts and more ministers are needed to carry it out.[23] And Paul has to scold the Corinthians for circumventing this ministry.[24]

Christian concern for the poor and the hungry has remained to the fore. Today liberation theologies once more stress God's option for the poor and call the Church to be the voice of the poor. Far from being other-worldly, Jesus and Israel, in this prayer as in all traditions, unite obedience to God with service to the world.

The Christian is also nurtured by the bread of God's word[25] which catechumens begin to receive at the table of the word.[26]

> We all receive our daily bread from God, whether we are Christians or not. Without it we could not live. But there is another kind of bread, the bread God's children ask of him. Our Lord referred to it in the gospel when he told the Sa-

---

22. Jn 6:33
23. Acts 6:2ff
24. 1 Cor 11:20–22
25. Mt 4:4
26. Intro 7; Way 20

maritan woman, "It is not good to take the children's bread and throw it to the dogs."[27]

This is the bread of God's word. Yes, the inspired scriptures are also our daily bread during our life on this earth. Man does not live by bread alone, but by every word that comes from the mouth of God. Bread for our stomachs, food for our minds: we ask both of our heavenly Father.[28]

The fully initiated Christian is sustained as well by the Eucharist—our supersubstantial (another possible translation of the phrase) bread.

It is good to pray for this bread, and to ask that we may never be deprived of it on account of our sins. The faithful will understand what I mean, and you too will understand once you are baptized.

When our earthly life is over we shall no longer need to make this petition. We shall no longer have any use for bread, because we shall never be hungry again. We shall no longer need the sacrament of the altar, because we shall be wholly united with Christ. We shall no longer need to read the scriptures, because we shall see the Word of God himself through whom all things were made.[29]

And forgive us our trespasses as we forgive those who trespass against us

What bread is for the body, forgiveness is for the spirit. The work of Christ, his sacrifice, forms the new humanity. Christ transforms human beings in the very deepest core of their being. And that transformation extends through the Church to humanity in its widest compass. That transformation is nourished by the Eucharist which is celebrated for the forgiveness of sins.[30]

Jesus offers total forgiveness. Whatever we have done is reconciled, but that forgiveness does not stop with us. Just as Christians pray for and in turn supply daily bread, they in turn forgive those who have wronged them.

While we pray for forgiveness, it does not end with prayer. The

27. Mt 15:26
28. Augustine, Sermon 58
29. Augustine, Sermon 58
30. Mt 26:28

Lord's Prayer presumes that we in turn have been forgiving in our own life. And if we find it difficult to forgive (as is usually the case) we might pray about it.

Christian prayer is intimately connected with ordinary life. Prayer does not remove us from life but rather provides the insight, grace, and consciousness to live more by the kingdom vision and less by the world's values.

Lead us not into temptation, but deliver us from evil

Various kinds of temptation exist within the Judaeo-Christian tradition. God tested (one translation for this phrase) the Hebrews.[31] Job and even Jesus was led by God into the wilderness to be tested.

But while God tests humanity so that he may deepen and enrich us, enabling us to fulfill his purpose for us, he does not tempt us to evil. In the wilderness it is Satan who tempts Jesus, not God who led him there to be tested. Humanity is tempted also by Satan and by demonic forces and powers. We are also tempted from within ourselves. Jesus shows how the Pharisees have missed the mark since they reduce religion to keeping the outside of the cup clean, but are unmindful of what is within it.[32] John speaks of people preferring the darkness to the light.[33]

The path toward the kingdom is not easy. The world is hostile to the kingdom and its values. Conflict sometimes arises between loyalty to the kingdom and the world's demands. Naturally we ask not to be put to the test. The journey will be long and difficult. But we also trust God. Asking not to be led into temptation expresses that trust.

Caught in the web of original sin, sometimes we do not even know how to respond to a situation. Evil is not just a problem for others. Our knowledge of ourselves gained from Jesus throws God's light on our actions and thoughts. Our own evil is unmasked.

As this knowledge grows we rely upon God to deliver us from this evil. This deliverance is not a condemnation of the world and a fleeing to some safe Christian place. The world being God's creation is inherently good. But evil has infested it. And that tendency toward evil manifests itself not only in villains but in every human being including ourselves: from that we ask deliverance.

And at the end as in the beginning, notice the plural forms used.

---

31. Jdt 8:25
32. Lk 11:37–41
33. Jn 3:19

It is the Church praying for daily bread, for forgiveness, for deliverance from evil. Christianity presumes conflict and temptation.[34] There is war between God and evil. The powers of evil are the first to recognize Christ—they know what is afoot.

Although many Christians today are far from suffering or persecution they should not fall into the fallacy that such is to be expected. Indeed their acceptance might goad them into examining how they are failing to follow Jesus fully. For Jesus promises rejection and persecution to his followers. The kingdom is not fully here. The world still opposes the light. And history according to the Christian viewpoint is moving toward a final conflict. This petition calls upon God to save us from evil and to bring us safely into God's Kingdom.

> If you feel sure that you are standing firm, beware! You may fall. So far you have faced no trial beyond what man can bear. God keeps faith, and he will not allow you to be tested above your powers, but when the test comes he will at the same time provide a way out, by enabling you to sustain it.[35]

TO DEEPEN—

Show how the concerns and petitions of Christian prayer can be understood as the way Jesus teaches us to pray.

How might Paul's exhortation to "pray without ceasing" (1 Thes 5:17) be understood in the light of the Lord's Prayer?

How do the various prayers of the liturgy give concreteness to the phrases of the Lord's Prayer?

Rewrite the Lord's Prayer, putting it into your own language so that it becomes more a formula for how you are to pray.

Attend prayer services (charismatic, scriptural, the divine office, rosary, benediction) and see each kind of prayer in the light of Jesus' teaching in the Lord's Prayer.

Further Reading:

Augustine. *On the Lord's Prayer.* St. Paul Editions, 1961.
Crosby, Michael H. *Thy Will Be Done: Praying the Our Father as a Subversive Activity.* Orbis Books, 1977.

---

34. Heb 2:18; 4:15
35. 1 Cor 10:12–13

Louf, Andre. *Teach Us To Pray*. Paulist Press, 1975.
Origen. *On the Lord's Prayer*.

TO CONTINUE—

You might explore the official prayer of the Church in the liturgy in Way 9ff and Life 38ff.

Prayer styles and spiritualities are explained in Life 6ff.

51. THE WAY OF ACTION

TO PREPARE

Some acquaintance with the importance of mission in Christian life is advisable (Way 15, 36ff).
In general this section should be left until one is acquainted with material toward the beginning of the Way and Truth.

How does the Church fulfill its mission to build up the kingdom of God? The works of mercy listed actions of the Christian apostolate.[1] However in this section we have reached the pinnacle of Jesus' teaching. What does Jesus send out the apostles to do?

Evangelization and Worship

Go therefore and make disciples of all nations, baptizing them in the name of the Father and of the Son and of the Holy Spirit, teaching them to observe all that I have commanded you.[2]

At the heart of Christianity lies the good news—the proclamation of and about Jesus known as the **kerygma.** An early example occurs in Peter's speech at Pentecost.[3] The Church's central task is to proclaim the good news so that people might hear it and be saved. **Evangelization** is accomplished by preaching, writing, and today by the media.

---

1. Way 36ff
2. Mt 28:19–20a
3. Acts 3:11–26

From the day of Pentecost the church has recognized that its primary function, entrusted to it by its founder, was to reveal Jesus Christ and his Gospel to those who did not know him. The whole of the New Testament and especially the Acts of the Apostles show us that this time was ideally suited to evangelization and in a certain sense offers us a prototype for the accomplishment of this work, a work of which the whole history of the Church furnishes a splendid counterpart.[4]

Evangelization is not reserved solely to missionaries but calls ordinary Christians who, when asked, share the Gospel which provides meaning for their life. "Laypeople have countless opportunities for exercising the apostolate of evangelization and sanctification. The very witness of a Christian life, and good works done in a supernatural spirit, are effective in drawing people to the faith and to God."[5]

While evangelization proclaims the definitive arrival of God's reign in Jesus Christ, the Church's worship celebrates Jesus as the focus of God's reign in sacrament. The Eucharist manifests the body of Christ. It incorporates and transforms people into Christ. The Eucharist is the "summit and source" of the Church's mission. The Church proclaims to the world what has been accomplished in its midst.

Fellowship and Witness

For where two or three are gathered in my name, there I am in the midst of them.[6]

The Church manifests community, known as **koinonia.** Jesus calls people to be united in him through his body on earth. In this body of Christ[7] we find unity with God and one another, the essence of God's kingdom. Unity proclaims the new order of being in the kingdom. Our boundaries have been lowered. We share all in the love of God. As Church we are commissioned to create and manifest this community for the sake of the world.

Now the company of those who believed were of one heart and soul, and no one said that any of the things which he possessed

---

4. Paul VI, Evangelization in the Modern World, n. 51
5. Decree on the Lay Apostolate, n. 6
6. Mt 18:20
7. Truth 41

was his own, but they had everything in common. And with great power the apostles gave their testimony to the resurrection of the Lord Jesus, and the great grace was upon them all. There was not a needy person among them, for as many as were possessors of lands or houses sold them, and brought the proceeds of what was sold, and laid it at the apostles' feet; and distribution was made to each as any had need.[8]

The Church is a sacrament of God's kingdom. It is not the kingdom, but it is inseparable from that kingdom. In evangelization the Church calls people to experience the presence of God's reign today. The Church is a sign of what God is actually doing in history and of what humanity should be doing in response to God's saving action.

The present sad state of Christian disunity belies the truth we witness in Christ. And so we must seek with God's grace once more to become one. This **ecumenical** movement has grown in the last century among Christian churches, including the Roman Catholic. Each Christian has a task of healing the wounds of our divisions without forsaking the Truth and in a spirit of true love.

Among the other faiths of humanity, the Church also has a mission. Of course it must always be faithful to its mandate to announce the Gospel. But it also seeks to enter into **dialogue** with other religions so that all may grow in unity.

True community is a taste of the kingdom. So Christians are called to create and nourish community and solidarity in their neighborhoods, schools and other areas of public life. As Christians we recognize our relationship with all people as children of one God. We work to eradicate prejudice and discrimination. We heal divisions and strive for justice so that through community people might turn toward the light.

The community has been called a sign of the kingdom. And that sign quality is known as "witness" or **martyria** from which comes the word "martyr" for those who give their lives as a witness to the faith. The Church and Christians are signs to the world—salt for the earth, light for the world. Jesus inaugurates a new way of being. Already through the Church that kingdom is flooding into the present world and transforming all. The Church is called to make present God's love and compassion for all peoples.

Although the martyr is a rather spectacular example of witness, Christians witness in infinite ways. Indeed sometimes witness is given without knowing one is doing so. The best witness is the common life

8. Acts 4:32–37

lived by Christian values. There is no rank in God's kingdom. Each life and task is equally loved. Charles de Foucault provides a unique example of witness. He spent much of his life living among the Moslems of northern Africa. He did not preach or teach Christ. Instead he attempted to live Christ. It is said that not one person ever came to him and converted to Christianity. But how many people saw in him the Christ and were warmed and enlightened by his example?

Service

You know that those who are supposed to rule over the Gentiles lord it over them, and their great men exercise authority over them. But it shall not be so among you; but whoever would be great among you must be your servant, and whoever would be first among you must be slave of all. For the Son of Man also came not to be served but to serve, and to give his life as a ransom for many.[9]

The Church acts in the world through **diaconia** or service. Jesus is a person for others. He washes his disciples' feet and tells them that their leadership must be more of the servant than the worldly model of the master.[10] As Jesus reached out toward the poor and marginalized, so the Church continues his ministry today. The Christian is sent by Jesus, gifted with the Holy Spirit, to continue showing forth Christ through service.

Christians in some way serve their fellow human beings. How this service takes shape, and its extent in our life, must be decided by each person. But if there is no service dimension we are failing our Christian mission. And, further, we deny ourselves the opportunity to be converted more fully.

For Christian service itself provides experience of the kingdom. Serving others we discover for ourselves that the happiness Jesus promises in this action is real. And through our commitment toward service we open ourselves to our brothers and sisters. Community becomes possible.

Hopefully our service aids the coming of God's kingdom. We wake up to the plight of the poor. Recognizing them as our brothers and sisters we take steps to help them move out of poverty and oppression and we become heralds of the good news.

---

9. Mk 10:42b–45
10. Jn 13:3–20

TO DEEPEN—

What are some ways in which you might enter into the Christian witness?

How do you see your local parish undertaking the mission of Jesus?

What examples of Christian witness have inspired you?

How does the Christian or the Church show forth the good news?

Enter into some aspect of Christian mission and reflect then upon its relationship to your faith and experience.

Further Reading:

Bea, Augustin. *Church and Mankind.* Franciscan Herald. Cardinal Bea was one of the great ecumenists, heading the Secreteriat for Christian Unity.

Dulles, Avery. *Models of the Church.* Doubleday, 1974.

Dulles, Avery. *A Church to Believe In: Discipleship and the Dynamics of Freedom.* Crossroad, 1982.

Kress, Robert. *The Church: Communion, Sacrament, Communication.* Paulist Press, 1985.

Ratzinger, Joseph & Lehman, Karl. *Living with the Church.* Franciscan Herald, 1978. An interesting book, since presently Cardinal Ratzinger heads the Congregation of the Faith in Rome.

Prayer:

Lord, make me an instrument of your peace!
Where there is hatred, let me sow love;
where there is injury, pardon;
where there is doubt, faith;
where there is despair, hope;
where there is darkness, light;
where there is sadness, joy.

Divine Master,
grant that I may not seek so much
to be consoled, as to console;
to be loved, as to love;
for it is in giving that we receive,
    in pardoning that we are pardoned,
    and in dying that we are born to eternal life.

(Prayer of St. Francis of Assisi)

TO CONTINUE—

The way of mission (Way 36ff) gives other examples of how the Christian is to live.

Other results of Christian life are seen in Life 10ff.

The Church's witness is also explored under Catholic Social Teaching and Action (Life 44–45).

The highest expressions of the Christian life and love are seen in Life 49–50.

THE TRUTH

◇ **Revelation**
◇ **The Truth of Scripture**
◇ **The Truth of the Tradition**
◇ **The Truth of the Christian Path**

◇

1. *Revelation*

Christianity is a way of living according to the covenant established by God in Jesus Christ and open to all. The various ways are explored in Part One.

But the covenant reveals a new vision of reality which is the content of the Christian faith. Thus Part Two concerns the key theme of revelation—what God reveals.

A concise summary of Christianity is found in the First Letter of John: "We proclaim to you the eternal life which was with the Father and was made manifest to us—that which we have seen and heard we proclaim also to you, so that you may have fellowship with us; and our fellowship is with the Father and with his Son Jesus Christ."[1]

The substance of Christianity is eternal life offered us by God. And this offer has been made manifest to us. Thus Christianity is based upon a revelation—a making manifest of what was formerly unknown.

The description of revelation changes throughout the various epochs of Christianity. For although the revelation of God does not change, human beings and our situation changes. Vatican II expounds revelation to our time, as seen in the following excerpts from the *Constitution on Divine Revelation*, n. 1. As the bishops stated, they want "the whole world to hear the summons to salvation, so that through hearing it may believe, through belief it may hope, through hope it may come to love."

---

1. 1 Jn 1:2–3, as translated in the Constitution on Divine Revelation

God Reveals Himself in Revelation

It pleased God, in his goodness and wisdom, to reveal himself and to make known the mystery of his will.[2] His will was that people should have access to the Father, through Christ, the Word made flesh, in the Holy Spirit, and thus become sharers in the divine nature.[3] By this revelation, then, the invisible God,[4] from the fullness of his love, addresses people as his friends,[5] and moves among them[6] in order to invite and receive them into his own company. . . . The most intimate truth which this revelation gives us about God and the salvation of humanity shines forth in Christ, who is himself both the mediator and the sum total of revelation.[7]

The History of God's Revelation

God . . . provides people with constant evidence of himself in created realities.[8] And, furthermore, wishing to open up the way to heavenly salvation, he manifested himself to our first parents from the very beginning. After the fall, he buoyed them up with the hope of salvation, by promising redemption;[9] and he has never ceased to take care of the human race. For he wishes to give eternal life to all those who seek salvation by patience in well-doing.[10] In his own time God called Abraham, and made him into a great nation.[11] After the era of the patriarchs, he taught this nation, by Moses and the prophets, to recognize him as the only living and true God, as a provident Father and just judge. He taught them, too, to look for the promised Savior. And so, throughout the ages, he prepared the way for the Gospel.

---

2. Eph 1:9
3. Eph 2:18; 2 Pet 1:4
4. Col 1:15; 1 Tim 1:17
5. Ex 33:11; Jn 15:14–15
6. Bar 3:38
7. Mt 11:27; Jn 1:14, 17; 14:6; 17:1–3; 2 Cor 3:16; 4:6; Eph 1:3–14
8. Rom 1:19–20
9. Gen 3:15
10. Rom 2:6–7
11. Gen 12:2

Jesus Is the Fullness of God's Revelation

> After God had spoken many times and in various ways through the prophets, "in these last days he has spoken to us by a Son."[12] For he sent his Son, the eternal Word who enlightens all people, to dwell among humanity and to tell them about the inner life of God. Hence, Jesus Christ, sent as "a man among men,"[13] "speaks the words of God,"[14] and accomplishes the saving work which the Father gave him to do.[15] As a result, he himself—to see whom is to see the Father[16]—completed and perfected revelation and confirmed it with divine guarantees. . . . He revealed that God was with us, to deliver us from the darkness of sin and death, and to raise us up to eternal life.

Our Response to God's Revelation

> "The obedience of faith"[17] must be given to God as he reveals himself. By faith a person freely commits his or her entire self to God, making "the full submission of his or her intellect and will to God who reveals,"[18] and willingly assenting to the revelation given by him. Before this faith can be exercised, a person must have the grace of God to move and assist him or her; he or she must have the interior helps of the Holy Spirit, who moves the heart and converts it to God, who opens the eyes of the mind and "makes it easy for all to accept and believe the truth."[19] The same Holy Spirit constantly perfects faith by his gifts, so that revelation may be more and more profoundly understood.

---

12. Heb 1:1–2
13. Epistle to Diognetus, c. 7, 4
14. Jn 3:34
15. Jn 5:36; 17:4
16. Jn 14:9
17. Rom 16:26; Rom 1:5; 2 Cor 10:5–6
18. Vatican Council I, Constitution on the Catholic Faith, c. 3
19. Denz. 180 {377}

TO DEEPEN—

How do the bishops of Vatican II describe revelation?
What is the very core of God's revealed truth?
How does revelation relate to covenant (Way 1)?

Further Reading:

Dulles, Avery. *Models of Revelation.* Doubleday, 1983.
Dulles, Avery. *Revelation Theology.* Herder & Herder, 1969.
Latourelle, Rene. *Theology of Revelation.* Alba House, 1966.
Vatican II, *Dogmatic Constitution on Divine Revelation,* 1965.

TO CONTINUE—

The major deposit of revelation is found in Scripture (Truth 3ff).
The summary of Christian revelation is the Creed (Truth 25ff).

◇

2. *The Truth of Scripture*

The contents of Christianity comprise the total revelation (Truth 1) as found in the traditions of Israel and brought to fulfillment in Jesus Christ. This revelation is communicated through two streams—sacred Scripture and sacred tradition. This section explores the contents—or rather the stories—of Scripture. But first what does Catholicism believe regarding the Scriptures?

3. Introduction to Scripture

TO PREPARE—

The Way of Scripture (Way 2–7) complements the material here.

While The Way of Scripture dealt with the practical issues (versions and ways to read Scripture), this section considers the Church's teachings concerning Scripture—what it is and how it is to be understood, and what part it plays in Christian revelation.

Inspiration

Christians regard the holy Scriptures as inspired writings: the only inspired writings in our tradition. Inspiration means that God enlightened and directed the biblical authors in their writing. These writings communicate God's revelation as no other books or words can.

But inspiration does not imply that God overrides the ideas, concepts, philosophy or world view of the human authors. God instead works through them with all their individual and social limitations and expresses the revelation through these limited conditions. Just as in Jesus God takes flesh in a thoroughly human manner and appears in the limitation of human form, so the Scriptures reveal God through these thoughts, words, and concepts.

But there is more than merely a human work in these sacred texts. God has granted a special assistance to these writers to express in a fitting manner the faith of the people of God at a given stage of salvation history. Because God does not abolish or lift the authors above their present stage there is an evolution in the growth of the Scriptures.

The insights at a more primitive level are taken up into succeeding higher levels. Much early biblical material reveals a rather bloodthirsty God whereas Jesus shows a face of love, compassion and forgiveness. God has not changed but rather humanity is growing and maturing in its insight into God. But such maturing does not deny God's inspiration to earlier materials.

Inerrancy

Catholics believe that the Scriptures do not err in matters of faith. But inerrancy does not apply to all other knowledge contained in the Scriptures. Thus common opinions of the day, historical knowledge, scientific theory, even facts are not covered by the doctrine of inerrancy.

For example, Genesis 1 describes the creation. The inerrant teaching in this passage includes the revelation that all that exists is the creation of God, and that creation is inherently good, being of God. The details arise from common speculation in the author's day. They are not considered part of the inspired teaching and so are not inerrant. A Catholic might hold different opinions concerning the genesis of the universe, so long as they do not contradict any teaching of the faith.

But how does one in many cases separate revelation from the opinions of the time? It is necessary to consider Scripture as a whole to determine the true character of revelation. The Church provides guidance in such discernment.

Canonicity

The sacred Scriptures are a collection of works composed over centuries in various languages. A decision by the Church guided by the Holy Spirit determined which works would be included in these Scriptures. This list is called a canon. The Council of Trent first defined the full Roman Catholic canon in opposition to Protestant reformers who challenged the canonicity of certain Old Testament books and threatened the same to the New Testament.[1]

The decision as to what constitutes Scripture cannot be determined by Scripture alone. The Church originally selected the components. And the Church has the authority to determine their interpretation.

The question of canonicity was not finally addressed by a Church council until Trent. Luther selected a canon of the Hebrew Scriptures, accepting only those books extant in Hebrew. The Roman Catholic Church in response to this action determined the canon to consist of those books plus the deutero-canonical books of Jerome's Vulgate translation. So the Catholic canon for the Hebrew Scriptures contains more books than the Protestant canon. The Orthodox Churches have not defined a canon. So their Hebrew Scriptures contain the same books as the Roman Catholic, plus some others. All churches maintain the same canon for the New Testament books.

TO DEEPEN—

Would a Catholic have to believe that Jonah was really swallowed by a big fish? What does it mean to say that a Scripture is inspired?

---

1. Way 4

Is inspiration the same as infallibility (Truth 22ff)?

Are there mistakes in Scripture?

Further Reading:

Farmer, William & Farkasfalvy, Denis. *The Formation of the New Testament Canon. An Ecumenical Approach.* Paulist Press, 1983.

Gnuse, Robert. *The Authority of the Bible—Theories of Inspiration, Revelation and the Canon of Scripture.* Paulist Press, 1985.

Kersten, John. *Bible Catechism.* Catholic Book Publishing.

TO CONTINUE—

The Catholic Church as teacher of the faith is examined in Truth 22ff.

4. The Scriptures of Israel

TO PREPARE—

The position of these and the following Scriptures in the liturgy is discussed in
Way 22.

Our tradition finds truth first and foremost in our history. For our
God reveals himself in human history, particularly that of Israel. This
section briefly introduces the shape of Scripture. There the first-hand
truth is found.

Jesus[1] and the Jews of his time referred to the corpus of writings
Christians called the Old Testament as the law and the prophets. There
was as well a third category known as the writings.

Jesus and his message must be seen in the context of Israel. For
Jesus is a son of Israel and his message is addressed primarily to Israel
and cannot be understood properly outside that context. Further,
Christians consider themselves the continuation of Israel. Our ancestors too are Abraham, Moses and the prophets—if not by blood, then
by adoption. Israel's history is our history at least until the time of Jesus
and the split of Christianity from Judaism.

The history of ancient Israel is considered sacred since through it
God reveals himself. Israel's history records God's actions in our world.
God becomes involved in human history to the extent of finally becom-
ing a human being.

This sacred history is not the same genre as the modern conception, however. Israel's history concerns primarily the meaning of life.
The facts are not primary to the telling; rather their significance is crucial. This is mythic history rather than factual. This does not deny that
many of these events actually happened. But their significance is par-
amount.

To convey that primary meaning, sometimes events are narrated
using elaboration, rhetoric and exaggeration—tools of any good story
teller. Modern scholarship attempts to discover what lay behind the
stories, what the author wished to communicate, and what elements of
the story are based on fact. But for our purposes the important thing is
not that the event happened as described, but that we grasp its meaning
as the sacred author intends.

---

1. Mt 5:17

TO DEEPEN—

Further Reading:

Andersen, Bernhard. *Understanding the Old Testament.* Prentice-Hall, 1986.
Barron, Sr. Mary. *Unveiled Faces: Men and Women of the Bible.* Liturgical Press, 1981.
Boadt, Lawrence. *Reading the Old Testament.* Paulist Press, 1984.
Castel, Francois. *History of Israel and Judah in Old Testament Times.* Paulist Press, 1985.
McKenzie, John. *Theology of the Old Testament.* Doubleday, 1976.

5. TORAH—THE LAW OF ISRAEL

The first and most sacred category of Scripture for Israel is the law or the Torah—the first five books of the Bible. The events narrated in the law tell Israel who she is and inform her of her mission and destiny. These events are crucial for Christians since they foreshadow Jesus, the fulfillment of the law.

The Torah in its present shape weaves together different strands of tradition from both the northern and southern kingdoms of Israel. The final form of the Scriptures both preserves the original traditions and offers interpretation as well as reinterpretation of the tradition.

The law should not be understood in the narrow sense of the laws of Israel. It is first the covenant[2] entered into between God and Israel. The Torah tells of the different covenants leading up to Mount Sinai and details God's continuous reaching out to Israel. The major covenants are with Adam,[3] Noah,[4] Abraham,[5] and finally Moses.[6] Christians believe that in Jesus a new covenant[7] supersedes the others.

6. Legends Concerning the Human Condition

Our story begins in the legendary time. The first human couple, Adam and Eve, sin in the Garden of Eden.[8] Subsequent stories con-

---

2. Way 1
3. Gen 2:16
4. Gen 9:1–19
5. Gen 15:1–21
6. Ex 20
7. Heb 8:6
8. Gen 2:4b—3:24

cerning Cain and Abel, their children,[9] Noah,[10] the tower of Babel[11] and others tell how human rebellion and sin grew. These stories of origins explain mythically the human condition.[12]

7. The Patriarchs of Israel

Then follow the legends of the patriarchs, the ancestors of Israel.[13] Abraham and Sarah are the parents of Israel because of Abraham's faith. He follows God's call to leave his homeland for another land which God will give to him and his descendants.[14] When God fulfills the promise by granting a child in their old age, Abraham is again put to the test and told to sacrifice Isaac. At the last minute an angel intervenes and saves the child.[15] Once again Abraham has trusted God. On the basis of this trust he becomes the father of faith.[16]

His descendant Jacob receives the name Israel when one night he struggles with God.[17] Israel, the nation, throughout her history will struggle with God. God enters into relationship with us. And relationships involve struggle. Struggling with God, like Jacob, we are wounded in the wrestling. But that wound is not our undoing but our blessing. Israel means "he who struggles against God and prevails."[18] Such struggling leads to understanding, growth in wisdom and blessing.

The patriarch Joseph, Jacob's last born and most beloved son, is envied by his brothers and sold into slavery in Egypt.[19] But Joseph is able to read dreams and comes into Pharaoh's favor by interpreting Pharaoh's troubling dreams. When famine strikes the surrounding lands, the brothers come to Egypt seeking help. Joseph sees them, reveals his identity to them and aids them. For Christians Joseph is a forerunner of Jesus who also saves and forgives his brothers. Matthew models his account of Joseph, the father of Jesus, upon Joseph the patriarch who follows his dreams and takes his people down to Egypt.[20]

---

9. Gen 4:1–26
10. Gen 6:5—8:22
11. Gen 11:1–9
12. Truth 57
13. Gen 11ff
14. Gen 12:1–8
15. Gen 22:1–19
16. Rom 4:16
17. Gen 32:24–32
18. Gen 32:28
19. Gen 37—50
20. Mt 1:18—2:23

TO DEEPEN—

Further Reading:

L'Heureux, Conrad. *In and Out of Paradise. The Book of Genesis from Adam and Eve to the Tower of Babel.* Paulist Press, 1983.
Vawter, Bruce. *On Genesis: A New Reading.* Doubleday, 1977.

8. The Exodus—God's Saving Action

Joseph relocates his family in Egypt, and many generations later a Pharaoh reigns who does not remember Joseph and enslaves his descendants. God appears in a burning bush to Moses telling him of his concern for the people in their suffering.[21] God will through Moses lead the people out of bondage and give them a land of their own. When Moses asks God's name the reply is, "I am who am."[22]

Returning to Egypt Moses demands the people's freedom. When Pharaoh proves obstinate plagues are sent upon Egypt.[23] The last plague is the death of the Egyptian first born. The slaves' first born are spared since at God's direction they sprinkle the blood of a lamb over their doorposts. The angel passes over the land, sparing those houses.[24]

Pharaoh, broken by his son's death, relents. The people leave, led by Moses and Aaron his brother. However Pharaoh changes his mind and sends his troops in pursuit. The people are led by a pillar of cloud by day and fire by night. At the Red Sea they are blocked before and behind. But the sea parts and the people pass through. The pursuing Egyptian chariots catch in the mud and are drowned as the sea closes in.[25] Moses and his sister Miriam lead the people in songs of thanksgiving to God for their liberation and victory over the Egyptians.[26]

The people eventually come to Mount Sinai and Moses goes up the mountain to commune with God.[27] There God gives the ten commandments,[28] the charter for Israel—who, unlike any other nation, were created solely by God and are to live under God's guidance.

When Moses comes down from the mountain, the people have reverted to the old gods. In despair he destroys the tablets of the law. But

---

21. Ex 3:1–22
22. Ex 3:14
23. Ex 5—11
24. Ex 12:1–28
25. Ex 13:17—14:22
26. Ex 15:1–21
27. Ex 19:1–29
28. Truth 45

the people are brought around again. For their sin they are condemned to wander in the wilderness for a generation.[29] There God tests them and they in turn try God. They are fed by manna—a bread-like substance—which at night appears on the desert floor.[30] They are quenched by water flowing from a rock.[31] Finally, the time of their wanderings over, they are led to the land prepared for them.[32] Moses, for his sin,[33] is prevented from going into the land and dies on the outskirts.[34]

9. The Law

Finally the Pentateuch contains the law of Israel. For Christians the most important aspect of this law is the core known as the ten commandments.[35] In addition there are many laws governing the new people, their customs, celebrations, ethics and ritual. These laws are found in the later portions of the Book of Exodus which expound the covenant. Leviticus for the most part describes the laws regulating the priesthood drawn from the tribe of Levi and the religious cult. And Deuteronomy is a second presentation of the law with its own plan—it outlines both civil and religious laws—placed in the context of a long discourse of Moses.

Further Reading:

Buber, Martin. *Moses.* Harper and Row, 1958. A great modern Jewish philospher's examination of Moses and Exodus.

10. THE PROPHETS

Modern Christians differ from Jesus and the early Church in what is included in this category, the older classification being more inclusive. Today we consider as prophetic only those books bearing a prophet's name. The older numbering included all those books which provide the continuation of Israel's history after Moses' death through the exile

---

29. Num 14:26–38
30. Ex 16:1–36
31. Num 20:2–13
32. Ex 33—34
33. Num 20:12
34. Deut 34:5–7
35. Ex 20:1–17; Truth 45

(former prophets), as well as the writing prophets (later prophets). This arrangement is not arbitrary since two major prophets—Elijah and Elisha—as well as Samuel are found among the former. This tradition points out that next to the law, the prophets are held most sacred.

TO DEEPEN—

Further reading:

Brueggemann, Walter. *The Prophetic Imagination.* Fortress Press, 1978.
Heschel, Abraham. *The Prophets.* (2 vols.) Harper & Row, 1962. A study by a great modern Jewish writer and theologian.
Reid, David P. *What Are They Saying About the Prophets?* Paulist Press, 1980.
Roberts, William. *The Prophets Speak Today.* St. Anthony Messenger Press, 1981. Selections from the prophets.

11. Historical Books

There are two sets of royal histories. The first is known as the Deuteronomist's history since it comes from the same source as Deuteronomy. This continues the story of the migration into Canaan under Joshua and the conquest of the land.[36] It then details the rise of kingship and continues until the exile.[37] The second account, the Chronicler's history, covers the monarchy until the exile[38] and continues with the return.[39] These books should not be mistaken for histories in the modern sense. They are concerned with theological themes: their history illustrates their theology.

Conquest of Canaan

Joshua, Moses' successor, leads the people into the land.[40] Years of struggle ensue with the indigenous people over control of the land. During this time judges, charismatic leaders, inspire the people in the fighting. Samson—the strong warrior—is brought low by Delilah, the Philistine woman who discovers that his strength lies in his uncut hair

---

36. Jos, Jgs
37. 1 and 2 Sam, 1 and 2 Kgs
38. 1 and 2 Chr
39. Ezra, Neh
40. Jos 1:1–9

which dedicates him to God.[41] Other judges are Gideon[42] and Deborah.[43]

Rise of Kingship

Established in the land, Israel begins to compare herself with other nations and desires a king. Samuel reluctantly accedes and Saul becomes Israel's first king.[44] His tragic story leads to his downfall and the rise of Israel's greatest king—the shepherd boy David.[45] In him Israel senses her finest hour. However David is a real human being, with flaws as well as greatness.[46] His son Solomon builds a temple for the Lord in Jerusalem and becomes the symbol of the wise king.[47]

But after Solomon, Israel declines. With the rise of Babylonia, first the northern[48] and then the southern kingdoms fall[49] and Israel's glory as a nation (at least in the ancient world) comes to an end. The focus shifts from the kings to the prophets.

12. The Writing Prophets

Prophecy precedes the monarchy and outlasts it. The prophet is called by God and given a message. Unlike the monarchy or priesthood this is a charismatic office. But distinguishing real from false prophets was not easy. Often only time separated the wheat from the chaff. The prophets preserved in Scripture are not the only people claiming the office, but rather those who have in the light of history been proved of God.

The prophet Samuel gives Israel her first king in Saul and later seeks out the boy David to make him Saul's successor. Israel's greatest prophet Elijah lives during the reign of King Ahab.[50] He struggles with unbelief in Israel and opposes not only the king and his queen Jezebel, but the fickle people as well. He confronts the priests of Baal in a contest on Mount Carmel.[51] Later in distress he experiences God as a still small

---

41. Jgs 13–16
42. Jgs 6:11—8:35
43. Jgs 4:4—5:15
44. 1 Sam 10:1–8
45. 1 Sam 16ff
46. 2 Sam 11:1—12:25
47. 1 Kgs 3:6–9; 6
48. 2 Kgs 17
49. 2 Kgs 24
50. 1 Kgs 17ff
51. 1 Kgs 18:20–40

voice.[52] And at the end of his life he is taken up to heaven in a fiery chariot,[53] giving rise to the legend that he (like Moses) never died since their death is not described in Scripture. Thus he becomes the symbol of the prophet as Moses is of the law.[54] His successor Elisha continues his work.[55]

Throughout the rest of sacred history the prophets, speaking in God's name, call the people to return to the Lord and to his covenant.[56] They accuse Israel of having violated the covenant upon which her existence is based. Amos speaks out against social injustice.[57] Hosea must marry an unfaithful woman and live out existentially God's anguish over Israel's infidelity.[58] Isaiah[59] echoes this message, and his great poetry foresees a time of fulfillment which Christians apply to the coming of Christ.

But affluent Israel does not heed the prophets' messages. As time goes on, the message becomes harsher. If the Israelites do not change their ways God will abandon them;[60] he will no longer shield Israel but will deliver her up to her enemies. Jeremiah lives out the death of Israel in his own life, for he is rejected and suffers greatly for God's word.[61] Christians see in his prophecy a foreshadowing of the rejection and suffering of Jesus.

The prophets experience God as all-powerful shaper of history. Slowly the idea develops that this God is more than one tribal God among many. The story of Jonah tells of a reluctant prophet, sent to Nineveh. But he does not believe that these non-Israelites deserve to hear the Lord's word.[62] The Lord must rebuke and punish him: thrown overboard he is swallowed by a great fish.[63] God has control over and concern for all nations, not just Israel, but he loves Israel and chose her. This universalism develops in prophetic thought, particularly in Second Isaiah,[64] and finds fulfillment in Jesus.

But Israel collapses. Splitting first into two small nations, she is finally conquered by the Babylonians. Her land burned, most of the

---

52. 1 Kgs 19:9–18
53. 2 Kgs 2:1–11
54. Truth 17
55. 1 Kgs 19ff
56. Ez 16:59–63
57. Truth 24
58. Hos 1:2–9
59. Is 1—39
60. Am 8
61. Jer 11:18—12:6
62. Jon 1:2–3
63. Jon 1:17
64. Is 40ff

people are taken into captivity in Babylonia. Ezekiel, the most visionary of the prophets, sees the Lord's glory departing the temple, and he knows that all is over.[65] The dream of Israel has come to an end; gone is the glory and the power. Once again they are slaves, their freedom something to weep over. God has forsaken his people.

But even in exile the prophets continue to interpret events. In their prosperity and glory Israel had no use for God, so he has delivered them over to the enemy. Now in their captivity they may once more be ready to hear God and return to him. In exile Ezekiel's prophecy proclaims hope for the future when God will anew free his people.[66]

The prophets saw Israel's defeat as punishment for her failure to live up to the covenant. Now her captivity purifies and remolds the people—they realize their dependence upon God and experience God's power over all nations.

At the same time Israel begins to experience the mercy of God. In spite of everything he loves this people, and he is unable to forsake his nation forever. God does forgive, and after the exile God will again establish Israel. In exile Israel learns hope; the future depends not on her but on God who shapes events. And she realizes the great love of God. He can be wrathful and angry but also loving and ready to forgive.[67]

With the rise of Persia and Cyrus, Babylon falls and the people are freed to return to their homeland. Second Isaiah[68] sings of this new exodus with Cyrus the new liberator. Christians see in his prophecy a foreshadowing of Christ's coming and liberation. The figure of the suffering servant[69] looks forward to Jesus' redemptive suffering. Indeed through this figure the first Christians came to understand the work of Jesus.

13. THE WRITINGS

The third category is a catch-all. Included are the books of the chronicler's history,[70] as well as the later history of the Maccabean revolt.[71] There are poems, stories and books of wisdom; some called scrolls were read on important feast days, including Ruth and Esther as

---

65. Ez 1:1–22; 11:22–25
66. Ez 36—39
67. Jer 31:34
68. Is 40ff
69. Is 42, 49–50, 52:13—53:12
70. Truth 11
71. 1 and 2 Mac

well as the love poem, the Song of Songs. Christians particularly cherish the Book of Wisdom and the collection of Psalms as beloved, key texts.

A collection of Israel's songs and hymns to God, the psalms cover every situation and emotion in the human condition. Tradition ascribes them to David, the shepherd boy, poet and king, and indeed some may go back to him. These psalms contain Israel's faith. They record how Israel responded to God. Israel's experience of prayer led her to meditate upon her historical traditions and to interpret and reinterpret them in the light of her further experience of God. Christians pray these psalms today in Christ—seeing Jesus foreshadowed, and praying them as the prayer of Jesus, who is the perfection of Israel.

Through contact with Egypt and other cultures Israel in her royal period cultivated and cherished wisdom. A group connected with the royal court probed the implications of a good and God-fearing life. Proverbs and maxims were collected guiding the people in right living.[72] The wise meditated upon the infinite wisdom of God who creates the entire universe and governs the lives of people as well as nations.[73]

In wisdom Israel confronts questions that arise as she discerns God's influence upon the world. Why does God allow evil to flourish? The Book of Job asks: Why do the good suffer? Through meditation upon such difficult problems Israel enriched her faith, experiencing more deeply life's mystery. Her faith in God's guiding wisdom comes to fulfillment in Christianity, in Jesus whom Christians see as the incarnation of God's wisdom.[74]

There is no natural continuity between the Old and New Testaments. A long time spans the death of the last prophet and the appearance of John the Baptist. Some books (Maccabees) recount Israel's latter history. Others shed valuable light upon this time.

Many **deutero-canonical**[75] books belong to this intertestamental period and are valuable not for their contributions to revelation but in tracing the history of revelation. For example, the additions to the Books of Daniel and Esther come from this later period.

Another group of writings, not considered Scripture by Catholics, also illuminate this time. Although not considered inspired, these books are read for information concerning their times. Known as **apocrypha**[76] by Catholics, these include 3 and 4 Maccabees, the Books of Esdras, the Odes of Solomon, and others.

---

72. Prv 10—22
73. Sir 1:1–10
74. 1 Cor 1:20–24
75. Way 7
76. Way 7

One genre of biblical literature does bridge the covenants: **apocalyptic**. The most famous example is the Christian Book of Revelation, but its thought is also found in the Gospels and Paul, as well as in some sections of the Hebrew Scriptures (notably some prophets). Apocalyptic forms a bridge from Israel to the Christian revelation.

Apocalyptic literature arises in the time of crisis. A literature of the extreme, it arose in Israel's suffering and exile,[77] and continues when in disappointment her return did not renew her former glory, but brought further conquest from Alexandrian Greece and then Rome. Apocalyptic speaks of disaster; it foretells the end of the nations in terrifying images of bloodshed, famine and desolation.

But it is actually a literature of hope. To those oppressed it promises the collapse of their enemies' power. It offers the hope that God will again rescue his people and lead them out of slavery's darkness into the light.

The word is from the Greek meaning "revealing" or "uncovering," and this literature claims to reveal the secrets of how God is bringing history to an end. The writings are usually ascribed to an ancient holy person or prophet. And often an angel interprets heavily symbolic vision to the seer.

The Book of Daniel (168 B.C.), a late work presented as the words of an earlier prophet, actually speaks of the situation during the Alexandrian period. Fantastic figures, such as the Son of Man[78] riding on the clouds, promise a new day when justice will prevail.

This literary form also appears in sections of other prophets such as Isaiah.[79] But it comes to dominate the period around Jesus and thus colors early Christian thought and literature.

TO DEEPEN—

Further Reading:

Bergant, Dianne. *What Are They Saying About Wisdom Literature?* Paulist Press, 1984.

Familiarize yourself with these key stories:

The Creation of the World (Gen 1)
Adam and Eve in the Garden of Eden (Gen 2—3)

---

77. Way 10
78. Dan 7:13–14
79. Is 24—27, 55—66

Noah and the Flood (Gen 6—8)
The Call of Abraham (Gen 12:1-8)
Abraham and Isaac (Gen 22:1-19)
Moses and the Burning Bush (Ex 2:23-4:17)
The Passover (Ex 12:1-28)
The Crossing of the Red Sea (Ex 13:17—14:22)
The Giving of the Covenant on Mount Sinai (Ex 19:1-25)
The Manna from Heaven (Ex 15:22—16:36)
Joshua and the Battle of Jericho (Jos 6)
Samson and Delilah (Jgs 14—16)
The Call of Samuel (1 Sam 3)
The Anointing of David (1 Sam 16)
Elijah (1 Kgs 17—2 Kgs 2)
The Call of Isaiah (Is 6:1-13)
The Story of Jonah (Jon)
The Story of Job (Job)

Look at the first reading for next Sunday's Mass. How does the story look forward to the day's Gospel?

14. The Gospel of Our Lord Jesus Christ

Gospel and Gospels

Gospel means both the good news that Jesus brings and the good news that Jesus becomes. It forms the very heart of Christian faith and the climax of the liturgy of the word.[1] It is not primarily a book but rather the act of proclaiming the good news. Paul uses "gospel" to describe his own preaching which did not encompass Jesus' words or actions at all but focused exclusively upon his passion and resurrection. Finally the term has been applied to the literary form of the first four books in the Christian Scriptures.

The Gospel exists concretely as four accounts: Matthew, Mark and Luke are called the Synoptic Gospels because they share common material; John differs significantly in material and emphasis. Each is the Gospel of our Lord Jesus Christ. Although differing, each authentically proclaims the good news. They resemble four perspectives on the same event—Jesus' life, death and resurrection. Each has unique insights, and together they provide a more rounded picture than any one account.

"Gospel" has different meanings: first, the proclamation of the good news in all its fullness: the proclamation and preaching of Jesus, his actions and life, and above all his passion and resurrection—the cornerstone of Christian faith. Then it refers to the separate Gospels through whose concrete words and images we hear the good news. Then, although no other Gospels are inspired,[2] any proclamation of the good news through preaching or through ministry is "gospel" or "evangelization"—to announce the good news.

The four Gospels in Scripture share a general shape in spite of their differences. All begin with some presentation of Jesus' ministry—his works, his teaching. They then present his passion—his last days, including his betrayal, trials, and death. And they conclude with his resurrection from the dead. These elements are all necessary to a Gospel. Many of the non-canonical "gospels" such as the gospel of Thomas include only the teachings and so do not really qualify as "gospels."

The Synoptic Theory

Matthew, Mark and Luke share much common material. However "synoptic" does not mean identical: it means that they see with a com-

---

1. Way 21
2. Truth 3

mon vision as opposed to John who often stands on his own. But in addition each has a different insight into Jesus and his meaning.

Source criticism traces the process leading to our current Gospels. In the earliest Christian communities, the disciples proclaimed the good news by telling the story of Jesus' death and resurrection. This proclamation is known as kerygma.[3] These stories were cherished and handed down.

At a certain point someone collected them and created the Gospel literary structure: the ministry, passion and resurrection of Jesus. The manuscripts may have passed through a number of hands and modifications before assuming final form. Since scholars assume that Mark's was the first to appear, he defines the overall genre.

Matthew and Luke are dependent upon Mark: they often use his stories, word for word, while other events are modified to fit their own theology but show a reliance upon Mark. Other material, not included in Mark but common to Matthew and Luke, is thought to come from a common source (called "Q" after the German for "source"). Matthew and Luke also have unique material assumed to come from their own community's treasure and reflecting the evangelists' theology.

The Individual Gospels

The Gospel of **Mark** (ca. 70 A.D.) is the shortest and earliest Gospel. And he is most concerned with telling the stories, events, and signs of Jesus' ministry. Very little of Jesus' teaching is in Mark, although he certainly regards it as important and constantly remarks that people were astonished not only at Jesus' signs but at his teachings.[4] Perhaps at this early period Jesus' teachings were considered too sacred for a public book. Reserved for those already in the community, they were passed on orally.

The so-called "messianic secret" is another key element of Mark. Jesus often instructs people healed by him not to tell what happened.[5] Scholars believe that this device may have been used to explain why the Jewish people did not recognize Jesus as Messiah in spite of his works—Jesus chose to keep it quiet. This motif also appears in Matthew and Luke, but only in passages common to Mark, indicating that it is Mark's theology rather than a shared idea.

For Mark, the true significance of Jesus' actions cannot be understood unless they are seen as the deeds of the Son of Man who came to

---

3. Cf. Acts 3:11–26; Way 51
4. Mk 1:27
5. Mk 1:43

suffer. He presents Jesus' life and deeds always in the light of the cross. Jesus is the hidden and suffering Messiah.

Because of its constant references to suffering, people used to think that Mark was written during Nero's persecution in Rome. Now further study and archaeology reveal the extent of suffering in Palestine during the Jewish war against Rome (66–70 A.D.). Many scholars today suggest that Mark was written for Christians in that situation.

The Gospel of **Matthew** (ca. 70 A.D.) is the "Gospel of the Church," presenting much of Jesus' teaching and concerned with the set-up of the early community. For this reason he has been given pride of place in the Christian Scriptures. His community is composed of Jewish-Christians. He sees Jesus as a new Moses and shows how Jesus fulfills the prophecies of Israel.[6]

The Gospel of **Luke** (ca. 90 A.D.) is regarded as the Gospel of the Gentiles. Tradition names him a Greek disciple of Paul and a physician. Only Luke has the elegance and ease of literary Greek. Only Luke's Gospel includes some best loved stories such as the shepherds in the fields at Jesus' birth,[7] the good Samaritan,[8] and the prodigal son.[9] His special themes are the poor of the Lord and prayer, and he gives special prominence to women—he provides most of our information about Mary, Jesus' mother. He also tends to double things and events—two angels instead of one, etc.

Finally the Gospel of **John** (ca. 90 A.D.) might seem the most spiritual, mystical or symbolic Gospel. And the Church in a sense reserves John to expound the deeper levels of faith. In John more than the others the Easter light flows back to the very beginning of Jesus' ministry, illuminating his whole life in glory. But if John is symbolic and at odds with the others, his is not necessarily the least historic.

John differs in his chronology from the Synoptics. Here Jesus has a three year ministry, cleanses the temple at the beginning of his ministry rather than the end, and celebrates the Last Supper on the night preceding Passover. It has been argued that John changes chronology to fit his theological frame. But the other evangelists do the same thing. Indeed some scholars believe that John may be more factual than the Synoptics.

John has a unique structure preceding the passion-resurrection narratives where he shares more in common. But the first part is a series

---

6. Mt 1:22; 2:17 etc.
7. Lk 2:1–20
8. Lk 10:29–37
9. Lk 15:11–32

of seven signs, each followed by sometimes extensive commentaries: the conversation with Nicodemus concerning being born again,[10] with the Samaritan woman concerning living water,[11] with the Jews over the bread of life.[12]

The Church reserves John for Lent and Easter to prepare and initiate the elect into the Easter sacraments.[13] John's discourses disclose the deeper significance of these mysteries.

TO DEEPEN—

Which are the Synoptic Gospels and what does this term mean?

What are the different meanings of the word "Gospel"?

Compare the different accounts of the Last Supper (Mt 26:20–29; Mk 14:17–25; Lk 22:14–38; Jn 13ff; 1 Cor 11:23–27, the earliest written record). What are the differences? What might they reveal concerning the various theologies of the evangelists?

Read the Gospel for the coming Sunday. Look up the parallel accounts, if they appear in the other Gospels. What distinguishes this account?

Further Reading:

Badia, Leonard. *Jesus: Introducing His Life and Teaching.* Paulist Press, 1985.
Boff, Leonardo. *Jesus Christ, Liberator.* Orbis, 1978.
Brown, Raymond. *Jesus, God and Man.* Macmillan, 1976.
Fitzmyer, Joseph A. *A Christological Catechism.* Paulist Press, 1982.
McEleney, Neil. *Growth of the Gospels.* Paulist Press, 1979.
Wahlberg, Rachel. *Jesus According to a Woman.* Paulist Press, 1975.

TO CONTINUE—

The liturgical presentation of the Gospel is explained in The Christian Year (Way 28ff).

The Creed—another proclamation of the Gospel—begins in Truth 25.

The liturgical setting for the Gospel is found in Way 22.

---

10. Jn 3:1–21
11. Jn 4
12. Jn 6:22–71
13. Way 33–34

15. PRELUDES TO THE GOSPEL

Preaching of John the Baptist

None of the gospels, not even Mark's which is the briefest, begins with Jesus. Each first sets the scene. Mark and the others following his example present John the Baptist before Jesus. John is the forerunner—Jesus' herald. This wild ascetic comes out of the desert announcing the coming new age. His imagery evokes the coming catastrophe.[1] He demands conversion through a baptism of repentance.[2]

Infancy Narratives

The other evangelists preface John the Baptist with other material to further situate Jesus. For **Matthew**, coming from the Jewish tradition, Jesus is the fulfillment of the law, the new Moses. His infancy narrative concerns Joseph, Jesus' foster-father, prefigured in the patriarch Joseph who also listened to his dreams.[3] Matthew's first five chapters echo Israel's history in the Pentateuch:[4] led into Egypt,[5] called out of Egypt,[6] passage and baptism in water,[7] tested in the wilderness,[8] and receiving the law on the mountain.[9] Jesus recapitulates Israel's history but, unlike Israel, is faithful. He fulfills the law, becoming the new Israel.

Luke concentrates on Mary, Jesus' mother. She symbolizes Israel—the handmaid of the Lord.[10] Through her obedience and faith she gives birth to the Savior. Luke introduces his favorite themes: the poor to whom Jesus is sent seen in the shepherds,[11] prayer in the three great canticles[12] prayed daily by the Church,[13] and women in the figures of Mary, Elizabeth[14] and Anna.[15]

Luke's poetic narration make his the most cherished Christmas

---

1. Mt 3:1–12; Mk 1:1–8; Lk 3:1–18
2. Mt 3:7–10
3. Mt 1–2 cf. Gen 40
4. Truth 5
5. Mt 2:13; Gen 46
6. Mt 2:20; Ex 12:29–50
7. Mt 3:13–17; Ex 13:17—14:22
8. Mt 4:1–11; Num 11
9. Mt 5–7; Ex 24
10. Lk 1:38
11. Lk 2:8–18
12. Lk 1:46b–55, 68–79; 2:29–32
13. Life 38
14. Lk 1:39–45
15. Lk 2:36–38

stories. Much of his poetry, including the three canticles, is built up of traditional material from the Hebrew Scriptures. For example, Mary's song[16] echoes the song of Samuel's formerly barren mother as she learns she is with child.[17] His infancy narrative concludes by foreshadowing the end of the Gospel itself: the finding of Jesus in the temple with its symbolic clue of "three days" anticipates the resurrection where the one presumed dead is found alive.[18]

The Prologue of John[19]

John's prologue is set on the cosmic stage, befitting his Gospel's grand symbols: Christ the light,[20] the living water,[21] the bread of life,[22] the vine,[23] the good shepherd.[24] To introduce these symbols Jesus is first identified as the Word of God himself, made human flesh,[25] dwelling among us, unknown to his own,[26] yet conferring eternal life upon those who come to recognize and acknowledge him.[27]

TO DEEPEN—

How do these preludes proclaim the Gospel?

How is their story another way of telling the essential good news?

Catholics enter into the Lukan stories through the joyful mysteries of the rosary. You might pray those after reading the passages they are taken from (Life 42).

Look up the story of Joseph (Gen 37—50) and compare him with Jesus' foster father in Matthew's infancy narrative.

Further Reading:

Brown, Raymond. *The Virginal Conception and Bodily Resurrection of Jesus.* Paulist Press, 1973.

16. Lk 1:46–55
17. 1 Sam 2:1–10
18. Lk 2:41–52
19. Intro 3
20. Jn 1:4
21. Jn 4:14
22. Jn 6:35
23. Jn 15:5
24. Jn 10:11
25. Jn 1:14
26. Jn 1:11
27. Jn 1:16–17

TO CONTINUE—

These stories are presented liturgically in the Advent-Christmas seasons (Way 29–30) and they are celebrated as well (Life 40).

The figure of Mary is further explored in Truth 41.

The significance of these events form the doctrine of the incarnation explained in the Creed (Truth 29–31).

16. THE TEACHING OF JESUS

Preaching:
The Kingdom of God

Jesus' message begins: "Repent and believe in the kingdom of God."[1] As his ministry develops he shows how that kingdom is with him breaking into the world. His miracles are evidence that the kingdom is already coming. The new age has already begun. In the disciples' preaching after Easter, the emphasis shifts to Jesus himself embodying the kingdom. In him they experience that kingdom's presence. Just what is this kingdom? Where is it?

The kingdom of God is an ancient Judaeo-Christian theme. Israel was called to be God's kingdom. But as Israel failed in one way or another to measure up to the kingdom, she dreamed of a future when God would establish his kingdom. This dream centered upon the Messiah—a new David[2] who would inaugurate the kingdom, bringing about the new age. In apocalyptic thought, Israel's current subjugation and distress heightened her hope in the day of the Lord.

Jesus believes that the kingdom is imminent and indeed already imploding into this world. Through signs, parables and teachings he awakens his listeners to the kingdom's advent. A new reality is dawning in our present existence. God's reign has not fully come. There is still an expectation of its final coming both in Jesus and in Christianity. But to some extent it is within reach.[3]

Jesus brings images of God inherited from Israel into sharp focus. God is a liberator setting captives free; he sides with the poor and oppressed.[4] He is a God of justice—but not a human justice polluted by sin and pride. The kingdom is not a continuation of the present situa-

---

1. Mk 1:14–15
2. Truth 10
3. Lk 17:20f
4. Lk 4:18–21

tion. The powerful here will not hold their place in God's kingdom. Traditional powers will be overthrown.[5]

Jesus calls God "Father." But this Father is not the traditional patriarchy written large. Indeed Jesus asks his disciples to call no one Father other than God.[6] God is most intimately called "Abba"—a word close to "Dearest Father." Jesus reveals him as the awesome Creator with parental care, love, and intimacy.

God's reign is caring and compassionate. God's heart goes out to the poor, the lost, the sick, the outcast. And in the kingdom each creature experiences God's care and outreach to support, nourish and raise up. Love is the very center of reality, the only and the true power of God. God creates, sustains, and reaches out to us because God is love.

The Reign of God

The kingdom is not so much a place as a state of being. It is better translated as the "reign" of God. For the word kingdom should not imply a special place, nor does it resemble earthly kingdoms with the implications of monarchy and patriarchy.

To speak of God's reign recaptures the dynamic thrust of the phrase. We live within the care and power of God. Our lives are given shape and force through God's grace. The healing and forgiveness of God's reign are available now.

With Jesus God's reign breaks into our present world. The kingdom's advent spells trouble for our present situation. The outcome should not cause fear but hope of a better situation for all creation. The reign of God is already present, but not yet fully realized.

Jesus provokes crisis; a note of warning pervades his message. God's reign goes against the world's ways. Embracing the world and its values we will experience the kingdom's advent as wrath. God does not become angry or rejecting, but by placing ourselves in antagonism to the kingdom we go against the grain, and we are hurt.

The reign of God restores and fulfills creation, which again resembles Christ in whom it was originally created. But the world today often stands opposed to God—the poor suffer injustice, the greedy feed off the hungry. Jesus reveals the injustice of the world. He calls for conversion toward the reign of God. If we do not heed that call we may find ourselves fit only for the garbage pit of Gehenna.[7]

---

5. Lk 1:51–55
6. Mt 23:9
7. Mt 25:46

The reign of God is characterized by healing and forgiveness. Jesus heals the blind,[8] the deaf,[9] the leprous.[10] He even raises the dead.[11] He points out the intimate connection between physical and spiritual wholeness: he heals the lame man by forgiving his sins.[12]

Israel had thought that on the day of the Lord, God would avenge her enemies. She looked forward to the destruction of sinners. Much of apocalyptic imagery is based on exclusion. This is understandable when we consider the suffering and persecution these people were suffering at the hands of their oppressors.

But Jesus does not feed this hope for vengeance. He preaches a radical forgiveness. He forgives those whom his society does not want to forgive—the prostitutes, the tax collectors. He shows how extravagant, even unjust God's mercy is. As long as people continue to see things in terms of good and bad, they are blinded to God's reign. God causes rain to fall on the just and unjust. Jesus tells his followers to stop thinking in terms of enemies. To hate one's foes is the way of the world. What good is that? He tells us to love those who oppose us.

Jesus shows God as reconciler and healer. He tells his disciples to continue that ministry. As Christians we look to God for our ultimate healing, confident that in Jesus we are reconciled. The world goes on. Injustice flourishes. But Christians know that this time is passing. A new day will dawn.

The reign of God is already coming into our world. And we can have a part of that advent. But to do so we must change—repent and believe not in the world but in the kingdom. Certain "realities" must be examined and replaced by clearer perceptions. Jesus challenges our belief in fear,[13] worry,[14] judgment,[15] vengeance.[16] He questions the verity of our anger,[17] our sense of righteousness.[18] To participate in this reign, we must die to ourselves.

---

8. Mt 9:27–31
9. Mk 7:31–37
10. Mt 8:1–4
11. Lk 7:11–17
12. Mk 2:1–12
13. Lk 12:32
14. Mt 7:31
15. Lk 6:37
16. Mt 5:39–42
17. Mt 5:44–46
18. Jn 8:7

Parables

Jesus' stories introduce God's reign. Parables reverse "common sense." The kingdom of God is not the same as the kingdom of this world.[19] In this world shepherds do not forsake their flocks for one lost sheep.[20] Farmers do not cast expensive seed to the winds.[21] Laborers are not paid a full day's wage for an hour's work.[22] The parables are windows through which to view this new reality.

In reading the parables we should keep in mind the original audience who heard these stories. They often depend upon these people for their impact. The rich and powerful might be offended by them. The poor might be amused at the discomfort of the principal characters or encouraged. The images used in the parables do not correspond to other things. The story itself is a whole, not an allegory which "teaches" some doctrine. The parable often contains an element of surprise—it turns common sense on its head.

Jesus criticizes people's accepted views and attitudes through his parables. He wants us to share these stories by entering into them. In doing so we come to adopt and live the vision embodied in them.

The parables were also modified, changed, and rewritten as they were passed down in the communities before taking their present written form in the Gospel accounts. Examining a parable is similar to an archeological dig—there are various layers. What did the evangelist mean by the parable? What was Jesus' original point? Sometimes there are strata in between with other meanings.

Teachings and Sayings

Jesus also explains the kingdom and its working through his teachings. He tells us how to look at our relationships[23] and emotions. He teaches us the necessity of an inward purity as well as an outward conformity with the law.[24] He teaches ways of transformation[25] so that, re-created, we might perceive God's kingdom already among us.

The society of Jesus' time is based on the oral rather than written

---

19. Jn 18:36
20. Mt 18:10–14
21. Mk 4:1–9
22. Mt 20:1–16
23. Mt 5:23–26
24. Mt 15:17–20
25. Way 47

word. So Jesus' sayings are designed to be remembered. He uses parallelism, repetitions, special emphases. The best comparison in our own society is the methods of advertising which use some of these same devices. Jesus' sayings are not factual statements or principles to be rigidly applied. They are metaphors to be lived. He is trying to persuade us to look at the world and ourselves in a new light, rather than imposing a new set of laws upon us.

Jesus and the Day of the Lord

Many of that time believed they were living in the last age before the day of the Lord. Then the present age would pass away and God's kingdom would be inaugurated upon earth. Christians understood Jesus' death and resurrection as the dawn of this new day. The time remaining until the final establishment of God's kingdom formed a period of waiting which provided people the opportunity to convert to the Gospel. Jesus and the early Christians used images from the apocalyptic tradition to describe and understand what had happened in Jesus.

Jesus employed the apocalyptic[26] image of the coming Son of Man, a heavenly avenger who would come riding on the clouds in judgment over the world.[27] If Jesus did not identify himself as this Son of Man, his disciples bestowed the title on him in light of his resurrection.

The appropriate moment is an integral part of Jesus' message concerning God's kingdom. The time is at hand.[28] Act as if this were your only day. Wake up or it may be too late.[29] You may have stored up your treasures on earth and the earth will not last.[30]

Christians should not be fatalistic. The images provide hope to the downtrodden, promise ransom to captives, offer sight to the blind. In the face of almost insurmountable odds God's plan is still in effect: the kingdom comes.

These images do not pre-figure specific events. Jesus specifically refuses to give the time and the hour.[31] They should not be taken as what will be—apocalypse, armageddon, end of world, etc. They give hope even in the darkest struggles to Jesus' despised disciples.[32]

---

26. Truth 13–14
27. Dan 7:9–27
28. Mt 4:17
29. Mk 14:33–37
30. Lk 11:13–21
31. Mt 24:36
32. Mt 5:11–12

TO DEEPEN—

What is the core of Jesus' message?

In what ways does he communicate that message?

Read the parables of Matthew 13. What do they tell concerning God's reign?

Read the sermon on the Mount—Matthew's collection of Jesus' sayings (Mt 5—7). What kind of life does Jesus call us to? What are his basic values? His attitudes toward life? What is God like?

Further Reading:

Kaspar, Walter. *The God of Jesus Christ.* Crossroad, 1986.

Miller, John W. *Step by Step through the Parables. A Beginner's Guide to the Stories Jesus Told, Their Meaning in His Time and Ours.* Paulist Press, 1981.

Nolan, Albert. *Jesus Before Christianity.* Orbis, 1978.

Norquist, Marilyn. *Thy Kingdom Come: The Basic Teachings of Jesus.* Liguori, 1986.

Sanford, John. *The Kingdom Within.* Harper and Row, 1970.

TO CONTINUE—

The way that Jesus' teaching tells us to live and be changed is found in *The Way of Conversion (Way 47ff)* and *The Foundations of Christian Living (Life 3).*

17. THE MINISTRY OF JESUS

Baptism by John

The appearance and preaching of John the Baptist inaugurates the Gospel proper.[1] Jesus comes to John for baptism.[2] In doing so he confirms the Baptist's ministry and receives his own commissioning from God.

Jesus' baptism is treated quite differently from Gospel to Gospel. Mark and then Matthew describe the scene in full. Luke places it offstage. John banishes it altogether. Followers of the Baptist believed that he and not Jesus was the Messiah. Christians needed to defend and vindicate Jesus. Submitting himself to John's baptism might imply that

---

1. Mt 3:1–10; Mk 1:1–8; Lk 3:1–20
2. Mt 3:13–17; Mk 1:9–11; Lk 3:21–22

John was the greater. Matthew even makes John question Jesus: Is it not you who should baptize me?

Temptation in the Wilderness

After his baptism Jesus retires to the desert to test the call he has received.[3] And in the desert he is tempted by Satan. Matthew and Luke fill out the story by using the example of Israel in the wilderness. When Satan tempts Jesus to turn the stones to bread, the story of Israel's demand for food and God's giving of the heavenly manna is recalled.[4] Where Israel failed, Jesus succeeds. He now is ready to begin his ministry proper.

Call of the Disciples

Moving through the countryside Jesus invites certain people to follow him.[5] They become his disciples. He instructs them, and they witness his works. Eventually he sends them out with his message so that they might continue his ministry and spread the good news.[6] Luke in addition to the sending of the twelve has a sending of seventy.[7]

The call symbolizes each person's encounter with Jesus.[8] It changes a person's life which now breaks with the past. A new way of living arises. Sometimes this change is represented by a new name.[9]

Signs and Miracles

Jesus proclaimed the coming reign by various means. His ministry is filled with miracles and wonders. He heals the sick.[10] He has power over the elements.[11] He evokes awe and wonder from those who encounter him.[12] He is a man of power and authority.

To Israelites who felt that history was going against them Jesus' signs show that God is still God. And God's reign defeats sin, disease, and the powers of evil. To those who felt that God was only on their side, Jesus' signs of healing and forgiveness toward lepers and non-Jews showed that God accepts such people as well as the righteous.

---

3. Mt 4:1–11; Mk 1:12–13; Lk 4:1–13
4. Ex 16:2–31
5. Mt 4:18–22; Mk 1:16–20
6. Mt 9:35—10:16
7. Lk 10:1–16
8. Intro 2
9. Mt 16:18
10. Mt 9:1–8
11. Mt 8:23–27
12. Mk 7:37

Jesus' miracles are not simply works of wonder or shows of magic. They reveal the kingdom's dawning presence. They disclose God. God's reign heals and forgives. These signs are only miraculous from this present world's viewpoint. Jesus' signs point to a new reality and introduce a different way of perceiving, believing and ultimately of living.

The New Community

At Caesarea Philippi Jesus asks the disciples who they believe him to be. When Peter acclaims him as the Christ, Jesus in turn makes him the head of the community of disciples.[13] Roman Catholics believe that Peter's office is continued in the papacy.[14]

The Easter section of the Gospels present other commissionings.[15] In John, Peter is appointed as shepherd of the new community.[16]

The Transfiguration

Finally an event in Jesus' life reveals to his disciples his glory. Is he a lawgiver like Moses,[17] or a prophet with a new vision like Elijah,[18] or something more? Jesus takes Peter, James and John up a mountain,[19] where he is transfigured before their eyes. He shines with a glory attributed only to God. And appearing by his side, Moses and Elijah by gesture acknowledge him to be their superior. The transfiguration foreshadows the final revelation of Jesus' glory in his resurrection.

TO DEEPEN—

What are some of the things the disciples learn from Jesus?

How is Jesus like Moses? How is he like Elijah?

What does Jesus train the disciples to do?

Read the apostolic discourse (Mt 10). How does this passage describe the disciple?

---

13. Mt 16:13–23
14. Truth 22
15. Mt 28:16–20; Jn 21:22
16. Jn 21:15–19
17. Truth 8
18. Truth 12
19. Mt 17:1–8; Mk 9:2–8; Lk 9:28–36

Further Reading:

Fuller, Reginald. *Interpreting the Miracles.* SCM Press, 1963.
Lewis, C. S. *Miracles.* Macmillan, 1978.
O'Grady, John. *Models of Jesus.* Doubleday, 1982.

TO CONTINUE—

The significance of baptism is described in Intro 13 and Truth 75.

The temptation story forms the basis for Lent (Way 32) and the Christian's con-
version (Way 47).

18. THE PASSION OF JESUS

The passion (the last events of Jesus' life leading up to and including his death and burial) and resurrection narratives form the very core
and probably the earliest Gospel strata to assume written form. Here
the four written Gospels are most harmonious. And these narratives are
sizable—almost half of Mark.

Unlike the previous material the passion is not made up of smaller
units. It forms a single narrative, and the Church respects this unity by
proclaiming it as such during Holy Week. Jesus' entire ministry finds
its fulfillment and vindication in his death and resurrection.

Select one of the passion narratives to read. A basic appreciation
of Christianity is impossible without a first-hand acquaintance with this
central story. Although the various accounts agree substantially there
are differences as well. Mark emphasizes the isolation of Jesus; he is
betrayed, denied and forsaken by his disciples, mocked and tortured by
his persecutors, even taunted by the thieves crucified with him, and at
the end he lacks even the sense of his Father's presence.

Matthew focuses upon Christ's royalty. But the royalty is paradoxical—it appears in Jesus' humiliation. Luke takes a different approach.
It becomes a story of martyrdom and can be compared with the account
of Stephen's martyrdom.[1] Jesus even in the hour of death goes out in
sympathy for others: to the daughters of Jerusalem, to his executioners,
to one of the thieves.

John shows how the kingship of Jesus shines even through his humiliation. In spite of outward appearances Jesus is in command of the

---

1. Acts 7:54–60

situation. He sets events in motion by voluntarily coming forward for the arrest. When Peter wants to intervene he is rebuked. Jesus even decides on the moment of his death: he gives up his spirit. "I lay down my life, that I may take it again. No one takes it from me, but I lay it down of my own accord."[2]

Each of these accounts is not merely intended to tell what happened, but to interpret what happened as Gospel. As you read the particular account, try to sense the particular perspective of that evangelist. Compare episodes with their parallels in the other Gospels. How does this evangelist understand Jesus' death?

Predictions of the Passion

The passion is preceded by three predictions of his coming death and resurrection.[3] But his disciples do not understand;[4] why should death and betrayal be a part of his ministry? Peter is rebuked for trying to dissuade Jesus just after he has confessed him to be the Messiah.[5] Here is a different Messiah than Israel anticipated.

Entry into Jerusalem[6]

On his entry into Jerusalem, the crowd acclaims Jesus. They hail him as Messiah and strew palm branches before him as he rides on a donkey. The story prefigures Jesus' eventual messianic triumph in the resurrection. But it ironically highlights human fickleness—acclaiming as king today one whom tomorrow they reject and crucify. Paradoxical images of kingship—the world's and God's—are juxtaposed.

The Last Supper[7]

Jesus sends his disciples ahead to secure a room for Passover.[8] Celebrating the feast, he takes bread and wine and institutes the new covenant on the morrow sealed with his blood.[9]

Although his description contains details and elements of a Passover meal, John places the Last Supper on the evening before the Pass-

---

2. Jn 10:18
3. Mt 16:21; 17:22–23; 20:17–19
4. Mt 18:23
5. Mt 16:23
6. Way 33; Mt 21:1–9; Mk 11:1–10; Lk 19:28–38
7. Truth 78: Mt 26:17–19; Mk 14:12–16; Lk 22:7–20
8. Truth 8
9. Mt 26:26–29; Mk 14:22–25; Lk 22:15–20

over.[10] In place of the account of the Eucharist, John tells how Jesus washes the disciples' feet and instructs them in the ministry of service.[11] He then gives a final discourse.[12]

It is not that John does not value the Eucharist. He has already written about it at length in connection with the multiplication of loaves.[13] But at this point in his Gospel he identifies Jesus with the Passover lamb. To understand the passion it is necessary to see it in the light of the Passover and exodus from Egypt.[14] Then God instituted the first covenant with Israel. Now in Jesus God establishes an everlasting covenant with all peoples.

Judas and the Betrayal

Jesus foresees betrayal by Judas, the group treasurer.[15] Judas, for whatever reason, has arranged with the Jewish leaders and the Romans to hand Jesus over this night.[16] After the event, Judas realizes what he has done.[17] He attempts to give the money back to the priests. And then he goes off and kills himself.

In the Garden of Gethsemane[18]

Now Jesus and his disciples go to the Garden of Gethsemane to pray. He takes Peter, James and John aside, asking them to keep vigil, but they fall asleep three times. In his prayer Jesus asks that the cup of his coming suffering and death be taken away. Yet he prays that God's will, not his own, be done.

The guards come with Judas, who betrays him with a kiss. The disciples flee in terror. The soldiers lead Jesus to trial.

Peter's Denial[19]

During the trial Peter is outside in the courtyard. Some people suspect that he is a disciple. Peter denies this three times, as Jesus had earlier predicted.[20] Then Peter had vowed his fidelity. When the cock

10. Jn 13:1
11. Jn 13:3–20
12. Jn 13:21—17:26
13. Jn 6
14. Truth 8
15. Mt 26:23
16. Mk 14:10–11
17. Mt 27:3–10
18. Mt 26:36–46; Mk 14:32–42; Lk 22:40–46
19. Mt 26:69–75; Mk 14:66–72; Lk 22:56–62; Jn 18:15–27
20. Mt 26:33–35

crows Peter realizes what he has done and runs away in agony. All Jesus' disciples have forsaken him. He is left alone in the hands of his enemies.

Trial[21]

Jesus meanwhile has been brought before the high priests, who want to convict him of blasphemy. They try various charges against him, including his claim to be the Messiah. The trial does not go smoothly. Determined to do away with Jesus, in the morning they take him to Pilate. The Jewish leaders could not put a person to death unless he were a Gentile who had violated the sanctuary of the temple.

Roman legal historians give credence to the trial narrative in Matthew and Mark. Someone had to bring the case before the prefect. The Roman officials usually conducted business early in the day in order to be finished by afternoon. The prefect could conduct the trial as he saw fit. Most people brought into the court could expect to be beaten. Even if you were cleared, you might be given a light beating as a warning.

Jesus' refusal to defend himself is unusual. For failure to do so meant that the person was presumed guilty. Notice too that Jesus had warned his disciples not to defend themselves when dragged into court.[22] Jesus chooses to be condemned rather than resist evil.

To convince Pilate of Jesus' criminality the Jewish leaders must make him seem a political threat. They accuse him of claiming to be the King of the Jews. The Romans worried about Jewish liberators who might try to wrest control of their homeland from the Romans. The Zealots were one such party. So this charge against Jesus is serious.

These trial scenes become high irony in Christian eyes. Jesus is indeed a King in Christian eyes. But his kingdom is not of this world. For Christians, Jesus is not on trial here but the Jewish church and the Roman state: this world's so-called "powers." John's Gospel carries the irony furthest.

Since there is a Passover custom of releasing a prisoner, Pilate asks the crowd whom to free: Barabbas, a murderer, or Jesus. Stirred up by the priests, the crowd demands the release of Barabbas and the death of Jesus. Pilate sends Jesus to be scourged, where he is mocked by the soldiers—dressed in a purple robe and crowned with thorns.

---

21. Mt 26:11–26; Mk 15:2–15; Lk 23:2–25; Jn 18:28—19:16
22. Mt 5:38–48

Crucifixion[23]

The cross-beam placed on his shoulders, Jesus carries it outside the city to the place of execution. On the way he stumbles in exhaustion. At Golgotha he is crucified along with two criminals: a common Roman means of execution, but so barbarous that no Roman could be subjected to it: it was limited to non-citizens.

The guards attempt to hasten death—a person might survive for days—not to pollute the sabbath and offend the Jews. They break the legs of those crucified, but Jesus is already dead. The body is removed and Joseph of Arimathea lays it in his own tomb. Since it is near sundown of the sabbath, there is no time now to prepare it with spices, so it is left until Sunday to complete the burial preparations.

This account merely outlines the passion story. Each evangelist emphasizes certain events and themes to shape his own interpretation. Events themselves are not alone crucial for our tradition. Rather the meaning is disclosed in the event. These meanings perceived in the actions reveal the depth and richness of the story.

TO DEEPEN—

What is the overall message of the passion account in the evangelist you read?

Why is the passion and death of Jesus so important to Christians?

When is the new covenant instituted by Jesus? What event seals that covenant? What covenant does it fulfill?

Compare a certain scene in the various Gospels. What do they all share? What details are unique to each?

Further Reading:

Blackwell, John. *The Passion as Story—The Plot of Mark*. Fortress Press, 1986.
Metz, Johannes & Moltmann, Jurgen. *Meditation on the Passion*. Paulist Press, 1979.
Sloyan, Gerard. *Jesus on Trial*. Fortress Press, 1973.

---

23. Mt 26:33–44; Mk 15:22–32; Lk 23:33–43; Jn 19:17–37

TO CONTINUE—

This material forms the basis for the celebration of the pasch (Way 33).
The Christian meaning of this story is explained in the Creed (Truth 32–33).
For the significance of the Eucharist see Truth 78.

19. THE EASTER GOSPEL

Resurrection

The story would seem to be over with Jesus' death. But it is not so. Christians believe that God raised Jesus from the dead. And this event is so important that all other teachings and events are seen in its light.

The resurrection truly occurred. How it occurred is another story, given to differing interpretations, no one of them entirely satisfactory. But that it happened is affirmed by the entire New Testament and Christian tradition.

However, belief in the resurrection is open only to those who have faith. The guards at the tomb do not witness it. Jesus does not reveal himself to strangers (except Paul). And there is no incontrovertible proof. It must be grasped by faith.

But what converted these disciples? Could it be merely a hope? Only a mass hallucination? What enabled these weak men who abandoned their master and fled for safety on Good Friday to embrace martyrdom rather than deny their conviction that Jesus had been raised from the dead? And the resurrection throughout history has transformed people, beginning with St. Paul on the Damascus road[1] down to the present day.

The resurrection narratives should not be taken literally. They point toward this great truth. Since resurrection surpasses our understanding, the stories too cannot fully articulate the event. Thus sometimes Jesus seems to have a physical body: Thomas is asked to put his hand in the wound;[2] Mary is told not to hold him back.[3] In others he appears incorporeal: walking through walls,[4] disappearing into thin air.[5]

The earliest resurrection stories center upon the empty tomb.[6] The sabbath rest over, the women go to prepare the body properly for

---

1. Acts 9:3ff
2. Jn 20:27
3. Jn 20:17
4. Jn 20:26
5. Lk 24:31
6. Mt 28:1–10; Mk 16:1–8; Lk 24:1–12

burial. At the tomb they are astonished to find the stone which sealed the entrance rolled away and the body gone. They are told that Jesus is risen. Alive he goes before them. The women relay the message to the men in hiding. Unbelieving, Peter and John run to the tomb themselves. But the women's story is confirmed.

Other stories describe Jesus' appearances to his disciples. He appears to Mary in the garden.[7] He appears in the upper room with the disciples[8] and to others on the road to Emmaus.[9]

Whatever their specific shape, these narratives share a similar structure. They begin with the disciples' confusion, despair, and sorrow. Did his death not spell the end of their hope in Jesus? The messianic prophecies did not speak of betrayal and death.

Then in the midst of their despair breaks the resurrection—the empty tomb, the testimony of witnesses such as those first women, and the appearances of Jesus himself. Jesus has triumphed over death. There is no doubt that he was dead. The Roman authorities were competent to determine that. Yet now his followers are convinced that he is risen. This good news transforms their lives. No longer the fearful ones who fled his arrest, they boldly testify to his resurrection. And they keep faith even in the face of their own torture and death.

Finally these stories end with a commissioning. The witnesses are told to spread this good news. The women are told to tell the disciples.[10] And the disciples are sent to the ends of the earth.[11]

The resurrection narrative shapes all Christian experience. It is the Gospel's fulcrum. The written Gospels proclaim the life and teachings of Jesus in the light of Easter. It may be necessary for historical purposes to discover Jesus' original teachings. But for the Christian all of Jesus' life and teachings are given authority and color by his resurrection.

Or consider the Christian liturgy. We gather together, confused and perhaps depleted by our struggles with life and the world. Then the good news is proclaimed: Jesus is Lord and giver of new and everlasting life. We witness the presence of the living Lord in our midst through the Gospel proclamation and the sacramental actions. Strengthened and confirmed in our faith that God is making all things new in Christ, we are sent as witnesses. The resurrection becomes the

---

7. Jn 20:1–18
8. Jn 20:19–29
9. Lk 24:13–35
10. Mt 28:7
11. Mt 28:19

very center of our faith: the source of our life, that which renews and recreates us and through us the entire creation.

Ascension

While the resurrection climaxes the Gospel story, other events complete the sequence. Mark's Gospel, especially in its original form, ends abruptly: the tomb is empty, Jesus is risen. Matthew provides a commissioning of the apostles to go forth to all nations and baptize in the name of the Father and the Son and the Holy Spirit. We have seen above that the resurrection itself includes the commissioning of the disciples. Matthew simply expands upon that theme.

Similarly the ascension is included in the concept of the resurrection. Luke's story presents pictorially Jesus' transition from earthly life to glory implicit in the resurrection. After a series of appearances and post-Easter teaching, Jesus joins his Father. Luke provides concrete shape by laying the new liturgical sequence of Easter-Ascension-Pentecost over the old Passover-Enthronement-Pentecost liturgy of Israel. John places the ascension on Easter Sunday itself. In any case this is not an historical, but a theological event—the return of Jesus to his Father preparatory to sending the Holy Spirit.

Sending of the Holy Spirit

The sending of the Holy Spirit differs between Luke and John. John places it on Easter.[12] Luke makes it the Christian fulfillment of Pentecost—the feast of first fruits, and the giving of the law.[13] The tongues of flame and mighty wind echo events in the Sinai theophany.[14]

The action itself—the descent of the Holy Spirit and the formation of the Christian Church—is of crucial importance, not the time sequence. The sending of the Holy Spirit completes Jesus' work and inaugurates the Church's mission by which his presence permeates subsequent time and space.

TO DEEPEN—

What is the basic shape of the resurrection narratives?

What does the resurrection mean to Christians?

What is the significance of the ascension and the sending of the Holy Spirit?

---

12. Jn 20:19
13. Acts 2:1–47
14. Ex 19:16–25

Further Reading;

Brown, Raymond. *The Virginal Conception and Bodily Resurrection of Jesus.* Paulist Press, 1973.

Fuller, Reginald. *The Formation of the Resurrection Narratives.* Fortress Press, 1980.

Richards, Hubert. *The First Easter, What Really Happened?* Twenty Third, 1986.

TO CONTINUE—

These stories form the basis for the celebration of Eastertime (Way 33–34).

The dogmatic teachings arising from these stories are explored in the Creed (Truth 35–36).

20. The New Testament Writings

TO PREPARE—

A cursory knowledge of the Christian story would be helpful, such as The Good News in Brief (Intro 3) or the Creed (Truth 25).

This category includes Christian Scripture outside the Gospels. Sunday and solemn liturgies[1] use them as the second reading, the epistles in particular. However the Acts of the Apostles sometimes occurs as the first reading.

The Acts of the Apostles

The Acts of the Apostles is a sequel to Luke's Gospel. It tells the story of the founding of the Church. Luke shows how the Holy Spirit led the apostles—in particular Peter and Paul—to spread the Gospel from Jerusalem to Rome, the world center of that day. Paul's letters show conflict between him and Peter. But in Acts, Luke, writing years later, makes Peter and Paul very similar, indeed allies. The earlier issues have been resolved. Luke here reflects issues important to his own time.

Acts is not history in the modern sense. Luke shows Jesus' power continuing to work after Pentecost through the Holy Spirit dwelling in the apostles. Furthermore Luke, like other Scripture writers, is concerned more with the theological meaning of history than with a narrative of events. Acts is not a factual but rather a theological account. Luke's Gospel sees the Gentiles as a development in the spread of the Gospel. This book is structured to present the inevitable progress of Christianity from Jerusalem where it was viewed as a Jewish sect to Rome where it is seen to be a universal religion.

The Epistles

An epistle is a letter, but at that time a letter was much more important and thought out than today—for this was the only means of long-range communication. There are other scriptural epistles—a letter connected with Jeremiah (Baruch)—but in the Christian Scriptures the epistle becomes a crucial tool to evangelize and educate the developing Christian communities.

---

1. Way 22

These apostolic letters were cherished and circulated to share the teaching. They form a major portion of the Christian canon.[2] They are seldom doctrinal or moral treatises such as an introduction to the faith. Rather they arise out of particular circumstances in the community which the apostle—usually that community's founder—is forced to address. They are not systematic treatises. And sometimes scholars are uncertain of the original circumstances. We must reconstruct the entire picture with half the possible evidence—the apostle's response.

These letters have authority as the earliest written records of Christian preaching and teaching. Many precede the Gospels which are later creations.

Pauline

And at least in Paul's case, a key shaper of Christianity, only his letters show his thought. **Romans, 1 and 2 Corinthians, Galatians, Philippians, Philemon** and at least **1 Thessalonians** present Paul's vision—a normative presentation of the faith. Obviously the only way to comprehend Paul's thought is through first-hand experience.

Paul's central theme is faith in Jesus Christ.[3] He speaks of human experience as confused and wandering. Israel's law acts as a guide since through the law we come to see our sinfulness.[4] But the law becomes a kind of curse. Although it reveals sin and shows the way of righteousness, when we try to follow this way we fail and thus are convicted. Before the law we could live in ignorance. But the law shows how far short of truth and goodness we fall. The law reveals the extent of human disobedience which heaps sin upon sin.

But how are we to turn ourselves around? As Paul discovers, it is impossible for us to do this.[5] But in Jesus Christ God himself fulfills the law for us. And joined to him in baptism we become co-heirs.[6] Using the story of Adam and Eve,[7] Paul tells how in Adam all sinned, so in Jesus Christ's obedience all are made whole.[8] We cannot save or make ourselves whole. Any attempts result in failure and greater sin. But God has reached out in Jesus and in him establishes our righteousness. Christ frees us from the law.

----

2. Truth 3
3. Phil 1:21
4. Rom 2:12–16
5. Rom 7:19
6. Rom 6:1–14
7. Gen 2:5—3:24
8. 1 Cor 15:22

We are joined to Jesus Christ through baptism. Under the water we are baptized into his death and joined; thus God raises us up in his resurrection to new life. We die to ourselves so that Christ may live in us.[9] We are no longer bound to sin and death. Having already died we now share in his resurrection.

Christians then live not for themselves, but Christ lives in them. And, transformed by Christ, they are made whole. In Christ they find that they can do all things which were impossible under their own will. Christ's grace makes all things possible. They can risk all things because failure, sin and death no longer have a hold. Secure in the knowledge that they belong to Christ, Christ will bring all home to the Father. Christian life then cooperates with grace which recreates and sanctifies so that through Christ we are made new.

Deutero-Pauline

Some scholars, detecting a development of Pauline thought in **Ephesians, Colossians** and perhaps **2 Thessalonians,** argue that these letters were written by students of Paul and therefore should be called Deutero-Pauline. In these letters greater Church structure emerges as the communities develop, becoming more organized. Such evolution is natural to any organism such as a community. With time the early Church perceived deeper implications and ramifications of what had happened in Jesus.

Pastoral

The pastoral epistles (**1 and 2 Timothy, Titus**), still later developments of Pauline thought, are concerned with ministry, Church organization and function. They show the development and emergence of the deaconate and the episcopacy[10] as the communities realize that they may be more permanent than first anticipated.

Catholic

Finally **1** and **2 Peter, James, 1, 2** and **3 John,** and **Jude** are called "catholic" because they address not a specific community or individual but the Church at large. These letters are not by the apostles. Their language is that of a later generation. Their authors want to preserve the apostolic tradition given them by the great apostles. They do not

---

9. Gal. 2:20
10. Truth 22ff, 84

want to break new theological ground. They are written under the names of the apostles to guard the tradition against misinterpretation.

Hebrews is more a systematic theology than an epistle. It is addressed to Hebrew Christians whose theology and faith are different from the Pauline Gentile churches. Two images from this book have greatly influenced Christian spirituality and liturgy: that of the Church as a wandering people of God which was reclaimed by Vatican II, and the image of Christ as high priest after the order of Melchizedek.[11]

Apocalyptic

The Christian Scriptures conclude with a book of apocalyptic. The early community under Nero's persecutions envision the end of this world which gives way to the age of the Lamb.[12] Jesus[13] had shared in apocalyptic hope and predicted the fall of the temple.[14] As a work of imagery and poetry, it may still inspire visions of the world and the problems that Christians encounter as they try to live in it.

Apocalyptic thought occurs in the early strata of the Christian Scriptures. Christians have come to see Jesus and his message in a wider context and have found different ways to express that message than in these vivid images.

TO DEEPEN—

What is the earliest written Christian material?

Read Paul's Epistle to the Galatians. What major Pauline themes are set forth there?

How does Paul view baptism?

Why don't we find fully articulated theologies in the epistles?

Do the letters of Peter present Peter's theology in the same way that the letters of Paul present his theology?

How do the authors of the Catholic epistles see their relationship to the faith?

In which category of Scripture is next Sunday's second reading? Look up the book in your Bible and read the introductory remarks to learn some of its background.

---

11. Gen 14:18
12. Rev. 21
13. Truth 16
14. Mt 24:4–36; Mk 13:5–37; Lk 21:8–36

Further Reading:

Brown, Raymond. *The Churches the Apostles Left Behind.* Paulist Press, 1974.

Collins, Raymond. *Introduction to the New Testament.* Doubleday, 1983.

Dupont, Dom Jacques. *Salvation of the Gentiles. Studies in the Acts of the Apostles.* Paulist Press, 1979.

Fiorenza, Elisabeth Schussler. *The Apocalypse.* Franciscan Herald Press, 1976.

Fuller, Reginald. *A Critical Introduction to the New Testament.* Longwood Pub. Group, 1979.

Marrow, Stanley B. *Paul. His Letters and His Theology.* Paulist Press, 1986

Perkins, Pheme. *Reading the New Testament. An Introduction.* Paulist Press, 1977.

Stanley, David M. *Apostolic Church in the New Testament.* Paulist Press, 1965.

TO CONTINUE—

Christian dogma and theology continue the teaching and thought of the epistles. The teaching function of the Church is found in Truth 22ff. The Creed— the authoritative summary of the faith—is explained beginning with Truth 25.

◇

21. *The Truth of the Tradition*

Tradition is the second means by which revelation is communicated. "Tradition" is the entire handing down of the Christian faith, while "traditions" refer to something specific from the tradition. By tradition the Church transmits the word of God. It is necessary because we have no primary contact with the historical Jesus—God's revelation. The Church whose experience goes back to Jesus himself shares what it has received and preserved.

Tradition is older than Scripture. For Scripture begins as oral tradition that at some point assumes written form. Tradition which originally produced Scripture now interprets it. How are they to be understood?

Tradition is the life of the word of God in the Church: the history of Christian exploration and reflection upon the Word. But it includes more than the Scriptures. It encompasses the whole of Christian life: beliefs, customs, prayers, worship, celebrations.

During the catechumenate[1] the Church officially presents the elect with the Lord's Prayer[2] and the Creed[3]—two major traditions. And the entire catechumenate is actually a passing on and entering into the Christian tradition.

Finally tradition is the result of this life. We are becoming part of the Christian tradition—part of what is handed down. And in the future what we are today is passed to future generations. As Catholic Christians we are the tradition.

Deposits

This tradition is found nowhere other than the Church as a whole. But the traditions of the Church (which are part of tradition) exist in various places within the Church.

Tradition is first in sacred Scripture which is a unique treasure of the Church.[4] This deposit of tradition the Church claims to be inspired.[5] Scripture of course forms a center for Christian life.

The tradition embraces worship and the sacraments.[6] It includes ways of prayer, rites to celebrate, feasts and seasons to observe, sacraments to heal and transform. These traditions assume written form in

---

1. Intro 6
2. Way 50
3. Truth 25
4. Truth 2
5. Truth 3
6. Way 8; Truth 74

the Church's liturgical books, but the tradition is found not in the books but celebration.

Throughout the Church's life tradition has produced statements, dogmas, creeds and conciliar texts. These too give written form to the tradition.

Tradition is found in the various customs and practices of the Catholic people. Christmas gift-giving testifies to the tradition—which tells of the gift of Christ who has come into our world.[7] Catholic practices—the rosary, the stations of the cross, feast days and fast days—all form tradition.[8]

---

7. Life 40
8. Life 41–42

22. The Church as Teacher

Since Christianity includes a content of revealed wisdom, it is a teaching. Jesus chose disciples as students. He is the original and primary Christian teacher. He defines what is taught and how it is to be taught. Jesus himself becomes the central teaching of Christianity.

Toward the end of his ministry he chooses Peter to head the twelve, and he passes his power and authority on to them.[9] These apostles are the primary witnesses to the resurrection, and when they select a man to fill the position vacated by Judas, they choose from those witnesses.[10]

The **apostles** with Peter at their head comprise the original structure of the new community. Since only the apostles received their teaching directly from Jesus, they possess an authority not passed on to their successors: the apostles are inspired by the Holy Spirit. That authority today resides only in Scripture.[11]

These apostles proclaimed the Gospel, won converts and set up local churches. They ordained men to oversee these communities, and the office of bishop, the "**episcopacy**," was established. Bishops are not of the same order as apostles.

Peter's office remains in the Church as the **papacy**. Thus the Pope is the bishop of Rome (where Peter died) and the head of the college of bishops. The teaching office of the Church is manifested most fully in the Pope and bishops gathered in **ecumenical council.** There have been twenty-two councils, the last being the Second Vatican Council of 1961–1965. Councils are named after the place where they meet. Conciliar teachings have primary authority after the Scriptures.

In the course of history the papacy developed. Such growth is not a falling away from an original Church. The Holy Spirit dwelling within the Church guides its actions; this development is part of God's plan.

In time the Church came to see that **infallibility**, always regarded as characteristic of conciliar teaching, applies to the Pope himself. Papal infallibility does not affirm that the Pope is always infallible, but only when he speaks in his official capacity[12] on an issue of faith and morals. Since the definition, only the assumption[13] and the immaculate conception have been so proclaimed. Infallibility means that God will not

---

9. Truth 17
10. Acts 1:15–26
11. Truth 3
12. Ex cathedra, i.e., from his cathedral chair
13. Truth 41

allow the Church to be led into error and that the officially declared teaching of Pope or Pope and council bears this mark.

The **bishops** are the pastors and teachers of the Christian Church. They stand in the lineage of the apostles and hand on their teaching. Their teaching (including the Pope's) is not authoritative in the same way as apostolic teaching. They are the guardians of the apostolic tradition. The Church's teaching office resides with the Pope, the councils, and the bishops. They in turn establish teachers or catechists who teach by their permission.

The Teachings

Christianity's most authoritative teaching resides in Scripture. Church teaching seeks to show how the truth of Scripture illumines the many circumstances through which the Christian people move on their pilgrimage toward the kingdom of God. No other teachings have the same weight and authority as these Scriptures, although even Scripture itself is subservient to God who originally inspired it.

Traditionally Christian teaching is divided into two components— faith and morals. In these two areas the Church is assured of infallibility. Two traditional statements set forth the contents of faith and morals: the Apostles' Creed defines faith, the ten commandments ground morality.

23. THE FAITH TRADITION

The creeds summarize authentic Christian belief. A creed is an official collection of beliefs authored by the Church. A number of creeds exist—some more binding than others. Among these two assume key authority as signposts of orthodoxy—the Apostles' Creed and the Nicene-Constantinople Creed.[14] Others include the Creed of St. Athanasius and a modern attempt by Pope Paul VI to put the faith as seen by Vatican II into a credal format.[15]

Creeds are the central definitions of Christian faith. Orthodoxy (correct faith) is determined by one's allegiance to a creed. However, as with Scripture, so a creed needs interpretation. One is obliged to believe in a creed only as its authors intended. Just as Scripture scholarship determines the intended meaning of Scripture, so historical theology ascertains the intended meaning of credal statements.

A **dogma** is a statement of belief. The creeds are composed of dog-

---

14. Way 22
15. Truth 29

matic statements—for example, Jesus is "true God, true man." These dogmas are sometimes called symbols. Although not symbols in the sense of the sacramental symbols of water or bread, words are basically symbolic—they refer to a meaning beyond themselves. Symbolic language points rather than defines. So in the above example we should explore just what the original framers meant by "God" and "man." Assuming that their intention is identical to modern usage can lead to misunderstanding.

Furthermore, **development of dogma** occurs as faith passes through history. Catholic faith today is not exactly the same as that of the first century. Two thousand years of experience, meditation, study and living have deepened the Church's insight into revelation. Deepened insight leads to dogmatic development—the full doctrine of the Trinity[16] does not emerge until the third century and later. It also gives rise to dogmas not part of the original deposit[17] such as papal infallibility.[18] These add nothing new, but are the result of deeper insight and appreciation.

Finally the multiplicity of dogmas and doctrines within the Church raises difficulties. Are all considered equal? No, there is a **hierarchy of dogma**. Certain dogmas are more central to the faith than others. In general the beliefs stated in the Apostles' and Nicene Creeds are central to the Christian tradition. Other doctrines growing out of these are of less consequence. This does not imply that they are unimportant.

The Church has defined certain dogmas during the course of its history. If these have been defined officially either by a council (as creeds) or by a Pope, they are considered infallible.[19]

However many dogmas more central to the faith at other times or places are not so central today. For example, the stress upon the other world, lacking in current Catholicism, in past times developed doctrines such as purgatory. These doctrines, while not denied, are not as much to the fore as they once were. No one age, person, or place encompasses the whole of Catholicism which extends to include the full diversity of experience both in space and time.

Finally, **theology** seeks to speak and expound revelation to its age and culture. Thus theology is an enterprise of every age and culture. Early Christian theology used Platonism and Greek philosophical terms

---

16. Truth 27
17. Truth 41
18. Truth 22
19. Truth 22

to expound the Gospel. Thomas Aquinas made Aristotle's philosophy the basis for his articulation of the faith. Modern theologians ask how God's word might address problems of liberation, or how Christianity might speak in the language of psychology or the other sciences.

Creeds and dogmatic statements arise out of the Church's theological enterprise. But the particular theological language is not intended to become the exclusive language of the faith. Dogmas point behind their language and philosophy to define as Christian truth the realities to which the words and statements point. Thus although the doctrine of transubstantiation is couched in Aristotelian language, theologians today understand the Eucharist using modern terminology and philosophy. They must prove however that their theology is consonant with the original dogmatic statements.

TO DEEPEN—

What is the difference between a creed, a dogmatic statement and a theology?

What does it mean to say that a statement is infallible?

Who are the primary teachers in the Catholic tradition?

What is the difference between inspiration (Truth 3) and infallibility?

Is Scripture infallible?

Further Reading:

Dulles, Avery. *The Survival of Dogma.* Crossroad/Continuum, 1982.
Miller, Michael. *What Are They Saying About Papal Primacy?* Paulist Press, 1984.
McKenzie, John. *Authority and the Church.* Sheed and Ward, 1985
Reiser, William E. *What Are They Saying About Dogma?* Paulist Press, 1978.
Sullivan, Francis A. *Magisterium. Teaching Authority in the Catholic Church.* Paulist Press, 1983.

TO CONTINUE—

The Creed is presented beginning in Truth 25.

The history of theology is covered in the sections on Christian history (Life 29ff) and modern thought and theology in The Life of the Christian Spirit (Life 13).

24. THE MORAL TRADITION

There are four basic sources for Christian moral teaching. First Israel's experience with God has revealed the true course of human action. This tradition is symbolized by the ten commandments[20] but includes the prophetic and wisdom traditions as well. Second, the moral tradition of Greece and Rome provides another stream of Christian morality. Much New Testament morality is based upon Greco-Roman, particularly stoic ethics. This tradition is symbolized by the cardinal virtues.[21] Jesus and the Christian Scriptures provide the third source symbolized by the theological virtues.[22] Finally the Christian tradition itself meditates upon and refines its understanding of morality as in the capital sins.[23]

The Mosaic Covenant

The Mosaic covenant grounds our entire tradition. This law established Israel and prescribed much of her life. Upon this law the entire Jewish tradition is based and Jesus builds upon this tradition bringing it to fulfillment.

The strain of moral teaching from the time of Moses to the present reveals an evolution. What was allowable in Moses' time may not be appropriate to a later period; similarly some prohibitions of earlier days are no longer mandatory at a later stage. Thus in the light of Jesus and his teaching the early Christians abrogated the ritual law of Israel.[24] On the other hand Jesus himself tightens the divorce laws.[25] And as humanity progresses it comes to see institutions such as slavery (accepted in the course of things by the early Church) as against the will of God.

The Prophetic Tradition

The prophetic tradition complements the law. While the law established a new society and provided fundamental guidelines and protection for that society and its institutions, the prophets addressed concrete issues and crises.

Israel's God from the beginning identified with the poor and oppressed. God had compassion upon the slaves of Egypt[26] and liberated

20. Truth 45
21. Truth 67–70
22. Truth 71–73
23. Truth 58
24. Gal 3:1–9
25. Mk 10:1–12
26. Ex 3:7–10

them. As Israel becomes a power she resembles other nations. The rich get richer and the poor get poorer. And the rich walk upon the rights of the poor. Prophecies reveal these injustices and demand that Israel rectify the situation. Amos speaks out against those who overcharge the poor and are deceitful in their business practices.[27] Zechariah pleads for the widow and the orphan, the powerless victims of society.[28] Such injustices are not peculiar to Israel; the prophet's word challenges modern situations, not only on behalf of the poor within a society, but the poor nations among the wealthy few.

The prophets' challenge is not meant to condemn Israel or other sinners. They call for repentance, a return to the law, a rededication to justice. They call for a commitment to the spirit of the law, for it is easy to be convinced that one is following the law by observing the letter while totally failing the spirit.

Jesus raises the law's demands to a level at which no one could humanly fulfill them. The Christian ethic is not a minimum of what we should do but a description of the kingdom whose arrival alone brings the longed-for peace and happiness. Although that ethic makes great demands, it does not result in condemnation when we sin. Rather a constant assurance and experience of reconciliation enables us to begin again, to try again, to learn from mistakes, and slowly to grow in grace.

Finally the prophets challenge Israel's understanding of her vocation. Israel is chosen by God. But often that choice was understood as rejecting others, or as dependent upon something unique to Israel. Some prophets remind Israel that she is chosen to be a sign to the nations of God's love and compassion.

Christians too have often seen their vocation as a sign of God's special favor. But that favor does not arise from something we have done. Nor does it imply disfavor for others. We are chosen for a mission: to be Christ for the world, leaven for the bread, salt for the earth. In that great mission our real glory lies, not in ourselves or our accomplishments.

The Wisdom Tradition

The third great source of ethics derives from Israel's meditation upon wisdom. Part of wisdom is understanding the proper way to behave, and many scriptural proverbs provide guidance for social relations.

---

27. Am 8:4–7
28. Zech 7:10

But wisdom goes far beyond the coining of proverbs. This tradition regards the height of human accomplishment as knowing the wisdom of God—the true nature and order of creation. At times our tradition is seen as arbitrary. People regard laws as simply the whim of the lawgiver—in this case, God. But Israel's meditation upon wisdom like China's meditation on the Tao shows the order, the blessing, the creativity, at the very heart of creation when we are at one with it. And the law is designed not to curtail freedom, but indeed to promote real freedom and liberation by being harmonious with God and creation rather than going against the grain which is sin.

The highest form of wisdom consists in meditation upon and living by the law. Law is much more than a set of rules and regulations. The law is the truth. And to live according to the law is to find fulfillment and happiness. For Israel that law is the Mosaic covenant. For Christians the law is Christ. By conformity to Christ we find fulfillment.

Jesus' Ethical Teaching

Jesus approached the Mosaic tradition in two ways. On the one hand he criticized the leaders of his day for making the tradition more burdensome than necessary. He deplored the tendency to warp the law to the advantage of the elite. He warned of keeping the letter while going against the spirit—this was especially the case with the sabbath observance.[29] For Jesus the heart—the interior of the law and of the person—determines the exterior.[30]

On the other hand, Jesus raises the old law to a new level. He goes to the source of the problem—thoughts of adultery lead to adulterous actions, the passion of anger leads to the crime of murder. Jesus' commands are not to be taken in the same light as the original commandments. The originals laid the minimum foundation for a society. The perfections of those commands in Jesus' teaching show what is necessary to achieve the happiness and peace of the kingdom.

Jesus ends the series of new commands in the Sermon on the Mount with two commands that far surpass the old law. First he says:

> You have heard that it was said, "An eye for an eye and a tooth for a tooth." But I say to you, Do not resist one who is evil. But if any one strikes you on the right cheek, turn to him the other also; and if any one would sue you and take your coat,

---

29. Lk 6:1–5
30. Mk 6:14–23

let him have your cloak as well; and if any one forces you to
go one mile, go with him two miles. Give to him who begs
from you, and do not refuse him who would borrow from
you.[31]

Jesus speaks of the *lex talonis*, (an eye for an eye) in that day a part
of most law, including the Mosaic. But Jesus turns that seeming model
of human justice on its head. This command demonstrates the extent of
human wrongheadedness. For the height of our justice is not justice at
all in the kingdom of God. The extremity of our situation can be gleaned
from the fact that few Christian churches have dared impose this command on their members.

Only recently in history has the force of this law been shown. Mo-
hatmas Gandhi and then Martin Luther King have trusted non-violent
resistance to challenge unjust structures. Their success has led others
to reconsider these teachings not just as ideal definitions of God's reign
but as strategies for helping that kingdom come.

The true radical change Jesus has in mind comes forth in his last
new command:

You have heard that it was said, "You shall love your neighbor
and hate your enemy." But I say to you, Love your enemies
and pray for those who persecute you, so that you may be sons
of your Father who is in heaven; for he makes his sun rise on
the evil and on the good, and sends rain on the just and on the
unjust. For if you love those who love you, what reward have
you? Do not even the tax collectors do the same? And if you
salute only your brethren, what more are you doing than others? Do not even the Gentiles do the same? You, therefore,
must be perfect, as your heavenly Father is perfect.[32]

Jesus stands human nature on its head. It is only natural to love
one's friends and hate one's enemies. Yet what has such an attitude produced but bloodshed and misery? In the kingdom of God there are no
enemies—no boundaries between what is mine and yours. Such a vision far exceeds our ability to contemplate in this world today. Yet Jesus
invites commitment to just that vision. Become perfect, become whole,
just as God is. Only that perfection can usher in the beatitude characteristic of God's reign. Responding to Jesus and becoming his followers,

---

31. Mt 5:38–42
32. Mt 5:43–48

Christians bind themselves to these commandments as guidelines for living their lives.

For Jesus, the proper foundation of all life is to be like God. And God is love. Therefore Christianity is basically an ethic of love—love that is concerned for the other, that is sacrificial, that is freely given, and that bears great fruit. This passion should motivate all Christian behavior.

The Catholic Tradition

Scripture reveals a wealth of ethical teaching which is not set down in any real order. How are Christians to arrive at a practical ethical standard? Are we to adopt the teachings of the Sermon on the Mount as a new binding law? In the area of ethics there is certainly a need for an authority that articulates standards of acceptable behavior.

The Catholic moral tradition is based of course upon these authoritative scriptural teachings. The Greco-Roman culture into which Christianity plunged soon after her birth contributed its ethics as well. The concept of natural law[33] comes from this source. All these streams as well as consequent Christian developments comprise a complex moral teaching.

The magisterium is the fullest moral teacher of the Roman Catholic Church.[34] Although the promise of infallibility rests with Church moral pronouncements, there has never been such a moral pronouncement. Nevertheless Church teachings, encyclical letters, and moral theology provide guidance.

Traditionally Christians present ethics in the context of the ten commandments. In exploring these commandments we shall discuss their relevance to today and the way they are interpreted by Catholic tradition. Thus we shall look at ways in which Jesus brought these commandments to perfection, and also how these have been understood in terms of foundational morality. The discussion will continue as we explore the moral foundations for the Christian path in the succeeding section. For while the ten commandments chart out the course of societal morality, the Christian Church has also developed an individual morality.

---

33. Life 12
34. Truth 22

TO DEEPEN—

In what ways is the Christian ethic the same as others? What makes it different?
What are the sources for the Catholic moral teaching?
Who are the primary moral teachers in the Church?
How does Jesus' teaching differ from the law?

Further Reading:

Schnackenburg, Rudolf. *Moral Teaching of the New Testament.* Crossroad.

TO CONTINUE—

*The moral teaching is presented in The Ten Commandments (Truth 45ff), The
Deadly Sins (Truth 58ff), The Seven Virtues (Truth 66ff) and Catholic Social
Teachings (Life 44).*

*The way in which a Christian goes about acting and deciding morality is found
in The Way of Morality (Way 41ff) and The Christian's Relation to Society
(Life 12).*

25. The Apostles' Creed

I believe in God the Father almighty,
Creator of heaven and earth,

and in Jesus Christ,
his only Son our Lord,
who was conceived by the Holy Spirit,
born of the Virgin Mary,
suffered under Pontius Pilate,
was crucified, died, and was buried;
he descended into hell;
the third day he rose again from the dead;
he ascended into heaven,
sits at the right hand of God the Father almighty;
from there he shall come to judge the living and the dead.

I believe in the Holy Spirit,
the holy Catholic Church,
the communion of saints,
the forgiveness of sins,
the resurrection of the body,
and life everlasting.

We call this formula the Creed. It consists of twelve brief articles which have been collected from the scriptures and drawn up in a way people can easily memorize.

The time has now come for me to teach it to you. I want you to commit it to memory word for word. Do not write it down on paper; write it in your hearts so that you never forget it. Say it over every day among yourselves. Before you go to sleep at night, before you go out of your house during the day, fortify yourselves with the Creed. And as I explain it to you, believe it, and be ready to recite it publicly next week.

The Creed is part of your Christian armor. It is a provision for your journey that you must retain as long as your life lasts. Never accept any other faith than this, not even if I should change my mind and say something that contradicts what you are now being taught. . . . Faith, you might say, is like cash paid over the counter. I am handing over the cash to you now, but God will require an account from you of what you have received. Remember what St. Paul says to Timothy: "I charge you before God, who gives life to all, and before Jesus Christ who gave testimony before Pontius Pilate, to keep this faith that is committed to you spotless until our Lord Jesus Christ appears. A treasure of life has been entrusted to you, and at his coming the Master will look for the deposit."[1]

Further Reading:

Chesterton, G. K. *Orthodoxy.* Doubleday, 1959. A classic defense of Orthodox Christianity by this early twentieth century convert.

Field, Anne. *From Darkness to Light. What It Meant To Become a Christian in the Early Church.* Servant Books, 1978. A collection of the early Fathers' writings for catechumens, explaining the Creed, the Lord's Prayer, and the ceremonies of initiation.

Harned, David B. *Creed and Personal Identity: The Meaning of the Apostles' Creed.* Fortress, 1981.

Ratzinger, Joseph. *Introduction to Christianity.* Crossroad, 1970.

THE CREED: BELIEF IN GOD
26. I BELIEVE

Importance of Meaning to Human Existence

Christianity claims to reveal the truth concerning ourselves and our world. Throughout its history humanity has sought to know itself and its world. Is our existence meaningful? Which way of life leads to fulfillment and satisfaction? What is the purpose for our own and the universe's existence? We search for meaning—and indeed, deprived of meaning, life shrivels and dies.

Our quest has taken various forms in history. The religions address our need for meaning—products of our eternal search. Some are primitive; some are high teachings reflecting human wisdom at various stages of evolution.

The human quest has also been refined into philosophy—the love of wisdom. And in modern times the rise of science has unraveled many mysteries and pushed back the boundaries of the unknown.

In the midst of things, coping with the daily cycle of events we can lose sight of this quest just trying to stay above water. But in times of leisure and in crises, the question rises again: What kind of life provides a sense of wholeness?

---

1. 1 Tim 5:21; 6:13-15; Augustine, *On the Creed for the Catechumens*

Faith

Christians believe that God has responded to this eternal search for meaning. In the history of Israel and in Jesus of Nazareth, God's gift of faith provides meaning, tells how things truly are, and reveals a way leading toward wholeness. God's response is a free gift—it cannot be discovered using intellect or science. It is a revelation[1] concerning the nature of creation, God and ourselves.

In offering this gift of faith, God invites us into a covenant.[2] Through this covenant God agrees to lead and transform us as we journey toward his kingdom. We agree to the conditions of the covenant—following God's law, growing in the love and knowledge of Jesus, and being transformed by the Holy Spirit, giving our lives in service. We enter into this covenant through baptism,[3] becoming members of Christ's body.

But just what is faith from our side? It is similar to and sometimes confused with knowledge, wisdom, belief, or, on the other hand, superstition or magic. And it is thought to be the opposite of doubt.

First of all faith is **trust**. We trust God and his revelation. We do not know that it is true. It cannot be proven. What faith points to cannot be demonstrated by **scientific method**. Faith certainly has a component of **knowledge**, but such knowledge does not come from our senses or reason but as a gift from God. Entering the covenant we trust God's word as true.

However, while faith can not be gained by knowledge, it is not unreasonable. We cannot **reason** to the contents of faith, but, given those contents, they accord with reason. Faith transcends but does not contradict reason. St. Anselm[4] defined theology as faith seeking understanding.

Depending upon trust, faith is not absolutely certain. There is always an element of risk; were that not so, faith would be knowledge. But what about difficulties of belief? Questioning? Confusion? Uncertainty? Are these defects? **Doubt** is not opposed to but a healthy component of faith.

What we believe is sometimes difficult—contrary to worldly sense. Such difficulties give rise to doubts. But the life of faith includes an endurance of doubting. We pray then that God sustain and strengthen us. Our doubts often prepare the way for a deeper vision and commitment.

---

1. Truth 1
2. Way 1
3. Intro 13
4. Life 33

The opposite of faith is not doubt, but **despair**—the belief that God does not care and will not sustain us.

Sometimes faith is likened to **superstition** and magic. And faith sometimes degenerates into superstition—reliance upon something to save one. We rely upon a rabbit's foot, or whatever fate, to turn the trick. Superstition lies lower than faith since it trusts in some abstract force. Faith relies upon God. Furthermore superstition implies no responsibility for the creation of one's life which is ruled by the stars, or the runes. Faith calls to responsibility for our life, to co-create our life and our world.

Magic attempts through rites, words, or actions to gain power over one's life, others, God, or the world. It manipulates instead of engaging in life. Faith calls us to enter into life and to be created through our encounter. Magic refuses to enter this relationship, preferring instead to dominate from without.

Faith is an action, a response to God's revelation. But **belief** is expressed in doctrines—statements setting the limits of belief. These doctrines, gathered into a Creed, summarize the truth God has revealed in calling us into the covenant of faith. Catholics believe the dogmatic statements and creeds of the Church. But we have faith in God and Jesus Christ. These two should not be confused.

TO DEEPEN—

What is the difference between faith and belief?

What is the opposite of faith?

Can a Christian have doubt?

Does faith contradict reason?

Further Reading:

Haught, John F. *The Cosmic Adventure. Science, Religion and the Quest for Purpose.* Paulist Press, 1984.

Newman, John Henry. *A Grammar of Assent.* Doubleday, 1955. A study by a great nineteenth century theologian and convert that attempts to explore just what it means to believe.

O'Collins, Gerald. *Fundamental Theology.* Paulist Press, 1981.

Tillich, Paul. *Dynamics of Faith.* Harper & Row, 1957. A simple yet profound analysis of faith by one of the great modern Protestant theologians.

27. IN GOD THE FATHER ALMIGHTY

Christians believe in one God. Our knowledge of God comes foremost from revelation in the history of Israel and in Jesus. But in the light of that revelation Christians also have developed a philosophical approach to God.

Philosophical Approach

St. Thomas Aquinas taught that human reason can discover the existence of God. Reason could not prove God's existence, but could demonstrate that it is reasonable to posit God. Thus the famous "proofs" are really demonstrations that God's existence is in accord with human reason.

Reason can further discover certain qualities of God, such as that he is omnipotent (almighty) and omniscient (all-knowing); that he is the source of unity, truth, beauty, and goodness; that he is not a being, like other beings, but is being itself: *ipsum esse subsistens*—that Being which is the cause of its own existence. God's being is self-sustaining, unlike everything created which God sustains in being.

The Catholic philosophical tradition also points out limitations to human knowledge of God. The apophatic tradition stemming from Dionysius the Areopagite states that we can know nothing of God as he is in himself.[5] All we can know of God is what God is not. And whatever is posited about God is not really positive knowledge but simply qualification of what God is not. We are prevented from falling into the fallacy that a limited creature can comprehend the unlimited. No matter how much we know about God, God is still more unknown than known—and will always remain so.

Thus theology is actually anthropology. We do not learn about God as he is in himself. We truly know nothing of the "selfhood" of God. But we do know how God relates and wishes to relate to us. Revelation is not first of all knowledge, but an invitation to enter into relationship with God.

Knowledge from Revelation

Primary knowledge of God comes from revelation. God is the **Creator** of all that is.[6] The universe is entirely God's creation. Whatever exists was created out of nothing. There is no opposing principle or power which God must struggle against. God's is the only real power.

---

5. Life 8
6. Gen 1:1

God reveals himself to Moses as Liberator.[7] God is **Yahweh**. God has compassion upon the slaves and wills to free them. God is involved in the struggle for liberation wherever it occurs.

And God is aligned with the weak, the oppressed in this struggle. God reveals that he has chosen the poor as his people. He reveals himself to slaves. He makes his home among the homeless. And he does this in order to liberate those oppressed by the sinful structures of the world.

Through Moses God enters into a covenant with Israel. God becomes **Lord** (Adon) of Israel. Indeed God's name is so holy that it cannot be uttered. Instead Israelites use the euphemism "Lord" to speak of God. Thus we acknowledge God's authority over us, looking to him for nurture and protection.

Being a nomadic people, God is seen as the **shepherd of Israel**. The shepherd boy David becomes Israel's great monarch (1 Sam 16:1-13). Later the prophets speak of God as the shepherd who watches over his flock.[8]

The prophets more fully reveal God's passion for **justice**[9]—but not human justice, which more often than not gives advantage to the powerful. God's justice is above politics and society. And again the option is preferential toward the poor and oppressed, the outcast and the stranger over those in power who more often than not create rather than alleviate injustice.

Jesus' life and teaching bring these themes to fullness and completion.[10] He teaches that God is **Father** (Abba).[11] God is personal, not a law or power. God acts out of compassion. God seeks out what is lost.[12] God rejoices in creation. God is love itself[13]—not love in the sense of grasping and trying to possess what is loved, but love to the extent of laying down one's life for the beloved.[14]

While traditionally God has been spoken of in masculine language, present-day feminist theology is opening our eyes to the wealth of feminine imagery for God in the Scriptures.[15] Christians do not believe that God has a sex. The masculine imagery is culturally conditioned and was meant to assert the personal nature of God rather than God's gender.

---

7. Ex 3:7ff
8. Ez 34:1–31
9. Am 5:21–24
10. Truth 16
11. Mk 14:36
12. Lk 15:1–10
13. 1 Jn 4:16
14. Jn 15:13
15. Truth 16

Trinity

The Trinity makes the Christian concept of God unique among religions. The Trinity is the highest mystery of our faith. It cannot be understood or grasped just as God himself cannot be comprehended.

The Trinity is not simply knowledge about God. It reveals the way we encounter God. It profoundly shapes Christianity. It forms the basis of our prayer—to the Father, through the Son, in the Holy Spirit.[16]

Theologically the Trinity is often put forward through a number of seeming contradictions. Christians affirm the absolute oneness of God, yet claim that within the one Godhead there are three persons. We confess that God the Father is not God the Son nor God the Holy Spirit. Yet at the same time we assert that these three persons are all one God.

There is some danger in using the word person, especially in light of modern understanding. To say that God is manifested as a person does not imply that God is a person like us. To make God a person makes God a being like other beings and so contradicts the basic definition—that God is not one among many but one alone. Applying attributes to God, especially personal ones, makes clear that God's qualities can be likened to human qualities. Thus God is loving, compassionate, caring, jealous, etc. But these terms are applied by analogy to God. In God such qualities are not the same as in humans.

In terms of the Trinity the concept of person really speaks about a way of being rather than of personality. Thus there are three ways of being in God defined as Father, Son and Holy Spirit. These three are equal—one is not better than another. They are different in their relationships to one another. And their relationships are determined by their origins. The Father is not generated or spirated. The Son is generated from the Father. The Holy Spirit is spirated by the Father and the Son.

The three persons are also differentiated by their function in our salvation. The universe is created by God the Father. It is however created in the image of the Son. We are redeemed by the Son incarnated[17] as Jesus of Nazareth. And the Son when he returned to the Father sent the Holy Spirit to be our sanctifier and Paraclete.

Since the very core of the Godhead manifests this Trinity in unity, Christians also perceive this pattern in the creation bearing the Creator's marks. Thus various Trinitarian features disclose the inner essence of things. For example, this guide uses the triple division of Way, Truth

16. Way 8
17. Truth 30

and Life to reveal not three things but the unity of Christianity. If God is at core Trinitarian, what does not reflect this structure of threeness in oneness?

TO DEEPEN—

What are some of your images of God? How do these help you to know God? Where do they come from?

Can we prove that God exists?

What are some major images of God found in the Hebrew Scriptures?

What does the Trinity say about God?

How does the Trinity influence all perception for a Christian?

Further Reading:

Bracken, Joseph. *What Are They Saying About the Trinity?* Paulist Press, 1979.

Edwards, Denis. *Human Experience of God.* Paulist Press, 1983.

Galligan, Michael. *God and Evil.* Paulist Press, 1976.

Haught, John F. *What Is God?* Paulist Press, 1986.

Küng, Hans. *Does God Exist? An Answer for Today.* Doubleday, 1980.

Mollendott, Virginia Ramey. *The Divine Feminine: The Biblical Imagery of God as Female.* Crossroad, 1984.

Panikkar, Raimundo. *The Trinity and the Religious Experience of Man.* Orbis Books, 1973.

Quoist, Michael. *Meeting God.* Dimension Books, 1985.

Rahner, Karl. *The Trinity.* Herder & Herder, 1970.

Rahner, Karl. *Foundations of Christian Faith.* Crossroad, 1978.

Ruether, Rosemary. *Sexism and God Talk.* Beacon Press, 1983.

Schillebeeckx, Edward. *God Among Us.* Crossroad, 1986.

Shea, John. *Stories of God. An Unauthorized Biography.* Thomas More Press, 1980.

28. Creator of Heaven and Earth

The universe is a creation rather than chaos without form or meaning. What exists owes existence and is sustained in existence only by God. Only God, Catholic philosophy says, is the cause of his own existence. Everything else is dependent upon God for its coming into being and its sustenance.

Christian tradition also speaks of the extent of the creation. God is Creator of all that is visible and invisible. Included is the entire material universe. In addition our tradition speaks of forces of good and evil which are spiritual rather than material. These forces and powers also depend upon God.

Over the centuries Israel came to see **Satan** as the key force opposed to the good and to God. Experience showed at times a power of evil greater than human evil. While other traditions spoke of creation as a contest between powers of good and evil, Israel ascribed all real power to God alone. Satan's power, or the powers of evil, are not real—they are allowed to exist only by God's permission. That their powers are illusory will be revealed on the day of the Lord.[18]

Aligned with Satan are **demons**, other powers opposed to God. Although considering themselves God's adversaries, their being is totally dependent upon God's will. The continuance of their power in the universe consequent upon the saving act of Jesus is a mystery. Christian teaching says that on the coming of God's reign, these forces of evil will be unmasked in their true powerlessness as the light of God's goodness permeates and transforms creation.

There are powers of good as well called **angels**—messengers (of God) who carry out God's will throughout the universe. Christian belief in angels and demons need not take up the imagery of past generations: angels with wings and demons with pitchforks are only images of popular imagination. Spiritual beings need none of these characteristics. The tradition asserts only the existence of created realms outside our own nature which straddles the material and the spiritual.

Christian belief in these spiritual powers calls into question the dominant materialism of our culture and calls us to expand our horizons as to the wealth of beings in God's creation. The nature of evil in our world cannot be completely understood simply as the actions of evil or deluded people. Forces of evil help to understand instances of evil beyond the human such as Auschwitz. And similarly forces of good aid in our struggle to overcome sin.

Modern science relies upon the theory of **evolution** to understand the present proliferation of creatures on earth. This theory is not intrinsically in conflict with Catholic teaching on creation. Evolution explains how species have arisen during the course of the earth's history. The Christian doctrine of creation asserts that whatever is owes its existence to God. It does not attempt to explain how the various beings have come to birth.

Teilhard de Chardin's[19] evolutionary vision of creation has inspired

---

18. Truth 37
19. Life 13

the present-day school of process theology in both Catholicism and Protestantism. Process theology also speaks of change within God. Such an idea seems strange because of the dominant Greek notion in Western theology that what changes is not perfect, but it fits better with the images of God from Scripture.

TO DEEPEN—

What does a Christian think about the world? Is it good or evil?
Is there a proof that God exists?
Can a Christian believe in evolution?

Further Reading:

Hayes, Zachary. *What Are They Saying About Creation?* Paulist Press, 1980

TO CONTINUE—

The biblical teachings about God are found in Truth 4-20 and should be consulted to fill in the picture presented here.

THE CREED: JESUS CHRIST
29. AND IN JESUS CHRIST, HIS ONLY SON, OUR LORD

Jesus' teachings, works and life form the very center of Christianity. Pope Paul VI in his Creed written after the Second Vatican Council summarized Catholic belief concerning Jesus.

The Christ

> We believe in our Lord Jesus Christ, who is the Son of God. He is the eternal word born of the Father before time began, one in substance with the Father . . . through whom all things were made. He was incarnate of the Virgin Mary by the power of the Holy Spirit and was made man—equal, therefore, to the Father according to his divinity, his unity deriving not from some impossible confusion of substance but from his Person.

The Teaching of Jesus

> He dwelt among us full of grace and truth. He announced and established the kingdom of God,[1] enabling us to know the Father. He gave us the commandment that we should love one another as he loved us. He taught us the way of the Gospel beatitudes,[2] according to which we were to be poor in spirit and humble, bearing suffering in patience, thirsting after justice, merciful, clean of heart, peaceful, enduring persecution for justice's sake.

The Redemption

> He suffered under Pontius Pilate, the Lamb of God taking to himself the sins of the world, and he died for us, nailed to the cross, saving us by his redeeming blood.[3] After he had been buried he rose from the dead of his own power, lifting us by his resurrection to that sharing in the divine life which is grace.[4] He ascended into heaven whence he will come again to judge the living and the dead, each according to his merits.[5] Those who have responded to the love and compassion of God will go into eternal life. Those who have refused them to the end will be consigned to the fire that is never extinguished.[6] And of his kingdom there will be no end.

The human being, Jesus of Nazareth, is the very center of Christianity. Christians give their life and its direction over to this man. Our exploration begins with the different titles given Jesus in the New Testament and early Church. From these titles subsequent Christian meditation blossoms.

The most prominent title has become the **Christ.** This is not Jesus' name, but a description of his office. It is the Greek equivalent of **Messiah** and means "anointed." Israel was promised a Messiah as her future

1. Truth 16
2. Life 47
3. Truth 32–33
4. Truth 35
5. Truth 36–37
6. Truth 44

king who would usher in the day of the Lord when this age will pass away to be replaced by God's reign. The disciples saw Jesus' life as a fulfillment of messianic prophecies and so came to recognize him as Messiah.

However Jesus was not the commonly expected Messiah. While he fulfills certain prophecies he fails to fulfill others—for example he does not become a political leader who frees Israel from foreign domination. The New Testament writers therefore are concerned to show how, although Jesus is not the expected Messiah, he is indeed the Messiah. Since Christianity quickly entered the Greco-Roman world, the term Christ is more common than Messiah.

Two scriptural titles are confusing today since they mean quite different things than their names imply. Christians call Jesus both the **Son of God** and the **Son of Man**. Originally these referred to just the opposite of their implied meaning. Every Israelite would be considered a son of God, whereas the son of man is a special figure of Jewish apocalyptic[7]—a semi-divine being who was to appear at the end of the present age to inaugurate the reign of God.

Christians called Jesus the Son of God—meaning that he enjoys a special relationship with God as his only-begotten Son.[8] Jesus himself speaks of the Son of Man who is to come.[9] He does not equate himself with that figure, but early Christians, in the light of the resurrection, do, and then look forward to his future coming to inaugurate his kingdom.

The early Christians called Jesus **Lord**: a title also bound up in Israelite history. Israel used the euphemism of "Lord" (Adonai) instead of God's name.[10] Christians using this title ("Kyrios" in Greek) purposely identified Jesus with the God of Israel. This same identification appears in Gospel stories such as the calming of the storm[11] where Jesus exhibits power proper only to God.[12]

John has contributed a key title: the **Word of God**. God's word alone has power to call into being. God creates through speaking. God's word in the prophets is the power of God calling out of sin and bondage into justice and freedom. Jesus is that Word of God in its fullness. In him radically this Word, which is and expresses God, takes on human flesh and dwells among us.[13]

7. Truth 17
8. Jn 1:14
9. Mt 16:27
10. Truth 27
11. Mt 8:23–27
12. Ps 29
13. Jn 1:14

30. Who Was Conceived by the Holy Spirit

These titles become the basis for subsequent reflection on Jesus and his work. **Incarnation**, a key doctrine, describes Jesus' person. Jesus is God who has come among us in human flesh. Therefore not only his words, but his actions, indeed his very being, are fully divine.

But at the same time Jesus is also fully human. He shares our humanity in everything except sin. Thus he is not a superman—an alien being. Our humanity is fully present in Jesus, including human limitations. The incarnation asserts that Jesus is fully human and fully divine, not a mixture of the two. Each quality finds full expression in him. How this (or any other dogma) is to be understood according to contemporary ways of thought is the task of theology.

31. Born of the Virgin Mary

The incarnation is complemented by the **virgin birth** of Jesus. This teaching arises out of the infancy Gospels.[14] Christian reflection upon these stories believes that in the conception of Jesus, Joseph can not be called the natural father. Mary conceived by the power of the Holy Spirit. Basically Jesus is not simply a descendant of humanity, but is equally of God.

Catholics also attach great importance to the title Virgin applied to Mary, the mother of Jesus. Mary, in Catholic thought, is a symbolic as well as historical figure. Her importance lies in what she has come to represent as well as who she was.[15]

Luke's infancy narrative sees Mary as the flower of Israel—the rose of Sharon, the daughter of Sion, the faithful hearer of God's word. Her virginity emphasizes her dedication to God: the virgin is faithful to God rather than to a husband. And the virgin is the image of the bride—a powerful metaphor of God and Israel.[16] Mary's fidelity, the spiritual significance of her virginity, is manifested in her "yes" spoken to the angel.[17] In spite of all obstacles, she assents to God: Be it done to me according to your will.

In Jesus God makes a new beginning, the start of a new creation.[18] Mary is the final flowering of the old creation in Israel, giving birth to

---

14. Truth 15
15. Truth 41
16. Ez 16:1–63; Hos 1:2–9
17. Lk 1:38
18. Truth 15

the new in Jesus. Thus virginity is not only biological, but a spiritual quality.

In the Church's reflection upon the person of Jesus and the controversies over his nature as both human and divine, Mary received the title "God-bearer" or "Mother of God." To protect the person of Jesus from dogmatic schizophrenia—a mixture of God and humanity—Mary is declared to be the full mother of Jesus, not just of his humanity. Such a title originally referred more to Jesus than to Mary. Only as the cult of the Virgin developed did it become a focus for further reflection upon the figure of Mary.[19]

32. Suffered under Pontius Pilate

Although no doctrine arises out of this phrase, the mention of Pontius Pilate locates Jesus concretely in human history. Christianity is not a philosophy; it is not simply a wisdom however divine that guides our life. It centers around a concrete human life lived in history. Pontius Pilate occupied a public position. We can date his governorship. That dating pinpoints the moment of our salvation in Jesus' death on the cross. Christians believe that the gift of wholeness and salvation was won through Jesus' obedience to God in accepting death on the cross.[20]

Without this event there would be no reconciliation, no offer of new life, no possibility of beatitude. The life of Jesus utterly changes creation. For this reason Christians reckon time before or after Jesus.

Jesus' suffering is crucial to understanding his mission. Christianity reveals a path through suffering leading to glory. Suffering is not automatically redemptive: many are simply crushed by its weight. But it need not be so. Jesus confronts suffering at its most extreme—death. His life is lived toward his death. And his death has become almost more significant than his life. For his suffering and death, in obedience to God, reveals to all creation the glory of God's reign. Joined to Jesus in his death we have hope of sharing in his resurrection.[21]

Jesus' confrontation with suffering provides a model for his followers. We do not avoid suffering or evil. Rather we confront it in the name of Jesus. In him is the power to overcome suffering and death and usher in God's reign.

---

19. Truth 41
20. Phil 2:8
21. Rom 6:5

33. Was Crucified, Died, and Was Buried

The Cross

The **cross**, the instrument of Jesus' death, has become the central Christian symbol.[22] From a fearful vehicle of torture it has become the Christian's glory and hope. In the cross opposites are united: up and down, right and left, heaven and earth, east and west. Jesus' crucifixion reconciles God and humanity.

The cross is a sign of contradiction as it reaches out in opposite directions. It divides at the same time that it unites. And the cross is always a stumbling block.[23] The cross prevents Christianity from becoming a philosophy. It anchors Christianity in history—it is an actual event, not a doctrine. Here God was at work reconciling creation to himself.[24]

And the cross remains the great stumbling block. It forces us to admit we are saved, made whole, not by anything we have done but by what Jesus has done. It forces us to swallow what was blasphemy to the Jews—that God took flesh in a specific human being. And it makes us wrestle with what was folly to the Greek rational mind—this God does the unthinkable: God dies. Christians believe both the blasphemy and the folly. But we regard it as the profound wisdom of God and the glory of humanity.

Jesus' Obedience

A Christian sees human history in all its glory. Human thought, culture and accomplishment are a source of wonder. But there is an underside: pride and selfishness lead to acts of evil and atrocity that balance the good. A wondrous and fearful being is humanity.

Christianity speaks of our penchant for evil as disobedience. If the law[25] reveals the innermost workings of the creation—the way that reality truly is created to be—then humanity often unconsciously and sometimes consciously chooses to swim against the current. Indeed we are incapable of swimming for long with the current. And the source of this incapacity is our attempt to define ourself as a law unto our self and to believe that everything including our own fulfillment lies within our power.

---

22. Way 8
23. 1 Cor 1:23
24. 2 Cor 5:19
25. Truth 5

Thus we attempt to fix things and ourselves. We feel that with good will and effort the problems of life and the world can be solved. But this is pride,[26] stemming from a basic choice to think of ourselves as the center rather than as creatures dependent upon God and looking to him for guidance and the grace to evolve toward wholeness.

Jesus' death manifests a total obedience toward God. He does not choose death himself: it is part of God's plan for his life and ministry.[27] He would prefer to avoid his confrontation with death. But he is faithful. And his obedience becomes the model for all. Death does not destroy him, but God instead raises him up to the height.[28] By accepting him as our Model, Teacher and Savior, we are seen by God not as we are in our sinful fragmented rebellious nature, but in the light of Christ into whom we are incorporated.[29]

Jesus' suffering, crucifixion, death and burial blaze a path through death, revealing it not as the end, but as a new beginning. This great action provides a metaphor for confronting and going through every death. The sting of death—that threat which prevents our really ever living is removed. Only a Christian could perceive the supreme irony as the poet John Donne did: "And you, poor death, shall die."

Through his obedience unto death Jesus reconciles God and humanity. Through our disobedience we have fallen into sin. This willful choice now warps our nature—it is part of our human inheritance. And this fundamental disobedience, this refusal to be part of creation, this demand to be like God, has poisoned our relationship not only to God but toward creation itself. Our relationship to nature and creation is largely a history of rape rather than stewardship.[30] Our disobedience threatens the universe. We already have the capacity to annihilate all life on our planet. What might we threaten when we travel to the stars?

This disobedience has now become part of our nature. It cannot be cured by us. Only a free action of God could put things right again. In Jesus God comes into the world to reconcile us to himself and to creation itself. This is the meaning of the **atonement.** Jesus makes us one with God again. It does not mean that Jesus atones to an angry God— paying off some debt; such is a common perversion of the doctrine. Rather Jesus restores harmony. And through his obedience he wins the power to enable us in him to be transformed so that we may become truly whole and healthy.

---

26. Truth 59
27. Mt 26:39
28. Phil 2:9
29. Truth 76
30. Truth 52

34. He Descended into Hell

This phrase, not in the original formulation of the Apostles' Creed, was added early in Christian history. Jesus' action of salvation penetrates to the very core of the universe. "He descended into hell"—the nether regions, the kingdom of the dead.

A myth speaks of Jesus' cross being at the very navel of the world. Golgotha means the place of the skull.[31] And Christians believed that the skull was Adam's—the first man, the father of the race.[32] The center of the world is the point of connection with the underworld where the spirits of the dead were thought to dwell in many ancient cosmologies. Thus Jesus slid down the cross pole to enter the underworld. There he confronted Satan who had won power over creation through his successful temptation of Adam and Eve into sin.[33] And with his cross now grasped as a sword, Jesus frees those enslaved and leads them into paradise.

Jesus' work is not limited to those who come after him. Instead that work spreads out in both time and place to reconcile the entire creation. Jesus through his death on the cross has already reconciled all creation to God. We are not saved when we come to accept Jesus as our Savior. At that point we realize our salvation. And from that point, following Jesus, we discover how this reconciliation and wholeness already bestowed in Jesus' death and resurrection might be actualized.

35. The Third Day He Rose Again from the Dead

In response to Jesus' fidelity God did not allow him to be destroyed, but raised him from the dead. **Resurrection** is not resuscitation of a corpse, but life in a new dimension. It belongs to the new creation which Jesus inaugurates. The material body is transformed—glorified—a term describing the presence of God.

The resurrection is the event of central significance for Christians. It gives validity to all that Jesus said and did. Jesus reinterpreted the experience of Israel and claimed his interpretation as true against conflicting views of the Pharisees and scribes. His teachings were rejected by the religious establishment and he was put to death. Had there been no resurrection we might wonder whether he had been deceived in his

---

31. Mt 27:33
32. Gen 2:4ff
33. Gen 3

basic convictions. That God raised him from the dead gives authority to Jesus.

Second, the resurrection is the final development of Jesus' person. All of his life and teachings comes to be seen by Christians as leading to his vindication through resurrection. Through his resurrection he comes to possess that personhood which was being fashioned all through his life by God's gifts and his own faithful response. The story of Jesus' life is not a pre-written script which he merely follows like an actor. Like all human beings he creates his life through his struggles, decisions, and responses to people and events. His resurrection is won through his obedience to God, even in the face of death on a cross. By his faithfulness, witnessed by God's raising him up, he becomes the Savior.

Third, the resurrection is a transition into a new mode of existence. Formerly, Jesus like all human beings was enfleshed as an individual. In this state he was bound as we are to concrete limitations of time and space. Now Jesus continues to live embodied in the community of believers; he is able to be present now to persons everywhere. He is among us, present in Spirit, word and sacrament. The resurrection signifies a transition from individual historical existence to a new spiritual presence in a community of persons.

Finally, Jesus' death and resurrection proclaims God's response to the eternal riddle of existence. Why do we suffer and die? How are we to live in the face of death? The resurrection is not simply an event that happens to Jesus, but a promise of what will happen to each individual. Jesus' story becomes the story in terms of which Christians understand and live their lives. Our own suffering and death is not final, but rather a passage from death to life as seen in Jesus' passion and resurrection. The resurrection provides a glimpse of our final destiny. Jesus is the first fruits of this new creation,[34] but, joined to him, we will share in those fruits and be transformed as he is.

Although the fullness of resurrection will not be ours until the coming of the kingdom, its power is present now. In becoming Christians we share in Jesus' resurrection. The final glory streams even now into our fragmented world. Through that grace poured out we are transformed and share in Jesus' mission to cooperate with God's reign already appearing.

---

34. 1 Cor 15:23

36. He Ascended into Heaven, Sits at the Right Hand of God the Father Almighty

Even more than in the resurrection, figurative language describes the ascension. This language comes from the Old Testament passages[35] used in the enthronement liturgy.

The ascension speaks of the completion of Jesus' ministry. After his resurrection he instructed his disciples in the fullness of his mission.[36] Then he sent them forth while he returned to his Father.[37]

His mission, teaching, his very presence on earth today take place not in his human body, but in his followers. The ascension, as John sees it, is the necessary prelude to the sending of the Holy Spirit.[38] Only through the Spirit would Jesus' mission transcend space and time. Limited to one body, he would be limited in space—in what distance the message could cover—and in time—all bodies are subject to death. But through his followers, inspired with his Spirit, the message spreads to the corners of the earth, and echoes down the corridors of time.

As we believe that Jesus comes from the Father, so after his ministry he returns to the Father where he receives the favored place. Again this imagery is not literal: it metaphorically describes the completion of Jesus' mission. Sitting at God's right hand means that Jesus has been made Lord of all the creation. He does not cease being fully human, however, and so we now have an intercessor, a friend, an intermediary with God.[39]

37. From There He Shall Come to Judge the Living and the Dead

That the imminent return of Christ in glory to inaugurate the reign of God has not yet occurred does not imply that Christians do not still wait in hope for this great day of the Lord known as the **second coming**. In the resurrection the new age has already dawned. The resurrection is a foretaste of the kingdom. But until the final passing of this world, we are commissioned to bring the message and the reality of the good news to our brothers and sisters.

This world is not our final resting place. Here we can never ex-

---

35. Ps 24:7–10, etc.
36. Acts 1:2–8
37. Acts 1:9–11
38. Jn 16:7
39. 1 Tim 2:5

perience the fullness of God's reign. So Christians even today, twenty centuries later, look forward to the coming judgment, when Christ will come again in glory to judge the living and the dead, inaugurating the kingdom in glory and power. This event is known as the *parousia*.

The early Church was filled with expectation for the coming of Christ.[40] Their prayer was "Maranatha—Come, Lord."[41] Outcasts from their world, they had nothing to lose and everything to hope for in the Lord's coming. Often today Christians have lost that early enthusiasm. We are tempted to make our peace with the world. At times Christians have dreamed of Christ's kingdom somehow coming in this world: they spoke of the Holy Roman Empire, or of Christendom. But that is a false hope.

Further, for many Christians the idea of the **last judgment** has become fearful, a thing of terror. Yet it should inspire us with confidence. For Christ's judgment will exhibit a love that is more than mere justice. That judgment will separate out the evil of this world and redeem what is of God and shines forth with God's love.

The basis of Christ's judgment will be love itself. How have we turned toward love? How has that love been manifested in our relations with others? To what extent have we been transformed in the radiance of love? Damnation is a turning from, a rejection of love. Its effects are not felt in the afterlife in some hell—it is first experienced in the very hell which selfishness creates in this life.

We may fear the judgment because we are not transformed sufficiently. We are sinful, caught in bonds of selfishness, blinded to the truth. But the judgment is also a discernment. What is quick—lifegiving—will be raised up into God's kingdom, whereas what is dead will be left behind, to be burned on the garbage dump of Gehenna.

Yes the judgment provokes a crisis. We can extinguish the light of God's love within us. It is possible to be damned not because of broken rules, but because we have hardened our hearts, denying love access, sealing ourselves up from God and our fellow creatures. This is damnation—not any falling short of perfection.

The final judgment ushers in the kingdom of God, the wedding feast of the Lamb,[42] the new creation. And this reality, as opposed to the present age, will never end.

---

40. 1 Thes 4:13—5:11
41. 1 Cor 16:22
42. Rev 21

TO DEEPEN—

What does the incarnation say about who Jesus is?

How does this part of the Creed summarize the story of Jesus?

In what way is Jesus' death seen as an atonement?

Compare the shape of the Gospel story with the Creed. How does the Creed help a Christian to read the Gospel accurately?

Further Reading:

Anselm of Canterbury. *Why God Became Man.* Magi Press, 1969.

Cook, Michael L. *Jesus of Faith. A Study of Christology.* Paulist Press, 1986.

Galot, Jean. *Who is Christ? A Theology of the Incarnation.* Franciscan Herald, 1981.

Kasper, Walter. *Jesus the Christ.* Paulist Press, 1977.

Kelsey, Morton. *Resurrection: Release from Oppression.* Paulist Press, 1985.

O'Collins, Gerald. *What Are They Saying About Jesus?* Paulist Press, 1982.

O'Collins, Gerald. *What Are They Saying About the Resurrection?* Paulist Press, 1978.

Sloyan, Gerald. *The Jesus Tradition: Images of Jesus in the West.* Twenty Third, 1986.

White, Leland. *Christ and the Christian Movement: Jesus in the New Testament, the Creeds and Modern Theology.* Alba House, 1985.

Williams, H. A. *True Resurrection.* Harper & Row, 1972.

Wilson-Kastner, Patricia. *Faith, Feminism and the Christ.* Fortress, 1983.

TO CONTINUE—

If you have not already done so, you should explore the sources of Christian faith in Jesus in the Gospels (Truth 15ff).

Christians enter into the experience which the Creed articulates in the liturgy (Way 9ff).

The Creed supports the Christian's way of life (Way 47ff).

THE CREED: HOLY SPIRIT
38. I BELIEVE IN THE HOLY SPIRIT

The Holy Spirit is the third person of the Trinity.[1] The Spirit is generated by the love between the Father and the Son. The Spirit dwells within Christians transforming them into the likeness of God.

---

1. Truth 27

Symbols and Images

Many images offer insight into the mysterious realm of the Spirit. The Holy Spirit is imaged as **breath**—in the beginning God breathed upon the waters, drawing forth the creation.[2] God breathed into Adam, bringing him to life.[3] The Holy Spirit is the vivifying breath of God. The Holy Spirit sustains all creation in being. Should God remove the Spirit from anything created it would cease to exist. The Holy Spirit is the very foundation of our being—as basic as breath.

The Spirit is pictured as a **dove** descending over Jesus after his baptism.[4] After the flood this bird of peace brought back an olive branch showing Noah that the waters had receded.[5] The Spirit brings us God's peace—that peace which only comes through being brought home to our source in God. And the oil of the olive becomes a sacramental symbol of the Holy Spirit and the gift of peace.

But quiet and gentleness do not always signify the Holy Spirit. The Spirit is in the **gale** and the **wind** as well. The Spirit is the power of God—the only true power. The Spirit builds up creation, sanctifies it, and brings it home to the Father. The Spirit levels all that stands opposed to God and the truth—it is indeed a gale wind. And that wind purifies as it blows—cleansing the creation and preparing it for its redemption. And like the wind the Spirit blows where it will.[6] It cannot be imprisoned; free like the wind, it will not be contained within any narrow word, institution or idea. The Spirit frees and liberates from all oppression and tyranny—even that imposed in the name of God.

Finally the Holy Spirit is **fire** or **tongues of flame** such as descended upon the apostles' heads at Pentecost.[7] This flame sets the creation on fire with the power of God. By its power the apostles do what they could not do before: Peter remains steadfast; Peter and John heal in Jesus' name.[8] And these men carry the Gospel message to the ends of the earth. The Spirit's flame purifies, burning out the dross.

---

2. Gen 1:2b
3. Gen 2:7
4. Mk 1:10
5. Gen 8:11
6. Jn 3:8
7. Acts 2:3
8. Acts 3:1–10

The Domain of the Holy Spirit

In Creation

The Holy Spirit is universally encountered in creation. The creation is brought into being by the Spirit's power. The Spirit breathing in the creation sustains all in being. The aspect of God encountered shining forth from the created realm is the Holy Spirit—and that Spirit reveals God to all who are open.

But if the Spirit dwells at the heart of creation, bringing all back to the Father, our knowledge of the Spirit is still not clear. For the creation is tragically flawed—fallen from its original blessedness.[9] Ignorance and sin cloud our perception of truth and prevent us from doing the good. The Spirit is all too often misunderstood or misappropriated.

Indeed it is possible to sin against the Holy Spirit—against life itself.[10] For this sin alone forgiveness is not possible because as long as we sin against the Spirit we pit ourselves against love itself. God cannot touch us since we have sealed God and everything else out.

In the Religions of Humanity

The Spirit knows no boundaries. And it is not rationed by God.[11] Thus no one group, Christian or Jew, has a monopoly upon the Holy Spirit.

The Holy Spirit at the heart of creation draws all home to the Father.[12] Thus all aspirations for that homecoming as witnessed throughout human religions are the work of the Spirit. Whatever in these traditions proclaims the truth is the work of the Holy Spirit. Thus truths in other faiths can complement and enrich the Christian faith. And Christians have much to contribute to other faiths.

The works and glories of the Spirit are infinite. And they are not contained by or reserved for any one person or group. Whatever is true, good, beautiful, and one is of God and inspired by the Holy Spirit—the love of the Father and Son who brings the immense diversity of creation, alienated and separated by sin, into unity. But this unity does not destroy the diversity. Rather it preserves and shows forth the magnificence of God's riches.

---

9. Truth 57
10. Lk 12:10
11. Jn 3:34
12. Rom 8:23

In Israel

The history of Israel more clearly reveals the Holy Spirit. There the Spirit works in human **history**—liberating those enslaved, revealing the law of God, dwelling among the poor. On leaving Egypt Israel is led by a pillar of cloud by day, of fire by night[13]—again symbolism of the Holy Spirit.

Israel's history is sacred history because it is inspired by the Holy Spirit—in these deeds and actions, and in the men and women who mediate God's word to Israel. The **prophet** speaks God's word, consoling the oppressed and challenging institutions. God calls the prophet, conferring the Spirit's power to prophesy to Israel. Isaiah's mouth is purified by a fiery coal[14]—another symbol of the Spirit.

The Spirit is God's **wisdom**—the essence of the law. Meditating upon God's law, one comes to truth in this confusing and sinful world. The wisdom of God is the foundation of creation; it is the beauty of creation seen as the firstborn daughter of God.[15] The Holy Spirit has a feminine dimension stemming from "ruach" and "sophia," feminine in Hebrew and Greek.

In Christianity

Jesus is conceived by the Holy Spirit which as a cloud of glory overshadows Mary.[16] The Spirit inspires Jesus in his mission: calling him at his baptism,[17] sustaining him during his testing in the wilderness.[18]

Jesus tells his disciples that he must return to the Father to prepare for the **sending of the Holy Spirit** to guide them in the truth.[19] Thus the Spirit which inspired Jesus now dwells in his community and guides us in fulfilling Jesus' mission.[20]

John's Gospel calls the Holy Spirit the **Paraclete**—the advocate of Christians in their mission to proclaim the Gospel. The Paraclete is our guide and counselor, our helper and comforter, our advocate and defender. Christians should not grieve that Jesus is no longer physically present. His indwelling Spirit enables us to carry on Jesus' ministry if we only have trust and confidence.

---

13. Num 14:14
14. Is 6:6–7
15. Prov 8:22–31
16. Lk 1:35
17. Mt 3:17
18. Lk 4:1–2
19. Jn 14:26
20. Acts 4:31

Today the Christian Church is the key domain of the Spirit. The Holy Spirit **inspired**[21] the authors of sacred Scripture and led the Church in the formation and selection of the scriptural canon.[22] The Spirit preserves the Church in truth, making it **infallible**.[23] The Spirit **sanctifies**[24] Christians, making them saints. The Spirit works in the entire creation, in all creatures, in history, in religions, drawing all into unity.

In all its actions the Church **invokes** the power of the Holy Spirit. Before reading Scripture Christians pray that the Holy Spirit reveal its truth.[25] And in the sacraments[26] the Church prays God to send the Holy Spirit to bless the elements and to quicken them for our salvation. In no time or rite does the Church not call upon the Holy Spirit to be present to guide it.

TO DEEPEN—

What are some of the primary images of the Holy Spirit?

What is inspiration? Sanctification? Invocation?

Where is the Holy Spirit manifested?

Is the Holy Spirit found outside the Christian Church?

Further Reading:

Congar, Yves. *I Believe in the Holy Spirit*. (3 vols.) Seabury, 1983.
DeCelles, Charles. *The Unbound Spirit—God's Universal, Sanctifying Work.* Alba House, 1985.
DeValle, Francisa. *About the Holy Spirit*. Lumen Christi.
Ford, Francis X. *Come, Holy Spirit*. Orbis, 1976.
Massabli, Charles. *Who is the Holy Spirit?* Alba House, 1979.
Montague, George T. *Holy Spirit: Growth of a Biblical Tradition*. Paulist Press, 1976.
Swift, Mary Grace, ed. *With Bright Wings. A Book of the Spirit.* Paulist Press, 1976. A collection of the writings of theologians and poets on the Spirit.

---

21. Truth 3
22. Truth 3
23. Truth 22
24. Way 46
25. Way 6
26. Truth 74

TO CONTINUE—

The works of the Spirit are found in Way 37.

The history of the Spirit is found first in Israel's history (Truth 4-13) and subsequently in the Church's history (Life 29-37) as well as in other traditions (Life 23-28).

Life in the Spirit fills in concrete details of the Christian spiritual path (Life 1-13).

THE CREED: THE CHURCH
39. THE HOLY CATHOLIC CHURCH

The Greek word for Church, "Ekklesia," makes clear its original meaning: those "called out" of society to form a new community. The Church is the society of those called by Jesus Christ. Consequent upon following Jesus, the disciple is baptized in his name: thus the Church is the community of those baptized.

The Second Vatican Council focused primarily upon the Church itself. Two key documents speak first of the Church renewing Catholic understanding, and then of the Church's relationship to the modern world. Other documents (such as that on the liturgy) actually reform and renew the life of the Church. Our exploration begins with the Council's Constitution on the Church.

The Church in Salvation History

The eternal Father, in accordance with the utterly gratuitous and mysterious design of his wisdom and goodness, created the whole universe, and chose to raise up people to share in his own divine life; and when they had fallen in Adam, he did not abandon them, but at all times held out to them the means of salvation, bestowed in consideration of Christ, the Redeemer, "who is the image of the invisible God, the firstborn of every creature" and predestined before time began "to become conformed to the image of his Son, that he should be the firstborn among many brethren."[1] He determined to call together in a holy Church those who should believe in Christ. Already present in the figure at the beginning of the world,

---

1. Rom 8:29

this Church was prepared in marvelous fashion in the history of the people of Israel and in the old alliance. Established in this last age of the world, and made manifest in the outpouring of the Spirit, it will be brought to glorious completion at the end of time. At that moment, as the Fathers put it, all the just from the time of Adam, "from Abel, the just one, to the last of the elect," will be gathered together with the Father in the universal Church.

The Presence of Christ in the Church

The one mediator, Christ, established and ever sustains here on earth his holy Church, the community of faith, hope and charity, as a visible organization through which he communicates truth and grace to all people. But the society structured with hierarchical organs and the mystical body of Christ, the visible society and the spiritual community, the earthly Church and the Church endowed with heavenly riches, are not to be thought of as two realities. On the contrary, they form one complex reality which comes together from a human and a divine element. For this reason the Church is compared, not without significance, to the mystery of the incarnate Word.[2] As the assumed nature, inseparably united to him, serves the divine Word as a living organ of salvation, so, in a somewhat similar way, does the social structure of the Church serve the Spirit of Christ who vivifies it, in the building up of the body.[3]

This is the sole Church of Christ which in the Nicene Creed we profess to be one,[4] holy, catholic and apostolic, which our Savior, after his resurrection, entrusted to Peter's pastoral care,[5] commissioning him and the other apostles to extend and rule it,[6] and which he raised up for all ages as "the pillar and mainstay of the truth."[7] This Church, constituted

2. Truth 29
3. Cf. Eph 4:15
4. Truth 40
5. Jn 21:17
6. Cf. Mt 28:18
7. 1 Tim 3:15

and organized as a society in the present world, subsists in the Catholic Church, which is governed by the successor of Peter and by the bishops in communion with him. Nevertheless, many elements of sanctification and of truth are found outside its visible confines. Since these are gifts belonging to the Church of Christ, they are forces impelling toward Catholic unity.

The Mission of the Church

Just as Christ carried out the work of redemption in poverty and oppression, so the Church is called to follow the same path if it is to communicate the fruits of salvation to people. Christ Jesus, "though he was by nature God . . . emptied himself, taking the nature of a slave,"[8] and "being rich, became poor"[9] for our sake. Likewise, the church, although it needs human resources to carry out its mission, is not set up to seek earthly glory, but to proclaim, and this by its own example, humility and self-denial. Christ was sent by the Father "to bring[10] good news to the poor . . . to heal the contrite of heart," "to seek and save what was lost."[11] Similarly, the Church encompasses with its love all those who are afflicted by human misery, and it recognizes in those who are poor and who suffer the image of its poor and suffering founder. It does all in its power to relieve their need and in them it strives to serve Christ. Christ, "holy, innocent and undefiled,"[12] knew nothing of sin,[13] but came only to expiate the sins of the people.[14] The Church, always in need of purification, follows constantly the path of penance and renewal.

---

8. Phil 2:6–7
9. 2 Cor 8–9
10. Lk 4:18
11. Lk 19:10
12. Heb 7:26
13. 2 Cor 5:21
14. Cf. Heb 2:17

The Pilgrim Church

> The Church, "like a stranger in a foreign land, presses forward amid the persecutions of the world and the consolations of God,"[15] announcing the cross and death of the Lord until he comes.[16] But by the power of the risen Lord it is given strength to overcome, in patience and in love, its sorrows and its difficulties, both those that are from within and those that are from without, so that it may reveal in the world, faithfully, however darkly, the mystery of its Lord until, in the consummation, it shall be manifested in full light.[17]

40. The Four Marks

Christians identify Christ's Church as having four marks: it is one, holy, catholic and apostolic. These marks, affirmed in the Nicene Creed and elsewhere, are acknowledged by all churches which cling to that central Creed.

First the Church is **one**. There is one Christ and he delivered one teaching, baptized with one baptism and sent one Holy Spirit.[18] Thus the community established by Jesus Christ is one. This mark is hard to recognize in the face of a Christianity split into many conflicting and competing communities. Yet the divisions are due not to different teachings of Christ but to human sin and ignorance. And their healing, through the charity of Christ, remains a priority of Christians.

Yet in spite of the divisions, Christians profess that the true Church maintains the unity of Christ. For Roman Catholics this unity is symbolized by communion with the Pope, the bishop of Rome, successor of Peter the head of the apostles.[19] Throughout Christian history the Pope acts as a sign of unity above all local variants in doctrine and practice. And today the papacy figures in any realistic attempt at Christian unity. The office itself may and has already changed over the course of time. It need not be exercised as it is today or has been in the past. But the Pope is the central figure of any united Christendom. And Roman Catholics believe that being in communion with this central figure they

---

15. Augustine
16. Cf. 1 Cor 11:26
17. Constitution on the Church 2, 8
18. Eph 4:4–5
19. Mt 16:18

are in communion with the one true Church of Christ throughout history and on earth today.

How Christian unity is maintained has varied throughout our history. At times the Church has clung to a unity that has imposed a common liturgical language upon all. Today a large measure of diversity is again seen as consonant with our unity. Augustine said that Christians should manifest unity in the essentials, diversity in all other things, and charity in everything.

The Church's second mark is **holiness**. Although composed of and governed by sinners, it is nevertheless holy, for it is Christ's body on earth. Its holiness is not its own or that of its members, but the holiness of Christ who purifies it, when necessary castigates it, and perfects it in all its members. And in spite of a sinful membership at all times, the Church's testimony to holiness and sanctity is great. In every age Christians, allowing the Spirit to work in them, provide examples of the sanctity possible to those who trust in Christ. The Church's saints, throughout the ages, across the globe, and in our midst today, attest to its holiness.[20]

The third mark is **catholicity**—a Greek word meaning "universality." The Church is not restricted to one group or time. Jesus' call extends to everyone. The Church encompasses Gentile and Jew, male and female, white, yellow, red and black, Easterner and Westerner, rich and poor, nobles and outcasts.[21]

Catholicity results in the great diversity of the Church. If religions search for God, then Christ is God's response to our quest. That response is not a religion in itself—it is rather the Gospel.[22] Christianity forms when the Gospel encounters our quest and responds by providing through our religious structures access to and unity with God.

Thus the first preaching of the Gospel was addressed to Israel in terms of her experience of God. This preaching remains normative, but Christianity became a much different religion. Western Christianity is the Gospel response to Greco-Roman culture and then to the cultures of Northern Europe. This form should not be considered normative for all peoples.

Today the catholicity of Roman Christianity is again manifesting itself in Africa and Asia. New forms and customs are arising as the Gospel reveals the fullness of the truth to these people. This Gospel then inspires the adaptation of customs and traditions—their way of wor-

---

20. Life 46
21. Gal 3:28
22. Intro 3

shiping God—leavened by the Gospel and enlightened by the sacraments. Nothing of the essence of Christ is lost in this great catholic variety. Indeed only through an extension of this mark to all peoples will the full extent of Christ's richness be revealed. For other cultures and traditions uncover riches neglected in our own.

Apostolicity is the final mark. The Church begins as Jesus calls certain people to become apostles. To them he entrusts his teaching and mission—sending them to the ends of the earth to proclaim the good news.[23] The Church is apostolic because it can trace its lineage back to those apostles. There is a continuous line of teaching—and it is the same today as then.

Apostolicity is symbolized within the Church in the ordination of bishops. The key gesture is the laying on of hands. The ordaining bishop and other bishops in attendance place their hands on the head of the candidate, thus passing on the power of office. Any bishop should be able to trace his lineage back to the apostles.

Apostolicity means that the faith professed is identical in essence with that of the apostles. While many elements are due to the Church's christening of local customs as a mark of catholicity, the essence of the faith is crucial. The Gospel alone gives life, having the power to convert us to God's reign. Thus that Gospel cannot be allowed to be perverted or corrupted. The proof that such is not the case lies in the Church's fidelity to the Creed and Scriptures. And that fidelity is affirmed in the bishop's conformity to the teaching of the apostles, and by his ordination in their lineage.

41. Images of the Church

Pilgrim People of God

The Second Vatican Council renewed understanding of the Church through the use of certain traditional images not prominent in recent history. The Church is the **pilgrim people of God**: a society whom God has chosen for his work in the world. It has been given the Gospel and it journeys through history with its eyes set on the coming kingdom. It is in history with a mission—to represent Christ to the world. It is not perfect. It does not have all the answers. It is on pilgrimage. It has no fixed abode, no resting place in this world. And on pilgrimage it encounters people and events which change it; its medi-

---

23. Mt 28:19–20

tation upon the Gospel grows in wisdom and insight. And it is transformed by Christ's light which it carries and clings to.

The Church is the **body of Christ**, or, as it is sometimes called, the mystical body of Christ. Jesus Christ is present upon earth today in his Church. There his Gospel is preached, his sacraments administered, his values enfleshed.

Paul provided this image.[24] We are all part of this body of Christ—and we have different roles and missions dependent upon our talents and resources, and dependent upon our call. This body has a structure as do all bodies. The head does not act in the same way that the eye does. But together all who are part of the Church represent Christ to one another and to the world.

The Pauline literature also speaks of the **bride of Christ**.[25] This continues the imagery of Israel as a woman and bride.[26] The Church is feminine in relation to God who is masculine. Each Christian—male or female—is receptive rather than initiating toward God. Christ came and won us as bride. He loved us so much that he died to win us. And we respond to this love as a bride responds to her husband. This image has flowered in meditation upon the love metaphor in the Song of Songs, and in the great mystical tradition of John of the Cross and Teresa of Avila where the goal is mystical marriage.[27]

The New Israel

These images reveal the meaning of Church. Its story actually begins long before Christianity. God first calls a person in Abraham.[28] Abraham's faith and trust in God's call makes him father of all the faithful in our tradition. Then God calls Israel out of slavery to become God's people.[29] Israel becomes God's sign to all nations. She is God's beloved spouse. Even in her infidelity God cannot abandon her but remains faithful.[30]

The Church as the new Israel is the continuation of God's chosen people. Jesus calls beyond the boundaries of Israel to all who would follow him. He is the perfect embodiment of Israel: where she is faithless he is faithful; where she is tempted and falls, he remains steadfast.[31]

---

24. 1 Cor 12:27
25. Eph 5:25
26. Is 62:5
27. Life 8
28. Gen 12:1–9
29. Ex 20:1
30. Hos 1:2–9
31. Mt 4:1–11

Israel is brought to fulfillment in Jesus and passed on now as a rich heritage for his followers.

The old Israel is not rejected. Her failure to accept Jesus as Messiah is a profound mystery.[32] Israel is still God's chosen people. But the new action inaugurated in Jesus is mediated by the new Israel—the Church, the current sign to the nations of God's steadfast love and fidelity.

Israel is often represented in the Hebrew Scriptures as a woman: the **daughter of Jerusalem**,[33] the **rose of Sharon**,[34] the **wife of Hosea**.[35] Luke sees Mary as the culmination of Israel herself—the bride prepared for her husband, totally faithful and trusting in God.[36] Continuing this reflection the Church applies the images of Israel to Mary. She is the image of Israel as seen in the eyes of God her beloved. This identification begins in Scripture itself.

Mary, Mother of the Church

The Second Vatican Council bestowed upon Mary the title "**Mother of the Church**" and understood Mary primarily as a symbol for the Church. Conversely, the Church is to be seen under the image of Mary. Thus while our imagery of God is heavily masculine, the imagery of the Church is primarily feminine and includes the entire Marian imagery.

The first image, **Lady Wisdom**, develops in the wisdom tradition.[37] Wisdom represents God's primal plan for creation. She symbolizes God's love for creation. She is the creation unsullied by sin and unperverted by disobedience. Wisdom gathers her children around her and prepares her table.[38] The Church is community: holy, sacred, and of God. In our world fragmented by sin community is often impossible, or exists only weakly. Yet God intends creation to be an expression of real community—of diversity in unity—and of the joy which such community brings. The imagery of Lady Wisdom preparing a meal for her children flowers in the Christian community gathered as children of God around the table of the Eucharist.

The second great image of the feminine is **Eve**.[39] St. Irenaeus, the

---

32. Rom 9–11
33. Is 51:17—52:2
34. Song 2:1
35. Hos 1:2–9
36. Lk 1:26–38
37. Truth 13
38. Prov 9:1–6
39. Gen 2:21ff

great Church Father, completed Paul's analogy. Paul compared Christ to Adam and spoke of Christ as the second Adam who through obedience restores us to God.[40] Irenaeus speaks of Mary as the second Eve. Whereas Eve disobeyed God in eating of the fruit, Mary assents to God's will and turns things around. Irenaeus puns on Eve's Latin name: Eva. In Mary, "Eva" becomes an "Ave"—the Latin word beginning the angel's salutation: Hail, Mary.[41] As Eve is the mother of all the living, Mary becomes the mother of the new creation in Christ—again the Church as mother.

In the figure of Mary as developed in Catholicism we can now glimpse the meaning of the Church. Through her fidelity to God in her assent to the annunciation Mary gives birth to Christ.[42] She is first of all the faithful **daughter of God**—this quality prepares her for her great role. Then Mary is the **bride of the Holy Spirit** just as the Church is bride. The Church, like Mary, through trust in God constantly gives birth to Christ. And as Mary was the **mother of Jesus**, so the Church is mother to all Christians, teaching, nourishing, correcting, and helping us to grow in the Lord.

Two doctrines have been officially defined concerning Mary in the Roman Catholic tradition: the **immaculate conception** and the assumption. These too aid deeper understanding of the Church. Mary, because of her role in our salvation, was preserved from all sin from the moment of her conception. This was accomplished not through her own merit but by anticipation of the redemption Christ would accomplish. So the Church in its nature is preserved from all sin. While all of her members are sinners and sinful, the Church itself is preserved from sin not by our accomplishments but through the power of Christ.

The celebration of the **assumption** of Mary dates from the third century although only defined as dogma in 1950. Mary, on her death, was assumed body and spirit into heaven. We glimpse in Mary the hope of our own final end. On the day of the Lord we shall all be resurrected, body and spirit. God will gather up what has been scattered and all shall be transformed and brought into God's kingdom. Thus the assumption is a way of speaking about the destiny of the Church. We may hope that nothing will be lost, but that all of God's beloved creation—symbolized in the figure of Mary—will be brought home to the Father.

---

40. 1 Cor 15:22
41. Lk 1:28
42. Lk 1:26–38

What are the four marks of the Church and what do they mean?

Why is the Church important?

Is it possible to be a Christian without being a member of the Church?

What are some of the key biblical images of the Church?

How did the Second Vatican Council see Mary?

What do the Marian doctrines tell us about the Church?

Prayer: The Hail Mary

Hail, Mary, full of grace, the Lord is with thee. Blessed art thou among women and blessed is the fruit of thy womb, Jesus. Holy Mary, Mother of God, pray for us sinners now and at the hour of our death.

Further Reading:

Brown, Raymond et al., eds. *Mary in the New Testament: A Collaborative Assessment by Protestant and Roman Catholic Scholars.* Fortress Press and Paulist Press, 1978.

Buby, Bertrand. *Mary, The Faithful Disciple*, Paulist Press, 1985.

Buhlmann, Walbert. *The Coming of the Third Church.* Orbis, 1976.

Dulles, Avery. *Models of the Church.* Doubleday, 1974.

Greeley, Andrew. *The Mary Myth: On the Femininity of God.* Seabury Press, 1977.

Herr, William. *This Our Church.* Thomas More, 1986.

Küng, Hans. *The Church.* Doubleday, 1976.

Segundo, Juan. *The Community Called Church.* Orbis, 1973.

Tambasco, Anthony J. *What Are They Saying About Mary?* Paulist Press, 1984.

Thistlethwaite, Susan Brooks. *Metaphors for the Contemporary Church.* Pilgrim Press, 1983.

42. THE CREED: THE COMMUNION OF SAINTS

"Communion of saints" calls attention to the inner nature both of the Church and of the process of redemption. Neither Church nor Christian can be fully understood through any external description. At heart the Christian community is the gathering of God's saints. While not identical with the Church which includes all manner of people, including some who may be members in name only, this communion reveals the true nature of God's people.

Order and Charism

While order and structure are crucial for the establishment of any institution such as the Church, the inner spark of the communion of saints is the Holy Spirit who pours gifts upon the people for the furtherance of the Gospel. These gifts, known as charisms, have played a crucial role in the Church's history. While office is an institutional structure, charism cannot be legislated. The Spirit blows where it will.

Israel's history shows the balance and tension between charism and office. Office is the king and the priesthood, established by law with defined modes of operation. It provides order and continuity. Charism flowers in the prophets who receive a personal call from God. Their word is not their own but God's. It often challenges complacent or corrupt offices. The prophet calls Israel out of her ritualism and formalism, reminding her of the heart of the law when she is content with the mere letter. Often the prophet is the gadfly of conscience.

This natural tension does not suppose that office and charism are always at odds or that one excludes the other. Pope John XXIII was elected to fill an office. Yet John's charism called the Second Vatican Council and changed the Church profoundly.

With the coming of the Holy Spirit at Pentecost a new age begins. While before the Spirit was limited to a few, in the Christian community the Spirit's outpouring suffuses all. Although the official Church has been cautious and often fearful of the Spirit (for the very fact that it cannot be controlled) and although the charismatic is sometimes opposed by the authority of office, the Spirit's voice has leavened the Christian community greatly.

The tension is healthy. When the community veers toward an over-dependence upon office, it becomes stodgy and moribund. Order is defended at the expense of vitality. And when charisms gain the upper hand the vitality threatens to tear the group apart in sectarian quarreling. Truth is found in the middle—an order which grounds and provides stability and charism which allows the Spirit to inspire.

The tension is sometimes impossible to resolve at the time of crisis. Only with time is the charism tested. Christian history is filled with saints suspected and even persecuted by an office that later canonized them. The Church can do little to alleviate this conflict since there our salvation is worked out.

Kinds of Charism

The crucial text on the charisms is from St. Paul. The charisms are not given for our own glory, but to show forth the love of God and the glory of the coming kingdom through these special gifts.

> Now there are varieties of gifts, but the same Spirit; and there are varieties of service, but the same Lord; and there are varieties of working, but it is the same God who inspires them all in every one. To each is given the manifestation of the Spirit for the common good. To one is given through the Spirit the utterance of wisdom, and to another the utterance of knowledge according to the same Spirit, to another faith by the same Spirit, to another gifts of healing by the one Spirit, to another the working of miracles, to another prophecy, to another the ability to distinguish between spirits, to another various kinds of tongues, to another the interpretation of tongues. All these are inspired by one and the same Spirit, who apportions to each one individually as he wills.[1]

The Full Extent of the Church

The communion of saints also points to the full extent of the new community of which the Church is a part here and now. Through the Church we are joined not only to all Christians on earth today, but as well to those dead gathered to the Lord.

Thus Catholics honor those men and women proclaimed saints by the Church.[2] Having exhibited heroic sanctity they are models for others. We ask their prayers and aid on our journey, just as we would ask friends to pray and aid us. We are one with the Church's saints. We are also joined with those who, although dead, have not completed their conversion.[3] Our prayers help them complete their journey of purgation.

God seeks to gather all into unity. This unity does not obliterate individuality. Through unity in community individuals are made one in love.

---

1. 1 Cor 12:4–11
2. Life 46
3. Truth 44

TO DEEPEN—

What does the "communion of saints" tell us concerning the essential nature of the Church?

What is the difference between "office" and "charism"?

Is every Christian granted some kind of "charism"?

What charisms have you seen at work in the Christian community?

Further Reading:

Boff, Leonardo. *Church, Charism, Power.* Crossroad, 1986. One of the key texts of liberation theology.

Lohfink, Gerhard. *Jesus and Community, The Social Dimension of Christian Faith.* Paulist Press, 1985.

Rahner, Karl. *Shape of the Church to Come.* Crossroad, 1974.

TO CONTINUE—

The institutional aspects of Church are covered in Life 15ff.

The saints are treated in Life 46.

43. THE CREED: THE FORGIVENESS OF SINS

TO PREPARE—

Jesus' ministry of forgiveness of sins is discussed in Truth 18.

A clause devoted to "forgiveness of sins" shows its importance to Christian faith. Forgiveness lies at the very foundation of God's work in us. Jesus' ministry was characterized by forgiving and healing[1] as much or even more than his teaching.

A true encounter with Jesus Christ leads persons to become aware of their sin and alienation from God and from society. Our admission of sinfulness is the first effect of the process of redemption.

Jesus calls us into a new reality—God's reign. This kingdom prom-

---

1. Truth 18

250   Catholic Christianity

ises a new life eventually blossoming in a new creation. He calls people to embrace this new way of living now. The past is dead.[2] Leave it behind and begin again.

But we must first be freed from our past. Tied to our past and its consequences, we may find it impossible to begin this new life. So Jesus forgives our sins. Only from this new foundation of innocence will we be able to cooperate with God's grace.

Although sin is a fundamental Christian teaching and reality, the emphasis is rather upon God's forgiveness. Christianity uncovers the sinful nature of much human conduct not to plunge us into despair but to offer God's reconciliation which incorporates us into the kingdom.

A grave sin is an action resulting from a free decision of a person to go against the will of God as this is revealed in the creation, in grace and in revelation. Such acts kill the spirit. To be considered a mortal sin three conditions must be met.

True mortal sin involves some rejection of God. Modern moral theology speaks of a fundamental option—a basic commitment which orients our lives toward either self-centeredness or other-directedness. Christians try to act in accordance with the will of God as revealed through the commandments and the Church's moral teaching.[3] What if a person commits an objectively serious wrong but in so acting the person does not intend to reject God? To the extent that this is so, the action's seriousness is diminished.

Pastorally the person should be counseled to be enabled to acknowledge the truth of Catholic teaching and embrace that truth to the extent they are able. Catholicism has ethical rules but in discerning specific actions Christ's compassion and reconciliation take precedence over any legalism.

The person must know that the action is seriously sinful. Ignorant actions, causing serious problems and harm, are not regarded as mortally sinful for that person. Furthermore, if the person knows that this action is considered sinful by the Christian tradition, and yet cannot see it as sinful in conscience, sinfulness is diminished. An action may be morally wrong and yet, because of ignorance, not be a sin.

The action must be freely done. If compelled by force to commit a sin, one's sinfulness is diminished to the extent that conditions limit one's freedom. Stealing a loaf of bread might be gravely sinful for a person who could afford to buy it, but not as sinful for a starving person

---

2. Mt 8:22
3. Truth 45–70, Life 44

with no money. The objective act is wrong in each case, but the second situation is not really the act of a free agent.

Finally the action must have serious matter—it must be objectively and seriously wrong. Believing it sinful to step on the crack in a sidewalk does not make such action sinful since no objective evil is involved.

The Catholic community experiences forgiveness of sins today through the sacraments. Baptism forgives all sins and allows a fresh start.[4] And after baptism sin is healed in the Eucharist.[5] In the case of serious sin penance reconciles the sinner again with God and the Christian community.[6]

Scrutinized in the light of the kingdom most human activity is sinful. Catholic tradition calls this common sinfulness "venial sin." Included are acts due to selfishness or simple unconsciousness or objectively sinful actions which are diminished through lack of freedom or knowledge. Venial sins do not break our communion with people. But they strain our relationships and over time may prove too great a burden to community. We are reconciled within the Christian community primarily through the Eucharist.[7]

But forgiveness of venial and mortal sin does not pierce to the core of the problem. Humanity is deformed by original sin.[8] This is a state of being rather than an action. Original sin signifies a tendency toward sinful actions when left to one's own devices. We have a propensity toward evil in spite of the fact that we are created good.

Original sin is the ground out of which actual sin arises. Christians primarily regard sin as infidelity toward the covenant we have entered into with God.[9] Sin also injures the social fabric—either between the person doing the wrong and the person wronged, or between the sinner and society itself.

While forgiveness of sins enables the Christian to begin again and turn toward God, we still find ourselves in a sinful world and we are tempted in that environment toward further sin. But the grace of God, if cooperated with, liberates us even from original sin. The Christian is able with the help of Christ even to overcome the world. And this liberation from sin is the proper definition of salvation. Liberated from the pull of original sin we are able to assist in the coming of God's kingdom.

---

4. Truth 76
5. Truth 78
6. Truth 80
7. Truth 78
8. Truth 57
9. Way 2

TO DEEPEN—

Why is forgiveness of sins specifically mentioned in the Creed?
What is the difference between original and mortal sin?
What factors must be present for a sin to be mortal?
Under what conditions does God forgive sins?
How do Christians concretely experience forgiveness of sins?

Prayer: The Confiteor

I confess to almighty God, and to you, my brothers and sisters, that I have
sinned through my own fault, in my thoughts, and in my words, in what I
have done, and in what I have failed to do; and I ask blessed Mary, ever Virgin, all the angels and saints, and you, my brothers and sisters, to pray for
me to the Lord our God.

Further Reading:

Donnelly, Doris. *Learning To Forgive.* Abingdon, 1982.
Gaffney, James. *Sin Reconsidered.* Paulist Press, 1983.
Menninger, Carl. *Whatever Became of Sin?* Bantam Books, 1978.
Taylor, Michael J. ed. *Mystery of Sin and Forgiveness.* Alba, 1971.

TO CONTINUE—

The contents of Christian moral teaching are presented in Truth 45–73 and in
Life 44.
The moral life unfolds into the spiritual life presented in Way 46ff.
The forgiveness of sins is further explored in Truth 43, 76, 80.
The Christian view of the human condition is found in Truth 57.
The nature of penance is discussed in Way 48.

44. THE RESURRECTION OF THE BODY, AND LIFE EVERLASTING

This statement which looks forward to the future consummation of
the world, has already been encountered in the discussions of apocalyptic. Here the focus shifts to the Church's teaching concerning the

last things—human destiny, the kingdom of God, death, judgment, hell, purgatory and heaven.

The End of History and the Coming of God's Kingdom

Revelation is concerned with human destiny or the end of history. The Hebrew Scriptures point toward the kingdom which God would inaugurate to replace the present age. Apocalyptic made this coming kingdom one of its key terms. Jesus announces that the kingdom of God is at hand.[1] The early Church expected Jesus' quick return and the imminent coming in power of God's kingdom.

As the end did not come, ideas concerning the kingdom began to change. Interest in the Middle Ages turned to the individual's fate. Medieval theology which contributed substantially to the teaching on the last things is concerned not with the outcome of history, but with the individual's death.

Christians still await the full coming of God's kingdom in God's time and through God's power, although we can help in its building up and preparation through cooperation with the Holy Spirit. The Church is not the kingdom, but a sacrament—a sign of that kingdom present in our midst.[2] Other signs of the kingdom's presence are not linked to the Church. And history, while it cannot bring about the kingdom through its own efforts, nevertheless produces seeds which will eventually bear fruit in the kingdom's coming.

The kingdom will be ushered in by the **second coming** of Jesus Christ known as the **parousia**. At that time all creation will be subject to the **general judgment** which applies to the consummation of the whole world and of history itself. This is referred to as the **last judgment**.

The Last Things:
Death

Medieval concern with the individual added certain details to this New Testament picture. For example, **death** in a sense replaced the world crisis of apocalypse. Although the world may not end soon, each person is subject to death and so stands in a particular crisis vis-à-vis God. "It is in the face of death that the riddle of human existence becomes most acute. . . . All the endeavors of technology, though useful in the extreme, cannot calm his anxiety."[3] Death completes one's life,

---

1. Mk 1:15
2. Truth 74
3. Constitution on the Church in the Modern World, n. 18

concludes one's history. Whether our life reflects the life of God's coming kingdom or the sin and selfishness that characterize worldly existence determines our destiny. We do not achieve our place in the
kingdom—it is given us as a gift of God through Jesus Christ. But we
must cooperate with Christ's grace to be transformed into citizens of
God's kingdom.

Judgment

The crisis toward which all life moves in the Christian world view
is the imminent judgment of God which will usher in the kingdom.
While the Christian Scriptures saw judgment at the end of the present
world age inaugurating the kingdom wherein all creatures will be
brought before the throne of God, the Middle Ages saw rather a **particular judgment** of the individual immediately after death which determines salvation or damnation. Thus there are two judgments in
Catholic teaching. These are not really separate—what happens in the
particular judgment will be repeated on a world scale at the general
judgment.

Hell

There are two ultimate destinies: hell or heaven. Catholicism
teaches the possibility of **hell.** God does not save us against our will.
God does not damn people to hell. But if a person refuses God's love,
refuses to die to self, then that person will be allowed to choose hell—
a state of radical alienation and isolation without love.

Jesus' use of the imagery of hell and damnation does not describe
a particular place but emphasizes the urgency of his message and the
seriousness of our decisions for or against the kingdom. Jesus views life
as a crisis demanding decision. We can refuse God and thus risk damnation. "Open your ears and hearts to God's word before it is too late."

Popular Christian imagery envisions hell as the dwelling of the
devil and demons. Again the Church does not teach that hell is a place,
but only a possible state of being. However the Church does teach of
Satan and of demonic powers. There is evil which is not solely dependent upon human beings. Forces of evil can draw individuals and communities up into their power.

But these forces do not have any true power.[4] Their illusory power
is allowed to run its course in our world through God's forbearance. But
the victory over evil has already been won in the cross of Christ.[5] Thus

---

4. Gal 4:8–9
5. Col 2:14–15

Christians should not adopt a paranoid attitude toward the world—sniffing out Satan in all things not specifically Christian. The world, being creation, is basically good. Indeed Satan and the demons are also creatures. Created good, through free will they chose evil.

A theological opinion held by some states that the unbaptized free from mortal sin go to a state of **limbo**. Such an opinion was never defined by the Church. And the Second Vatican Council's insistence upon the universality of grace from the very beginning of each person's existence makes the idea of limbo less and less tenable today.

All infants in danger of death should be baptized. But this is not so much to save them from limbo as to join them to Jesus' death and resurrection and bring them into membership in Christ's Church.

Everlasting Life

Those gathered to God's kingdom in the final judgment pass on to what is variously called **heaven**, the beatific vision or eternal life. This imagery is evocative rather than descriptive. This new life is beyond our present ability to conceive. Thus all attempts must be acknowledged as just that.

We shall be joined in full union with God. Our individuality is not swallowed up; we shall still recognize ourselves and others. But we shall be in communion with creation and God. We will become fully like God with no hint of selfishness remaining, fully transformed in the love of Christ.

And our destiny is not as a disembodied spirit. We are enfleshed spirits. Our bodies are part of us—they are not simply vehicles for our being or, worse, prisons for the spirit. This destiny is expressed in the **resurrection of the body**. God's creation is not left behind in the kingdom but resurrected and glorified. We experience now through our bodily existence. Then we shall experience again through a glorified bodily existence. More than this we cannot know, but to these beliefs we pin our hopes.

Purgatory

But what about those who, although they do not turn their backs upon God or love, yet have not been wholly transformed by the time of their death? Catholics believe that the process of purification continues after death. **Purgatory**, like hell, is not a place but a state which purges our residual selfishness becoming like God totally oriented to others. Purgation cleanses this selfishness, drawing us into the selflessness of God. Such a process is painful because of attachment to our ego.

Purgation involves all people as they move from self-centeredness to love-centeredness. It begins in this life and continues if necessary after death. All humans must pass through this process. But we need not feel alone or isolated in this suffering. For we are moving out of isolation and into the communion of saints where mutual sharing in love directs us. This mutual sharing occurs in the process of purgation. Thus we may pray for the dead and through our prayers and works help their purgation.

The Church and the coming kingdom are a community where all live as one. We support one another in our suffering now and in our joy then. This is the basis for the practice of **indulgences**. Although in the Middle Ages and into the Reformation this practice became overly economized and even degenerated into simony (the selling of sacraments), these excesses should not cloud over the original meaning.

While the last things seem to point to future realities, whether taken in the biblical understanding of the coming of God's reign or the Church's later development of the afterlife, heaven, hell and purgatory are not states limited to an afterlife but also describe present existence. A life rejecting love is condemned to hellish sufferings here and now. A life converted to Jesus is filled with beatitude that shares already in the life of the kingdom. And most lives swing between these two extremes, hopefully in the process of purgation—conversion to the Kingdom of God.

Nor should these teachings cause a Christian to act or believe that everlasting life comes only after death. Everlasting life is a present possibility. Jesus offers us now a depth of living of which we were previously unaware. After death that existence blossoms into the kingdom, but we participate in its coming right now. This richness of life to be enjoyed here and now is the great gift offered by Jesus.

TO DEEPEN—

How did the understanding of human destiny shift from the New Testament times into the Middle Ages?

What does a Christian believe will happen at the end of the world?

What is the difference between the particular and general judgment?

Does a Catholic have to believe that anyone is actually consigned to hell?

Are heaven and hell places?

What does purgatory allow for?

How are heaven, hell, and purgatory present in our lives today?

Further Reading:

Hayes, Zachary. *What Are They Saying About the End of the World?* Paulist Press, 1983.
Hellwig, Monica. *What Are They Saying About Death and Christian Hope?* Paulist Press, 1978.
Kelsey, Morton. *Afterlife: The Other Side of Dying.* Paulist Press, 1978.
Küng, Hans. *Eternal Life?* Doubleday, 1984.

TO CONTINUE—

The process of conversion which purgatory images is described in Way 47.

45. The Ten Commandments

TO PREPARE—

The Way to Morality (41ff) should be covered before or along with this material.

The essence of the law for Christians lies in the ten commandments. There are various ways of numbering: the traditional Catholic numbering is followed below, but the numbers are not that important. For convenience in this section the essence of the commands is summarized. Here are the commands as they appear in Scripture:

And God spoke all these words, saying,

1. I am the Lord your God, who brought you out of the land of Egypt, out of the house of bondage.

You shall have no other Gods before me.

You shall not make for yourself a graven image, or any likeness of anything that is in heaven above, or that is in the earth beneath, or that is in the water under the earth; you shall not bow down to them or serve them; for I the Lord your God am a jealous God, visiting the iniquity of the fathers upon the children to the third and the fourth generation of those who hate me, but showing steadfast love to thousands of those who love me and keep my commandments.

2. You shall not take the name of the Lord your God in vain; for the Lord will not hold him guiltless who takes his name in vain.

3. Remember the sabbath day, to keep it holy. Six days you shall labor, and do all your work; but the seventh day is a sabbath to the Lord your God; in it you shall not do any work, you, or your son, or your daughter, your manservant, or your maidservant, or your cattle, or the sojourner who is within your gates; for in six days the Lord made heaven and earth, the sea, and all that is in them, and rested the seventh day; therefore the Lord blessed the sabbath day and hallowed it.

4. Honor your father and your mother, that your days may be long in the land which the Lord your God gives you.

5. You shall not kill.

6. You shall not commit adultery.

7. You shall not steal.

8. You shall not bear false witness against your neighbor.

9. You shall not covet your neighbor's house; you shall not covet your neighbor's wife,

10. or his manservant, or his maidservant, or his ox, or his ass, or anything that is your neighbor's.

The law serves as a framework for Christian morality. What do these commands say in themselves and how are they understood in the light of Jesus' teaching and in Catholicism?

When asked about the law, Jesus replies with a summary: "You shall love the Lord your God with all your strength, with all your mind, with all your heart, and your neighbor as yourself."[1] The law basically speaks of our relations first with God and then with our neighbor. These summary statements are not original to Jesus, but he seems the first to join them together.

46. LOVE OF GOD

A new relationship with God is the foundation of this Mosaic covenant:

And God spoke all these words, saying, I am the Lord your God, who brought you out of the land of Egypt, out of the house of bondage.

While the Mosaic covenant builds upon the natural law in articulating relations with the neighbor, in setting forth our relationship with God this law proceeds from the covenant which God initiates with Israel.[2] That covenant determines the very being of Israel—who she is. She exists only because of the liberating action of God which led the slaves out of Egypt and provided first the law and then the promised land.

Thus the law begins by reminding Israel that God has liberated Israel from slavery in Egypt, delivered her from bondage and oppression. God freely enters into history and liberates Israel, claiming her for his people. This claim is based upon God's liberating action.

In response to what God has done the covenant then details the obligations falling upon Israel. The first is to keep in mind Israel's relationship with God. This is commonly done in the prayer called the **"Shema"** which Jesus refers to in his response. "Shema" is the first word

---

1. Mt 22:34–40
2. Ex 19:3–8

of the prayer: "Hear, O Israel, the Lord your God is one."[3] This revelation in liberating actions which establish Israel is the very foundation of her life. The Christian through being joined with Jesus Christ shares that tradition and looks to God as the foundation of his or her life as well.

47. You Shall Have No Other Gods Before Me

Originally this command exists in a context of many competing gods. There were the gods of Egypt, and there would be the indigenous gods of Palestine. How does the God of Israel relate to these other gods? God claims exclusivity with Israel—there can be no competition.

Eventually this command gives rise to the understanding that not only is God to be our God, but this God is the only God who exists. Such a belief is called monotheism. God is not in competition with other gods. But rather these other gods do not exist in their own right, and any power they seem to have comes from the one true God.

Since monotheism is today an accepted fact of religious life there might seem no real need for this command. Yet the idea of God has a larger meaning than its religious use. A person's God is what that person regards as the essence of life, what is most valuable, your ultimate concern.

God has revealed himself to Israel and in Jesus. God is not simply a cipher, but has certain values and characteristics. These revealed values struggle with other often contradictory values in our world. It makes a difference which values a person or group places trust in. And the values determine which God one is worshiping.

The God of Israel reveals his passion for liberation by freeing the slaves. God reveals his ultimate nature as love in Jesus. If liberation and love and compassion and the other values of God are not central to our life, is this God of Israel and Jesus Christ truly our God? Or have we in actuality placed another god in God's place?

This commandment demands that in our life certain values be central. There is no room for competing gods whether they be success, the state, or the individual's ego. God alone has the ultimate claim upon us.

This command against **idolatry** has had a long stormy history within our tradition. Again its origin is easy to understand. It would be generations before humanity evolved to the stage where it could separate the image from the power. For primitive humanity the image itself was the power of God. Thus there was the danger of reducing God to God's image. And once that is done one is tempted to use that power

---

3. Dt 6:4–5

for one's own ends: to manipulate God. Such manipulation is usually unconscious but it is nevertheless a terrible perversion.

Once we reduce God to an idol we assume that we have a handle on God. But we have lost the true God. God is beyond our power to imagine, too big to be encompassed by any idol or image. All idols are too small even to represent God. And this prescription against idolatry also applies to the idolatry of believing that God can be limited by words or definitions as much as by images. When describing God one must always be aware that the words say more about what God is not than they do about what God is.

Idolatry takes another form when humanity projects itself into God's image. Often this happens by picturing God in the guise of a human representative. God is seen as a great king, or in the Pope's vestments. If taken seriously this too is idolatry. For the human representative is appropriating what is truly of God. God is indeed a king, but God is very different from human potentates. God's kingship is most fully revealed in Jesus who washes his disciples' feet, and who dies rejected by his people. This is not the kind of kingship that kings appropriate. Claiming that God acts in their arrogant manner, they set themselves up as an idol that must be smashed.

The ultimate intention is to prevent the diminishment of God through any human representation. The ban on idolatry does not apply to a ban on images altogether. If it did, not only images but all words and concepts about God should be banned, for they all fail to communicate the true God. The proscription prohibits taking any image, word or concept concerning God ultimately. These point toward God if they are authentic, but do not adequately comprehend whom they point toward. God is greater than can be imagined.

48. Do Not Take God's Name in Vain

In this society the name was a sacred entity. Near the very dawn of language the power of the word was much more obvious than today. For these people one's name was directly related to one's being. If your enemies knew your name, they had power over you.

God's name is the most sacred of words, since it names the ultimate power of the universe. In Israel God's name was uttered only by the high priest on a certain day in the temple. When Moses asks for God's name, God responds, "I am who I am."

This commandment is not a prohibition against **swearing** or **cursing** in their modern understanding. Expletives are usually not meant today to be taken literally. They are a way of expressing anger, blowing off steam, and often no more than a semi-conscious habitual expression.

Such language and swearing is not against this commandment, although a person might want to be aware of reliance upon such language. Is it appropriate? And is it becoming simply a part of one's linguistic baggage, in which case it loses its ability to express rage etc., and becomes an inappropriate linguistic tick best removed.

As he often does, Jesus deepens this law, raising it from a moral command to a spiritual discipline. The commandment guards against using God's power and authority for vain ends. Oaths often attempt to put God on our side. It is but a short step to believing that God is in our power. Jesus asks the disciple to surrender the whole concept of the oath.

> I say to you, Do not swear at all, either by heaven, for it is the throne of God, or by the earth, for it is his footstool, or by Jerusalem, for it is the city of the great King. And do not swear by your own head, for you cannot make one hair white or black. Let what you say be simply "Yes" or "No"; anything more than this comes from evil.[4]

Jesus wishes us to rely upon our own power. It is too easy to become inflated, believing that we have much more power than we actually do. The way to happiness involves a realization of who we are and what we are capable of, as well as a willingness to work within those limits.

49. Keep the Sabbath

The sabbath rest is one of Israel's great contributions to spirituality. We do not exist only to eke out a living or to prove ourselves through work. This command establishes a cycle of six days for work and one of rest during which we regain perspective, are refreshed, and draw closer to God.

Christians shifted the sabbath observance to Sunday to celebrate the resurrection. They refrain from servile work on that day. And the Christian community joins together to thank God in the Eucharist.[5] The rest of the day should be for our rest and relaxation, for the family, the spirit.

---

4. Mt 5:34–37
5. Intro 16

Catholics today do not observe the sabbath law as strictly as Judaism or other forms of Christianity. Sometimes people must work on Sunday. But the heart of the law should be preserved. The person is expected to join in Christian worship. And it would be helpful and healthy to set aside another day for rest. As Jesus pointed out, the sabbath was made for man, not man for the sabbath.[6] It is given to benefit us spiritually.

50. Honor Your Father and Mother

This commandment falls under those commands speaking about our relationship to God. God is the foundation of our new society, and God identifies himself as a parent. The family is the foundation for human society; values and traditions are handed down through parents to their children. This bond is one of the most important in any human society. Our parents are key images for God. And we owe them respect and honor for having given us life, nourished and raised us.

This commandment is addressed to adults concerning their parents, not primarily children. And it does not demand obedience to our parents but rather honor. It speaks to a current situation. Due to a greatly extended life span, many old people are not treated with respect. They are shunted out of the mainstream and placed in impersonal rest facilities rather than cared for by their family.

This command certainly does not dictate our response. It does not say that placing a parent in a rest home is bad. But it does raise our obligation as children to honor our parents. They are not to be forgotten or put out of the way now that their "usefulness" is over. Indeed America's obsession with youth wastes a most precious resource—the wisdom that comes from age and is embodied in our senior members.

Jesus realizes that our ties to family can become an excuse not to follow him. Thus he speaks of coming to set father against son.[7] He tells a would-be disciple who claims family obligations to let the dead bury the dead.[8] He does not abrogate the original commandment, calling his disciples to dishonor their parents. Indeed Jesus deepens the concept of God as parent by calling God "Abba."[9] But he challenges our excuse that "obligations" do not allow us to embark upon the path of discipleship.

---

6. Mk 2:27
7. Lk 22:36
8. Lk 9:60
9. Truth 16, 27

TO DEEPEN—

What do the ten commandments arise out of in Israel?

What forms might idolatry take today? Why is this a sin?

Is swearing considered a sin by Catholics?

How does the sabbath observance help a person spiritually?

What obligations do we have toward our parents?

Further Reading:

Israel, Martin. *The Discipline of Love—The Ten Commandments for Today.*
   Crossroad, 1986.
McDonald, Perry and Odell, William. *Laws of Christian Living—the Com-*
   mandments. Our Sunday Visitor, 1986.
Spong, John. *The Living Commandments.* Seabury, 1977.

TO CONTINUE—

The basic demands for active membership in the Catholic Church are discussed
   in Intro 15ff.

51. LOVE OF NEIGHBOR

The second part of the decalogue refers to obligations toward the
neighbor. Jesus deepens this aspect of the law, putting it on a nearly
equal footing with the first part. "You shall love your neighbor as yourself." Love of neighbor is second only to love of God. (Love of oneself
is presumed as the foundation upon which this morality and spirituality
is based, although our failure to love our neighbor is often a consequence of our inability to love ourselves.)

Jesus announces God's love for each one of us. With this knowledge we begin the Christian path. Only in the reality of God's love can
we in turn overcome the obstacles placed in our way by a fallen world
to loving ourselves. And only when we are able to accept and love ourselves as God does can we fulfill this command to love our neighbor.

The Christian ethic is extremely demanding. But it is not a law that
judges us for not measuring up. Failure is met with forgiveness and reconciliation with God and the community that allows a fresh start and
renewed commitment. The ideal does not condemn us for failing to realize it. It points to true fulfillment. The law guides toward real hap-

piness. It is fulfilled only when we allow God through the Holy Spirit to transform our existence.

52. Do Not Kill

Subsequent Israelite and Christian history shows that obviously this command is not taken literally. There has always been a distinction between lawful and unlawful killing. This commandment applies only within the context of Israelite society. It says nothing about the external or internal (criminal) enemies of society, or animals.

This commandment is the foundation of our tradition's **reverence for life** which as it is evolving today extends toward all life. All life is a sacred gift from God and to be valued as such. While, in general, human society (including modern America) sees some life as more valuable than other life, the Christian tradition stresses that all life—and especially that of the poor, the oppressed and the defenseless—is a sacred trust. Thus Catholics consider abortion, violence, euthanasia, and, increasingly, capital punishment and economic, political, or religious oppression as well as war itself to be an infringement on this basic right to life.

The earliest Christians thought of **suicide** (in the form of martyrdom) as the highest act a person could perform. "Greater love than this has no man, that he lay down his life for his friends."[1] The great Church Father Tertullian called Christ the suicide. But Augustine stemmed this tide; the Church adopted the thinking of Northern pagans which regarded suicide the greatest of crimes.

Today we realize that those who commit suicide are often not in full control of their reasoning faculties and not to be judged as though they were. Also we recognize that suicide might also have an altruistic end. Thus the feeling behind suicide is no longer as uncompromising as before. It is still a serious sin, but there is compassion for the person.

Abortion has become a volatile issue in America and elsewhere today. Catholicism teaches that abortion involves the taking of innocent life and therefore is morally evil. But there must be regard for the mother and her well-being as well.

At the other end of the life-scale is the question of **euthanasia**. Catholic tradition asserts that it is immoral to kill a patient. But there is no need to prolong life by extraordinary means when the quality is sufficiently diminished that the patient and family do not want to prolong treatment. Catholics affirm a person's right to a death with dignity.

---

1. Jn 15:13

Death for Christians is not the ultimate evil to be avoided at all costs, but a holy passage from this world home to the Father. A person allowed to linger, supported by costly machines, is robbed of that dignity, and the family is subjected to needless torment.

Traditionally Catholicism gave the state the right to protect itself from criminals through **capital punishment**. However recent Catholic teaching is changing. Capital punishment is not perceived as a valid means for protecting the state. Capital punishment and imprisonment are often directed at the oppressed and poor within a society. Justice becomes simply a more covert and extended form of prejudice and oppression.

Catholics today are aware of and attempting to lessen other forms of violence against life. There is political and religious **coercion** and **oppression** and above all economic oppression. Our God has made a fundamental option for the poor.

The powerful in society are obliged to care for the underprivileged and oppressed. Included among others are women who do not yet enjoy an equal status with males, and the mentally and physically handicapped. Today an expanding lifetime places the elderly in this category.

Respect for life extends also beyond human life to **ecology**. It includes respect for the earth and its creatures. According to the Genesis story[2] we are placed on earth for its care. It has been given to us, not for rapine, but for our enjoyment and development.

Earth and its resources are limited. We are obliged to care for its creatures and resources. We may enjoy them but we must also consider those who come after us. Will they thank us for making another species extinct every ten years, for enabling the rain to corrode metal, for exhausting the mineral resources, for replacing trees and plants with concrete and plastic?

Catholic teaching on the morality of **war** is also evolving today. Although at first the soldier's career was considered incompatible with following Jesus, the Church soon accommodated to the world, especially when it became the established religion of the Roman Empire with responsibility to preserve it.

The traditional just war theory gives a nation the right to defend itself when attacked. The same applies to an individual under attack. But in the light of the nuclear arsenal and the probability that a major war would obliterate humanity and much of the earth's ecology, Catholic teachers including the Pope and the American bishops are questioning the feasibility of a just war with nuclear weapons.

---

2. Gen 1:26

While the Catholic Church does not impose upon anyone the necessity to be a pacifist, it does state that an individual may and indeed must refuse to fight in a war that that individual considers unjust. Further, if persons find that they cannot fight but must be pacifist, the Church supports them in that stand. Pacifism is certainly included in the teaching of Jesus, but it is not binding at the level of common morality considered here; it belongs to the realm of spiritual transformation.

Catholic teaching on the respect for life is broad and covers a number of significant areas. Recently this teaching has been compared to the seamless garment which Jesus wore to his crucifixion. All too often today groups that are pro-life in one issue are anti-life on another. The only true Catholic stance is pro-life in all its forms. To over-emphasize one at the expense of others shreds the seamless garment and creates an untenable position.

Either all life is sacred or no life is sacred. In our tradition life is not dependent upon what a person has accomplished with it. We are not saved by our good works but by the overwhelming reality of God's love that extends to unborn children, to endangered species, and to the derelict on the streets. All of this life is a sacred gift redeemed by Christ's sacrifice.

Having examined the Church's understanding of respect for life does not exhaust or bring to its highest level this commandment. Jesus raises the issue to the spiritual level—that level of transformation that ushers in the kingdom of God.

> You have heard that it was said to the men of old, "You shall not kill; and whoever kills shall be liable to judgment." But I say to you that every one who is angry with his brother shall be liable to judgment; whoever insults his brother shall be liable to the council, and whoever says, "You fool! You shall be liable to the hell of fire." So if you are offering your gift at the altar, and then remember that your brother has something against you, leave your gift there before the altar and go; first be reconciled to your brother, and then come and offer your gift. Make friends quickly with your accuser, while you are going with him to court, lest your accuser hand you over to the judge, and the judge to the guard, and you be put in prison; truly, I say to you, you will never get out till you have paid the last penny.[3]

---

3. Mt 5:21–26

While the original command and much of Catholic teaching simply prohibits violence against other life, Jesus goes to the heart of the problem. Killing is simply the final sin arising from a much deeper division within the human being. The disciple who would be perfected must look beyond social prohibitions and root out the disease at its source. Jesus asks us to look at our anger.

Anger is certainly permitted a Christian. Jesus himself became angry in chasing the money-changers from the temple.[4] But anger is appropriate or inappropriate. Unfortunately most anger is inappropriate.

Jesus brings us face to face with anger and shows how to understand and move out of it. Of course this is no longer basic morality. Jesus is not concerned with that. It is presupposed in anyone undertaking the spiritual journey. What is meant here is spiritual work. And this, beyond the pale of lawful or unlawful, sin or not, is the task of Christian conversion.[5]

53. Do Not Commit Adultery

Family and marriage constitute society's foundation. This commandment protects that institution. Adultery refers to intimacy and sexual relations between two people at least one of whom is married. The sin is not sexuality, but infidelity to the marriage covenant.

Adultery is the most serious way of betraying this covenant[6] which institutes a relationship of trust between the partners. They give themselves freely to one another. Only with one another will they celebrate the full extent of human love symbolized by sexual intercourse. Adultery, betraying that trust, weakens the covenant.

The original proscription was against the act of adultery. Jesus, in his fulfillment of the law, reinterprets this command also:

> You have heard that it was said, "You shall not commit adultery." But I say to you that every one who looks at a woman lustfully has already committed adultery with her in his heart. If your right eye causes you to sin, pluck it out and throw it away; it is better that you lose one of your members than that your whole body be thrown into hell. And if your right hand causes you to sin, cut it off and throw it away; it is better that you lose one of your members than that your whole body go into hell.[7]

4. Mt 21:12–17
5. Way 47
6. Truth 83
7. Mt 5:27–30

The real cause of adultery is lust,[8] a passion that exists in the heart, in the inside of a person, before it manifests in any outward actions. Thus Christians in following Jesus should look to their passions as well as actions.

The issue of **divorce** has a long history in our tradition. In the Mosaic law divorce was a rather simple issue. If the man became tired of his wife he could through a certain formality divorce her. To Jesus this teaching reflects the stubbornness, or we might say, the primitive civilization, of those times.[9] Jesus liberates women by abrogating the Mosaic divorce customs. No longer is it permitted for a man to put aside his wife.

> It was also said, "Whoever divorces his wife, let him give her a certificate of divorce." But I say to you that every one who divorces his wife, except on the ground of unchastity, makes her an adulteress; and whoever marries a divorced woman commits adultery.[10]

Catholics believe that marriage between two Christians creates a covenant dissolved only by death. There is a possibility of separation—of living apart from one another for the good of the individuals involved. But the marriage still binds, and the people are not free to enter into a new marriage covenant.

However the Church also recognizes that Christian marriage is a very high ideal. Often people are not capable of understanding what is involved or lack psychological maturity when entering the covenant. Catholic marriage tribunals examine failed marriage covenants to determine the possibility for a true marriage in the first place. If the tribunal finds that one or more conditions for marriage were lacking or insufficient, that marriage is annulled and the people are free to marry if they so choose.

54. Do Not Steal

This commandment refers to the third foundation of human society—property. Community cannot be established without protection of what people regard as their own. Thus laws regarding property make up the bulk of civil law.

8. Truth 65
9. Mk 10:1–12
10. Mt 5:31–32

The commandment condemns stealing—taking what does not belong to one. Included under this command would be actions such as falsifying an insurance claim, cheating on taxes, copying materials for use or sale without permission of the copyright owner, or unfair business practices.

The commandment applies to groups and countries in their practices as well. It is not just for developed countries to take the resources of underdeveloped peoples while paying a fraction of their value. Two-thirds of the world's resources are unjustly enjoyed by one-third of the world's peoples. This is greater than many other acts of theft, since it abandons millions to misery, poverty and squalor.

Only through our acknowledgement of the social contract through ideas such as this command do we make it possible for human society—which enriches us—to exist. Only a mutual recognition of human rights will enable our world to become one community rather than the present situation of the many robbed of their heritage through the greed of a few.

The Catholic tradition, especially recently, takes a stand against those who place property as the highest value, over the human person.[11] This is the stance of classical capitalism. And Catholic teaching asks whether the economic system is fair to all or only to a small group of capitalists.

55. Do Not Bear False Witness

This commandment considers relations between people in a society. It is concerned with truth, tolerance and respect. Human community depends upon a level of truth between members. The Catholic tradition teaches that fellow human beings are due honor and respect as a basic natural right. It is not a question of charity but of justice.

The following actions are against this commandment. **Contumely** or insult treats another person with contempt for no reason or for an irrelevant reason such as race, color, nationality, social position, sex or sexual orientation. **Calumny** is a lie told or spread which intends to deprive a person of the due esteem and respect of his or her neighbors. Third is **rash judgment**: judging and discriminating against a person without sufficient reason. For instance, this man is lazy because black people are by nature lazy. Finally **detraction** destroys or weakens a person's reputation and position by revealing secret defects of that person without sufficient reason.

---

11. Laborem Exercens

This command enjoins against false witness. But what of the obverse? When does one need to tell the truth? Is a person always obliged to speak only the truth? Language and society are by nature designed not only to tell the truth but to promote harmonious intercourse. Various levels of seriousness exist in truth-telling. At times telling the truth is not only not necessary but can involve an injustice.

Social amenities are not so concerned with the truth as with social intercourse. If asked how we are today, there is no need to give a detailed and truthful answer. This is merely a social convention. Indeed to launch into one's medical history could be quite inappropriate when all that is expected is a conventional reply.

Increasingly sophisticated means of information gathering make privacy a modern concern. People have a right to privacy and secrecy in certain areas of their lives. In such cases telling the truth could be an infringement of that right.

Counselors or service persons have access to information. In the Church the matter of confession is sealed. Currently our society is debating which professions should have the right to their clients' confidentiality. Also, how much information does government have the right to know concerning its citizens? These questions, like many moral issues, cannot be easily resolved since their consideration involves deeper issues such as the extent of personal freedom.

56. Do Not Covet Your Neighbor's House, etc.

This last group of commands concerns the issue of coveting. On the surface it seems of less import for societal well-being than previous commands affecting killing, adultery, stealing, and truth-telling. To covet means to desire for one's own what belongs to another. This command brings to the surface the deep structure that gives rise to infringements on the other commands. Indeed Catholic teaching places cupidity or desire at the root of original sin. And one sign of one's blessedness is the ability to be perfectly content with one's lot in life.

Thus the ten commandments, which establish the possibility of the new society created by God from slaves who fled Egypt, ends by looking beyond the merely social level of sin to its deeper causes in human nature. How many wars have been fought over this very issue of covetousness? How many relationships have been brought to an end because of envy? These last of the commandments, rather than being less relevant than the others, are indeed more profound, for what leads to the action of adultery but the desiring of another's spouse?

272 Catholic Christianity

What basic societal needs do the commands against killing, adultery and stealing protect?

What are some issues surrounding reverence for life?

What is the traditional Catholic viewpoint on war?

How and why is this changing today?

Why is adultery considered a grave sin?

What does it mean to covet something? Why is it wrong?

Further Reading:

Burtchaell, James T. *Rachel Weeping: The Case Against Abortion.* Harper & Row, 1984.

Cahill, Lisa Sowle. *Between the Sexes. Foundations for a Christian Ethics of Sexuality.* Paulist Press, 1985.

Campbell, Dennis. *Doctors, Lawyers, Ministers: Christian Ethics in Professional Practice.* Abingdon, 1982.

Carmody, John. *Ecology and Religion. Toward a New Christian Theology of Nature.* Paulist Press, 1983.

Gula, Richard M. *What Are They Saying About Euthanasia?* Paulist Press, 1986.

Haring, Bernard. *Free and Faithful in Christ.* Crossroad, 1978, 1984.

Heyer, Robert, ed. *Nuclear Disarmament: Statements of Popes, Bishops, Councils and Churches.* Paulist Press, 1982.

Hollenbach, David. *Nuclear Ethics. A Christian Moral Argument.* Paulist Press, 1983.

Shannon, Thomas A. *What Are They Saying About Genetic Engineering?* Paulist Press, 1983.

Shannon, Thomas. ed. *Bioethics.* Paulist Press, 1980.

Stevens, Edward. *Business Ethics.* Paulist Press, 1983.

Young, James J. *Divorcing, Believing, Belonging.* Paulist Press, 1984.

Williams, Oliver and Hauck, John. *Full Value: Cases in Christian Business Ethics.* Harper and Row, 1978.

TO CONTINUE—

Moral teachings are continued in considerations of The Capital Sins (Truth 58–65), The Virtues (Truth 66–73) and Social Justice Teachings (Life 44).

◇

57. *The Truth of the Christian Path*

The Human Condition
    Humanity as the Image of God
    Sin
    The Essential Nature of Man
    The Excellence of Freedom
    The Mystery of Death
Christian Living and Growth
58. The Path of Purgation—The Seven Deadly Sins
    59. Pride
    60. Envy
    61. Anger
    62. Sloth
    63. Greed
    64. Gluttony
    65. Lust
66. The Path of Illumination—The Seven Virtues
    The Cardinal Virtues
    67. Prudence
    68. Temperance
    69. Justice
    70. Fortitude
    The Theological Virtues
    71. Faith
    72. Hope
    73. Love
74. The Path of Unification—The Seven Sacraments
    75. Sacraments of Initiation
    76. Baptism
    77. Confirmation
    78. Eucharist
   79. Sacraments of Healing
    80. Penance
    81. Anointing of the Sick
   82. Sacraments of Vocation
    83. Holy Matrimony
    84. Holy Orders

The ten commandments' main concern is the good of society. Human beings are primarily social animals. Society must be set up so that individuals can achieve the liberty and happiness intended by God as their birthright. Only on such foundations can the transformative path of Jesus be built.

Having considered the ethical foundations for society, attention now shifts to the individual's path toward the kingdom. How does the Catholic tradition view the individual? Who are we? What are we like? Upon what truths of our existence does the path of Jesus build?

The Human Condition

The most recent Catholic understanding of the human condition is found in Vatican II's document, "The Church in the Modern World."

Man as the Image of God

> For sacred Scripture teaches that man was created "to the image of God," as able to know and love his Creator, and as set by him over all earthly creatures so he might rule them, and make use of them, while glorifying God.
> But God did not create man a solitary being. From the beginning "male and female he created them."[1] The partnership of man and woman constitutes the first form of communion between persons. For by his innermost nature man is a social being; and if he does not enter into relations with others he can neither live nor develop his gifts (n. 12).

Sin

> Although set by God in a state of rectitude, man, enticed by the evil one, abused his freedom at the very start of history. He lifted himself up against God, and sought to attain his goal apart from him. . . . What revelation makes known to us is confirmed by our own experience. For when man looks into his own heart he finds that he is drawn toward what is wrong and sunk in many evils which cannot come from his good Creator. Often refusing to acknowledge God as his source, man has also upset the relationship which should link him to his last end, and at the same time has broken the right order that should reign within himself as well as between himself and other men and all creatures.
> Man therefore is divided in himself. As a result, the whole life of men, both individual and social, shows itself to be a struggle, and a dramatic one, between good and evil, between light and darkness. Man finds that he is unable of himself to overcome the assaults of evil successfully, so that everyone feels as

---

1. Gen 1:27

though bound by chains. But the Lord himself came to free
and strengthen man, renewing him inwardly and casting out
the "prince of this world,"[2] who held him in the bondage of
sin.[3] For sin brought man to a lower state, forcing him away
from the completeness that is his to attain.

Both the high calling and the deep misery which men experience find their final explanation in the light of this revelation
(n. 13).

The Essential Nature of Man

Man, though made of body and soul, is a unity. Through his
very bodily condition he sums up in himself the elements of
the material world. Through him they are thus brought to
their highest perfection and can raise their voice in praise
freely given to the Creator. For this reason man may not despise his bodily life. Rather he is obliged to regard his body as
good and to hold it in honor since God has created it and will
raise it up on the last day. Nevertheless man has been
wounded by sin. He finds by experience that his body is in
revolt. His very dignity therefore requires that he should glo-
rify God in his body, and not allow it to serve the evil incli-
nations of his heart.

Man is not deceived when he regards himself as superior to
bodily things and as more than just a speck of nature or a
nameless unit in the city of man. For by his power to know
himself in the depths of his being he rises above the whole
universe of mere objects. When he is drawn to think about his
real self he turns to those deep recesses of his being where
God who probes the hearts awaits him, and where he himself
decides his own destiny in the sight of God. So when he recognizes in himself a spiritual and immortal soul, he is not
being led astray by false imaginings that are due to merely
physical or social causes. On the contrary, he grasps what is
profoundly true in this matter (n. 14).

2. Jn 12:31
3. Jn 8:34

The Excellence of Freedom

That which is truly freedom is an exceptional sign of the image of God in man. For God willed that man should "be left in the hand of his own counsel"[4] so that he might of his own accord seek his Creator and freely attain his full and blessed perfection by cleaving to him. Man's dignity therefore requires him to act out of conscious and free choice, as moved and drawn in a personal way from within, and not by blind impulses in himself or by mere external constraint. Man gains such dignity when, ridding himself of all slavery to the passions, he presses forward toward his goal by freely choosing what is good, and, by his diligence and skill, effectively secures for himself the means suited to this end. Since human freedom has been weakened by sin it is only by the help of God's grace that man can give his actions their full and proper relationship to God (n. 17).

The Mystery of Death

It is in regard to death than man's condition is most shrouded in doubt. Man is tormented not only by pain and by the gradual breaking-up of his body but also, and even more, by the dread of forever ceasing to be. But a deep instinct leads him rightly to shrink from and to reject the utter ruin and total loss of his personality. Because he bears in himself the seed of eternity, which cannot be reduced to mere matter, he rebels against death.

While the mind is at a loss before the mystery of death, the Church, taught by divine revelation, declares that God has created man in view of a blessed destiny that lies beyond the limits of his sad state on earth. Moreover, the Christian faith teaches that bodily death, from which man would have been immune had he not sinned,[5] will be overcome when that wholeness which he lost through his own fault will be given

---

4. Sir 15:14
5. Rom 5:21

once again to him by the almighty and merciful Saviour. For God has called man, and still calls him, to cleave with all his being to him in sharing forever a life that is divine and free from all decay. Christ won this victory when he rose to life, for by his death he freed man from death. Faith, therefore, with its solidly based teaching, provides every thoughtful man with an answer to his anxious queries about his future lot. At the same time it makes him able to be united in Christ with his loved ones who have already died, and gives hope that they have found true life with God (n. 18).

Christian Living and Growth

A range of ethics in the Scriptures forms the foundation for our tradition. The ten commandments lay down a minimum necessary for the well-being of society, and on the other hand Jesus promulgates the law as a description of life in the reign of God not yet fully present among us. So how is the Christian to live and be guided?

First the Christian's primary purpose is not to live a moral life. That is a prerequisite for becoming a Christian. The Christian is called to constant conversion and transformation, becoming a focus for the kingdom of God appearing in this world.[6] The primary Christian task is the development of the spiritual life built upon a moral foundation.

The spiritual life is traditionally considered in three stages: the purgative stage during which the person is purified of passions which lead to sinful actions. This stage too is connected with morality. In the second illuminative stage the person's life is enlightened by Christ's values. Finally the unitive stage is the process by which the person becomes joined in unity with God.

These three paths have traditionally been associated with mysticism: three stages in the ascent to God. Mysticism provides a rich legacy, and although most do not give their entire lives to the quest for perfection, those who do inspire and illumine the rest.

However Christianity is not primarily for the mystic or ascetic. Jesus' path applies to the common life. He shows how in the course of our relationships and everyday activities we may find wholeness.

The path of purification as presented here consists of work with the seven capital sins. The illuminative path is guided by the seven virtues. And the unitive path explores the Christian sacraments. These paths are not exclusive or meant to map out a temporal sequence: one does not begin with the purgative, moving on to the others. These paths guide us in their various ways throughout our Christian life. The sacraments help us to move from sinful behavior into the life of virtue. Working on one implies the others.

TO DEEPEN—

How does Catholicism view the human animal?
What is original sin?

---

6. Way 47

How does Catholicism view human destiny?

What are the three classical stages of the spiritual path?

Further Reading:

Chesterton, G. K. *The Everlasting Man*. Doubleday, 1974. Chesterton's exposition of the human predicament and how we are saved in Christ.

Lauer, E. and Miecko, John. *A Christian Understanding of the Human Person: Basic Readings*. Paulist Press, 1982.

Viladesau, Richard R. *The Reason for Our Hope. An Introduction to Christian Anthropology*. Paulist Press, 1984.

TO CONTINUE—

The way of morality is discussed in Way 41ff.

The forgiveness of sins is found in Truth 43.

The Christian teaching on death and afterlife is found in Truth 44.

58. The Path of Purgation—
The Seven Deadly Sins

TO PREPARE—

The ten commandments (Truth 45ff) should be covered before this material.

The spiritual life considers what must be changed so that we may live according to God's reign. This process of purification concerns repentance and a coming to see and understand what forces in us act against our best interests and create our misery. Purgatory concerns this same process.[1] If the person does not complete the process in this lifetime, it is continued somehow after death.

Dante in his *Divine Comedy* constructs Purgatory to mirror the different stages of Christian purification. He begins with the most serious sins and moves toward the less serious. The expression "seven deadly sins" uses the word "sin" in a slightly different way than previously. There and here to a certain extent sin means an action which ruptures the bond between that person and society or a member of society. In our tradition sins must be actions which alienate us from one another. And actions must be regulated for a community (whether society or Church) to occur.

But now we have moved out of the realm of actions, where the sin actually occurs. Here is a deeper level of human existence—tendencies giving rise to the sinful action in the first place. A sin does not usually come out of the blue. Before actions come patterns of thought, passions, tendencies. Jesus considered these at the root of the commandments, and in his fulfillment of the law he tells his disciples to root out these tendencies—to nip sin in the bud.

The Catholic tradition calls these tendencies the seven deadly sins which may result in sinful actions. But the seven deadly sins actually refer to those passions which lead to sinful actions and must be worked with so that we no longer are in bondage to sin.

These tendencies can be grouped according to their attitude toward the key Christian virtue of love. Pride, envy and anger are perversions of love—they consciously work toward our neighbor's harm. Sloth, greed, gluttony and lust are distortions of love—either defective, or an excessive love for a secondary good.

---

1. Truth 44

59. PRIDE

The most deadly capital sin is pride—the belief that one is the center of the universe. All of us share these tendencies to a certain degree. In some, one sin takes precedence and becomes the major struggle, but we have all the sinful tendencies. Pride is deadliest, because in truth we are not the center of the universe. We are not God. Pride in its fullness is the belief that one is God. Christian asceticism tames the ego— that part of our psyche which has arrogated all power to itself and believes that it is all of us, and that it is truly God.

Pride thinks or believes that we are self-sufficient. We are our own maker—the image of the self-made man. Pride prevents us from seeking help or admitting that anyone can be our superior. And since we have seen that the Christian journey can not possibly be made on one's own power, pride negates the journey's possibility to begin with.

There is only one God. But there are as many egos as people. In truth we are of God. We exist because of the Holy Spirit breathing in us, carrying us home to the Father. The Spirit unites us to God and to one another. But the Holy Spirit is not dominant in our psychology. Ego has assumed power and control. And when the ego attempts wholeness, it does so through power and dominance. The ego takes over spiritual teachings and applies them to itself.

Jesus provides a beautiful and powerful image against pride. At the Last Supper he the Master washes the disciples' feet.[2] No ego would deign to do this. Only the Spirit of God places service above all power or force.

In working upon pride, we do not want to destroy our ego—a necessary psychic component in this world. But we want to cease identifying with the ego. We are more than that part of us which has seized power. And we are not God but beloved creatures being transformed in Jesus Christ.

The attitude of knowing one's place and condition is called humility, which has a bad name in our society. Humility is often thought of as debasing, losing self-respect. But that is a false humility. True humility is the knowledge of who you are and contentment in who you are rather than an attempt to be or seem more.

60. ENVY

Envy differs from pride through an added element of fear. The envious person fears that someone else has something more or is better

---

2. Jn 13:3ff

and cannot look on the happiness of others with joy. The envious person poisons everything because he or she is afraid that in truth he or she may not be the center of the universe.

Envy as a tendency is not as dangerous as pride because it is unstable and unsatisfactory. The proud person may never awaken to reality. But the envious cannot enjoy satisfaction. They constantly fear that they will be surpassed.

Of course envy may lead to melancholy or resignation. What is the use of doing anything? Someone else will always be there to outdo me. It is better not even to try, to sit down in my misery and let the happiness of others rankle.

The corresponding virtue is equanimity. The envious are convinced that they have gotten a raw deal or been left out: the grass is always greener on the other side of the fence. Once over the fence naturally the grass yonder is greener. Truly there is enough for everyone. Into everyone's life a little rain must fall. No one is getting more than his or her fair share (at least in the spiritual realm). Besides, envy leads one to ignore and despise the gifts and graces one does have, like the little child who cannot appreciate his Christmas presents because his little sister has something different.

61. ANGER

Anger has a proper place in our life. Jesus became angry at the temple money changers.[3] So why is anger a deadly sin? And should all anger be considered sinful? But here our primary concern is not sinful actions, but their sources. The passion of anger is certainly a cause of much hurt and suffering in our world.

We might begin to examine our anger. Does it seem almost a constant state? Is it easy to trigger? Is our anger appropriate or does it easily become out of proportion to what initiated it?

Or we might consider our lack of anger if that is appropriate. Are we never angry? What do we do with our anger? Do we suffer depression which is repressed anger? In the spiritual journey the first step is recognition of our passions. Then we can decide what we wish to do with them. In human existence these passions are seldom examined. As a result we easily become their prisoner.

Others' actions that make us quite angry are often unaccepted characteristics of ourselves. Projected onto others we become righteously angry. We will never become whole if we do not learn to accept

---

3. Mt 21:10–16

and integrate these dark sides to ourselves. Our anger can alert us to these repressed aspects of our psyche.

Ego uses anger to bolster pride. At the beginning of a discussion you may be quite ambivalent about the question at hand. But as the discussion heats up your position grows more solid as the other side seems more wrong. Here anger is in service of the ego rather than truth.

On the other hand it does no real good to deny or repress anger. Repressed emotions will break out in other emotions, or in illness. Christianity does not counsel repression but self-knowledge that moves toward transformation.

Anger is called for and appropriate in many situations. It is healthy to express that anger. But a Christian should watch out for anger disproportionate to the offense. It is also advisable to become aware of when anger is appropriate, and when it is part of a power drive.

Our society not only has learned to tolerate anger but sometimes promotes it. "Winning through intimidation" is hardly an appropriate Christian response to life. At times a Christian must challenge the current lifestyle. Aggression is not a characteristic of God's reign.

Again anger appears both in the individual and in the culture at large. War is the result of national anger and aggression. What things in our culture promote anger? What is the impact of violence in the media not only upon children but upon the society at large?

62. SLOTH

Sloth is the neglect of what one should do. In the spiritual life it is the neglect of conversion and prayer. Under sloth's influence everything gradually becomes deadened. One loses motivation, any desire to do things. Life itself becomes dull and boring. It might seem wonderful to never work again, to lounge all day on the beach. But when such an opportunity presents itself, after the initial rest, boredom and a general deadening set in. Life loses its flavor and zest.

Early Christian monks considered sloth the most deadly of these tendencies. For the spiritual life does not provide a thrill a minute. It is a long, hard, gradual process. And it is easy to want to give up. The monks had to be continually exhorted to keep up their practices, to persevere in prayer.

And there is an element of sloth in all our lives. It is easy to give up the process of conversion. Sometimes we do not experience any results. "Is anything happening?" we ask. "Am I deceiving myself?" Sloth teaches us to recognize this temptation as a deception. Our faith should inspire us to keep going through periods of aridity and difficulty.

Sloth appears in our relationships too. Marriage, if not supported by continual communication and celebration, becomes arid. Friendships and talents lose their original zest if neglected.

Sloth can also manifest itself as acute busyness. Our lives can become immensely complicated, so much so that we forget what is truly important. Work keeps us from our family. We become "busy about many things."[4]

The cure for sloth is action. We are made to be active, to work. This is certainly not our only purpose in life, and to become a workaholic is as deadly to our well-being as to become slothful. The true way balances work and leisure. The true way promotes spiritual growth by finding support in community.

Consider the social consequences of sloth. Our society runs only by having a significant number of people unemployed and put on the margins of society. These people are taught to see themselves as useless. They are not needed or wanted. Unemployment takes away their dignity as human beings. Can Christians remain complacent about this situation?

Pope John Paul II declares that every human being has a right to express himself or herself in work.[5] Through work and creation we manifest the image of God. Take away our work, or our right to the benefits of our work, and you take away our dignity and sap our vitality.

In spirituality sloth is the sin of not loving sufficiently. We do not love God sufficiently to become more like God. We do not love our neighbor sufficiently to ensure that society becomes beneficial to all its members.

63. GREED

The last three capital sins are due to an excess of love, but love for the wrong thing. The proper love for a human being is love for God and for neighbor.[6] Greed is a love of money or possessions rather than people. A capitalist economy makes it difficult to view greed as a sin since it is made a prime virtue.

Greed is a sin not so much because it is wrong, but because it is a

---

4. Lk 10:41–42
5. Laborem Exercens
6. Truth 46

dead end. We cannot find real happiness in possessions or power. We are putting our love into something inadequate. The end result is frustration.

Our society is the greatest consumer in history—our rapacious appetite knows no bounds; it simply keeps growing. That commodity will make me happy. But once gained, the old gnawing appetite returns and only some other product or more money, power, or whatever will do the trick. The worst (or best) thing that can happen in this rat race is that the person finally gains everything he or she could possibly want. But the hunger is still there; happiness is still elusive. The problem is not in not having what you want: the problem is thinking that a secondary good can satisfy a desire that can only be met by a primary good. What will satisfy? What can? Only God, only real love.

Like the other sins greed is manifested on the social level. One-third of the world uses two-thirds of the world's resources. A few feed and overeat while many starve. Pope Paul VI warned that this situation is gravely sinful.[7] Christians should transform society and politics so that all might enter into the earth's wealth. Is it not sinful to eat a banana or drink a cup of coffee bought at the expense of the harvester's poverty and paid for with a fraction of its price in terms of human labor?

64. GLUTTONY

Gluttony classically refers to excess food and drink. Food and drink are necessary for our nurture. And eating and drinking, particularly in a social context, are enjoyable. But a sinful human tendency thinks that if a little of something is good, a lot is better.

Gluttony is an example of misplaced love. People with a weight problem eat to find satisfaction. But it cannot bring real and lasting satisfaction. And it has consequences as well in obesity.

Alcohol is a legal drug in our society. But it is a drug—one of the most dangerous known to humanity. If it were just discovered today, there is almost no possibility that it would be considered fit for society. In moderation it enlivens society. In excess it leads to wasted lives, suicide and murder.

Other legal drugs as well tempt toward immoderation. We can become addicted to coffee, cigarettes, and of course medically supplied substances. The Christian does not condemn the human drives offered

---

7. Progressio Populorum

expression through these drugs, but it does caution temperance[8] in their use so that our primary end—God—is not lost sight of.

Our society is based upon conspicuous consumption. Here is an instance of social greed. And the abundance is consumed by depriving others of sustenance, and with a regard for natural resources which may leave future generations with dead lakes, streams, oceans, unbreathable air, and inadequate resources for survival. What is the cost of our consumption? And is this price worth what we truly receive?

65. LUST

Finally there is lust which usually receives the greatest share of discussion. Yet lust is the least deadly of the seven. For at least lust is love—perverted from its true end, albeit, but love nevertheless, and love for a person.

Catholic teaching regards sexuality as a holy expression of love between two people reserved for marriage.[9] All other expressions of sexual intercourse fall short of this ideal, although the circumstances in each situation must be considered in weighing the gravity of the action.

Again this teaching goes against much modern thinking. But when sex is divorced from love, it is unable to satisfy our deep longing. Consider the sexual revolution today. As sex becomes more commonplace, more of a commodity, it must also become more kinky to preserve its spice. But sexual variations do not provide the ultimate satisfaction; it is sex as an expression of a deep, personal, caring and committed love that is only fully found in the relation of marriage.

In terms of the sexual action itself, Catholicism believes that since sexual intercourse is the physical expression of marital love it is sacred and should not be tampered or interfered with. While Catholicism teaches that a husband and wife have the duty to regulate their family to that number of children which they can adequately nurture and educate, it also teaches that unnatural means should not be used to limit the family. Of current birth control methods only abstinence, the rhythm method, and natural family planning are approved by the Church.

As with the other capital sins we can find a social manifestation of lust. At its most sinister lust becomes rape—sexual assault of another. In such a case lust is often mixed with anger or aggression. Just as rape

---

8. Truth 68
9. Truth 83

is one of the worst sins of lust, the ravaging of the earth has been one of the worst social manifestations of this sin. Rape almost always is committed by a man upon a woman. And the ravishing of the earth may be seen as an extension of the male value of aggression against the feminine.

TO DEEPEN—

What do the capital sins primarily refer to?

Which sinful tendencies express perversions of love, which are distortions of love?

Which is the deadliest of the capital sins? Why?

What is the Catholic position on alcohol?

What does Catholicism teach concerning sexuality?

Further Reading:

Groeschel, Benedict J. *The Courage To Be Chaste*. Paulist Press, 1985.
Keane, Philip. *Sexual Morality: A Catholic Perspective*. Paulist Press. 1977.
Lester, Andrew. *Coping with Your Anger—A Christian guide*. Westminster, 1983.
Sanford, John. *Evil—The Shadow Side of Reality*. Crossroad, 1981.

TO CONTINUE—

The basic moral teachings are presented in Truth 45ff.
Social justice teachings are found in Life 44.

66. The Path of Illumination— The Seven Virtues

Whereas the purgative way consisted of becoming aware of the passions imprisoning us in the worldly way of being, the second stage offers illumination of the proper way of being that leads toward the reign of God. Our discussion of morality so far has been largely negative—either laws prohibiting certain activities, or negative passions. Now we turn toward the positive: What kind of life is good?

Virtue comes from the Latin word for "strength." These strengths enable us to live a good life. They are powers rooted in God which enable us to become more like God. The Christian idea of virtue is also founded in the Greek concept that the good life is a matter of remaining in the middle—in the golden mean. Sin is excess on either side. Virtue consists not in never becoming angry which is as unhealthy as all-consuming anger. Rather virtue keeps anger appropriate to the injury.

As there are seven deadly sins, so there are seven virtues divided between cardinal and theological. The cardinal virtues deriving from the Greco-Roman tradition are the "hinges" upon which the moral life revolves. Prudence, temperance, justice and fortitude are not natural in the sense that they arise purely out of human effort—all human life is graced by God and thus all virtue is a response to grace. But they are natural in the sense that they are perceived by human reason to be virtues.

The theological virtues—faith, hope and charity—are so called because they arise in our tradition from the teaching of Paul[1] rather than from human reason. The ability to develop any virtue, however, consists in one's ability to respond to grace.

THE CARDINAL VIRTUES

67. Prudence

Prudence like many of the virtues and sins has fallen into hard times and become debased. It has nothing to do with being a prude. Prudence is the ability to discern the correct and best course of action in a situation: good common sense. Prudence mediates between abstract thought—What is the best way to act for the good?—and the concrete situation—What is the best way to act at this time?

---

1. 1 Cor 13

It is not enough as a Christian to do what is believed good. Intentions are not enough. We must try to discern what actually is the best way to proceed. It is not too difficult to decide upon abstract moral principles. But how does that abstract principle apply in this? Life seldom presents textbook examples. It is filled with ambiguous situations fraught with many different elements and values. Prudence enables one to make the best decision.

This virtue of prudence leads into the realm of **spiritual discernment**. How are we to evaluate our spiritual journey? Is some action or practice benefiting us? Is something the work of the Spirit or actually against the Spirit? Life's ambiguities and particularly the rarefied spiritual life make such discernment necessary and no easy task. For we are dealing with the invisible and transcendent and we are dealing as persons who have an innate tendency to see things to our best advantage—or sometimes to our worst advantage. How is the truth to be found?

Christians employ traditional criteria to discern the Spirit. These negative criteria expose false responses to the Spirit rather than tell us that we are actually responding to the true Spirit. But what more can we expect in this ambiguous world?

First, does the action lead to the fruits of the Spirit—love, joy, peace, patient endurance, kindness, generosity, faith, mildness and chastity?[2] Second, does the action or process lead to positions outside the accepted Christian theological, doctrinal or biblical teachings? Third, does the action under consideration lead to isolation, or does it intensify eccentricity rather than building up and enhancing the life of the whole the body of Christ?[3] Finally, does the action lead one to ignore pertinent factors and information involved, or reject the advice of others with wisdom and experience in this area, or does it lead toward an imposition of authority and power rather than consent? Negative responses make the action suspect.

68. Temperance

Temperance has also been degraded in common parlance, calling up stern condemnation of drink or other pleasures: women swinging axes in the temperance movement. But temperance is closest to our overall definition of virtue—a staying in the mean between extremes. The person totally adamant against all forms of alcohol is as intemperate as the drunk.

---

2. Gal 5:22–23
3. Eph 4:15–16

Temperance actually refers to our tendency—through original sin[4]—to seek secondary goods as ends in themselves. It refers to the three capital sins of greed, gluttony and lust. Temperance is not the repression of the appetites, which are good in themselves, but rather their temperance in the service of our overall good. Abstinence humanizes our appetite for food, sobriety humanizes our appetite for drink and drugs, and chastity humanizes our desire for sexual pleasure. These are only sins if pursued as ends in themselves rather than means toward human fulfillment.

Temperance underlies Christian asceticism. Asceticism is not by nature a religiously sanctioned form of masochism. It is not a means for expressing disgust with the body, the self or any created thing.

Asceticism leads toward knowledge and acceptance of ourselves and our human condition. Excess drink, food or sex is an attempt to deny that condition—to escape from actual life to a dream world of complete satisfaction. This false dream in truth does no good and much harm. The obese person or the drunk abuses body and mind. And the sexual profligate is seeking something that sex alone can not give.

The ascetic Christian comes to see the conditions of his or her life and accepts them. The ascetic patterns his or her life on Christ who through obedience even gave his life for others. The cross at the heart of our asceticism reminds us of our mortality and is at the same time assurance of God's victory over that mortality. The Christian is ready to face even death for the sake of the kingdom. The first sign of a genuine Christian asceticism is that the ascetic is accepting of the goodness of himself or herself, the body and life.

Also, is the asceticism ordered toward service of others or a means of avoiding service or commitment? The Christian does not work on himself or herself as an end in itself, but for the kingdom and so that he or she might more truly reflect the kingdom's reality. Finally, does one's asceticism make one freer to love, more creative, or does it isolate one, make one proud and closed off, more difficult to get along with? In Christianity even the hermit realizes that life is dedicated not primarily to one's own development, but to pray for the world and seek the good of others.

69. Justice

Justice means much more than is covered by our secular meaning. It means, at base, fairness and includes within its frame the ideals of

---

4. Truth 57

honesty, truthfulness, and honoring of commitments. Further in its Christian context it includes the concept of righteousness. Paul says that we are made righteous in Jesus.[5] This righteousness has nothing to do with a lofty attitude implying that we have something others do not—the sin of pride.[6] Rather our righteousness is Jesus Christ himself. Thus righteousness is the conforming of our life to Jesus—particularly with his death and resurrection and the new life in the Spirit flowing from the resurrection.

The virtue of justice extends outward into the community and the world. The Christian is not cut off from the rest of humanity. In putting on Christ we adopt Christ's compassion for all people. Thus the Christian is active, promoting justice in our world. Justice is to be sought among the poor, the weak, the cast off. Thus the Christian is concerned with social policies in regard to the poor. The Christian brings social sin to public consciousness. Social sin results when some organization or functioning of society works to the detriment of groups in that society. The Christian in such situations becomes the voice of the voiceless, and thus extends to all creatures God's healing compassion.

70. Fortitude

As can be inferred from the virtue of justice, the Christian is called to active involvement in building up the kingdom. To be a Christian, or a fully activated human being, requires the last cardinal virtue—fortitude. Fortitude is courage—the ability to overcome fear in order to pursue the good. It can be either active or passive. In its active sense, fortitude is the overcoming of evil for the sake of God's kingdom. Passively, fortitude is the endurance of pain, suffering and even death itself for the sake of the kingdom.

THE THEOLOGICAL VIRTUES

The theological virtues derive from St. Paul.[7] These virtues extend beyond the present life and concern the development of our spiritual potential.

---

5. Rom 1:16–17
6. Truth 59
7. 1 Cor 13

71. Faith

Faith is a virtue in three ways. First, it is a conviction. Our Christian faith is in Jesus Christ and in the beliefs concerning Jesus and his message. This is the faith referred to when we speak of our Christian faith. It centers upon the Creed and the other teachings of the Church. And it acts as a guide for our life and growth in the Holy Spirit.

The second dimension is faith as a trust. What we believe about Jesus leads us to trust him and the God he reveals. Faith is our relationship to God in Jesus Christ. Whereas the first dimension focused upon the contents of what we believe, this dimension stresses the relationship of trust by which the believer is gradually transformed and built up by the Spirit of God.

Finally Christian faith is commitment. Jesus has a mission—evangelization of the earth—which he entrusts to his followers. Jesus preaches clearly God's compassion for the poor. Jesus calls us to join in the work of preparing for the kingdom in our world. God's word challenges us to become liberating vehicles for God's grace. This dimension of faith is active. Faith does not allow us to sit back, confident that we have the answers to life. Faith calls us into the worldly arena to witness on behalf of the kingdom. Faith is our surrender of ourselves to God.

Faith is not a once-for-all commitment. I do not put my faith in Jesus, or affirm the Creed, and then move on to other things. Faith is a virtue—a strength—that grows in one through transformation in Christ. Faith has levels—from that of the child, to that of the new Christian, to the faith of the martyr. And all faith, like all virtue, is due not to our own effort, but rather to our cooperation with grace which establishes us in the arena of faith to begin with.

72. Hope

Hope is certainly the neglected theological virtue. Yet it is necessary for a full life. Hope allows us to imagine a future. When hope is removed a person becomes neurotic—unable to envision a future different from the frustrating present.

Christians live toward the future. We look toward the kingdom's advent. Hope allows us the power to work for that kingdom, dedicating our lives to what is now only a dream, but which our hope makes actual.

The first promise of that future kingdom is Jesus' resurrection.[8]

---

8. Truth 20, 35

This resurrection gives us hope in the rest of the Gospel. It is our pledge from God.

The kingdom is already bursting upon the present scene. Our hope allies us with the stirrings of the kingdom. We see in the tender shoots of liberty and equality the kingdom's first fruits. Although these shoots are fragile and often scorned by the world, Christian hope recognizes them and gives our lives to the service of this coming kingdom. Although the kingdom will come only in God's time, God calls us to further that kingdom, to make ready its way, by placing our hope in struggles for liberation, freedom and dignity.

73. Love

Love is the most celebrated of the theological virtues. But the word itself is ambiguous. And it is debased in current society.

Christians have used four Greek words to describe the kinds of love. First "epithemia" or desire is the capital sin of lust—sexual love is primary. Next, "eros" is the drive toward union with others in order to find self-fulfillment. Here sex is in service to a higher love that seeks a relationship with the other beyond intercourse. Third, "philia" is friendship, the love that is affection. It is the love of brotherhood and sisterhood. Finally, "agape" is the Christian form of love, implying total dedication and devotion to the welfare of the other. Agape lays down its life for the sake of its friends.[9]

Agape is the virtue of love. The fullness of that love is manifested in Jesus. Agape is not passive, but rather sacrificial. Agape gives without thought to receiving, because it knows that, being in a total relationship with God, God will sustain the person. Agape is also compassion for those who in ordinary society are the unloved, the neglected. It causes the shepherd to go in search of the lost sheep.[10] This love is the only true power in the universe; having created the world, it now sustains it in being.

TO DEEPEN—

What are the two types of virtue? Why are they so named?

What is prudence? How does it differ from prudishness?

How is temperance related to asceticism?

9. Jn 15:13
10. Lk 15:3–7

Why should a Christian need the virtue of fortitude?
How does the virtue of justice surpass the common understanding of the term?
What are the different meanings of faith?
Why is hope essential to a Christian or even a healthy person?
What are the four kinds of love? Which of these is the virtue?

Further Reading:

Crossin, John W. *What Are They Saying About Virtue?* Paulist Press, 1986.
Pieper, Karl. *The Four Cardinal Virtues.* Harcourt, Brace & World, 1965.

TO CONTINUE—

See the discussion of the gifts and fruits of the Holy Spirit (Life 4–5) and the works of mercy (Way 38–39) for a fuller picture of Christian life.

Faith is discussed more fully in Truth 26.

The object of Christian hope is discussed in Truth 44.

Love is further discussed in Life 48–50.

74. The Path of Unification—
The Seven Sacraments

TO PREPARE—

In general this section should only be approached after a thorough grounding in the basic *traditions* (see the list at end of Intro 9).

The purgative way reveals the passions which cut us off from God and one another and contribute to human misery. Then the illuminative way reveals those virtues which transform and allow us to continue Jesus' mission. Now we approach the pinnacle of Catholic spiritual life— the unitive way.

Christianity ultimately foresees the reunification of the cosmos in Christ. We are creatures of God, gone astray through sin. We no longer stand in the truth; indeed we hardly recognize what is true. In Jesus Christ that truth has appeared in our midst as one of us. Joined to him in the sacraments we are made one with God, and we journey toward God's reign.

Unity, our ultimate goal, is initiated and built up through the sacraments. This section considers Church teaching concerning individual sacraments and its celebration of them.

The Truth of Sacrament

Sacrament lies at the heart of the Catholic tradition. Sacramentality not only gives rise to the different sacraments, but informs our theology and our whole approach to Christianity and to life.

Jesus, the Primary Sacrament

The idea of sacrament is that some person, word, event, thing, can mediate an experience of God. Jesus is the ultimate sacrament since through this man we experience the living God. Through Jesus' concrete words and images, through his parables and signs, in his very being, we experience God himself. Jesus reveals God's human face. In Jesus God encounters us on our own terms, in flesh and spirit. And in Jesus God shows himself and the way in which we might return to him and find our true destiny.

But the flesh and blood Jesus is no longer here. Is it possible today to experience him as the sacrament of God? Yes, through his Church which is his body on earth.[1] The Church in its very essence is sacrament through his words passed on as Scripture, through his actions imitated by the Church, through the community bearing his name and witnessing to his transforming power, and through the sacraments.

Sacramentality arises from the incarnation. To reach us God has taken flesh. The incarnation leads to the atonement—that action restoring union with God.[2] Unity occurs because God has come into our world. That incarnational movement is not limited to Jesus Christ. Foreseen in God's shaping of history toward liberation, it continues in the sacraments. We find unity only because God sought us out through the incarnation, thus revealing our fulfillment and peace through unity with our source.

It is possible to read the above as putting obstacles between us and God. First there is Jesus, then the Church. Why can we not experience God directly? We can and do. But God's purpose in revealing himself in Jesus is to do more than merely make contact. Our fulfillment involves a new creation not only for ourselves as individuals but of humanity as community, and of the universe as cosmos. That restoration God reveals in Jesus, and an integral part of that fulfillment is the experience of real community that leads to the kingdom.

Thus the Church and even Christ are not mediators in the sense that we have to go through them to experience God. By becoming Christians we are the Church, and by being Church we are built into the body of Christ. Thus in the sacraments Christ himself as Church comes to the Father and receives the Holy Spirit for the furthering of mission.

The Church as Sacrament

The sacraments in their performance establish the Church in being. In celebrating them the Church finds its true essence. It becomes Church both for itself and for others. The sacraments nourish its mission, heal divisions within the community, and send us forth to continue the ministry.

Sacraments issue from the nature of the Church itself as the prime sacrament—the sacrament of Christ's continuing presence in the world. Jesus commissions his disciples to keep his message and to share it with the world. He promises to remain with them throughout this period.

---

1. Truth 41
2. Truth 30–33

The Church's first duty then is to show forth its Lord. Certain rites and actions—some coming from Jesus himself, others manifesting in the course of Christian history—are recognized as sacraments. Controversy provoked the Council of Trent to define seven sacraments. This definition does not restrict God's grace. But the Church guarantees these seven as encounters with Jesus Christ which effect our conversion and building up into God's kingdom.

These sacraments channel God's grace. We cannot find wholeness on our own. Only grace allows us to move from darkness to light. Grace is not restricted to sacrament or Church, but it is promised there. And grace is given not on the basis of merit, but simply because God unconditionally loves us and wills that we enter into union. The different sacraments channel grace so that the divine presence may be effective in particular needs: healing bodies, renewing life, nourishing spirit, providing strength for mission.

Being a Christian is not a question of being saved or being damned. A Christian can be damned; pagans are saved. The difference concerns knowledge and experience. The sacraments signify, celebrate, and effect what God is doing everywhere and for all. Christians are in on this action. We know who God is and what God wills.

But this privilege challenges us to join in God's word and to announce this good news so that others may come to this joy. And each sacrament effects our encounter with God not for ourselves only but so that we might become effective instruments of God's work. The sacrament is a sign of God's favor, and by entering into the sacramental relationship we become in turn signs of God's favor to our brothers and sisters who have not yet experienced the good news.

The Purposes of the Sacraments

The sacraments accomplish a number of things. First, celebrating the sacraments establishes the Church as Church. Through them the Church manifests itself as Christ's body present in the world.

The sacraments initiate the individual into the body of the Church. By encountering Christ the person is led to become part of Christ's body and join in his mission.

The sacraments also act upon the individual: initiating, confirming, nourishing, healing, forgiving, commissioning. They provide Christ's grace which effects transformation into the new creation.

Is a sacrament always effected when it is celebrated? For example, can an unworthy priest celebrate a valid and efficacious sacrament? As long as the sacrament is celebrated in a lawful manner it bestows grace, regardless of the priest. Not the priest but God acts.

And what of the recipient? If that person is not properly disposed toward the sacrament, if, for example, he or she receives the sacrament automatically, or while alienated from the community, it cannot be fully effective for that person.

Further, the sacrament is a sign not only to the receiver, but to the community and world. Witnessing baptisms at the Easter vigil renews and quickens the faith of initiated Christians. Our witness of a marriage awakens commitment to our own marriage, or our belief in the divinity of love.

Finally, the sacraments do not end with what they give the person receiving them. If the person in receiving the sacrament becomes a sign to the Christian community, he or she receives the sacrament to be a more transparent sign of Christ to the world. Each sacrament sends forth. We encounter Christ in the sacrament to be transformed more into Christ so that we may manifest that likeness in the world. We become more fully that which we receive.

TO DEEPEN—

What is a sacrament?

Who is the primary sacrament for the Christian?

How is the Church a sacrament?

Do sacraments restrict God's grace?

How are sacraments related to Christian mission?

Further Reading:

Bausch, William. *A New Look at the Sacraments*. Twenty-Third Publications, 1983.

Champlin, Joseph. *Special Signs of Grace, The Sacraments and Sacramentals*. Liturgical Press, 1986.

Cooke, Bernard. *Sacraments and Sacramentality*. Twenty-Third Publications, 1983.

Duffy, Regis. *Real Presence: Sacraments and Commitment*. Harper and Row, 1982.

Greeley, Andrew. *The Great Mysteries*. Seabury, 1976.

Guzie, Tad. *The Book of Sacramental Basics*. Paulist Press, 1981.

Martos, Joseph. *Doors to the Sacred.* Doubleday, 1981.

O'Neill, Colman. *Meeting Christ in the Sacraments.* Alba, 1964.

Rahner, Karl. *Meditations on the Sacraments.* Crossroad, 1977.

Roberts, William P. *Encounters with Christ: An Introduction to the Sacraments.* Paulist Press, 1985.

St. Cyril of Jerusalem. *Five Instructions on the Sacraments.* Eastern Orthodox Press, 1974. These are part of the mystagogic sermons given to the new Christians after Easter.

TO CONTINUE—

The individual sacraments are treated in Truth 74ff.

75. SACRAMENTS OF INITIATION

The sacraments of initiation (baptism, confirmation and Eucharist) are the heart of the sacramental system even though only one—Eucharist—is celebrated more than once for a person. They initiate into the Church—itself a sacramental manifestation of Christ in the world. Joined to Christ in his covenant, Christians embark upon a sacramental path that colors life and determines vision, values and actions.

Their celebration with adults in the context of the catechumenate and the Easter mysteries is normative. Outside this context these sacraments do not possess all the elements found there. Thus while infant baptism is the overwhelming practice, it does not fully comprehend the sacrament. For in being conferred upon infants, dimensions are missing that are only present in its normative form.

When the Council of Trent identified seven sacraments, it did not have in mind the Church's practice today. The Council only delineated which events should properly be regarded as full sacraments. Today when we celebrate the sacraments of initiation, although Catholics count three, there is only one action—Christian initiation. The individual sacraments are a result of historical circumstances which split initiation into baptism and confirmation. And although Eucharist is usually regarded as a separate sacrament it climaxes initiation: what baptism and confirmation initiate a person into—the inner life and sustenance of the community.

The sacraments of initiation first free men and women from the power of darkness. Dying in Christ, they are buried and rise again.[1]

---

1. Rom 6:3–4

They receive the Spirit of adoption, making them God's sons and daughters.[2]

Secondly, by these sacraments they are incorporated into Christ. They build up the Church, the body of Christ.[3] Through the gift of the Spirit they more perfectly reflect their Lord. Thus they are able to bear witness to Jesus Christ before the world.

Finally, they come to the table of the Eucharist to eat the flesh and drink the blood of the Son of Man in order to gain eternal life and show forth the unity of God's people. By offering themselves with Christ, they share in his universal sacrifice: the entire community of the redeemed is offered to God by their high priest. They pray for a greater outpouring of the Holy Spirit so that the human race may be brought into the unity of God's family.

76. Baptism

Meaning

Baptism enters us into the death, burial and resurrection of Jesus. This initiation unites us to him. He takes on our death, and we share in his resurrection. We are incorporated into him, becoming his body on earth.[4]

The baptismal bath cleanses from all sin. It is a bath of repentance. We have come in the light of Christ to see those actions and attitudes that are sinful, that miss the mark. Our baptism is an expression of repentance[5] that cleanses, offering a new beginning recreated in Christ.

As a sign of repentance, baptism signals a change of life—the outward sign of conversion to Christ. Baptized into him we no longer belong to ourselves but to Christ. And belonging to him, our lives should reflect his values and mind.

Finally baptism initiates us into full membership in the Church. This beginning of sacramental life prepares for the other sacraments which further conversion and nurture faith.

Celebration

Baptism is received after the adult has become a catechumen, has been instructed in the faith, and shows an understanding of Christianity

---

2. Rom 8:15
3. 1 Cor 12:27
4. Col 2:12; Eph 2:1, 4–6; Phil 3:10–11
5. Acts 2:38

and a desire to be initiated. A sponsor plays a role in the faith journey and takes part in the sacraments of initiation. It is celebrated at the Easter vigil[6] since it flows from the saving action of Jesus' passion and resurrection.

Following an expanded liturgy of the word, the candidates come forward with their sponsors to profess the Creed together. Then approaching the waters they are immersed three times as the minister says, "I baptize you in the name of the Father, and of the Son, and of the Holy Spirit."

Emerging from the water they are clothed in a white garment—a sign of putting on Christ[7]—and given a candle symbolic of their witness to the light of Christ. Then they are confirmed and celebrate together their first Eucharist with the community.

While this is the ideal, a number of variations occur. First, people for special reasons can be baptized by pouring water over the forehead. Until recently this was the normal method in Catholicism; Vatican II made immersion the norm since only there is the fullness of the symbol present.

Furthermore while the norm speaks of adults, more infants are baptized in the Church today than adults. Christians decided in the first centuries to receive children into the Church so that they might grow within a Christian environment.

Christian parents are obliged to baptize their children. Conferred upon infants, baptism does not share all aspects of adult initiation. Infants have not committed any sins and are not in need of cleansing. And the element of witness present in baptism (Christians are baptized to continue Jesus' ministry) obviously does not apply.[8] The godparents promise to take an active role in communicating the faith to the child.

Baptism is usually celebrated within the Mass. It occurs right after the prayer of the faithful and before the Eucharist proper. When celebrated apart from the Eucharist other elements such as the Lord's Prayer are taken into the rite, and certain prayers and minor ceremonies are celebrated more fully than during a Mass.

---

6. Way 33
7. Gal 3:27
8. For this reason the Roman Church separated confirmation from baptism, making it a separate sacrament.

77. Confirmation

Meaning

Confirmation became a separate sacramental moment in the Western Church because the bishop was not available at all baptisms to confirm. The practice of when to confirm has changed at various times. The teachings on confirmation are not as clear as with baptism. Confirmation actually completes baptism. There are not two sacramental actions—only one act, sometimes split into two to accommodate the Church's pastoral needs.

Baptism on the one hand applies the good news and Christ's grace to our own conversion. But we are baptized also to in turn undertake God's mission. Confirmation emphasizes that priestly and missionary aspect of baptism. When infants are baptized, confirmation at a later age can acknowledge the Christian's personal acceptance of the Gospel and its injunction to witness. In confirmation the Holy Spirit given at baptism comes to fullness within the mature Christian who moves from a passive faith stance to take his or her place among those who are also signs of Christ for the world at large.

Celebration

Originally confirmation concluded the baptismal action. It does so again when celebrated with the other sacraments of initiation at the Easter vigil.[9]

Confirmation is a simple action. The bishop (or priest) lays hands on the person and prays that the Holy Spirit be quickened in that person. During this action the sponsor places his or her hand on the candidate's shoulder, symbolizing his or her role in guiding to the faith. The person is anointed with sacred chrism as the minister prays, "N, receive the Holy Spirit, the gift of the Father." The sacrament proper concludes as the minister extends the kiss of peace.

Confirmation is delayed until a baptized child is ready to assume full membership. The Eastern Churches confirm infants at baptism. In the West confirmation was received right before First Communion until into the twentieth century. Pope Pius XII gave permission for non-confirmed Catholics to receive Communion so that confirmation might be delayed. Today the practice varies. Sometimes it is given at baptism. Otherwise it is received later, whether at age seven or eighteen.

---

9. Intro 13, Way 33

TO DEEPEN—

What are the sacraments of initiation? What is the action of initiation?
What does baptism do?
Why are infants baptized?
Why is a person only baptized or confirmed once?
When are the sacraments of initiation celebrated?
What does confirmation as a separate sacrament express?

Further Reading:

Austin, Gerard. *The Rite of Confirmation: Anointing with the Spirit.* Pueblo, 1985.
Coleman, William & Patricia. *Confirmed to Courage.* Twenty Third, 1976.
Cullmann, Oscar. *Baptism in the New Testament.* Westminster, 1978.
Davis, Charles. *Sacraments of Initiation: Baptism and Confirmation.* Sheed & Ward, 1964.
Freburger, William. *Baptism.* Alba, 1970.
Kavanagh, Aidan. *The Shape of Baptism: The Rite of Christian Initiation.* Pueblo, 1978.
Keating, Charles. *Infant Baptism and the Christian Community.* Twenty Third, 1977.
McIntyre, Marie. *Confirmation: Making of a Christian.* Twenty Third, 1977.
Schmemann, Alexander. *Of Water and the Spirit—A Liturgical Study of Baptism.* St. Vladimir's, 1974.
St. John Chrysostom. *Baptismal Instructions.* Paulist Press, 1963. A great doctor of the Eastern Church, these instructions were originally addressed to neophytes in the Easter season.

TO CONTINUE—

The process of initiation and the catechumenate is found in Intro 6ff.
The central story into which Christians are initiated is found in Truth 19–20.

78. Eucharist

The sacraments of initiation culminate with the central sacrament of Christian life, the Eucharist. But unlike the other sacraments of initiation which are not repeated and undergird the Christian, the Eucharist sustains the Christian throughout the journey.

In celebrating the Eucharist the Church most clearly shows itself and makes its essence manifest. "The liturgy . . . most of all in the divine sacrifice of the Eucharist, is the outstanding means whereby the faithful can express in their lives, and manifest to others, the mystery of Christ and the real nature of the true Church."[10]

Memorial Meal

The Eucharist is the memorial meal Jesus instituted among his followers on the night before he was killed. This meal in turn is modeled upon both the Jewish evening meal of blessing and the Passover meal. These meals call to mind (or cause us to remember) the events which brought both Israel and now the Christian Church into being—the exodus from Egypt[11] and now the passover of Christ.[12]

The Eucharist also celebrates the new covenant established between God and humanity in Jesus Christ. The eucharistic wine is the blood which ratified the covenants of old:[13] here, the blood of Christ shed on the cross.[14] The cup is at the same time the cup of blessing[15] which manifests the many blessings of this new covenant.

The Eucharist is a foretaste and participation in the great banquet of the kingdom. Thus it is reflected in the prophecies of the coming kingdom and its banquet,[16] as well as Jesus' banquet imagery[17] and his ministry from the wedding at Cana[18] to his image as bridegroom.[19] This is the feast of the Lamb.[20]

Sacrifice

The Eucharist is a sacrifice of praise and thanksgiving to the Father through Jesus Christ in the Holy Spirit.[21] This sacrifice further is a commemoration and also an expiation for the living and the dead. The Eucharist is the sacrifice of Jesus on Calvary. There are not two sacrifices or more, only one. The Eucharist makes present throughout time and

---

10. Constitution on the Sacred Liturgy, n. 2
11. Truth 8
12. Truth 18
13. Ex 24:6–8
14. Jn 19:34
15. 1 Cor 10:16
16. Is 25:6–10
17. Lk 14:15–24
18. Jn 2:1–11
19. Mt 25:1–13
20. Rev 21
21. Way 8

space in an unbloody manner Christ's sacrifice on the cross as both priest and victim. This sacrifice of the Mass is "properly offered not only for the sins, penalties, satisfactions, and other needs of the faithful who are living but also for the departed in Christ who are not yet fully cleansed."[22]

Celebrating the Eucharist draws us into that original sacrifice of Christ. We enter it as our way to the Father. And we bring our sins, our concern for friends and relatives to this sacrifice and join them with the sufferings and sins of all the world. And in return we are blessed, and God's grace won in Christ's cross flows out to the entire world in the Eucharist and though us who receive the Eucharist.

Christ's Presence

Catholics believe that Jesus Christ is truly present whenever the Eucharist is celebrated. This doctrine of the real presence finds its particular Roman Catholic articulation as transubstantiation (the substance of the bread and wine is changed into the body and blood of Christ although the accidents—external appearance and characteristics—remain those of bread and wine).

Christ's presence is not limited to bread and wine. Christ is present whenever two or three followers gather in his name.[23] Christ is present in the Gospel proclaimed, for the Gospel speaks his living word which calls, teaches, nourishes and challenges us today. Christ is present in the priest who imitates Jesus' actions at the Last Supper and presides in his name. Christ is present in his followers. And Christ commissions us, once nourished, to go forth to love and to serve one another.

The Eucharist has many other dimensions. These are simply meanings which the Church has proclaimed, often resulting from controversy. But the true power of sacrament communicates at a level deeper than word, sustaining our journey in times of gladness and suffering, community and alienation, health and sickness, consolation and desolation. The Eucharist touches all life's experience, nourishing our journey, sustaining our faith, promoting our conversion and growth into Christ.

Certain special occasions and events are made firm in the remaining sacraments. They are often celebrated in the context of the Eucharist. The particular sacrament may say something quite specific—a

22. Trent—Decree on the Mass, chapter II
23. Mt 18:20

marriage celebrates and inaugurates a new covenant between a man and a woman—but the underlying Christian experience of sacrificial love is encountered not only in the special sacrament of matrimony, but in a more general and universal manner in the Eucharist.

TO DEEPEN—

What is the Eucharist?
What does the doctrine of the real presence mean?
How is the Eucharist a sacrifice?
How is the Eucharist a meal?

Further Reading:

Balasuriya, Tissa. *The Eucharist and Human Liberation.* Orbis, 1979.
Bernier, Paul. *Bread Broken and Shared.* Ave Maria, 1981.
Bernier, Paul J., ed. *Bread From Heaven: Essays on the Eucharist.* Paulist Press, 1977.
Guzie, Tad W. *Jesus and the Eucharist.* Paulist Press, 1974.
Haring, Bernard. *The Eucharist and Our Everyday Life.* Crossroad, 1979.
Livermore, Penny. *Called to His Supper: The Biblical Eucharist.* Glazier, 1983.
Lussier, Ernest. *Living the Eucharistic Mystery.* Alba, 1976.
Merton, Thomas. *The Living Bread.* Farrar, Strauss, & Giroux, 1956. This monk became one of the most popular spiritual writers in the modern Church. Here are his meditations on the Eucharist.
Pennington, Basil. *The Eucharist Yesterday and Today.* Crossroad, 1983.
Seasoltz, Kevin. *Living Bread, Saving Cup: Readings on the Eucharist.* Liturgical Press, 1982.

TO CONTINUE—

The celebration of the Eucharist is found in Way 19ff.
The institution of the Eucharist is discussed in Truth 19.

79. SACRAMENTS OF HEALING

Certain sacraments apply to special situations in a Christian life. Thus they apply in a specific way grace generally mediated through the Eucharist. The first group concerns reconciliation and healing within the Christian community. These sacraments continue two important aspects of Jesus' ministry.

Jesus forgave sins[1] and healed the sick.[2] He passed these ministries on to the disciples. Jesus gives them the power to loose and bind in his name.[3] After Easter Peter and John heal in his name.[4] In Jesus' name the Church continues those ministries for its members and for the world as a sign of the kingdom.

80. Penance

Meaning

Since Christians are continuously converting toward the kingdom they are imperfect and do sin. The Church is holy and at the same time in constant need of purification. Baptism cleanses all past sins. But Christian life continues the pre-baptismal action of repentance and turning toward the Lord. Christians share in the sufferings of Christ enduring their own difficulties.[5]

Sinfulness is commonly healed through the Eucharist. Constantly throughout the ritual we confess our sinfulness of God, and in return are reconciled with God and one another.[6] Furthermore Vatican II provides for penitential services where through prayer and proclamation of God's word we come to repentance and renew dedication to Gospel values.

The sacrament of penance reconciles sin. The Eucharist also heals ordinary and sometimes seemingly all-pervasive selfishness. But what of those actions that deeply hurt or isolate us from others? In such a case, when in mortal sin,[7] the Roman Catholic is also cut off from the Christian community, even if that community is not the body sinned against. For the Christian undertakes to be a sign of Christ to the world. Serious sin ruptures one's association with the body of Christ because the world sees in that sin not a sign of Christ, but a betrayal of the covenant.

Could such a sin be forgiven? The early Church took a rather stern view of public serious sin. The sinner was only received back after

---

1. Mk 2:5
2. Mk 2:1–12
3. Jn 20:23
4. Acts 3:1–10
5. 2 Tim 1:8–13
6. Way 21, 26
7. Way 45

confession and public penance. Reconciliation after baptism was possible, but exceptional.

The evangelization of Europe added a different situation. Accomplished to a great extent by Irish monks with reputations of heroic sanctity, people sought these monks for confession and spiritual direction. The monks in turn imposed penances and absolved the people. This custom grew and flourished.

Since the Reformation[8] claimed that only two sacraments were instituted by Christ, Rome was forced to clarify the issue. Trent declared that confession, which had been celebrated in a number of ways, is a sacrament. Penance is necessary for a Christian in a state of serious sin and must be sought, if necessary, at least once a year.[9]

Penance manifests God's forgiveness and receives the penitent back into the Church community. The priest acts on behalf of the community. No sin is only against God; all sin is social in its consequences. So all sin needs reconciliation to the human community in addition to God's forgiveness. God's forgiveness is not restricted to this sacrament, but is assured by the Church each time the sacrament is celebrated.

The Second Vatican Council brought forward the community dimension of penance—this is not simply a person's reconciliation to God, but reincorporates into the community. Communal penance celebrations emphasize this dimension. Penance is also a wonderful help in the Christian's continuous journey of conversion. It provides solace, comfort, challenge, and healing for our continuing pilgrimage.

Celebration

Penance has had a checkered and colorful history within the Christian community. And reforms of the Second Vatican Council encourage its celebration in a number of ways.

Penance forgives sins, strengthening the continuing work of conversion and growth in holiness. While the Eucharist also reconciles, penance is necessary for those sins which break the social fabric. A Catholic is obliged to receive the sacrament when in mortal sin.[10]

A state of mortal sin is not necessary to partake of the sacrament. Penance helps us on the Christian journey toward wholeness. Taking periodic time out to consider one's life in the light of the Gospel is beneficial. After such an examination Catholics approach the sacrament to

---

8. Life 34
9. Intro 19
10. Intro 19

heal the rifts in relationships, and for the grace to continue turning toward Christ.

Four actions are involved in the sacrament. The first is **contrition**. We see our sins clearly, are sorry and wish to avoid future repetitions. Contrition is the foundation for metanoia or conversion.[11] Before turning toward the Lord one must come to accept one's sinfulness and desire change. Through contrition the person begins to consider, judge and arrange his or her life according to the holiness and love of God.

Confession itself forms the second action. Catholics avail themselves of the sacrament by going to a priest and confessing, knowing that they there encounter God's mercy.

In confession one tells the nature and number of sinful actions. There is no need to go into great detail. However the experience is dependent upon what is brought to confession and one's attitude toward the process. In bringing insignificant matters, how can one hope for significant healing? Confession demands a close look at one's life. Are we living like Christ? In what ways are we stuck in sinful behavior? What part does selfishness play in our life? These are hard questions. But they enable us to come to know ourselves and ask God's forgiveness which enables conversion.

Having confessed one receives a **penance**. This action helps restore the order disturbed by sin and furthers conversion. Penance is the beginning of renewal. "Thus the penitent, 'forgetting the things which are behind him,'[12] again becomes part of the mystery of salvation and turns himself toward the future."[13]

Absolution, spoken by the priest, extends God's forgiveness to the penitent. Speaking the words the priest places his hands on the penitent's head. Various images from Scripture echo this action and reveal its depths in meditation: the father receiving back the prodigal son,[14] the shepherd placing the lost sheep on his shoulders and bringing it back to the fold,[15] the Holy Spirit sanctifying the temple of God again.[16] Reconciliation leads to celebration at the Lord's table where there is great joy over the one returned from afar.

Normally this sacrament is celebrated privately between penitent and confessor. The penitent chooses whether to confess behind a screen or make the confession a dialogue with the priest. In any case the con-

11. Way 47
12. Phil 3:13
13. Rite of Penance 6c
14. Lk 15:11–32
15. Lk 15:3–7
16. Ez 43ff

fessor is strictly forbidden ever to disclose the contents. This is known as the seal of confession.

Today many churches celebrate penance services. These usually consist of a liturgy of the word[17] stressing penance in the context of the current liturgical season. A period for personal examination follows. Finally opportunity for confession is offered. When penance is celebrated privately, it is begun with a reading from Scripture. Then the penitent confesses his or her sins. In certain situations general absolution may be granted if it is impossible to hear all the confessions privately. But this is an exceptional situation, and if in mortal sin private confession should be sought in the future.

> The celebration of this sacrament is thus always an act in which the Church proclaims its faith, gives thanks to God for the freedom with which Christ has made us free, and offers its life as a spiritual sacrifice in praise of God's glory, as it hastens to meet the Lord Jesus.[18]

81. Anointing of the Sick

Meaning

> Is any among you sick? Let him call for the elders of the church, and let them pray over him, anointing him with oil in the name of the Lord; and the prayer of faith will save the sick man, and the Lord will raise him up; and if he has committed sins, he will be forgiven. Therefore confess your sins to one another, and pray for one another, that you may be healed.[19]

This ceremony is the source of the current sacrament. The sacrament offers the power of healing. And it shows how illness can be for our growth as well. It is not simply an evil that has befallen but can be a sacred time for drawing closer to the Lord. "From Christ's words they know that sickness has meaning and value for their own salvation and

---

17. Way 20
18. Rite of Penance 7b
19. Jas 5:14–18

for the world's; they also know that Christ loved the sick and that during his life he often looked upon the sick and healed them."[20]

Our society considers sickness only negatively. When sick, we often feel not only physically but in every way isolated and excluded from society. The sacrament proclaims that we are not cut off from the Christian community. We are still part of the Church. And through our sufferings and illness we participate in the redemptive sufferings of Christ. Our illness need not be without meaning even though we may not be able at this point to perceive its significance.

The Church's presence to us in the sacrament tells us of the special place we have in that community because of our illness. The Church prays for our healing in this specific sacrament as well as through on-going community prayers for all the sick.

The sacrament also offers the opportunity for confession. These sacraments of healing are tied together just as they are connected in life. Jesus points to a connection between sin and illness.[21] This should not be interpreted that illness is a punishment for what we have done. Often a spiritual or psychological component to physical sickness demands healing of the whole person, not simply the physical aspect.

The sacrament provides God's grace for the present situation. Sickness has many ramifications. It often brings on depression, feelings of isolation, unworthiness, despair. God's grace can meet these situations with faith and trust. This grace also provides hope and staves off anxiety which slows or interferes with healing.

The sacrament heals. This is not always the case, but our faith in the healing power of this sacrament is growing as the Church once more experiences this sacrament as a means of ministry to the sick.[22] Meant to continue Jesus' healing ministry within his community, it often does exactly that.

Finally the sacrament calls us back to our fundamental vision of life. Engaged in life we often come to think of ourselves in terms of what we can do, of what we have accomplished. Our boundaries narrow to the matter at hand. Sickness threatens this view. Suddenly all that was taken for granted is removed. Suffering confronts us anew with life's meaning and purpose. The sacrament presents our salvation through

---

20. Rite of Anointing 1
21. Mk 2:1–12
22. Until recently the Western Church reserved this sacrament for those in danger of death. Thus our experience with the sacrament as a healing action is very limited.

Christ's death and resurrection and shows how this illness, even if mortal, is part of our pilgrimage toward wholeness.

Celebration

The sacrament is usually celebrated individually. However today many churches have periodic public celebrations during the Eucharist. In a serious illness or before a serious operation the priest should be called to celebrate the sacrament. It is good for family and friends of the sick person to join together in the celebration representing the Christian community. The sacrament of reconciliation should, if possible, be celebrated beforehand so that the anointing itself may be more public.

The rite begins with a greeting and a sprinkling with holy water. A penitential rite follows, then the liturgy of the word. God heals through his word—the words spoken by Jesus, that Word which is Jesus.

Next all join in a litany asking God's healing and assistance of those who care for the ill. The priest lays his hands on the person's head in silence. The oil is then blessed. The forehead and hands are anointed as the priest prays:

> Through this holy anointing may the Lord in his love and mercy
>   help you with the grace of the Holy Spirit. Amen. May the
>   Lord who frees you from sin save you and raise you up. Amen.

A prayer follows, and then the Lord's Prayer. Communion may be given and a final blessing concludes the service.

In danger of death Catholics receive the last rites, the sacrament of the dying. The person receives Holy Communion, here called "Viaticum" ("going with"). If the person has not already received the sacrament of the sick, it is given as part of this rite.

TO DEEPEN—

How is sin reconciled within the Christian community?

Why should a person be obliged to confess to a priest?

What are the actions of penance?

What does the sacrament of anointing celebrate and do?

How are penance and anointing related?

When should a Catholic request penance? Anointing?

Further Reading:

Champlin, Joseph. *Together in Peace.* Ave Maria Press, 1975.

Drahos, Mary. *To Touch the Hem of His Garment—A True Story of Healing.* Paulist Press, 1983.

Foley, Leonard. *Your Confession: Using the New Ritual.* St. Anthony Messenger, 1975.

Gula, Richard M. *To Walk Together Again. The Sacrament of Reconciliation.* Paulist Press, 1984.

Haring, Bernard. *Discovering God's Mercy: Confession Helps for Today's Catholic.* Liguori Publications, 1980.

Jean-Mesmy, Claude. *Conscience and Confession.* Franciscan Herald Press, 1965.

MacNutt, Francis. *Healing.* Ave Maria Press, 1974.

Roccapriore, Maria. *Anointing the Sick.* Alba, 1980.

Sanford, John A. *Healing and Wholeness.* Paulist Press, 1977.

TO CONTINUE—

The way of conversion upon which the sacraments are founded is described in Way 47ff.

Jesus' ministry of healing and forgiveness is indicated in Truth 18.

The forgiveness of sins is discussed in Truth 43.

The general path of conversion is set forth in Life 3.

82. SACRAMENTS OF VOCATION

Two sacraments define certain lifestyles as encounters with God. Matrimony and holy orders focus upon basic experiences of God as love and service, and are defined by the Church as sacramental institutions.

83. Holy Matrimony

Meaning

Marriage is a universal human institution. Beginning in the Hebrew Scriptures and coming to a climax in the Christian Scriptures, God is imaged as a bridegroom entering into a marriage with humanity, either as Israel[1] or as the Church.[2] This metaphor makes Christian marriage a sign of Christ's relation to his Church.

---

1. Is 54:5
2. Eph 5:25

Catholic tradition sees marriage as a natural institution. In Christ that covenant is lifted up into a new dimension becoming sacramental. Through their love the couple experiences God. They become to their community symbols of God's love, fidelity and creativity. Marriage is a sacrament whenever entered into by two baptized people. Catholics must follow the Roman Catholic form for the wedding. The ministers are the man and woman. The priest or deacon, the Church's representative, along with the best man and maid of honor, witnesses the sacrament, and the priest then blesses the union. The ceremony initiates the covenant which is sealed by sexual intercourse.

Celebration

To enter into Christian marriage the couple must be unmarried and freely desire to marry. Three conditions are necessary. First, each person must decide freely. Second, each must affirm the Catholic teaching that marriage is a solemn covenant of total fidelity lasting for life. Third, they must be open to the possibility of children if it be God's will.

Most churches require a period of time before marriage for instruction in the responsibilities of married life. Further, if the couple is very young the Church may require counseling.

The sacrament is conferred by the couple upon one another. The priest and witnesses represent Church and state. The priest also blesses the couple, but the couple themselves minister the sacrament. In special circumstances a Roman Catholic may be married outside the Church. Such a marriage, provided that proper procedure is followed, is valid and legal.

The rite of matrimony is quite flexible. People are encouraged to personalize the ritual using customs from their cultural background. What follows sketches the official rites.

Marriage is often celebrated in the context of the Eucharist, but may also be celebrated separately. Either situation begins with an entrance procession and the greeting, prayers, readings and homily forming the liturgy of the word.[3]

The minister questions the couple concerning their freedom of choice, their faithfulness to one another and their acceptance and upbringing of children. Then he invites the couple to declare their consent. The minister witnesses their consent and blesses the rings given as signs of their love and fidelity.

---

3. Way 20

The Eucharist now follows and the nuptial blessing is given after the Lord's Prayer. Celebrated outside Mass, the nuptial blessing, in which the Church and all those gathered ask God to bless the couple and their new life together, ends the ceremony.

The couple may decide to incorporate other symbols into the ceremony. Some choose a common candle lit from tapers held by each: the two lights become one thus shine forth Christ. Some choose the ancient cup of blessing from Israel. A cup of wine is blessed, and the couple drink from it, promising to share life's sweetness as well as the bitterness that falls into every life together.

84. Holy Orders

Meaning

All Christians by initiation[4] share in the one priesthood of Jesus Christ. Thus all are commissioned to be evangelists of the Gospel in their lives—through love, service, healing, reconciliation, liberation of the oppressed, and all the other actions which proclaim and bring the kingdom to birth in the world.

But there is a further need for a specialized ministry within the Christian community. A community exists and is extended through time and space only through a certain order or structure. The Church's sacrament of holy orders concerns the ministry of Christ to Christians and to the world in specialized ways that do not supplant, but aid the mission of all Christians.

Holy orders ordains a man to serve in one of the Church's structured ministries. These are the episcopacy (the office of bishop), the presbyterate (or priesthood) and the diaconate. Men called and chosen for these offices are given in the sacrament the graces necessary to fulfill these offices. They in turn consecrate their lives to Jesus Christ under the sign of service to Church and world. As the married couple vows to journey toward Christ along the path of love, the ordained minister finds Christ primarily through service.

In turn the sacrament commissions the person to become a sign of Christ as servant for others. Jesus, in washing his disciples' feet,[5] gave his community a different relationship of leader and follower than prevails in the world.[6] The priest is committed to a life spent in service to

---

4. Truth 75
5. Jn 13:2-16
6. Mt 20:24-28

the Christian community. In addition, the priest is bound by a promise of celibacy in the Latin rite.

The fullness of the sacrament is found in the bishop: the priest, teacher, and shepherd of the local Christian community known as a diocese.[7] He leads the community in prayer and liturgy. He celebrates all the sacraments with his people, and he and the other bishops, with the Pope, the bishop of Rome, as their head, form a college which governs and is the authoritative teacher of the Church.[8]

The priest (or presbyter) participates in the priesthood of Christ and is ordained to help the bishop in the ministry. Thus the priest leads in prayer and worship and celebrates the sacraments necessary to parish functioning[9] (all but holy orders and, with exceptions, confirmation). He teaches and governs the local community in the bishop's name.

Finally the deacon (an order newly restored in its own right) assists the bishop and priests in the local ministry. The deacon preaches, teaches, celebrates the liturgy of the word and the sacraments of baptism and marriage, and conducts funerals. He does not celebrate the Eucharist although he has a role in its celebration, nor does he hear confessions or anoint the sick.

Celebration

As the name implies, holy orders comprises a number of rites and offices. The actual sacrament only refers to the major orders of bishop, presbyter and deacon.

In the Church's history a number of minor orders also evolved. Although not the sacrament proper, they commission specific ministries. Today lay people undertake these ministries such as lector or distributor of Communion although they are not formally ordained. A seminarian still receives these ministries as part of preparation for holy orders.

The ordination of presbyters is celebrated within the context of the Eucharist. After the liturgy of the word, those to be ordained are called forward. They are questioned as to whether they want to undertake the ministry; then the community prays over them. Finally the bishop and the other priests present lay hands on their head. Then they are given the symbols of their office and charged to carry out the ministry. Following the ordination the Eucharist is celebrated. The orders of deacon and bishop are slightly different.

---

7. Life 19
8. Truth 22
9. Life 18

TO DEEPEN—

What aspects of Jesus' teaching about God do matrimony and holy orders show forth?

What are the conditions necessary for Christian marriage?

What are the different major holy orders?

Who shares in the priesthood of Jesus Christ? How? How are the ordained ministries different from this overall priesthood?

Further Reading:

Aridas, Christopher. *Your Catholic Wedding: A Complete Plan Book*. Doubleday, 1982.

Brown, Raymond. *Priest and Bishop: Biblical Reflections*. Paulist Press, 1970.

Chrysostom, St. John. *On the Priesthood*. St. Vladimir's Press, 1977. The greatest Greek Father's exploration of priesthood.

Hart, Thomas N. *Living Happily Ever After: Toward a Theology of Christian Marriage*. Paulist Press, 1979.

Hewitt, Emily. & Hiatt, Suzanne. *Women Priests: Yes or No?* Seabury, 1973.

Le Maire, H. Paul. *Marriage Takes a Lifetime*. Twenty Third, 1981.

Mackin, Theodore. *What is Marriage: Marriage in the Catholic Church*. Paulist Press, 1982.

Mohler, James. *The Origin and Evolution of the Priesthood*. Alba, 1976.

O'Meara, Thomas. *Theology of Ministry*. Paulist Press, 1983.

Rahner, Karl. *The Priesthood*. Crossroad, 1970.

Schiappa, *Mixing: Catholic-Protestant Marriages in the 1980s*. Paulist Press, 1982.

Schillebeeckx, Edward. *The Church with a Human Face: A New and Expanded Theology of Ministry*. Crossroad, 1985.

Tremaine, Ann. *Gift of Love: Marriage as a Spiritual Journey*. Paulist Press, 1983.

Whitehead, Evelyn & James. *Christian Life Patterns*. Doubleday, 1983.

Woytyla, Karol. *Fruitful and Responsible Love*. Crossroad, 1979. Thoughts on marriage by Pope John Paul II.

TO CONTINUE—

Catholic ethics of sexuality and marriage are found in Truth 53 and 65.

The religious priesthood is described in The Religious Life (Life 11).

The organizational structure of the Church within which the ministry functions is found in Life 15ff.

THE LIFE

◊ **Life in the Spirit**
◊ **Life in the Church**
◊ **Life in the Kingdom**
◊ **Epilogue**

Introduction

Just how does Christianity fashion life in accordance with the Truth and the Way? This part focuses upon the practical matters of Christian life—customs, practices, attitudes which go to make up a concrete Christian existence.

Christian existence is explored under three broad categories: first, the individual: one's spirituality, prayer and life in the world. The next section considers life in the Church. Finally, life in the kingdom is explored as it has already manifested and continues to manifest in our world.

Most of this material is not as fundamental as the former parts, but fills in the picture of the lived Christian experience. While interesting, it should not replace knowledge of the major traditions.[1] Mostly trivia in its original sense, this third part covers what was left out of the previous material.

---

1. Intro 1

◇

1. Life in the Spirit

Here some key themes are considered under a new perspective—the actualities of Christian living. What is life in the Holy Spirit like? We return to the foundations of the path. Conversion is not left behind once one becomes a Christian but is the solid rock grounding all spiritual life.

The Christian lives in the Holy Spirit. This life is described in a number of lists (some going back to Scripture)—mnemonic devices which help make flesh something so abstract and diverse as human life. They do not exhaust Christian life, but are guidelines.

Allow them to point toward your own incarnation of the Holy Spirit, bringing together the Spirit's many fruits and works. We are dealing with experience difficult to communicate in words. The words are mere seeds which must be taken prayerfully into our hearts so that God might lead us into their reality which is truly the Spirit.

Then we consider just what forms the prayer life of the Christian might take: What are the prayer styles and spiritualities of the Catholic tradition? Finally we consider the actual shape of Christian life as it exists in our world. Here we consider some Catholic contributions to culture. We are not concerned here with the lives of saints[1] but those who have enriched human culture through their creativity in some way reflecting the Catholic tradition.

---

1. Life 46

2. Spiritual Life

Although Christianity centers upon conversion,[2] it need not always imply a radical uprooting. The change is often on a deeper level than one's physical life—what one does, one's family, one's lifestyle. These may seem to remain constant throughout the process of conversion.

But now a deeper dimension is perceived in life. One sees with new eyes, with a new heart. And in that new perception everything is subtly transformed. It is not always necessary to pull up roots, change one's living patterns, etc., to become a Christian. The difference is in how the Christian perceives and then responds.

A beautiful summary of Christian life comes from Israel. Christians have found in Psalm 23 a full expression of our life in Christ.

The Lord is my shepherd, I shall not want;
he makes me lie down in green pastures.
He leads me beside still waters,
he restores my soul.
He leads me in paths of righteousness
for his name's sake.
Even though I walk through the valley of the shadow of death,
I fear no evil;
for thou art with me;
thy rod and thy staff, they comfort me.
Thou preparest a table before me
in the presence of my enemies;
Thou anointest my head with oil,
my cup overflows.
Surely goodness and mercy shall follow me
all the days of my life;
and I shall dwell in the house of the Lord for ever.

"Shepherd" is a beautiful image Jesus used to describe God. He spoke of the shepherd who would leave the flock behind to search for the one lost sheep.[3] He noted the shepherd's care for the sheep.[4] And

---

2. Way 47
3. Mt 18:10–14
4. Jn 10:8–9

he takes the image up to new (and from a worldly point of view ridiculous) heights when he speaks of the Good Shepherd laying down his life for his sheep.[5]

The Christian begins from this image of God as a shepherd who cares for each creature. God reaches out to us when we are lost. We need never feel alone, abandoned, or rejected again.

Thus the Christian lives grounded in faith and trust in God. We believe that the universe in its depths cares and responds to all creatures. We believe that the foundation of all existence is a God called love.

I Shall Not Want

Meeting God as shepherding love, Christians believe that their needs will be met. Humans desire and dream. We are seldom truly satisfied with things as they are; we hope for better. We hunger and thirst for happiness. And much of life seems a futile pursuit of that happiness. For even when we attain what we seek, it often fails to satisfy fully.

For Jesus true happiness is not a cruel illusion. What we seek, God wishes us to have. But perhaps we have been seeking in the wrong place, or for the wrong thing. God will not leave us wanting. Jesus invites us upon a pilgrimage toward our heart's true desire. And Christian life is based upon the hope that we will come into our inheritance.

He Makes Me Lie Down in Green Pastures

Green pastures beautifully symbolize earth itself which God gives for our enjoyment.[6] The Christian comes to see life and all its varied panoply as a gift from God. We tend to take what we have for granted. Thus we are unsatisfied and long for what we do not have. But is not satisfaction within reach if we but awaken to the richness that is already ours? Seeing life as gift changes attitudes, feelings, and thoughts. We are able to enjoy the benefits of this moment instead of being blinded to what is present by anxiety to achieve what lies ahead.

Part of the Christian experience is the growing awareness of the present sufficiency of our life. Life is God's gift which awaits our gratitude to reveal its riches.

---

5. Jn 10:11
6. Gen 1:26

He Leads Me Beside Still Waters

The still waters refer to baptism.[7] In the sacraments we encounter God. Baptism begins Christian existence. But its waters are not left behind. Our baptism goes with us throughout Christian life.

Baptism reveals peace in the restful waters. Instead of grasping for life or our soul, baptism teaches us to let go, to sink under the waters. Only then do we find our peace.

The image of rest points toward another theme. Our rest is in the Lord. Rest describes our final goal. Christians speak of their heavenly rest. Augustine's heart was restless until it rested in God. The Christian values rest as a sign and experience of that final rest in the kingdom of God.

Christians keep the sacred rest one day a week on the Lord's day.[8] We do not live merely to work. What we create is a gift. We are not judged by what we have done. We are loved in that we simply are. And so we do not need to create ourselves, or find our justification for living in our labor. Our labor can be a gift, a praise of God, a joining in the work of creation. But that labor, that work is only part of the story. We are made also for the rest. The sabbath,[9] which reminds us who we truly are, restores us.

Christians find this rest in prayer as well. Meditation is time out from the world of doing: time for the world of simple being, the world that is God.

He Restores My Soul

In baptism we surrender. And it would seem that we die. But actually in losing, in letting go, God raises us up. Christian spirituality advises losing one's soul to find it restored in God.

Baptism reveals the Gospel's core. Buried with Jesus, in him we are restored, raised up into a new life. And belonging now to Christ, we continue to live out this baptismal action of dying and rising in the Lord. Here is the essence of conversion: the means by which we are gradually transformed and built up into the body of Christ.

He Leads Me in Paths of Righteousness for His Name's Sake

Jesus, the namesake of God, is our guide in this new life. He is God in human form. And he guides through his word in Scripture, through

---

7. Truth 76
8. Intro 16
9. Gen 2:3; Ex 20:8–11

his body the Church, through his action in our life, and through his response to our prayer.

The paths of righteousness are the ways to God's kingdom. These paths lead to light, to real happiness. And the paths are various, including the sacraments. But they also encompass the guidance of other Christians who walk these paths with us and show us their insights. The paths lead toward truth, toward what is right, toward God's justice experienced as mercy.

Even Though I Walk Through the Valley of the Shadow of Death

This present world is the valley of the shadow of death. The world is bent from its original purpose.[10] Now the domain of the prince of lies, God's light still shines out from creation, but our senses, dulled with sin, do not perceive clearly. And this world with its "realities" of rich and poor, master and slave, power and weakness, self and other, is but a valley in the shadow of death. Its only end is death. It cannot give us life or real happiness.

Jesus does not remove us from this world. His truth illuminates the world, revealing its illusions and turning us to the kingdom already dawning. And Jesus sends us into the world with his gift of truth and life. In this world we walk, guided in paths of righteousness, so that we in turn might shed light and be the gift of love to our brothers and sisters, liberating them from the dark valley.

I Fear No Evil; for Thou Art with Me

Christians are not simply sent into the world again. We have also begun to be liberated from that world. The world uses fear as a weapon of control. We are taught to fear. Some learn so well that they fear everything.

Part of Jesus' teaching liberates us from these controls. Scripture encourages us to "be not afraid." Seeing through other "realities" Christians find liberation from the suffering and misery which is the world's only gift to its inhabitants. Jesus asks his followers to put aside judgment,[11] to leave it to God. He teaches us to drop our notion of ourselves as separate entities and to come to see ourselves again in the unity of God's beloved creation.[12]

Thus even though Christians remain in the world, we are no longer

---

10. Truth 57
11. Lk 6:37
12. Mt 5:43–48

of the world. We do not take the world ultimately. Jesus' light dispels it. We have even seen through death to glimpse the new creation. We walk the shadowy valley without worldly fear, because we have Christ.

Thy Rod and Thy Staff, They Comfort Me

To discover a deeper meaning we must read these lines as the early Christians did in the Greek translation.[13] God speaks through not only the original Scriptures but through the specific Christian translation into Greek—the Septuagint.

There a pun appears, not found in the original Hebrew or in our English. Greek for "staff" is "parakleitos," very similar to the word "Paraclete," referring to the Holy Spirit.[14] Thus the guide through Christian life that gives us comfort on our journey, that supports us like a walking staff, is the Holy Spirit. And Christian tradition makes Comforter and Consoler a key characteristic of the Spirit.

Our life is transformed because God quickens the Holy Spirit within us. Our journey is actually the Spirit's pilgrimage home. The Father breathes out the Spirit who then returns to the Father, bringing home all creation. With faith in this great return, Christians take comfort even in life's vicissitudes. Whatever our present circumstances, we are truly homeward bound.

This image also recalls the staff of healing, the caduceus. And the Holy Spirit also heals. Bearers of that Spirit in the world, we are called to healing ministry—continuing Jesus' work. Having received comfort, we are sent to comfort our brothers and sisters.

Thou Preparest a Table Before Me

Here the Christian recognizes the Eucharist,[15] set before us along life's journey. From this table we receive nourishment and companionship. Its food strengthens us for ministry, replenishes our depleted energy, lifts our faith, and manifests in life's midst the fellowship of the Lord and his kingdom.

In the Presence of My Enemies

The table is set up in the presence of enemies. This food will sustain us in our darkest hours, surrounded by our enemies. Christ does

---

13. Way 7
14. Truth 38
15. Truth 78

not take us out of the world, but nourishes us in its very midst, so that we in turn might be a leaven, a salt for that world.[16]

And why are Christians placed in the presence of our enemies? To continue Jesus' mission of reconciliation. In Christ there are no enemies. Jesus counsels love of enemies. He prays for his executioners.[17] Living in Jesus and sustained by his eucharistic body, we too must come to see that we have no enemies. And toward those considered our enemies we must show Christ's forgiveness.[18]

Thou Anointest My Head with Oil

This phrase recalls confirmation.[19] Ancient peoples consecrated kings and priests by pouring oil upon their heads. The image is rich— perfumed oil, softening our skin, soothing away pain and tension, consecrating us to the Lord's work. For Christians are sent to preach the good news with their lives. Christians do not exist for themselves. Like Jesus we live to serve.

My Cup Overflows

What a rich description of Christian life! The image calls to mind the eucharistic cup, itself an image of the abundant wine in the great banquet.[20] Yet even now, in the Eucharist, in our life, the Christian tastes that cup's overflowing richness. Recall too the wedding at Cana where Jesus literally made the wine overflow.[21] This is life in the kingdom, and life now in service of the kingdom.

Surely Goodness and Mercy Shall Follow Me All the Days of My Life

Christians look forward to goodness and mercy as their experience of life. No matter what the circumstances we try to perceive beneath them God's sustaining mercy. God is leading all creation toward a kingdom founded on compassion. This is not to say that every Christian's life is easy. Jesus specifically identified with the poor and oppressed. But we look not simply to the present but forward toward the kingdom when all tears will be wiped away. Under that horizon our life shines in goodness and mercy.

---

16. Mt 5:13; 13:33
17. Lk 23:34
18. Way 50; Truth 80
19. Truth 77
20. Lk 14:15–24
21. Jn 2:1–11

And I Shall Dwell in the House of the Lord For Ever

The Lord's house is only secondarily a church or temple. In former days people felt that the Lord only dwelt in a certain place. When Jesus converses with the Samaritan woman, he tells her that the day is coming when God's temple will not be restricted to Jerusalem.[22] Those days are now upon us, for God's dwelling today is the Christian's body—the temple of the Holy Spirit.[23] To find God we need not journey toward some exterior shrine. God is as close as our very breath.

TO DEEPEN—

Memorize this psalm and make it part of your own prayer life.

Why has this psalm become so important to and beloved for Christians?

Can you think of any aspects of Christian life not included in this psalm?

Which sense of Scripture would read this psalm as treated in this section? (See Way 5)

How does this psalm prefigure the sacraments? And what does it say concerning the place of sacraments in Christian life?

TO CONTINUE—

The psalms are the basis for Christian daily prayer (Life 38).

3. THE FOUNDATIONS OF CHRISTIAN LIVING

TO PREPARE—

The process of conversion and penance should be covered (Way 46–48).

The Sermon on the Mount in Matthew presents Jesus' teachings concerning repentance and becoming members of God's kingdom. We

---

22. Jn 4:21–24
23. 1 Cor 6:19

must work upon ourselves in the context of our life. It means work upon our passions and emotions: lifting lust up to the human dimension of love,[1] moving beyond anger toward God's viewpoint which sees creation as one and his people as one family, seeing through the fictions of fear and worry which keep us imprisoned and afraid to risk truly living.[2]

This collection of Jesus' teachings is not a new law laid on our shoulders but an invitation to grow into a new creation. It is not easy or comfortable. But transformation promises a fuller life. And this work will enable us to experience wholeness we already enjoy in God's eyes thanks to Jesus' death and resurrection here and now in our life. To wait until life is over misses the precious opportunity of the present moment which Jesus constantly calls us live to.

Christians traditionally speak of three steps in conversion. At the beginning of his purgatory Dante depicts these steps literally. At Peter's gate, the entrance to Purgatory proper, Dante and Virgil, his guide, encounter first a white step for confession. God's light enables us to see ourselves clearly and acknowledge how we fall short. The second step, contrition, is black—the color of mourning. It is also cracked in the figure of the cross, for our sin killed Christ. The third step in red symbolizes satisfaction, for Christ's blood reconciled us with God and heals us.

Further detail in these stages of penitence is drawn from a practical way of living used by many people. The steps were originally drawn from the Oxford Movement, an evangelical and Catholic renewal in the Church of England. These twelve steps provide a means for anyone to live daily the Way of Jesus. They are primarily associated with Alcoholics Anonymous and other twelve step groups, but they can help people in all conditions to integrate the Christian vision into ordinary living.

Jesus' path involves working upon oneself in the context of daily life. An overall theme of such living might be defined as: one day at a time. "Sufficient unto the day is the evil thereof."[3] Such an idea might sound easy. Yet, examining our life, we discover that we indeed do not so live in this way. We live in the past and the future, but not the present. Yet to begin living in the present changes our life.

---

1. Mt 5:28ff
2. Mt 5:44ff
3. Mt 6:34

Confession

1. We admitted we were powerless over our life—that our lives had become unmanageable.

The first step of any spiritual path is to realize that one needs help in living. Most people believe that their lives are under their control, Yet such control is at best limited. As long as things are flowing well we can convince ourselves that things are in hand. But are they? How do we deal with death? Or sickness? Or addiction? Or accidental happenings? Truly we do not really have control over our lives or the world— the first hard truth we must realize before we can begin any spiritual path.

The good news is prefaced by bad news about ourselves, our world and our situation. The first step on the Christian journey acknowledges our sinfulness. This sin may become obvious as we awaken to our alienated situation. Or if we feel that there is no major sin we may come to realize our true condition through hearing of God's reign and coming to recognize factors which separate us from God and bind us to this world and age.

2. Came to believe that a Power greater than ourselves could restore us to sanity.

But what if our life is not insane? Few people acknowledge such a charge. We are so steeped in our sin, pride and ignorance that we are blind to our actual situation. Conversion is a long process because it takes time for us to begin to become conscious again of the truth which we lost sight of so long ago. If life and the world is not insane, of what use is a savior? Take away the bad news and Christianity has no reason for being. Yet, as G. K. Chesterton said, original sin is the Christian dogma proclaimed daily in every newspaper. Not only we, but the entire creation is out of joint, insane, and in need of restoration.

Jesus reveals God as a loving Father. Although we have no real control over our lives, God does, and he cares for us. Jesus announces God's reign in which a new way of life becomes possible— not life lived as before under our own power and control, but life lived as a gift from God, a life acknowledged to be in God's hands and under God's grace. Entering into relationship with God restores us to sanity.

3. *Made a decision to turn our will and our lives over to the care of God.*

The Christian surrenders to God. Baptism[4] expresses that surrender physically. Only thus can God heal and give us what he wishes to give us: the kingdom.

Coming to see that we have no real power over our life, we then are offered the opportunity of surrendering that fictitious power to God. Only now that God has control of our life can we begin to experience life as God's reign.

4. *Made a searching and fearless moral inventory of ourselves.*

Living in an unreal world, we cannot afford ordinarily to see ourselves as we truly are. We lie to others and even to ourselves. Yet as long as we cling to these lies, we cannot be helped. Thus the beginning and the foundation of our spiritual lives is an honesty about ourselves. We gain the courage to see ourselves honestly both in our strengths and in our weaknesses. We admit that we are far from perfection.

Most cannot face the truth about themselves. They prefer to repress that truth. But repression does not solve the problem. The repressed qualities are then projected onto others whom we self-righteously judge. But only when we gain the courage and ability to see ourselves in God's light, knowing that this leads not to condemnation but to salvation, are we able to change.

And not only do we hide our faults from ourselves, but we are often unable to appreciate our good qualities. The gift of seeing ourselves as others see us, both positively and negatively, is rare. And Jesus enables us not only to see our sins, but also to see our gifts and grace.

Contrition

5. *Admitted to God, to ourselves, and to another human being the exact nature of our wrongs.*

So far the steps have concentrated upon our consciousness. We have become aware that our lives are out control, and aware of a greater power. We have made a decision to hand our lives over and have looked

---

4. Truth 76

at our lives honestly. But for anything to happen we must move out of awareness and into action. Christianity is not limited to a way of perceiving and thinking, but is equally committed to acting. The first stage of action actually admits to God and another person the wrongs we have discovered about ourselves.

Catholics practice this step primarily in the sacrament of penance.[5] Confession to a priest helps us to see our sin objectively and to hear the forgiving words which cancel these sins, preparing for true healing and reconciliation.

6. Were entirely ready to have God remove all these defects of character.

It is one thing to admit our mistakes, another to want to forsake them. We cling to and even cherish something in our sin. Yet only true contrition—the willingness to leave the sin behind—opens toward healing. Without true contrition we find ourselves again committing the same sins. Over time we might hit bottom and recognize our insanity. Then we might find the contrition to ask God to remove them from us.

Also our ability to see ourselves honestly shows us how far short we fall of wholeness. Christian forgiveness does not exist to make us complacent in our sin. Rather it should move us out of sin. Conversion entails a true change of beliefs, values and life itself.

7. Humbly asked him to remove our shortcomings.

With contrition we need only ask and God will heal us. There is no condemnation—only forgiveness. And only that absolute forgiveness allows us to forsake our past for a new life.

And Christian life is a journey of transformation. We seek to amend our lives. We may fall back into sin. We at times may find ourselves stuck. But we are not content with such a situation. Amendment is our constant goal.

8. Made a list of all persons we had harmed, and became willing to make amends to them all.

While in the fourth step we took an inventory of our consciousness so that we might come to see our situation clearly, here we are moving out of that sinful situation. We recognize those we have wronged and

---

5. Truth 80

we approach them to make amends and ask forgiveness. Part of confession involves restitution for our wrongs. We help God heal what our sin has torn asunder.

Satisfaction

9. Made direct amends to such people wherever possible, except when to do so would injure them or others.

This is the traditional Catholic teaching on satisfaction. However, Catholics would add that persons should not be forced to make amends when that might injure them further. However they would certainly be encouraged to do so, and such amends would foster the conversion process.

Our sinful actions have hurt others, weakening the trust upon which society is built. In acknowledging sin, we face what we might do as we turn toward God to mend what our sins have broken. This reparation is considered a part of any real confession.

10. Continued to take personal inventory and when we were wrong promptly admitted it.

"So, if you are offering your gift at the altar, and there remember that your brother has something against you, leave your gift there before the altar and go; first be reconciled to your brother, and then come and offer your gift."[6]

Conversion is not a one-time action. Turning toward Jesus begins a lifelong process of penance. Being human, we will sin again. But we need no longer fear condemnation for our sins. There is no reason for us to hide our sins from ourselves or others. Indeed we find that life becomes richer and fuller when we are able constantly to take account of ourselves and admit our wrongs so that we do not recreate our bondage, but can experience the liberty of God's children. Since our wrongs are promptly forgiven, we enjoy a freedom we did not know before.

11. Sought through prayer and meditation to improve our conscious contact with God, praying only for knowledge of his will for us and the power to carry that out.

The Way of Jesus seeks God's will in place of our own. Only there is our true peace. Penance becomes the means whereby we continue

---

6. Mt 5:21–26

our journey toward wholeness. This journey is aided by our prayer and meditation—by all the means which foster the life of conversion.

12. *Having had a spiritual awakening as the result of these steps we try to carry this message to others and to practice these principles in all our affairs.*

This conversion is actually a spiritual awakening. We may have many significant conversions in our life's course. The journey to Christianity is simply that conversion which reveals the Way out of sin into life.

Finally the Christian knows that the Way of conversion is not just for oneself. Jesus calls us to ministry. The harvest is plenty, the laborers few.[7] Responding, we accept his invitation not only to discover the happiness his teachings bring but to further the kingdom by sharing this good news with others.

Only through giving what has been given do the teachings come alive and continue to challenge us. No one is worthy of this mission. But precisely to the unworthy, to sinners, does Jesus entrust it. Our mission gives purpose to our new life. We are to live no longer for ourselves (the way of sin left behind). Kingdom life is lived for others. And as we begin such a way of living we experience life as God's reign.

This plan for living hardly covers the extent of Christian existence. Our life is founded upon the forgiveness of sins, but moves far beyond that. Christians enjoy God's blessings and join in the hymn of celebration. This plan of life leads to the worship of God, to celebration and creativity, and to the giving of oneself in love and service.

Without this basic foundation in penance, the joy and celebration would be hollow, built upon a shaky foundation. Change is relatively easy. But true conversion is not. As long as we are in this world we must unceasingly begin again. Acknowledging our sins and experiencing forgiveness, we find the grace to leave our old selves behind. We know that we shall find our heart's desire only when we open up to the kingdom already given and present in Jesus Christ.

TO DEEPEN—

Take some time to reflect upon how these steps illuminate your own life.

Make the moral inventory of step four. What does this show you concerning the need for conversion?

---

7. Lk 10:2

Visit a twelve step meeting and observe how these steps are practiced.

Why is penance the foundation for Christian existence?

Further Reading:

Alcoholics Anonymous. Alcoholics Anonymous World Service, Inc., 1976. Also known as "The Big Book."

Twelve Steps and Twelve Traditions. Alcoholics Anonymous World Service, Inc., 1976.

4. THE GIFTS OF THE HOLY SPIRIT

The sacraments of initiation[1] incorporate us into Jesus Christ. And as God breathed the Spirit into Adam at the first creation,[2] so God bestows the Spirit upon Christians. Empowered by the Holy Spirit we are transformed.

God's Spirit confers gifts which aid this transformation and ministry in Jesus Christ. These gifts enumerated by the prophet Isaiah[3] and invoked in confirmation[4] are wisdom, understanding, right judgment, courage, knowledge, reverence, and awe and wonder in God's presence.

Like the Spirit, these qualities are not achieved or possessed naturally. Rather they are gifts of God which we may receive and then allow to guide our life. Nor does the Spirit compel us to grow in any of these gifts. Freedom is God's greatest gift. And the Spirit works within the realm of human freedom. The Spirit does not demand, threaten, or restrict liberty. The Holy Spirit calls us through Jesus and the Gospel, seduces us through love, and challenges us to realize our potential.

To enter into **wisdom** is to enter the domain of God.[5] Wisdom perceives the reality of the universe. Wisdom is the proper meditation of the Christian—wisdom not simply as knowledge, but rather as a perception of innermost reality. The pursuit of wisdom forms the basis for the Christian's continuing pilgrimage. The final wisdom is Christ, the image in which all is created.

With wisdom comes the second gift, **understanding.** We wish not only to discover and to know wisdom, but to stand under wisdom. A child of wisdom knows its protection.

---

1. Truth 75
2. Gen 2:7
3. Is 11:1–3
4. Truth 77
5. Prov 4:7

With wisdom and understanding, **right judgment** becomes possible. We begin to perceive reality truly. Only with such vision are we finally able to evaluate and perceive correctly. Without wisdom and understanding judgment is at best a shot in the dark.

The fourth gift, **courage**, is also a cardinal virtue.[6] The Christian life is not for the fearful and timid. The truth often sets us against the world which does not understand it. Courage or fortitude is necessary to accomplish Jesus' mission.

It may seem that the next gift, **knowledge**, has already been covered under wisdom and understanding. But knowledge is different. Wisdom is primary knowledge of God. Knowledge on the other hand is a secondary knowledge about things and the world. Knowledge is more allied with information, how to, technique, all of which is important in our life and our work for the kingdom. We need to know so that we might be able to shine the kingdom into the world, illuminating the darkness for ourselves and others.

Knowledge here is related to the virtue of prudence.[7] Knowledge is the know-how required to put wisdom to work. Knowledge is the means for incarnating wisdom.

The sixth gift is **reverence**. We come to see in our tradition that life itself is holy and sacred. There is truly no distinction between sacred and secular. Jesus is the most secular of spiritual teachers, the most sacred of liberators. Reverence keeps us mindful of creation's true nature. We are God's creatures, loved and lifted up. And because we are gifted in our very existence, we properly manifest a reverence for life which underlies all we do. We do not take life for granted, but recognize it as gift and respond in gratitude and reverence to all that happens.

The final gift returns this attitude of reverence to its source: **awe and wonder in God's presence**. We have a relationship with the living God. This communion fills us with awe and wonder. We try to drop the idea that we are experienced. Adults believe that they have seen it all. At best we delight in our children for whom all is new. But the Holy Spirit grants that same childlike attitude. Seeing everything held in God, and seeing through to the immensity of God that holds all in being, we recapture that spirit of awe and wonder in God's presence, which restores the excitement and glory we knew, but lost with childlike innocence. Jesus warns that without becoming again like little children we cannot experience the kingdom.[8]

6. Truth 70
7. Truth 67
8. Mt 18:3

TO DEEPEN—

How have you experienced some of these gifts of the Holy Spirit? What do these qualities say about the kind of life a Christian is called to lead? Take one of these gifts and meditate upon it. How does its meaning and significance deepen for you?

Further Reading:

Montague, George T. *The Spirit and His Gifts.* Paulist Press, 1974.
Shea, John. *An Experience named Spirit.* Thomas More, 1983.

5. THE FRUITS OF THE HOLY SPIRIT

Having examined the gifts of the Holy Spirit which commission us for Christian ministry, we turn to the fruits of life under the Spirit's direction and in the Spirit's service. The list is found in St. Paul[1] and the number seven is preserved by grouping in doubles. They can simply remain a list, or point toward the reality of Christian existence. They are of help in discerning whether a certain course of action is of the Holy Spirit. Let the scriptural texts presented here become guides to meditation.

Joy and Peace

Our life in Christ's Spirit is primarily characterized by **joy and peace.** Joy throughout Scripture applies to our salvation. Existence may not be easy, free of suffering or even persecution. Jesus says that we can expect rejection from the world for embracing his vision.[2] But in spite of sufferings, we know peace at having found what we were searching for, and joy at knowing that our search is successful. We have glimpsed our final destination. We have been to the mountain.

Joy is a key theme of Luke's infancy Gospel. The angel tells Zechariah, John the Baptist's father:

And you will have joy and gladness,
and many will rejoice at his birth;
for he will be great before the Lord.[3]

---

1. Gal 5:22
2. Mt 5:11–12
3. Lk 1:14–15a

338 Catholic Christianity

Elizabeth tells Mary, "For behold, when the voice of your greeting came to my ears, the babe in my womb leaped for joy."[4] Mary herself sings:

My soul magnifies the Lord,
and my spirit rejoices in God my Savior. . . .[5]

At Jesus' birth the angel tells the shepherds: Be not afraid, for behold, I bring you good news of a great joy which will come to all the people.[6]

Joy is our heritage as Christians. It is at the same time the pledge, possession and essential part of that day when the redeemed will praise God.

Hallelujah! For the Lord our God the Almighty reigns.
Let us rejoice and exult and give him the glory,
for the marriage of the Lamb has come,
and his Bride has made herself ready.[7]

In Scripture peace refers to total harmony with the community. It is founded on order and permeated by God's blessing. Thus humanity is able to develop and increase free and unhindered on every side. "And I will give you peace in the land, and you shall lie down, and none shall make you afraid; and I will remove evil beasts from the land, and the sword shall not go through your land."[8]

The wolf shall dwell with the lamb,
and the leopard shall lie down with the kid,
and the calf and the lion and the fatling together,
and a little child shall lead them.[9]

Jesus gives peace as his gift to his disciples.[10] The disciples refer to the Gospel itself as peace.[11] And Christians are charged to continue to "seek peace and pursue it."[12]

---

4. Lk 1:44
5. Lk 1:47
6. Lk 2:10
7. Rev 19:7
8. Lev 26:6
9. Is 11:6
10. Jn 14:27
11. Acts 10:36
12. 1 Pet 3:11

To set the mind on the flesh is death, but to set the mind on the Spirit is life and peace. [13]

For he is our peace, who has made us both one, and has broken down the dividing wall of hostility, by abolishing in his own flesh the law of commandments and ordinances, that he might create in himself one new man in place of the two, so making peace, and might reconcile us both to God in one body through the cross, thereby bringing the hostility to an end. And he came and preached peace to you who were far off and peace to those who were near; for through him we both have access in one Spirit to the Father. [14]

Patience and Kindness

Living in the Holy Spirit increases **patience and kindness**. The task entrusted to us is not our own. And we shall only succeed by remaining in God's will. So we learn patience. The kingdom will come not through our force and effort, but through our cooperation with God's will. And we have faith and hope that indeed God will be victorious against those forces opposing the kingdom.

Be still before the Lord, and wait patiently for him;
fret not yourself over him who prospers in his way,
over the man who carries out evil devices. . . .
For the wicked shall be cut off;
but those who wait for the Lord shall possess the land. [15]

More than that, we rejoice in our sufferings, knowing that suffering produces endurance, and endurance produces character, and character produces hope, and hope does not disappoint us, because God's love has been poured into our hearts through the Holy Spirit which has been given to us. [16]

Put on then, as God's chosen ones, holy and beloved, compassion, kindness, lowliness, meekness, and patience, forbearing one another and, if one has a complaint against another, forgiving each other; as the Lord has forgiven you, so you also must forgive. [17]

---

13. Rom 8:6
14. Eph 2:14–18
15. Ps 37:7–9
16. Rom 5:3–5
17. Col 3:12–13

Be patient, therefore, brethren, until the coming of the Lord. Behold, the farmer waits for the precious fruit of the earth, being patient over it until it receives the early and the late rain. You also be patient. Establish your hearts, for the coming of the Lord is at hand.[18]

And the kingdom shines in our kindness to others. Jesus teaches that we are united in one family and so we can show forth kindness (that attitude directed toward kin) to all people.

The stranger who sojourns with you shall be to you as the native among you, and you shall love him as yourself; for you were strangers in the land of Egypt: I am the Lord your God.[19]

Thus says the Lord of hosts, Render true judgments, show kindness and mercy each to his brother, do not oppress the widow, the fatherless, the sojourner, or the poor; and let none of you devise evil against his brother in your heart.[20]

But if any one has the world's good and sees his brother in need, yet closes his heart against him, how does God's love abide in him? Little children, let us not love in word or speech but in deed and in truth.[21]

Goodness and Trust

The Holy Spirit fills us with **goodness and trust**. Goodness is above all a characteristic of God. Jesus says, "No one is good but God alone."[22] God's goodness which is witnessed in creation and experienced in God's graciousness toward Israel leads to salvation in Jesus Christ. In Jesus all humanity experiences God's goodness. And the Spirit of Christ's goodness guides the life of the Church and is renewed in its members.

Praise the Lord!
O give thanks to the Lord, for he is good;
and his steadfast love endures for ever![23]

---

18. Jas 5:7–8
19. Lev 19:24
20. Zech 7:9–10
21. 1 Jn 3:17–18
22. Mk 10:18
23. Ps 106:1

And if you lend to those from whom you hope to receive, what
credit is that to you? Even sinners lend to sinners, to receive
as much again. But love your enemies, and do good, and lend,
expecting nothing in return; and your reward will be great,
and you will be sons of the Most High; for he is kind to the
ungrateful and the selfish. Be merciful, even as your Father
is merciful.[24]

As we experience the good we adopt a trusting attitude even when
goodness seems weak in relation to evil. Christians know the utmost
that evil can do—the killing of an innocent man. God's response to that
evil is the acquittal of the human race through the resurrection.[25] That
triumph gives reason to trust in ultimate victory.

It is better to take refuge in the Lord
than to put confidence in man.
It is better to take refuge in the Lord
than to put confidence in princes.[26]

Blessed is the man who trusts in the Lord.
He is like a tree planted by water,
that sends out its roots by the stream,
and does not fear when heat comes,
for its leaves remain green,
and is not anxious in the year of drought,
for it does not cease to bear fruit.[27]

And Jesus answered them, "Truly, I say to you, if you have
faith and never doubt, you will not only do what has been done
to the fig tree, but even if you say to this mountain, Be taken
up and cast into the sea, it will be done. And whatever you
ask in prayer, you will receive, if you have faith."[28]

Now faith is the assurance of things hoped for, the conviction
of things not seen. For by it the men of old received divine
approval. By faith we understand that the world was created

24. Lk 6:34–36
25. Rom 5:9
26. Ps 118:8–9
27. Jer 17:7–8
28. Mt 21:21–22

by the word of God, so that what is seen was made out of things which do not appear.[29]

For whatever is born of God overcomes the world; and this is the victory that overcomes the world, our faith. Who is it that overcomes the world but he who believes that Jesus is the Son of God?[30]

Gentleness and Humility

Life in the Holy Spirit produces **gentleness and humility**. Christ's Way is not of power but of surrender to Love. This Way reveals our true nature and dependence upon God. Through Jesus we learn to imitate God who acts gently and lovingly toward creation.

He will feed his flock like a shepherd,
he will gather the lambs in his arms,
he will carry them in his bosom,
and gently lead those that are with young.[31]

Take my yoke upon you, and learn from me; for I am gentle and lowly in heart, and you will find rest for your souls. For my yoke is easy, and my burden is light.[32]

Remind them to be submissive to rulers and authorities, to be obedient, to be ready for any honest work, to speak evil of no one, to avoid quarreling, to be gentle, and to show perfect courtesy toward all men.[33]

But the wisdom from above is first pure, then peaceable, gentle, open to reason, full of mercy and good fruits, without uncertainty or insincerity.[34]

As we discover our true center in God's will we grow in humility—not the art of putting ourselves down, but the art of coming to know our true nature: God's creatures sustained in God's love. Humility is a rec-

---

29. Heb 11:1–3
30. 1 Jn 5:4–5
31. Is 40:11
32. Mt 11:29–30
33. Tit 3:1–2
34. Jas 3:17

ognition of our total dependence upon God and a readiness to serve him selflessly, together with our neighbors.

> O Lord, my heart is not lifted up,
> my eyes are not raised too high;
> I do not occupy myself with things
> too great and too marvelous for me.
> But I have calmed and quieted my soul,
> like a child quieted at its mother's breast;
> like a child that is quieted is my soul.
> O Israel, hope in the Lord
> from this time forth and for evermore.[35]

> My son, perform your tasks in meekness;
> then you will be loved by those whom God accepts.
> The greater you are, the more you must humble yourself,
> so you will find favor in the sight of the Lord.
> For great is the might of the Lord;
> he is glorified by the humble.[36]

> For thus says the high and lofty One
> who inhabits eternity, whose name is Holy:
> "I dwell in the high and holy place,
> and also with him who is of a contrite and humble spirit,
> to revive the spirit of the humble,
> and to revive the heart of the contrite.[37]

So you also, when you have done all that is commanded you, say, "We are unworthy servants; we have only done what was our duty."[38]

For every one who exalts himself will be humbled, but he who humbles himself will be exalted.[39]

And being found in human form he humbled himself and became obedient unto death, even death on a cross.[40]

---

35. Ps 131
36. Sir 3:17, 18, 20
37. Is 57:15
38. Lk 17:10
39. Lk 18:14b
40. Phil 2:8

For consider your call, brethren; not many of you were wise according to worldly standards, not many were powerful, not many were of noble birth; but God chose what is foolish in the world to shame the wise. God chose what is weak in the world to shame the strong. God chose what is low and despised in the world, even things that are not, to bring to nothing things that are, so that no human being might boast in the presence of God. He is the source of your life in Christ Jesus, whom God made our wisdom, our righteousness, and sanctification and redemption; therefore, as it is written, "Let him who boasts, boast of the Lord."[41]

Poverty and Purity

The next fruits are **poverty and purity**. God is aligned with the poor and oppressed[42] who are first and foremost God's people. And those of us who are not poor enter the Church by joining in God's struggle on behalf of the poor. Poverty characterizes Jesus follower. There we realize our creatureliness and hope for God's kingdom to dawn and raise up all.

If there is among you a poor man, one of your brethren, in any of your towns within your land which the Lord your God gives you, you shall not harden your heart or shut your hand against your poor brother, but you shall open your hand to him, and lend him sufficient for his need, whatever it may be. . . . You shall give to him freely, and your heart shall not be grudging when you give to him; because for this the Lord your God will bless you in all your work and in all that you undertake.[43]

The Lord has taken his place to contend,
he stands to judge his people.
The Lord enters into judgment
with the elders and princes of his people:
"It is you who have devoured the vineyard,
the spoil of the poor is in your houses.
What do you mean by crushing my people,
by grinding the face of the poor?"
says the Lord God of hosts.[44]

41. 1 Cor 26–31
42. Jer 22:15–16
43. Deut 15:7–11
44. Is 3:13–15

Blessed are you poor, for yours is the kingdom of God.[45]

Let the lowly brother boast in his exaltation, and the rich in his humiliation, because like the flower of the grass he will pass away. For the sun rises with its scorching heart and withers the grass; its flower falls, and its beauty perishes. So will the rich man fade away in the midst of his pursuits.[46]

The Holy Spirit is pure. The pure in heart shall see God.[47] Through sin our lives are impure, our motives stained with self-importance, selfishness, and the deadly sins.[48] Conversion demands purification. With the fruits of purity our life becomes less scattered; we see our goal clearly; the Spirit draws us toward that reign where alone resides our joy and hope for justice.

Who shall ascend the hill of the Lord?
And who shall stand in his holy place?
He who has clean hands and a pure heart,
who does not lift up his soul to what is false,
and does not swear deceitfully.
He will receive blessing from the Lord,
and vindication from the God of his salvation.[49]

But who can endure the day of his coming, and who can stand when he appears? For he is like a refiner's fire and like fullers' soap; he will sit as a refiner and purifier of silver, and he will purify the sons of Levi and refine them like gold and silver, till they present right offerings to the Lord.[50]

If any one purifies himself from what is ignoble, then he will be a vessel for noble use, consecrated and useful to the master of the house, ready for any good work. So shun youthful passions and aim at righteousness, faith, love and peace, along with those who call upon the Lord from a pure heart.[51]

---

45. Lk 6:20b
46. Jas 1:9–11
47. Mt 5:8
48. Truth 58f
49. Ps 24:3–5
50. Mal 3:2–4
51. 2 Tim 2:21–22

For if the sprinkling of defiled persons with the blood of goats and bulls and with the ashes of a heifer sanctifies for the purification of the flesh, how much more shall the blood of Christ, who through the eternal Spirit offered himself without blemish to God, purify your conscience from dead works to serve the living God.[52]

Having purified your souls by your obedience to the truth for a sincere love of the brethren, love one another earnestly from the heart. You have been born anew, not of perishable seed but of imperishable, through the living and abiding word of God.[53]

Generosity and Mercy

Generosity and mercy were already explored in the works of the Spirit.[54] Like Jesus we turn from being people concerned first about ourselves, to being people for others. We have experienced God's overwhelming generosity. We now turn toward the world, extending this generosity to others.

When you reap your harvest in your field, and have forgotten a sheaf in the field, you shall not go back to get it; it shall be for the sojourner, the fatherless, and the widow, that the Lord your God may bless you in all the work of your hands. . . . You shall remember that your were a slave in the land of Egypt; therefore I command you to do this.[55]

When you give alms, do not let your left hand know what your right hand is doing, so that your alms may be in secret; and your Father who sees in secret will reward you.[56]

We are people of compassion—identifying with the poor and working to lift their burden. We are not superior to those who suffer—that would be pity. But we stand with them and share in their deprivation. This is one reason Christians fast. And compassion heals and lifts up into God's love.

---

52. Heb 9:13–14
53. 1 Pet 1:22–23
54. Way 37f
55. Deut 23:19–22
56. Mt 6:3

I will make all my goodness pass before you, and will proclaim before you my name "The Lord"; and I will be gracious to whom I will be gracious, and will show mercy on whom I will show mercy.[57]

How can I give you up, O Ephraim!
How can I hand you over, O Israel! . . .
My heart recoils within me,
my compassion grows warm and tender.
I will not execute my fierce anger,
I will not again destroy Ephraim;
for I am God and not man,
the Holy One in your midst,
and I will not come to destroy.[58]

He has showed you, O man, what is good;
and what does the Lord require of you
but to do justice, and to love kindness,
and to walk humbly with your God?[59]

Go and learn what this means, "I desire mercy, and not sacrifice." For I came not to call the righteous, but sinners.[60]

Woe to you, scribes and Pharisees, hypocrites! For you tithe mint and dill and cummin, and have neglected the weightier matters of the law, justice and mercy and faith; these you ought to have done, without neglecting the others.[61]

Justice and Truth

Justice and truth take on a meaning quite different from their worldly one in the light of Jesus. What passes for worldly justice does not necessarily reflect God's justice. God's justice is the voice of the poor and the outcast. God's truth is rejected by the world—a truth that seems a blasphemy in saying that a human being is God, and a folly in saying that this God dies.[62] Our justice and our truth is found only in the person and vision of Jesus Christ.

---

57. Ex 33:19
58. Hos 11:8a–9
59. Mic 6:8
60. Mt 9:13
61. Mt 23:23
62. 1 Cor 1:23

You shall not pervert justice; you shall not show partiality; and you shall not take a bribe, for a bribe blinds the eyes of the wise and subverts the cause of the righteous. Justice, and only justice, you shall follow, that you may live and inherit the land which your God gives you.[63]

Moreover I saw under the sun that in the place of justice, even there was wickedness, and in the place of righteousness, even there was wickedness. I said in my heart, God will judge the righteous and the wicked, for he has appointed a time for every matter, and for every work.[64]

Justice is turned back,
and righteousness stands afar off;
for truth has fallen in the public squares,
and uprightness cannot enter.
Truth is lacking,
and he who departs from evil
makes himself a prey.[65]

So if you are offering your gift at the altar, and there remember that your brother has something against you, leave your gift there before the altar and go; first be reconciled to your brother, and then come and offer your gift. Make friends quickly with your accuser, lest your accuser hand you over to the judge, and the judge to the guard, and you be put in prison; truly, I say to you, you will never get out till you have paid the last penny.[66]

Steadfast love and faithfulness will meet;
righteousness and peace will kiss each other.
Faithfulness will spring up from the ground,
and righteousness will look down from the sky.[67]

Pilate said to him, "So you are a king?" Jesus answered, "You say that I am a king. For this I was born, and for this I have

---

63. Deut 18:19–20
64. Eccl 3:16–17
65. Is 59:14–15
66. Mt 5:23–26
67. Ps 85:10–11

come into the world, to bear witness to the truth. Every one who is of the truth hears my voice." Pilate said to him, "What is truth?"[68]

Sanctify them in the truth; thy word is truth. As thou didst send me into the world, so I have sent them into the world. And for their sake I consecrate myself, that they also may be consecrated in truth.[69]

TO DEEPEN—

Use these words as seeds for meditation. How do they expand in meaning and significance for you?

What kind of life do these terms describe? How might it differ from other life-styles?

Which qualities do you seek most? Do any make you uncomfortable? Why?

TO CONTINUE—

The Works of Mercy are found in Way 37–38. The Way of Action is presented in Way 51.

---

68. Jn 18:37–38
69. Jn 17:17–19

6. Prayer Life

Tradition considers the spiritual life as either active or contemplative. For example, religious communities[1] view themselves as active or contemplative, or more commonly today as a combination. One withdraws from the external world to enter within and commune with God, the other goes into the world to do God's work confident that there one will encounter God. The two are not exclusive alternatives, but moments of authentic Christian existence.

Prayer Life and the Liturgy

Prayer, broadly defined, is whatever opens us to God. The various spiritualities, styles and prayers address specific individual needs. All Christians participate and find grace in the sacraments and worship, pre-eminently the Eucharist.[2] Any number of means complement this central worship. What might be appropriate for one might be a hindrance to another. Some find their strength and nurture from within, others from without. Prayers and spiritualities abound. Simply find those that best aid your transformation.

The overall shape of the Christian's prayer and prayer life are found in the Lord's Prayer which is more than a prayer; it is a way of praying.[3] This teaching shows us how to pray, what to pray for, and when to pray.

Spiritual Direction

Before considering various spiritualities let us examine some guidance available today. Many people are embarking upon a serious path of spiritual growth. While God is the ultimate guide, spiritual directors accompany our journey. Not every Christian has or needs a spiritual director. In many cases a friend, teacher, prayer group, or the community itself serves this role. A director oversees practice, guides in choosing a path, and provides help along the way. Since the spiritual life is concerned with intangibles, it is easy to become lost or distracted, or to diverge from the proper path. The spiritual director guards against such strayings.

In the past, spiritual directors were generally available only to priests and those in religious life.[4] But the renewed Church recognizes

---

1. Life 11
2. Truth 78
3. Way 50
4. Life 11

that all Christians are called to spiritual growth, so spiritual directors are becoming more generally available.

THE WAYS OF PRAYER

The Christian tradition agrees with other spiritual traditions in recognizing two key types of prayer: the way of affirmation and the way of negation. While the Christian tradition is founded in Jesus upon a way of affirmation, much prayer life has stemmed from the way of negation. Other than the liturgy and the sacraments a Catholic's prayer life is of one's own creation. It can fall into the traditional or use forms of prayer new to our tradition such as Eastern meditative practices.

7. The Way of Affirmation

The way of affirmation employs various images, signs and symbols which mediate the reality of God. In Scripture, events reveal God at work in our history. Jesus describes the kingdom through his parables and signs. Images such as salt or yeast disclose God's kingdom. These images are not meant literally. They, like the sacraments, speak of a reality and a truth beyond their literal form.

Prayer of this kind uses images, symbols or things to focus and mediate more deeply the reality of God. The **sacraments** through water, bread, oil, sexuality, etc., reveal in our lives the dawning of God's kingdom. Meditations on Scripture stories or Christian saints mediate in their own way the same experience. Since creation is the handiwork of God's love, God's grandeur shines forth in God's works.

A special scriptural prayer, **lectio divina** (divine reading), originated with the monastic communities. The person chooses a passage of Scripture for prayer. Then that passage (usually fairly short) is read slowly and prayerfully. As the prayer continues, focus upon a word or a phrase. Take the passage into yourself. St. Benedict[5] likens the process to a cow chewing her cud. Repeat the passage over and over. Let it suggest other allusions. You might simply be present to the passage. Today Scripture reading and in particular this practice is quite popular.

Of course Scripture stories, particularly the Gospels, are a source of prayer. The **Spiritual Exercises** of St. Ignatius Loyola—the basis of Jesuit[6] spirituality—present a thirty-day series of meditations to deepen

---

5. Life 31
6. Life 11, 34

conversion. Today many besides Jesuits use these exercises, usually in association with a spiritual director and modified for modern lifestyles.

A renewal of **creation-centered spirituality** opens Christians to sensual ways of prayer—activities not traditionally considered prayer but able vehicles nevertheless. For example, pottery making speaks about centering and the need for it. Art itself is a means of creative expression close to the heart of prayer. The entire creation reveals its Creator; when we use the creation, or when we create ourselves, we are drawn into the Creator's love and the exuberance and joy that lies at the heart of the universe.

Journal keeping might be traced back to St. Augustine whose *Confessions* reviewed his life in the light of God's grace. Our life story reveals the places where we are encountered by the grace of God. Journal writing helps us to recognize and celebrate these moments. We see our own story in the context of traditional stories—both scriptural narratives and the stories of others aware of being graced.

Throughout the ages many **devotions** have grown up within the Christian community. These are usually centered upon some person or object and greatly enrich the kinds of prayer available within the Church. They are entirely up to the individual as to whether they form part of his or her prayer life.

Among the most popular Catholic devotions is that to the Sacred Heart of Jesus—the heart being symbolic of Jesus' compassion and humanity. Devotions along this line include those to the Immaculate Heart of Mary, to Mary herself or one of her many aspects, or to one or more of the saints. In these devotions a special person or attribute symbolizes a central aspect of the Christian message and channels the person's prayer.

If a person has some particular concern, he or she might undertake a **novena**—a nine-day period of prayer usually centered around a special theme or in preparation for a feast. It originates from the nine days the disciples spent between the ascension and Pentecost[7]—this particular novena is in honor of the Holy Spirit.

Charismatic spirituality focuses upon the presence of the Holy Spirit's gifts and charisms within the person. Its history extends back to the dawn of Christianity.[8] And its prayer employs charisms of the Spirit such as the gift of tongues, the interpretation of tongues, the gifts of prophecy and healing. While in the past this prayer has been associated with evangelical and holiness Protestant groups, it arose in Catholicism

---

7. Acts 1:14
8. Acts 2:1–4

in the 1960s and has flourished since. People belonging to this spirituality usually belong to a charismatic prayer group.

A prayer style from the Eastern Church has entered into Western prayer life recently—the **Jesus prayer**. Following St. Paul's counsel to pray without ceasing,[9] the person takes a short ejaculation such as "Jesus, have mercy upon me, a sinner." This phrase repeated over and over again becomes the basis of one's prayer life. The prayer is said not only at times of prayer, but at any possible moment during the day. With time, the prayer which begins in the mind as an act of will sinks into the heart where joined to the breath it takes on a life of its own, transforming the person in Christ.

The **Stations of the Cross** ,[10] found in practically every Catholic church, meditate upon Jesus' passion[11] by walking this sacred way with Him. Finally the **rosary**,[12] one of the most popular Catholic prayers, combines repeated prayers with meditations upon mysteries in the life of Jesus and Mary. These are only a few of the literally hundreds of devotions and practices found in the Catholic tradition.

8. The Way of Negation

The image is not the reality, and to mistake it for such leads to idolatry. God is far more than can be imagined or comprehended. Indeed the created realm and human words actually betray as much as they reveal the true nature of God. Dionysius the Areopagite, the source of this negative way, insisted that whatever can be posited about God, its opposite can at the same time be posited. Thus it is better in one sense to describe God in negative rather than positive terms. The way of negation grounds much contemplative prayer. Here, rather than images which point to, yet betray God, images, words, and all created things are left behind to encounter the true God beyond and behind all images. This is the usual way of the mystic, although there are affirmative mystics also such as St. Francis of Assisi.

Centering prayer derives from *The Cloud of Unknowing*, an eleventh century English mystical classic. As in the Jesus prayer[13] the person takes a word or sound for the foundation of prayer. God is described as a cloud which the person enters, penetrating the mists of unknowing until finally illumined by God's radiant light.

---

9. 1 Thes 5:17
10. Life 42
11. Truth 18
12. Life 42
13. Life 7

Other meditation traditions stem from the great **Spanish mystics** St. Teresa of Avila and St. John of the Cross. St. John brings the way of negation to completion as he realizes that the search for God is a search into emptiness.

While the way of images is more naturally congenial to Christianity, the tradition itself has tended to emphasize the way of negation. Both are open to Christians. Indeed the only danger is in cleaving to only one. Our tradition beginning with Scripture and continuing through the sacraments mediates God to us through images. Jesus himself is the image of God made human.

Yet the way of negation also has its roots in our tradition. It is found in the hiddenness of God's name.[14] God cannot be encompassed or manipulated by human beings because he transcends all our attempts to comprehend him. Yet it is not the case that we know nothing of God. Our God has communicated in a totally human fashion through Jesus. But although God is revealed through these images, the Godhead yet lies in a cloud of unknowing beyond all images. Both ways are necessary to avoid false extremes.

9. THE CHRISTIAN SPIRITUAL CLASSICS

Christians have been inspired on their own journeys by some works which are cherished from generation to generation. Here are some of the essential spiritual classics.

Anonymous—*The Cloud of Unknowing*[15]

St. Augustine[16]—*Confessions*

St. Bernard of Clairvaux[17]—*On the Song of Songs*

de Caussade—*Abandonment to Divine Providence*

De Chardin, Teilhard—*The Divine Milieu and Hymn of the Universe*

St. Francis of Assisi[18]—*The Little Flowers*

St. Francis de Sales[19]—*Introduction to the Devout Life*

St. John of the Cross[20]—*Ascent of Mount Carmel: Dark Night of the Soul*

---

14. Is 45:15
15. Life 8
16. Life 31
17. Life 33
18. Life 33
19. Life 35
20. Life 8, 34

Juliana of Norwich—*Showings*

Merton, Thomas[21]—*New Seeds of Contemplation.*

Newman, John Henry[22]—*Apologia pro Vita Sua*

St. Teresa of Avila[23]—*Interior Castle: Autobiography*

St. Thérèse of Lisieux—*Autobiography*

Thomas à Kempis—*The Imitation of Christ*

TO DEEPEN—

Which of these ways of prayer have you experienced?

Which appeal to you?

Try out some of these ways? Experiment to discover what is helpful to you.

Attend a charismatic prayer meeting.

Attend some of the devotions offered at your parish.

Further Reading:

Bloom, Anthony. *Beginning To Pray.* Paulist Press, 1970.

Buckley, Michael & Castle, Tony, eds. *The Catholic Prayer Book.* Servant, 1986.

Champlin, Joseph. *Behind Closed Doors.* Paulist Press, 1984.

Cousins, Kathryn & Ewert, Payne, Dick. *How To Read a Spiritual Book.* Paulist Press, 1976.

Edwards, Tilden. *Living Simply Through the Day: Spiritual Survival in a Complex Age.* Paulist Press, 1978.

Fleming, E., ed. *The Fire and the Cloud.* Paulist Press, 1976.

Ford, J. Massyngberde. *Pentecostal Experience. A New Direction for American Catholics.* Paulist Press, 1970.

Happold, R. *Mysticism: A Study and an Anthology.* Penguin, 1970

James, William. *The Varieties of Religious Experience.* Mentor, 1958.

Johnston, William. *The Inner Eye of Love.* Harper & Row, 1978.

Kelsey, Morton. *The Other Side of Silence.* Paulist Press, 1976.

Quebedeaux, Richard. *The New Charismatics II.* Harper & Row, 1983.

Simons, George F. *Keeping Your Personal Journal.* Paulist Press, 1978.

Taylor, Jeremy. *Dream Work.* Paulist Press, 1983.

Vogel, Arthur. *The Jesus Prayer for Today.* Paulist Press, 1982.

---

21. Life 37
22. Life 36
23. Life 8, 34

10. Active Life

Christian prayer life was considered under the metaphor of contemplation. But prayer does not exist for itself. Prayer gives God glory, but this moment nourishes us to undertake mission. Christian life is not lived for itself. The Christian, like Jesus, exists for others, giving in loving service so that others might come to know God.

Many different lifestyles are found among Catholics, some approved, some not. Statistically most adults are married. Many Catholics, including all Latin rite priests, are celibate.

Christian life should witness to the world concerning Jesus' vision. We try to be of service to our neighbor, motivated by love. While each is called to manifest these qualities, certain traditional lifestyles founded upon the evangelical counsels embody them symbolically for the community and the world.

Second, we shall explore the relation between the individual Christian and various institutions. How does a Christian relate to the natural order of things? What does Christianity say about citizenship and civic responsibility? Finally, how does the individual relate to the Church as institution? For example, what is the place for dissent within the Church?

Third, we shall consider the impact which certain Christians have had upon our world. We are not concerned here with saints.[1] Our subject is those who, while not necessarily extraordinary in sanctity, have contributed to the life and culture of the world.

11. THE RELIGIOUS LIFE

Jesus calls his disciples to witness on behalf of God's kingdom. "Let your light shine before men."[2] And he speaks of some who might become eunuchs on behalf of the kingdom of God[3]—indicating a life that witnesses to the kingdom in its very being, willing to give up children and posterity, trusting instead in the abundant life in God's kingdom. In Catholicism life bound to the religious vows manifests this witness.

Religious life is defined most broadly by the **evangelical counsels** of poverty, chastity and obedience. Ordinary life can be consumed with preoccupations: sex and offspring, wealth and property, control and power. These three worldly goals, good in themselves, can deflect from

---

1. Life 46
2. Mt 5:16
3. Mt 19:12

the spiritual quest. People, binding themselves by these three vows, enter a religious community to devote themselves more intensely to the spiritual path. Such a person is a "religious."

Religious communities provide concrete ways for living the counsels. These communities are traditionally separated by sexes. Religious women are "sisters" or "nuns"; religious men are "brothers" or, if ordained, "fathers" or "priests."

A great variety of groups exist, divided into **active and contemplative** communities, according to an emphasis upon service or prayer. Actually there is no such thing as a totally active or a totally contemplative community—all are different blends of these two poles.

Older monastic communities are **orders**. These orders withdraw from the world into the monastery for prayer and contemplation. The head of a monastery is an "abbot" or "abbess" whose authority in his or her own community is equivalent to that of a bishop.

Communities have been founded at various times to foster a specific lifestyle or apostolate. Each community has a certain way of life and prayer as well as a definite apostolate. With the passage of time, orders are reformed due to changing circumstances. Thus many communities today claim to be in the Benedictine or the Franciscan lineage.

Some religious communities have **third orders**. These are open to lay people who continue to live in the world and may be married, but who embrace the ideals of the community in some way and bind themselves to certain practices through vows, just as the other members do.

Certain religious communities of men include or are exclusively made up of priests. Thus the clerical and religious lifestyles are combined. These religious priests contract with bishops to fulfill some ministerial need, but the order itself usually extends nationally or worldwide. Such communities may also include non-ordained males as well as women. Maryknoll, the order of American foreign missionaries, includes all three.

Finally **secular institutes** comprise people living in the world, pursuing secular careers but bound together by the religious counsels. They combine the lay with the religious lifestyle. They may be third orders, or groups solely constituted by lay people.

TO DEEPEN—

Speak with some members of religious communities about their lifestyle and ideals.

What are the evangelical counsels? How do they shape a person's life?

What are third orders?

Can a person living in the world follow a special religious lifestyle in the Church?

Further Reading:

Guinan, Michael. *Gospel Poverty: Witness to the Risen Christ.* Paulist Press, 1981.

Huddleston, Mary, ed. *Celibate Loving.* Paulist Press, 1984.

Metz, Johannes. *Followers of Christ.* Paulist Press, 1978. Vows in today's context.

The Response: Lay Volunteer Mission Opportunities. International Liaison, USCC, 1980.

Whitehead, Evelyn & Whitehead, James. *Christian Life Patterns.* Doubleday, 1982.

TO CONTINUE—

Christian marriage is found in Truth 83.

The minsterial priesthood is discussed in Truth 84.

12. THE CHRISTIAN'S RELATION TO THE WORLD

We exist not simply as individuals, but related to institutions and orders which make up our world. We have a basic and fundamental relationship to the created order. We also exist in a human society governed by laws and involving a number of institutions. And the Christian is also a member of the Church. How does the individual relate to these orders? And what is the relation of the various laws governing these different societies?

Systems of Law

Three different traditions of law arise out of three covenants between God and humanity. The first covenant with all humanity was initiated with Adam.[1] The moral teaching embracing this covenant is the natural law and is available to all. The second covenant—the Mosaic—includes the ten commandments and the law of Israel. The third is the Christian covenant fulfilling the law in Jesus Christ.

---

1. Way 1; Truth 6

What is the Christian's relationship to these various kinds of law? First, the natural law is basic to all true morality. Society's laws claim our obedience as citizens. And finally Church laws—not laws from God but laws made to enable the community to exist and fulfill its mission—are binding on its members.

The Natural Law

Since creation is in Christ's image, all truth, goodness and beauty is truly that of Christ. Reason enables us to know the natural law. And inasmuch as people discern what is truly good they discern Christ.

The natural law grounds all law. The other covenants built upon it deepen its insight into the good. Since by the natural law people perceive the true nature of creation, they also discover, however dimly, Christ.

But what is the natural law? What are its precepts? On one level it articulates a generalized perception of the moral good in axioms such as "Do good and avoid evil" or "Let your conscience be your guide." This fundamental precept to avoid evil and do good is not the tautology it might at first appear. It asserts that there are good and evil actions. Life is not morally neutral.

In the Catholic tradition other elementary notions of the natural law are based upon primal tendencies. Self-preservation is common to all organisms. Further, animals mate, produce and raise offspring. On the strictly human plane there is the tendency to seek the truth. And finally people, being social creatures, need communities. Natural law articulates these general rights: self-preservation, sexual and parental conduct, pursuit of ultimate truth and cultivation of communal life.

But specific laws such as "Do not commit murder" also arise from this general perception of the good. Natural law therefore helps discern the good, creating a harmonious society.

The natural law, based upon human perception of the good, changes and develops as human nature evolves. What was acceptable at one stage is later perceived as evil. Today slavery is intolerable. Humanity now perceives such an institution as evil, as its understanding of natural law has evolved.

In the Declaration of Independence Thomas Jefferson declared: "We hold these truths to be self-evident, that we are endowed by our Creator with certain inalienable rights: life, liberty and the pursuit of happiness." They are inalienable because they derive from the nature of things. But would a seventh century Celt consider them such? And even today do these rights extend to all people or just a few? Jefferson seemingly intended only free white males. What do these rights reflect if not Christ who gives true life, real liberty, and the opportunity not only to pursue but to enjoy lasting happiness?

Civil Law

A society's laws should be grounded in natural law. For example our Constitution's Bill of Rights is an outgrowth of our founders' perception of the natural law.

But in addition to natural law every society needs other laws for its harmonious working. Thus civil laws are legislated. For example, nothing in a red light intrinsically calls for people to stop, but in our society red and green traffic lights permit harmonious transportation.

Christians follow both the natural law and their society's civil laws. Only if a civil law is manifestly unjust is a Christian obliged to oppose it. Otherwise the law commands obedience for the good of society.

Church Law

Finally there are the laws of the Church—canon law.[2] When this spells out a matter of divine law—a command of God such as the ten commandments—it demands compliance at the risk of serious sin.

But much canon law concerns order and structure in the Christian community. Such law binds Catholics much as civil law binds citizens. It is sinful to break such law not because it is a sin against God per se, but because it disturbs the community order. However in some situations such a law does not bind because of other factors.

The bases of canon law and American and English common law differ importantly. American secular law is abundant, pervading all areas of social life. It is often very detailed, complicated, even confusing, taking into account many contingencies so that there are no exceptions. Canon law differs: the canons strive to express principles; they are usually concise and abstract. Since they are meant for Catholics all over the world, they often admit of varying applications and interpretations as well as exceptions. To apply the standards and philosophy of one code to another raises problems and misses the spirit in which that law was conceived.

Dissent and the Christian

At times the Christian may be at odds with one of these institutions or systems of law. While the appropriate response must take into ac-

---

2. Life 16

count the individual circumstances, a few general guidelines apply.

First, there is some discussion as to just what the natural law means when it is applied to specifics. Traditionally, the Catholic Church defined some morality in terms of the natural law. For example, birth control and sexuality have been based upon a particular understanding of natural law.

If it were truly a matter of going against nature, the person would be committing a sin and the action would be harmful. But certainty is not possible regarding many things stemming from natural law. And it is questionable in certain cases whether the argument is valid. In such cases the natural law simply is not clearly perceived.

The Christian is bound to obey civil law unless to obey would lead to moral evil. Today some Christians including a Catholic bishop break the income tax law, believing that the money's use in the arms race is immoral. Or young men refuse military service. Here the Christian is obliged to follow conscience, although one should also avail oneself of Church and other counsel.

What is the place for dissent within the Church? The Code of Canon Law allows somewhat for the communication and resolution of conflict within the Church. The Pope and on the local level the bishop are the key teachers and pastors. They are to receive the presumption of truth on the part of the faithful.

But on some issues today the Church is not a monolithic community. Although the American bishops have spoken out on both nuclear weapons and economic policy a number of American Catholics disagree with their teachings. A similar lack of unanimity within both the American and the world Catholic community obtains on certain issues, such as birth control and other sexual issues.

In their peace pastoral the American bishops distinguish between a statement of principle and a statement of policy or the application of a principle. So, while Catholics are called to affirm the principles in the letter, there may be disagreement concerning how those principles are applied in terms of policy. This leads back to a traditional distinction between the substance of a teaching and its formulation and application. All Catholics would affirm the substance of the Church's teaching on peace or sexuality, but they might dissent from the concrete applications of those teachings.

The official teaching on all these matters is that of the Pope and bishops. Thus if the question is what the Catholic Church teaches the answer is to be found in what they affirm. But there are within the Church today positions diverging from the official teachings.

There is a hierarchy of truths within the Church: some teachings are more fundamental than others.[3] It is one thing to challenge the Church's policy of celibacy for the clergy, another to question the restriction of holy orders to males, and yet another to deny that there exists an ordained ministry within the Church. The first challenges merely a Church law, the second questions the way the Church understands tradition, the third denies tradition itself.

The centrality of the issue determines the amount of leeway in interpreting that issue. Only one who has made every effort to be informed on the issue and has prayerfully studied the Church's position could be justified in dissent.

Dissent is not always welcomed or sometimes even recognized by the hierarchy. The Second Vatican Council initiated reforms both in Church structure (such as the collegiality of bishops) and in the concept of authority which have opened new windows and made Catholic life in the wake of the council often exciting as well as confusing.

The American bishops acknowledged some principles of dissent in their letter of response to Humanae Vitae (which dealt with birth control). They proposed three conditions for justifying public dissent from non-infallible teaching. First, the reasons for dissent must be serious and well-founded. Second, the manner of the dissent must not question or impugn the teaching authority of the Church. And finally it must not give scandal.

There is divergence within the Church upon a number of issues. While authorities may be unhappy with dissent, until now a workable means of dealing with and resolving it has not been found. Vatican II spoke of and initiated dialogue within the Church. Today the dialogue continues.

Although Church teaching seems intransigent on the issue of women priests, various people as well as organizations continue to lobby, educate and work for change in this teaching. While the Church teaching remains that the only lawful use of sex must be open to life and within matrimony, many Catholics today challenge this teaching or do not live according to it. These people remain loyal to the Church, but in wrestling with these questions their consciences do not allow them to assent to the official teaching.

Although there is a history of dissent in the Church, its shape today sometimes takes new forms. First, it is public rather than internal. Second, it encompasses masses of people. Third, the presence of media makes dissent much more a part of the public experience of the Church. But dissent has always been present in quieter forms. Even the old

3. Truth 22ff

moral theology manuals acknowledge dissent in the Church. Many martyred saints were put to death for their dissent. Other martyrs are still considered heretics. It would be well for modern dissenters to realize that the price of dissent could well be the same today.

The Second Vatican Council opened the windows upon a less autocratic Church. But many years will pass before we have learned how to live in this situation and to develop structures and processes that allow for the articulation of dissent as well as moving toward a consensus.

TO DEEPEN—

What different kinds of laws does the Church recognize?

What is the difference between divine law and canon law?

What should the Christian's relation to law be?

When is dissent necessary?

TO CONTINUE—

The structure and governance of the Church are discussed in Life 15ff.

13. THE LIFE OF THE CATHOLIC SPIRIT

Catholicism's two thousand year presence has profoundly shaped Western culture. At her best it is open to all the arts, inviting artists to lend their talents in communicating the Christian spirit. It is impossible to chronicle the extent of the Catholic spirit in the humanities, but it is necessary nevertheless to acknowledge that spirit as intrinsic to the Catholic experience.

Art is after all sacramental: the artwork mediates the artists' vision. Artists sometimes believe that their visionary experience is directly revealed by God. Through the arts humanity appreciates, praises and celebrates the supreme Creator.

Plastic Arts

Architecture

Most practical and necessary is architecture, for there is always a need of space to celebrate liturgy. The earliest Christian churches, once the persecutions ended, were modeled upon pagan temples. In a few cases the church was simply a modification of an existing temple. The basilica (major church) is modeled upon the emperor's throne room, modified by being built as a square cross.

Romanesque architecture dominates the early Western Middle Ages. Its huge, massive walls symbolize the faith's eternity and stability in a world otherwise unstable and dreamlike.

At the height of the Middle Ages the quintessential Christian architecture, **gothic**, in its soaring heights encompasses the entire universe within its walls. So wed is the gothic image to Christianity that to this day it is chosen for cathedrals and churches such as St. Patrick's in New York. There were subsequent styles of Church architecture such as the elegance of the baroque and the glitter of rococo, but none has been so identified with the religion as gothic.

The liturgical renewal of Vatican II provoked corresponding changes in church architecture. For example, the altar now is free standing. A wealth of new churches once again celebrates Catholicism's renewed vision.

Painting and Sculpture

As in architecture the earliest Christian painting and sculpture copied classical art. It is sometimes difficult to tell whether a representation is of Jesus or Orpheus.

The iconoclastic controversy of the Middle Ages raged over how and whether God, Jesus and the saints could be represented. The icon (a traditional rendering of the sacred images) has become the official style of Eastern Christianity. In the West a more representational and devotional art emerged in the Middle Ages. At the end of the Middle Ages in the West the artist emerged as an individual. **Giotto** is the first of modern Western artists with his own style and flavor.

Artistic enterprise flourished in the Italian Renaissance, showering Catholicism with some of its greatest treasures. **Michaelangelo** creates his David, Moses, and Sistine Chapel. **Raphael** inaugurates a style that became a touchstone for devotional kitsch into this century. And **Bernini** is the architect of St. Peter's among other sculpture and buildings. Among almost countless artists **El Greco**'s astigmatic visions stand out.

The modern era from the Renaissance on has seen its share of Christian inspired artists in spite of its generally secular character. The Protestant **Rembrandt** illustrated scenes from Scripture. In France **George Rouault** gives his art the flavor of stained glass. And **Salvador Dali** cannot be understood apart from his esoteric Catholic symbolism.

Performing Arts

Drama

Western drama was reborn not in the Renaissance, but in the Middle Ages from the Mass. The earliest modern dramatist is the nun **Hroswitha**; another being rediscovered is **Hildegard of Bingen**—plastic artist, theologian, dramatist, musician and scientist. Drama emerged from the responsorial—the psalm between the first reading and gospel.[1] And the Middle Ages witnessed its flowering in the **mystery** and **miracle** plays, of which the most famous are *Everyman* and the *Second Shepherds Play*.

Modern Christian dramatists in France include **Paul Claudel** (*Tidings Brought to Mary*) and **George Bernanos** (*Dialogues of the Carmelites*). **T. S. Eliot** (*Murder in the Cathedral, The Cocktail Party*), was an Anglo-Catholic American who spent his life in England. His contemporary **W. H. Auden** (*For the Time Being*) emigrated to America. **Christopher Fry** wrote *The Lady's Not for Burning*, and his *Sleep of Prisoners* is written for church performance. **Eugene O'Neill**, while not a practicing Catholic, was dominated by the Irish Catholicism which permeates his plays.

Music

Like architecture, music has been essential to liturgy. Spoken liturgy is a recent phenomenon. Through the Middle Ages liturgy was sung. Our praise of God employs music, word and image to celebrate God's grace and give thanks. As St. Benedict said "He who sings, prays twice."

Catholicism's official music is **Gregorian chant**, traced back to Pope Gregory the Great whose reforms gave Western liturgy its overall shape and structure. Some chant melodies derive from Hebrew psalmody used before Jesus; other melodies were adapted from medieval folk material. Chant is not intended to draw attention to itself. The music serves the words.

With the Renaissance, **polyphony** began to compete with the single line of plainsong. A number of melodic lines weave a rich texture. This liturgical music reaches its height in **Palestrina**. Others are **Orlando Gibbons** and **Gabrieli** whose compositions for St. Mark's in Ven-

---

1. Way 22

ice took account of space creating a quadriphony long before the advent of the phonograph.

Polyphony, originally resisted by Church leaders, won the day and became a new standard imposed on Church music until the present century. In the modern period other musical styles were banned and only Vienna was exempted. There composers were free to set the Mass texts to their own style, and thus resulted the musical settings by **Haydn, Mozart, Beethoven** and **Schubert**.

Protestants distrusted the lavish imaging of Catholicism, and only music found an honored place in their churches. The Protestant **hymn** has recently been adopted by Catholics as well. And the greatest composer of Christendom, **J. S. Bach**, spent much of his life writing music for church services, including the *St. Matthew* and *St. John Passions*, the *Christmas Oratorio* and the great *Mass in B Minor*.

Mass texts fascinated Romantic composers, though they were rarely practicing Catholics. A more operatic style evolved with **Hector Berlioz**. **Giuseppe Verdi**'s *Requiem* has been called with some justice his greatest opera. When criticized for his music's drama, Verdi asked, "Must our churches always be dimly lit?"

Benjamin Britten's powerful remembrance of the Second World War consecrated the new cathedral of Coventry, England rising phoenix-like from its bombed out shell. The *War Requiem* blends the Latin Mass text with poems of Wilfred Owen that comment upon them and speak of the horrors of war. **Leonard Bernstein**'s *Mass* blends the ancient texts with modern commentary. Both **Igor Stravinsky** and **Ralph Vaughan Williams** composed Masses for Church performance using polyphony in a quite modern way. When invited by Pope John XXIII to perform his Mass in the papal chapel, Stravinsky gasped, "But doesn't he know I'm not a Catholic?"

Some composers' work is illuminated by the Catholic tradition. **Gustav Mahler** was Catholic out of political expedience. But his symphonies such as the "Resurrection" often display Catholic themes and texts. While no Catholic, **Richard Wagner** blends his own exotic Catholic dream in "Parsifal."

Dance

Dance, too, has a close connection to Christianity. It may be the oldest art since it uses the body itself. There is powerful biblical testimony to its place as sacred art. The Second Vatican Council has once more allowed dance a place in the liturgy.

King David dances before the ark of the covenant as it is brought into Jerusalem.[2] Luke recapitulates this theme as John the Baptist leaps like David in his mother's womb in the presence of Mary, the new ark carrying the Lord.[3] Dance celebrates God with our whole bodies, with all our being. The sensuality of dance is not alien to God or spirituality. We are embodied beings.

Dance formed part of Christian liturgy from the earliest times through the Middle Ages and into the Renaissance. Only with the Protestant Reformation's negative reaction to dance did Catholicism begin also to question its place in liturgy and life. It still finds a place in many areas on special feast days, in processions, and in the movements of the liturgy itself. Following are testimonies from our tradition to the dance. First, John Chrysostom, the greatest of the Greek Fathers, asserts:

> Of those in heaven and those upon the earth a unison is made, one general assembly, one single service of thanksgiving, one single transport of rejoicing, one joyous dance. You danced those spiritual dances which are most modest; you circled and used musical instruments of the spirit, revealing your souls as do the musical instruments on which the Holy Spirit plays when he instills his grace into your hearts.[4]

And Bonaventure, the great Franciscan theologian, says:

> Blessed in soothe is that dance whose company is infinity, whose circling is eternity, whose song is bliss.[5]

Finally, Dante reminds us that the bliss of heaven itself was often imagined by Christians as a great dance:

> Hosanna! Lord God of Sabaoth! . . . Thus, revolving to its own melody, that substance was seen by me to sing, and it and the others moved in their dance. . . . And as wheels within the fittings of clocks revolve, so that to him who gives heed the first seem quiet, and the last to fly, so these carols differently dancing, swift and slow, made me rate their riches. . . . [6]

---

2. 2 Sam 6:14-16
3. Lk 1:44
4. Chrysostom, Hom 1, In illud, vidi Dom.
5. Bonaventure, Dieta Salutis
6. Paradise VII

Christian literature naturally begins with the Scriptures themselves, and in Catholicism pride of place is given to Jerome's translation, the Vulgate. **Augustine's** *Confessions* provided a new literary genre blossoming in innumerable autobiographies as people descry the meaning of their life's story.

The Middle Ages contributed the various sequences still sung at special Masses such as the "Stabat Mater Dolorosa," the Sequence for Corpus Christi by **Thomas Aquinas**, and the famous "Dies Irae" (no longer used). As the Middle Ages gave birth to the greatest Catholic theologian in Aquinas, so did it bear its greatest poet **Dante** whose *Comedy* is a poetic synthesis as vast and profound as the angelic doctor's *Summa*. Mention should also be made of **Chaucer** whose *Canterbury Tales* take place on a pilgrimage, and whose *Troilus and Cresside* puts a Christian understanding on a pagan tale.

The modern period has seen Catholic works from many cultures such as **Cervantes** and **Unamuno** from Spain, in France **Claudel, Bernanos, Mauriac**, from Sweden **Sigrid Undset**. England and America are not primarily Catholic cultures, but they also contribute. Before the Reformation **Piers Plowman** creates the medieval dream poem. The metaphysical poets are Catholic, although only one, **Crashaw**, is Roman Catholic. English neo-classicism numbers the Catholics **Dryden** and **Pope**. Among the Romantics **Wordsworth** and **Coleridge** are Christian, but they pale beside the visions of **Blake**, a prophetic visionary.

Catholic writers have only recently emerged again in England with specifically Catholic themes. The nineteenth and early twentieth century sees **John Henry Newman** and the apologist converts **G. K. Chesterton** and **Hilaire Belloc**. **James Joyce** may have left the Church but is impossible to understand without an inside knowledge of Catholicism. Poets include among Anglicans **T. S. Eliot** and **W. H. Auden**, and the Jesuit **Gerard Manley Hopkins**. Novelists and satirists number **Evelyn Waugh** (*Brideshead Revisited*) and **Graham Greene** (*The Power and the Glory*).

In America Catholicism is represented in literature by the poetry of **Thomas Merton, Robert Lowell** (who joined, then left, but whose early poetry is a continuation of the metaphysical tradition), Jesuit **Daniel Berrigan** and an angel of light verse, **Phyllis McGinley**. Flannery O'Connor's stories of the south do not contain obvious Catholic material but are informed by her Catholic vision. She is joined by fellow southerner **Walker Percy** (*Love in the Ruins, Lancelot*).

Beat poet **Jack Kerouac's** Catholicism, which he did not practice, nevertheless dictated his spiritual quest. And he was buried, as his friend Allen Ginsberg had predicted, with a rosary in his hands. Kerouac's definition of "beat" derived neither from jazz nor as a cop-out from the American dream of success but from "Beatitude"—the elusive happiness sought outside the deadly conformist society of the 1950s.

TO DEEPEN—

Go to an art museum and examine some of the works with Christian themes. Can you identify the various figures and themes?

Listen to a setting of Mass texts by a classical composer. How does the music help you appreciate the sacred words more deeply?

The novels mentioned and some poetry give a feel for the Catholic atmosphere hard to come by in other ways.

Further Reading:

Beckwith, John. *Early Christian and Byzantine Art*. Penguin, 1980.

Daniels, Marilyn. *The Dance in Christianity*. Paulist Press, 1981.

Davie, Donald. *New Oxford Book of Christian Verse*. Oxford University Press, 1982.

Deiss, Lucien. *Spirit and Song of the New Liturgy*. World Library of Sacred Music, 1970.

De Sola, Carla. *Learning Through Dance*. Paulist Press, 1974.

Ferguson, George. *Signs and Symbols in Christian Art*. Oxford University Press, 1966.

Schoof, Mark. *Survey of Catholic Theology, 1800–1970*. Paulist Press, 1970.

The Vatican Collections: The Papacy and Art. Abrams, 1983.

Watts, Alan. *Myth and Ritual in Christianity*. Beacon, 1968.

TO CONTINUE—

The history of theology and philosophy is covered in the history section (Life 29ff).

Catholic popular culture is discussed in Life 40.

◇

14. Life in the Church

TO PREPARE—

The section should be read only after familiarity with The Church as Teacher (Truth 22ff), The Holy Catholic Church (Truth 39ff) and Holy Orders (Truth 84).

This section considers life as found within the Catholic Church. First we look at how the Church is organized and structured. Then we examine the sociological makeup of the Catholic world, and finally the history of the Catholic Church. Thus this first part is entitled: "The Church in Time and Space." Then, in the second part, the Church's worship life is examined. Now, however, rather than considering how Catholic liturgy promotes our journey on the Way of Jesus,[1] we examine how it supports Catholic life. We consider the Church's daily prayer, its customs and celebrations, and the other liturgical calendars beyond the Sunday cycle.[2] Finally we look at how the Catholic Church relates to the world. Our topic is Catholic social teachings which touch upon life and conditions in our world.

---

1. Way 8ff
2. Way 28

The Church in Time and Space

Although the key meaning of the Church lies in its theological definition, its concrete organization and functioning are important: a definite structure, a quantifiable membership and an almost two-thousand-year history reveal much concerning Catholicism. Catholics believe that the vision of Jesus Christ subsists today primarily in this Church. Through flesh and blood existence in the Christian community we are converted more deeply and find fulfillment. Although many Church structures are not divinely mandated but the result of historical existence, they do influence how the Church functions and how it is perceived.

The Church's membership molds the Church's image in the world and especially in the local community. Just who belongs to this organization? What kind of people are Catholics? And what are the subgroups within the larger and more abstract Church?

Finally history determines much about what that institution is. What we are today is partly the result of our past. What is our history? While not essential to grasping the Gospel, these are important issues for understanding the present Church.

15. THE STRUCTURE AND ORGANIZATION OF THE CHURCH

The Church's present shape and existence are determined by two crucial factors. First, certain revealed truths determine the Church's essential nature and structures.[3] Being from God they are essential, although these structures have developed. Other structures which have evolved through history to flesh out the Church's organization are not divinely given and therefore are open to change. Without bishops or priests it would not be Church, but it could abolish the college of cardinals tomorrow as an act of reform. This section focuses primarily upon the non-essentials.

16. Law in the Church—The Code of Canon Law

The Church's structure and functioning are set forth in the Code of Canon Law by which the Roman Catholic Church is organized and governed. Based originally on ancient Church councils, it is quite dif-

---

3. Truth 39ff

ferent in philosophy and approach from American law. American Catholics should appreciate this difference. Canon law is really the practical application of theology. In fact, it was not until the twelfth century that theology and ecclesiastical law were taught as separate subjects in the schools. As theology developed through the centuries, the law had to be adjusted to keep pace. In the early Church, for example, reconciliation or penance was viewed as a last chance, a once-in-a-lifetime opportunity for forgiveness after baptism; now the law provides for frequent reception of this sacrament. Again, the recent progress in ecumenical theology has made it possible to share in worship with Protestants to an extent that would have been strictly prohibited before the 1960s. Civil law, on the other hand, does not depend upon a theoretical basis; it is much more empirical, growing out of lived experience.

This code (revised in 1983) determines Church structures and procedures. It details the rights and duties of Catholics from lay people to the Pope. It deals with the Church offices as well as associations connected with the Church—societies, religious groups, etc. It considers the organizational structures from the local parish community on up. It covers the various religious communities and institutes. It provides an order for the celebration of the sacraments and other official actions. It deals with Church properties. It covers instances in which a person or persons offend against the Church and the means of trial and penalty. It expounds Church authority and discipline. And it sets up the procedures for determining the sacramentality of marriage and the declaration of annulment in the cases of sacramental deficiency.

17. Orders of the Church

The Church is composed of orders, groups of people who have a special need or function within the community. Moving from the ground up, we begin with the newest members and work up to management.

Orders of Those Entering the Catholic Community

Catechumens[4] are unbaptized people preparing to be incorporated in the Church. The Church prays over them, blesses them through special rites and ceremonies, and shares its faith with them. Within the catechumenate the order of the **elect**[5] during Lent prepares for the

---

4. Intro 4ff
5. Intro 10

Easter sacraments. **Candidates**, an unofficial order, comprise Christians from other churches moving toward full membership in the Roman communion. After Easter the new Christians are **neophytes** for the Easter season.

Orders of the Faithful

The largest order within the Church are the baptized laity. They partake in its worship and sacramental life and may exercise a lay ministry to the Christian community or the world.

Vatican II opened several ministries to the laity. Key **lay ministries** are those of the **word**—the lector who proclaims the word of God in the liturgy or catechists who teach the faith—and the **Eucharist**—those who help distribute Holy Communion and bring communion to the sick, and, finally, the ministry of **service**, including all the charitable and social justice ministries.

Special Orders

This order includes all men and women in **religious life**[6] bound by the three evangelical counsels. Finally there are those men in **holy orders**[7] (deacon, presbyter, bishop) commissioned to carry out the ordained ministry. The Pope holds a special office, but belongs to the order of bishop.

Organizational Structure

18. The Parish

Again working up from the grassroots we begin with those people and structures encountered in the local community and then branch out into successively larger and more universal structures and offices. The **parish** is the local unit of the Catholic community. Parishes are usually territorial, embracing all Catholics within a certain geographical area. For people in special circumstances, for example college students or the military, other structures may be provided. In practice today some Americans join parishes other than their neighborhood parish through choice.

The central parish building is ideally the local church. In some

---

6. Life 11
7. Truth 84

cases there is no permanent church. Thus "parish" truly refers to the worshiping community rather than to any property.

The **pastor**, appointed by the bishop, is in charge of the care of the parish. His term of office may be indefinite or for the period of six years. He is responsible to the bishop for the parish's well-being, including its organizations and properties (which may include a school or community center in addition to the church and the rectory where the priests stay and a convent for sisters).

The pastor is responsible for the pastoral care of the people in the parish. He celebrates the liturgy and administers the sacraments, teaches, counsels, visits the people, organizes and participates in community functions. He is often helped by a staff that may include priests acting as the pastor's associates. Sisters and lay people may undertake specialized ministry within the parish such as conducting the school, supervising religious education, running the catechumenate, directing music, or helping in the various ministries.

The **pastoral team** forms the core of professional ministers. These specially trained people work full or part time. But the parish ministries extend far beyond a small team. Today many parishes have parish councils consisting of priests and lay people who help the pastor determine needs and goals.

Various groups and **committees** carry out particular ministries within the parish community and outside in the world. These include charitable organizations such as the St. Vincent de Paul Society which works for the poor rather like a Catholic Salvation Army. It also includes the catechists and catechetical teams teaching school children, teenagers, adults and catechumens. Other local organizations embrace social justice issues, community building, hospitality, visiting the sick and elderly, and service to the parish congregation as ushers or altar societies responsible for Church furnishings and vestments.

19. The Diocese

In most places the next unit of organization is the **deanery**—a group of neighboring parishes whose pastors work with the bishop on a regional basis.

The next structure after the deanery is the diocese—the territory entrusted to the **bishop**'s care. A diocese may be an area of land coextensive with a metropolitan or geographical area. Large cities are usually dioceses. Often the bishop of a large city is an archbishop who oversees adjacent smaller dioceses, each headed by a local bishop. In large dioceses auxiliary bishops aid the "ordinary" or diocesan bishop.

The bishop is the chief minister of the diocese. The priests function as his assistants and are responsible to him. The **cathedral** is the bishop's church, his seat, from which he presides and teaches.

A staff aids the bishop in managing the diocese. The **chancery**, the office building, houses diocesan organizations such as the offices of worship and of education, Catholic Charities, and organizations for priests and religious. Every diocese must have a **tribunal**, a local church court; in this country it deals almost exclusively with marriage cases brought by those seeking a declaration of nullity.[8] The court sometimes handles other legal proceedings including property and internal church processes.

A diocese is to have a presbyteral or **priests' council** to aid the bishop in the governance of the diocese; it is his chief consultative body. The bishop is obliged to consult the council in more important matters, especially in those cases specified by law. The council does not make binding decisions. The bishop holds the ultimate authority as teacher and pastor.

20. The National Level

The **National Conference of Catholic Bishops** (NCCB) includes all the bishops of the country. It is a canonical body mandated by Vatican II with defined juridical authority over the Church in America. This group meets one or more times a year to confer on Church matters. In the recent past the conference in addition to discussing and legislating on matters pertaining to ministry and liturgy, such as setting norms for Communion under both species or the age for the reception of confirmation, has studied and addressed contemporary issues such as the possibility of nuclear war and the American economy.

The **United States Catholic Conference** (USCC) is a civil corporation composed of all the bishops. Its purpose is to assist and coordinate "in the public, educational and social concerns of the Church at the national or interdiocesan level." A number of national agencies exist, most housed in Washington D.C., called into being by the American bishops to handle a special area or situation such as the liturgy or social justice, or to govern and direct groups within the national Church such as the various religious communities or the Catholic Veterans Association, etc.

Some multinational organizations exist such as the International Committee on English in the Liturgy (ICEL) which prepares liturgical

---

8. Truth 53, 83

translations for English-speaking countries. But these are for specific tasks and limited in authority and extent.

21. *Churchwide Structures*

Vatican City, a sovereign state within the city of Rome, is the hub of Roman Catholicism. The Pope is the chief teacher, pastor and legislator for the worldwide communion.

A large organizational structure aids the Pope in governance. First and foremost is the **ecumenical council**—the highest teaching body and legislative assembly in the Church. It is composed of the Pope and all the bishops. The last council was Vatican II (1961–1965) which reformed and mandated changes in many Church structures from the liturgy to canon law.

Another structure produced by the Second Vatican Council is the **synod of bishops** which the Pope calls at appropriate times to explore issues of concern. These synods comprise a selection of the world's bishops to advise the Pope. They are not legislative and do not have the authority of ecumenical councils.

The day to day running of the Church is largely in the hands of the Vatican bureaucracy: the **curia**. Here cardinals and bishops head congregations and agencies dealing with Church processes and relations to other worldly structures. These include: congregations for Bishops, Oriental Churches, Sacraments and Divine Worship, Clergy, Laity, Religious and Secular Institutes, the Evangelization of Peoples, the Causes of Saints; secretariats for Christian Unity, Non-Christians, and Non-Believers; commissions on Justice and Peace, the Laity, the Family, Culture. In addition three tribunals handle cases referred to the Pope.

22. *Honorary Titles*

The **college of cardinals** has the responsibility for the election of a Pope. The cardinals also assist by their advice in matters of major importance. For the cardinalate the Pope freely selects outstanding men who are at least priests; those who are not yet bishops must receive episcopal consecration.

The title of **monsignor** is conferred upon a priest who has been outstanding in his ministry and service to the Church.

TO DEEPEN—

Find out the names of your parish staff and the local bishops. Where is the cathedral? What is its name?

What is the concrete structure of your local parish?

Where would the validity of a marriage that has broken up be decided?

What groups are found within your parish?

What does a cardinal do? Is this an unchangeable structure?

Further Reading:

Coriden, Green, Heintschel, eds. *The Code of Canon Law: A Text and Commentary.* Paulist Press, 1985.

Place, E. *A Pastoral Guide to the Revised Code.* Chicago Studies, 1984.

THE EXTENT OF THE CHURCH

This section introduces some of the people and groups who make up the Church. Obviously a membership of more than eight hundred million incorporates much diversity. One might define Catholicism in the words of James Joyce as "Here comes everybody." "Catholic" refers to a universality which at its best the Church seeks to encompass. St. Augustine recommended, "In essentials unity, in accidentals diversity, in all things charity."

23. The Various Rites of the Catholic Church

Vatican II revised the rites of the Catholic Church. With the introduction of modern languages and other changes, variations in the Roman rite are now prominent. Gone are the days when the Mass was identical everywhere. Today variations occur between parish and parish, or priest and priest. Some churches have as yet failed to comply with the new rites, whereas others have carried the process of acculturation beyond what the current rites allow.

Although small in comparison to Latin rite Catholics, a number of Eastern rites exist within the Roman Church. These Eastern churches accept the primacy of the Pope, but maintain their own rituals, canon law, theology and customs. A number are found in major American cities.

24. Roman Catholicism in North America

Most Christians belong to the lay state: people who embrace Christianity and make their living and life in the public world. There are two major divisions of lay people in the Church—married and single.

A significant number of Catholics live in family situations either as spouses, children or relatives. Catholicism finds ways to minister to its members in the context of family life. Educational opportunities are geared toward the different family members. Organizations within the Church support families and enrich their lives.

The Church does not define or offer any specific Christian lifestyle for the unmarried. These include of course children and adults. Some adults embrace celibacy which the Church teaches as the only appropriate lifestyle for a single person. Others may be in relationships not confirmed in marriage or may be divorced or separated persons. Still other single people are widowed. Others are gay or lesbian.

Although the Church does not officially condone some of these lifestyles, a significant number of practicing Catholics are involved. Tension between Church, individuals and groups has become a factor of Catholic life. The American Catholic divorce rate is almost the same as the average. The number of single parent families and single people has dramatically increased. These and other significant demographic changes in the U.S. population present the Church with a great array of lifestyles. There seems to be no foreseeable reversing of these present trends.

Ethnic Groups

Like Americans generally we are a Church of immigrants, outside the few native American Catholics. And American Catholicism is shaped largely by immigration which over the last century has brought a number of ethnic groups to America. And these brought with them their national brand of Catholicism.

Historically the most dominant ethnic group has been the Irish. Other major immigrants during the last century include Germans and Poles who settled largely in the middle west and color Catholicism there. The French are prominent in eastern Canada and also in the northeastern United States. Italians along with the Irish populate the East Coast cities.

Recent Catholic immigrants have been largely Hispanics from Latin America. The largest populations on the east coast have been from Puerto Rico and the Caribbean area, while the largest numbers in the

West have come from Mexico. In the near future American Catholicism will be heavily influenced by Hispanic culture.

The Vietnam War brought many Vietnamese Catholics to the west coast and other areas to begin a new life. These groups bring their own perspective on Catholicism including customs, ways of thought and living, and attitudes toward their faith which can lead to misunderstanding at worst and toward a wonderful richness of the American culture at best.

Many black people have become Catholics in America and are adding their own voice. Although not sizable in terms of the overall Catholic population, blacks bring their own experience to the Church and finding ways of being Catholic and black rather than fitting into the white expression of Catholicism that has passed for the norm so far.

Regional Differences

Regional differences may be due to the peoples who have settled in an area and thus influenced the shape of the Church or to other regional factors. Anything said here is bound to be simplistic and should not be taken literally or as more than an attempt to highlight major trends.

American Catholicism has been an urban phenomenon since most immigrants were drawn to the cities. The northeast region, being the entrance point for most immigrants, has tended to be the premier Catholic area of the country until recently. Predominantly Irish it has accommodated the region's puritanism and also manifested the Yankee qualities of work and industry. But there is diversity as well, from the conservative tone of Philadelphia to the socially progressive thrust of Boston.

Midwestern Catholicism, heavily influenced by German immigrants, is more progressive than east coast Catholicism. Liturgical renewal in the early part of this century came from midwestern German Benedictines. Chicago developed a very progressive and socially conscious lay presence.

Catholicism has not been prevalent in the south, although originally Florida and Louisiana were colonized by Spanish and French Catholics who provided a rich culture preserved above all in New Orleans. Today shifts of northerners into the sunbelt increases the Church there. Without the primary ethnic ties or the long traditions of northern Catholicism, southern Catholics, often removed from family in the north, are creating a true progressive and community centered Church.

In the southwest Catholicism's dominant ethnic group is Mexican American. The churches often take on Spanish architecture and Latino customs. With the great westward migrations after the Second World War a number of other ethnic groups have also come west.

The Pacific northwest is still the primary unchurched area of the country. Catholics are a minority, as are Christians in general. But without the primary ties to the old world, Catholicism exhibits a progressive nature so that many of the ideas of Vatican II have been adopted and put into practice here that have not yet been widely accepted in more conservative areas.

In Canada Catholicism is largely determined by the French of Quebec. Among non-French Catholics are the various ethnic groups of the Canadian melting pot, including native Americans and Eskimo peoples.

Variety among Viewpoints and Commitment

Gone are the days when American Catholics were automatically assumed to be Democrats. Today American Catholic political opinion spans the conservatism of William F. Buckley, Jr. to the radical prophecy of Daniel Berrigan. The political and social thought of the Catholic hierarchy in both Rome and America tends toward socialism and welfare due to Christian concern for the poor, but an increasing variety of political and economic thought exists within the Church. Some question whether the bishops' teachings on nuclear war or the economy will even be granted a serious hearing by most American Catholics. In politics, economics and social problems a Catholic position does not imply that a majority of Catholics will be aware of the stance or adopt it themselves.

The spectrum of thought extends into the theological sphere. The greatest event in modern Catholicism, the Second Vatican Council, introduced vast changes and a new vision into the Church. These have not been without consequences and results. Today's Catholicism is much more diverse than the hierarchy might wish.

Some are disturbed and feel that the Church or certain Catholics have gone too far. Such attitudes can been seen in the newspaper "The Wanderer" and in the organization Catholics United for the Faith (CUFF).

On the other hand, some feel that the Church has not entered far enough into the spirit of Vatican II. They consider the agenda unfinished and look for further changes such as the opening of the priesthood to women, or a development in sexual teaching. Such thinking can be seen in publications such as "The National Catholic Reporter." This diversity leads to controversy and political maneuvering, and sometimes descends to name-calling. But it is also a sign of life and vitality.

A further variety is evident regarding involvement and concern with Catholicism itself. The Church allows membership to all professing a modicum of good faith. Some seem Catholics in name only; others are moderately committed, and a few are consumed by the spiritual quest and their commission to service: a Church of saints and sinners. And while the Church calls all to conversion and sanctity, people can continue to be members with a minimum of commitment. Of course it hopes that they may one day wake up, and if they do they will be in the right place to respond.

Certain groups have special needs. Increasingly the Church in America recognizes that Christ's Church belongs to the poor and exists to be with the poor in their struggle for liberation. Though many Catholics are not poor, the Church itself is the Church of and for the poor.

These include groups besides the economically poor. As women discover the extent of their oppression in a patriarchal culture, many are either leaving the Church or staying in the hope of changing that dominant ideology. The elderly can often be identified with the poor, for even if materially well off, they are often relegated to the margins of American life, as are the sick.

Catholicism is largely a family Church, and in America the concern for family has produced a great parochial school system as well as a system of religious instruction. Here, the Church confronts the danger that some expressions of American Catholicism seem designed primarily for children and that religion ceases to have an adult dimension.

Organizations and Groups

A number of service and support groups aid the American Church. Traditionally these have included the Knights of Columbus and other fraternal support and charitable groups. The St. Vincent de Paul Society collects food, clothing and goods for the poor. The Catholic Worker, founded by Peter Maurin, staffs food kitchens and other services for the homeless. Catholic Relief Services provide on-site emergency food and transportation. The National Catholic Rural Life Conference provides advocacy on behalf of issues pertaining to farming and natural resources. Various sodalities provide spiritual nourishment and service.

Modern support groups have arisen as needs occur. Credit unions provide a means of saving money and help one another through loans. The Cursillo movement originated in Spain as an intensive retreat which renews people. Marriage Encounter began in the 1960s to help Catholics appreciate the Christian dimension of matrimony and develop attitudes of listening to one another. Bread for the World finds Catholic chapters that form a lobby to government on behalf of the hungry. Most recently we have seen women's support groups, gay and lesbian groups (Dignity), divorced Catholics and others.

TO DEEPEN—

What has been your own experience of Catholicism's diversity?

How would you characterize your local parish community in terms of ethnicity, etc.?

Learn something of the history of Catholicism in your area.

Further Reading:

Hellwig, Monica. *Christian Women in a Troubled World.* Paulist Press, 1984.

Murray, John C. *We Hold These Truths. Catholic Reflections on the American Proposition.* Sheed & Ward, 1985.

Nouwen, Henry & Gaffney, James. *Aging: The Fulfillment of Life.* Doubleday, 1976.

Nugent, Robert, ed. *A Challenge to Love—Gay and Lesbian Catholics in the Church.* Crossroad, 1986.

Posey, M., ed. *Theology: A Portrait in Black.* National Black Catholic Clergy Caucus, 1980.

25. Catholic Europe and the Middle East

America is only one part of the Catholic world. And just as ethnic and regional divergences form the fabric of American Catholicism, the pattern proliferates when opened to the rest of the world.

Historically Catholicism received its present general shape as the Gospel encountered Greco-Roman culture and then that of pagan northern Europe. Until recently this model served Catholicism everywhere, but Vatican II encouraged other cultures to develop their own particular expression.

Today although much of Europe is still regarded technically as Catholic, the faith has eroded. Much of France, Italy and Germany are post-Christian. Their pre-eminence in the Christian world is primarily historical, although individuals from these countries may still hold powerful positions within the Vatican. While geographical and historical centers of the faith may still be in these countries, the vitality of Christianity is found better elsewhere.

European Catholicism exhibits its own varieties. It is a far cry from the Polish Church that struggles daily against a hostile government and therefore must cleave to the faith and traditions which are all that can sustain a people who have lost so much, to the progressive Dutch Church, faced with a world that it must engage and address compellingly, and feeling therefore that certain elements must be discarded to address the modern world.

The original Christian society was not Europe but the Middle East. Although sustaining a great loss to Islam, Christianity has survived there. This is the proper world of the Uniate Churches—the Eastern rite Catholics—of whom the Lebanese Maronites are a prominent example.

26. The Church of the Third World

Latin America

Today many believe that Christianity's future lies in the third world. Latin America has traditionally been Catholic, colonized by the Spanish and the Portuguese. Today liberation theology has arisen in these countries with its proclamation of the Gospel's power to aid the poor in their struggle for freedom. The Latin American Church is turning from its past, when it was part of the political establishment, toward the future, becoming a Church of the people and empowering them to claim freedom.

Africa

The Church is growing most rapidly in Africa and its emerging nations. While Christianity and its sense of transcendence has largely lost its power in sophisticated Europe, African Christians are founding vibrant communities. And the challenge is to create a Christianity which builds upon the African experience and heritage in the same way that European Christianity found its face through allowing the Gospel to transform its own heritage. In this area problems have arisen between a European understanding of the faith and the newly emerging African vision.

Asia

Finally Christianity in Asia is coming into its own. The Gospel was stunted in Asia because of the insistence that Western Christianity serve as the sole model. But today Asian Christians understand the Gospel in the light of their own experience and traditions. Christianity is in dialogue with Asian religions, being enriched and hopefully enriching in turn.

Vatican II abandoned the defensive and rigid expression of Catholicism of the last four hundred years. Although this process has led to some tension and misunderstanding, this rich diversity of expressions of the faith is one of the distinguishing features of Catholicism. And the tension offers a rich opportunity for growth and development. Jean Vanier has said in *Community and Growth:* "Tension or difficulty can be the sign of the approach of a new grace of God."[1] We are united in one Lord, one faith, one baptism, one hope,[2] but we express these unifying beliefs through the multitudinous colors of the human prism so that Christ may be all in all.

Further Reading:

Gibellini, ed. *Frontiers of Theology in Latin America.* Orbis, 1979.
Lernoux, Penny. *Cry of the People.* Doubleday, 1981.
Nouwen, Henry. *Gracias.* Harper & Row, 1983. Diary of six months in Bolivia and Peru, of the people, their poverty, suffering and hope.

27. The Roman Catholic Church and the Churches

Our journey now continues beyond the boundaries of the Roman Catholic Church to consider those who also claim the Christian heritage. These Churches will be presented as the Roman Church views them in relation to itself. The dominant Catholic model for understanding other traditions as well as other religions is that of concentric circles. At the center is the Roman Catholic Church with the Pope as the primary symbol of Christian unity.[3] Other Churches are grouped in terms of their conformity to the faith as Rome understands it.

---

1. Paulist, 1979
2. Eph 4:5
3. Truth 40

Orthodoxy

First and closest to the Roman position are the Orthodox Churches. These are in schism from Rome—they are not in union with the papacy. But Rome acknowledges their faith, theology and Church structures as valid. Among these Churches are the **Greek Orthodox Church**, the **Russian Orthodox Church** and smaller branches scattered throughout the Middle East, eastern Europe and northern Africa.

Other Catholic Communions

The second concentric circle includes other Catholic communions not in union with Rome. Foremost are the **Anglican** communions such as the Church of England, the **Episcopal Church** in America and the other Churches of lands linked to the British Commonwealth. These are not strictly Protestant Churches. Like the Orthodox they are in schism. However Rome does not regard them as it does the Orthodox, because they have at times come under the influence of Protestantizing forces.

Other much smaller Catholic communions called **National Catholic Churches** split off from Rome at various times. For example the Polish Catholic Church split as a result of the First Vatican Council. The Church of Cardinal Lefevre belongs among these groups.

Mainstream Protestantism

The third concentric circle encompasses the mainstream Protestant Churches—those which hold to the Nicene Creed: the **Lutheran, Presbyterian, Methodist**, and **Calvinist** traditions. Very generally Protestantism emphasized the authority of Scripture over the Church, and of the word over sacrament. Today ecumenical dialogue has re-established communication between the Churches. Dialogue explores issues in the hope of coming to an understanding of one another's doctrines and positions and moving toward unity.

Other Protestant Churches

The mainstream Protestant Churches do not exhaust by any means the Protestant world. Beyond these lie other bodies such as the **Baptist** traditions which do not affirm the Nicene Creed. Thus these groups make up another circle. Included here would be the various **Pentecostal** and **Holiness** groups as well as most **fundamentalist communities**.

Christian Groups

Beyond lie groups which are similar to Christians in some ways, yet differ so significantly that they fall outside the traditional definitions of a Christian Church. They may deny the Trinity, such as the **Unitarian-Universalists**. Or they may hold non-traditional doctrines, such as the **Mormon** ideas of pre-existence of souls or baptism for the dead. Other communities in this category are the **Jehovah's Witnesses**, **Christian Science**, and the **Unification Church** of Reverend Moon.

The Ecumenical Movement

Within the last century many Christian Churches have attempted to stem the splintering of Christians which has continued since the Reformation. Beginning in Protestant Churches, organizations and movements have arisen calling Christians to rediscover their common unity and join together again at least in works and witness if not at this time in reunification. The World Council of Churches is the most prominent organization of this kind.

The Roman Catholic Church supports the ecumenical movement. Although not a member of the World Council it is present now at meetings and is in dialogue with other Churches to restore Christian unity. Rome in an unprecedented gesture invited Protestant and Orthodox observers to the Second Vatican Council.

The ecumenical movement exists on many levels. In addition to the formal Church actions, innumerable activities by Christians aim at promoting unity and removing the misunderstandings and prejudices which have in the past divided the Church. Dialogues grew up such as the Catholic-Anglican and Catholic-Lutheran dialogues. And these exist both at the official levels and at the grass roots. At the grass roots as well, Christians are attending one another's churches, exchanging pulpits, joining together in ecumenical prayer services, and working together for social justice.

TO DEEPEN—

What is the Catholic attitude toward other Christians today?

Attend an ecumenical prayer service or study group.

Further Reading:

Hale, Robert. *Canterbury and Rome. Sister Churches. A Roman Catholic Monk Reflects on Reunion in Diversity.* Paulist Press, 1978.

Meyer, Harding & Vischer, Lukas. *Growth in Agreement: Reports and Agreed Statements of Ecumenical Conversations on a World Level.* Paulist Press, 1982.

Minus, Paul M. *Catholic Rediscovery of Protestantism.* Paulist Press, 1976.

Schmemann, Alexander. *Historical Road of Eastern Orthodoxy.* St. Vladimir's Press, 1977.

28. Christianity and World Religions

Throughout history even to the present day, there is found among different peoples a certain awareness of a hidden power, which lies behind the course of nature and the events of human life. At times there is present even a recognition of a supreme being, or still more of a Father. This awareness and recognition results in a way of life that is imbued with a deep religious sense. The religions which are found in more advanced civilizations endeavor by way of well-defined concepts and exact language to answer these questions.[4]

The Religions of the Abrahamic Covenant: Judaism

The Jewish people share with Christians a common heritage in Israel. The relationship between Christianity and Judaism has historically been largely antagonistic. The earliest Christians were ejected from the synagogues, and as the Christian Church became powerful and a primarily Gentile community, it spawned antisemitism, some of which can be traced back to the New Testament itself. Today the two faiths are in dialogue. John XXIII greeted a Jewish leader with: "I am Joseph your brother." John Paul II visited a Jewish synagogue in Rome. Vatican II condemned antisemitism and declared that the Jewish people were not responsible for the death of Christ, an insidious idea which fueled much hatred. The Jewish people remain God's chosen people.[5]

Islam

Islam also derives from Abraham.[6] It shares with Judaism and Christianity faith in one God. Born after Christianity, Islam acknowl-

---

4. Declaration on the Relation of the Church to Non-Christian Religions, n. 2
5. Rom 11:16-24
6. Gen 16:1-16; Truth 7

edges Jesus as a prophet and pays honor to Mary. Increasing evidence
shows its influence on Christianity. The Islamic renaissance reintro-
duced Aristotle to the West—an intellectual threat until Aquinas
showed how it might ground Christian theology. And the mystic Sufis
of Islam may have inspired the blossoming of the love mysticism of
Francis of Assisi and the troubadours of medieval Europe.

Other Religions

> For since Christ died for all, and since our ultimate vocation
> is in fact one, and divine, we ought to believe that the Holy
> Spirit, in a manner known only to God, offers to every man
> and woman the possibility of being associated with this paschal
> mystery.[7]

Beyond Islam we leave the Israelite tradition behind and encounter the other major religions, most notably the Indic strand of present
day **Hinduism** and **Buddhism**.

> In Hinduism people explore the divine mystery and express
> it both in the limitless riches of myth and the accurately de-
> fined insights of philosophy. They seek release from the trials
> of the present life by ascetical practices, profound meditation
> and recourse to God in confidence and love. Buddhism in its
> various forms testifies to the way of life by which people can,
> with confidence and trust, attain a state of perfect liberation
> and reach supreme illumination either through their own ef-
> forts or by the aid of divine help.[8]

Traditions of the Far East include **Taoism** in China and **Shinto** in
Japan. And finally shamanistic traditions still thrive in various cultures
from the Eskimo and American Indian to the South Pacific Islanders.
    The Church does not regard these faiths as on the same level. But
it appreciates the glimpses of God afforded in these traditions. Its mis-

---

7. Church in the Modern World, n. 22
8. Declaration on the Relation of the Church to Non-Christian Religions, n. 2

sionary activity distinguishes between higher faiths which raise humanity's mind toward the One and superstitions which bind humanity in darkness. To all it hopes to offer the light of Christ who illuminates all and reveals the oneness of creation.

The Catholic Church rejects nothing of what is true and holy in these religions. It has a high regard for the manner of life and conduct, the precepts and doctrines which, nevertheless, often reflect a ray of that truth which enlightens all. Yet it proclaims, and is in duty bound to proclaim without fail, Christ who is the way, the truth and the life.[9] In him, in whom God reconciled all things to himself,[10] people find the fullness of their religious life.[11]

TO DEEPEN—

How does the Church respond to other religions?

Which religions share a common foundation with Christianity?

How does the Catholic Church regard other religious traditions?

Further Reading:

Carmody, Denise Lardner. *What Are They Saying About Non-Christian Faith?* Paulist Press, 1982.

Coward, Harold. *Pluralism: Challenge in World Religions.* Orbis, 1985.

Knitter, Paul. *No Other Name? A Critical Survey of Christian Attitudes toward the World Religions.* Orbis, 1985.

Richard, Lucien. *What Are They Saying About Christ and World Religions?* Paulist Press, 1984.

Rudin, James, Fisher, Eugene, Flannery, Edward, Tanenbaum, Mark, eds. *Twenty Years of Jewish-Catholic Relations.* Paulist Press, 1980.

Waldenfels, Hans. *Absolute Nothingness: Foundations for a Buddhist-Christian Dialogue.* Paulist Press, 1980.

Thoma, Clemens. *Christian Theology of Judaism.* Paulist Press, 1978.

---

9. Jn 14:6

10. 2 Cor 5:18-19

11. Declaration on the Relation of the Church to Non-Christian Religions, n. 2

TO CONTINUE—

The Church's response to other Christians is seen in its ecumenical activity, its response to other religions in inter-religious dialogue and to the non-Christian world in evangelization. These activities are discussed in Way 51.

THE CHURCH IN TIME

This section makes no pretext to being a true history of Christianity. It only aims to refer to some key events and people as well as the overall shape of Christian history. Catholics are a people with a history. We trace back the Church to Jesus himself. And the people of history have helped to shape Catholicism. The following does no more than fill in a broad canvas with certain names, movements and dates. It is truly trivial. For more information and history, follow the references to various histories.

29. Christian Beginnings—The First Century

The Christian Church began at Pentecost[1] when the Holy Spirit descended upon the disciples.[2] At first they saw themselves as Jews who believed that Jesus was the Messiah. Their message was directed at their fellow Jews. But the message was not received gratefully, and soon Stephen the deacon became the first martyr.[3] Only later did they adopt the name "Christian."[4] Before, they were known as followers of the Way.[5]

The conversion of Paul[6] is the key event in this early period (ca. 34). A devout Pharisee active in persecuting the new sect, he became its most enthusiastic convert and began the missionary drive to the Gentile world of the Roman empire. Largely through Paul's efforts the new faith took root and definitive shape in the Gentile world. The original Jewish expression dried up quickly and Christianity's hope lay with the Gentiles.

Paul effected such rapid conversions because Jews, scattered throughout the empire, had attracted pagans to their high moral religion. But circumcision and adherence to the laws prevented many from

---

1. Way 34
2. Acts 2
3. Acts 6:8—8:1a
4. Acts 11:26
5. Acts 9:2
6. Acts 9:1–22; Gal 1:12–17

becoming Jews. These "bystanders" stood around the walls of the synagogues to hear the services. Paul extended the new covenant to them without demanding that they forsake their traditions or submit to circumcision. James, leader of the Jerusalem church, opposed Paul's radical vision. He demanded that all people entering the Church first conform to the law of Moses. Paul opposed such a restriction and won his case,[7] thus opening the Church to a huge influx of Gentiles prepared for the faith by Judaism.

Paul's journeys cover much of the Greco-Roman world (40–61). In Rome he and Peter were martyred under Nero's persecutions (64–67). Since Peter, the head of the apostles, died in Rome, the hub of the empire, it became also the new Church's center, leaving Jerusalem behind. Peter's first successor is Linus (67–76), commemorated with other early Popes in the first eucharistic prayer.[8]

This period (50–120) witnessed the composition of the different Christian writings.[9] At first treasured by the host community, they were also circulated to sister churches and read at assemblies. But they were not yet regarded as Scripture which was limited to the Jewish Scriptures.

Roman persecutions now disturbed the community. Christians refused to take part in the imperial cult—acknowledging the emperor as a god. Being small and uninfluential they could not gain exemption as the Jews did. Many saints commemorated in the first eucharistic prayer[10] are martyrs from this time.

"Martyr" means to be a witness to Christ. Because of the intense situation, Christians regarded the denial of one's Christianity a heinous sin resulting in excommunication. To become and remain Christian involved danger and risk. But from the martyrs' blood the community grew strong. Their faith and courage inspired others to examine the faith and find the truth of Christ.

30. Christian Expansion—Second and Third Centuries

The community rapidly expanded during the following centuries, penetrating into the outlying regions safer from persecution than great cities. The Roman Church was generally acknowledged as the "head of the alliance of love" (Ignatius of Antioch), the symbol for unity. However the papacy was not the power it later became.

---

7. Acts 15:1; Gal 2:11–14
8. Way 25
9. Way 4
10. Way 34

The Apostolic Fathers followed the generation after the apostles. The faith had to be communicated to members of the Greco-Roman empire in language they could understand. The **Didache**—the teaching of the apostles—expounds the faith for catechumens. The eucharistic prayer of **Hippolytus** is the earliest extant copy of such a prayer. The Fathers themselves include **Ignatius of Antioch, Clement of Rome**, and **Justin Martyr**—the first great apologist who appealed to intelligent Romans.

The faith was also threatened by heresies. The greatest threat came from gnosticism, more a general philosophy and spirituality awash in the empire before and during the advent of Christianity. Gnosticism was dangerous not because it opposed Christianity but because it shared much in common. The prime Christian defender is **Irenaeus of Lyons**—perhaps the greatest of the Apostolic Fathers and, until the discovery of the Dead Sea Scrolls in this century, our primary source for gnosticism.

Marcion provoked another crisis by drawing up a list of Scriptures and asserting that Jesus' God of love had replaced the angry Yahweh. The Church was forced to define the New Testament canon.[11] It also affirmed that the God of Israel is identical with the God of Jesus.

This period includes many brilliant theologians, some of whom stretched their theologies beyond the limits of orthodoxy. **Tertullian** (160–220) eventually left the Church to join the Montanist heresy—a conservative, purist party. On the other side, the most creative and imaginative theologian, **Origen**, reformulated the faith in terms of Platonism and speculated about reincarnation and other ideas since repudiated.

The Church was still primarily a missionary enterprise. As it penetrated the mainstream culture it adapted secular institutions. Great catechetical schools arose, such as Alexandria where Origen began, and which included among their masters **Clement of Alexandria**. The catechumenate[12] flowered in these schools, and many works of the Fathers were instructions to catechumens, or revealed the mysteries of the sacraments to the neophytes.

Throughout this period persecution alternated with tolerance for the faith. The years 202–249 saw a systematic persecution. And the great Diocletian persecution lasted from 303 to 311. Martyrs continued to supply models of courage.

---

11. Truth 3
12. Intro 6

31. The Birth of Christendom—Fourth and Fifth Centuries

In 311 an edict of tolerance put an end to the age of martyrs. The emperor Constantine's conversion shortly thereafter led to Christianity's becoming the established religion. In a short time (380) by decree of Theodosius I Christianity became the religion of all peoples of the Roman empire.

The threat of martyrdom had promised a heavenly crown in return for one's witness. But with the religion now tolerated and soon to become official, how could Christians prove devotion and faith? A new kind of martyrdom, not the red of blood, but the white of monasticism, was born. The Desert Fathers (and mothers) did battle for the faith not against external political authority but against inner demons. The biography of **St. Antony** (251–356) set a new model, and hundreds forsook the world. In the desert Antony battled his inner demons for Christ.

The Church as a whole, with persecution over, experienced dissension within as various interpretations proposed to phrase the faith in Greek (neo-Platonic) philosophical language. Such translation resulted in many errors. The great councils of this period debate the language of faith.

The most important councils are known by their meeting places. **Nicea** (325) worked out the divinity of Christ against the Arians who denied it. The Nicene-Constantinople Creed[13] was formulated there. **Ephesus** (431) defined that Mary is the Mother of God (Theotokos)[14] against the Nestorians. And the final great Council of **Chalcedon** (451) defined the two natures in the one person of Christ.

The Church's great theologians enable this translation into Greek thought. Still in the age of the Fathers, differences were growing between East and West. Among the Eastern Fathers were **St. Athanasius** (295–373) who influenced the Council of Nicea, the Cappadocian Fathers **St. Basil the Great** and his brother **St. Gregory of Nyssa** and **St. Gregory of Nazianzen**, and the greatest Eastern Father of this period, **St. John Chrysostom** (354–407), whose name "golden mouth" attests to his preaching eloquence.

In the West **St. Ambrose** (340–397), bishop of Milan, was responsible for the great Exultet of the Easter vigil.[15] **St. Jerome** translated the Scriptures into Latin, providing the official version for the Roman Church—the Vulgate. **St. Augustine** (354–430) was the most influential

---

13. Truth 23
14. Truth 31
15. Way 33

Western theologian and one of the greatest Western thinkers. His *Confessions* invented modern autobiography and his *City of God* provided an understanding of how civilization might survive the impending end of the Roman empire and thus created the first theology of history.

The defeat of Arianism did not end the danger. With the collapse of the Roman empire and the tribal migrations, Arianism appeared anew as the Christianity adopted by these tribes. The power of the papacy continued to increase. Pope Leo I could thus say that the "see of St. Peter became the head of the world" with the collapse of the secular empire. The papacy and Church were the only institutions remaining from the ancient world.

32. The Conversion of Europe—Sixth Through Tenth Centuries

The collapse of the Empire did not stop the spread of Christianity. The center shifted from the old cities of the empire into the mission fields of Europe. The missionaries took the faith to the backwaters of the empire and beyond. The more established churches now began to turn to Christian education from evangelization, since the area was now heavily Christian. Instead of the catechumenate and adult baptism, the normal practice is infant baptism and education.

St. Benedict founded Monte Casino (529) and drew up the Rule of St. Benedict—the model for most religious rules in the Western Church. With the expansion of the monasteries throughout Europe the faith was spread and the culture of the ancient world was preserved.

Pope Gregory the Great (590–604) undertook the evangelization of the Germanic peoples. This was accomplished largely through Benedictine monks such as **St. Boniface** who went to Germany to set up monasteries.

A new dimension to the missionary activity came into play. In the Germanic tribes the target for conversion was the ruler. Once the ruler converted, the entire tribe would become Christian. Clovis, king of the Franks, converted in 496. Such conversion was often more a political than a spiritual process, and as a result much of Europe was superficially converted. Needless to say this process did not involve a catechumenal experience; indeed there was often no catechesis at all. The catechumenate as a way of becoming Christian was now extinct. Superstition and pagan practices existed within the faith and distorted it.

The European dream of a resurgence of the Roman Empire also began. The Popes fomented the dream which further divided West from East where the Empire still existed. Charlemagne's coronation by the Pope in 800 was symbolic of this turning from the East.

The new religion of Islam swept across the Mediterranean region, wiping out formerly Christian areas of North Africa and Spain. The threat was not only military but intellectual, for Islam heralded an Arabic renaissance and the rediscovery of Aristotle threatened Christianity as an alien thought form until finally appropriated by Thomas Aquinas.

A second wave of missionary activity came not from Rome but from outlying areas not threatened by the Arianism of the tribal migrations. Christianity came to the British Isles in the sixth century through **Augustine** (another Augustine) and the legendary **Patrick**. In Ireland especially a monastic Christianity took hold and the Irish monks went as missionaries into voluntary exile, bringing their form of Christianity to the European mainland. With them they took such forms as their practice of confession which would later shape the sacrament of penance.[16]

The iconoclastic controversy (725–842) threatened the East. An icon is an image of Christ or a saint, and the controversy was generated by those who opposed the imaging of God. Eventually the Church approved icons, an important element of Orthodoxy. The Western Church did not help but rather interfered in this controversy, furthering tension and division.

The East began the great mission to the Slavs under **St. Cyril** (d. 868) and **Methodius** (d. 895). The Russian alphabet devised by Cyril is thus called Cyrillic.

33. The High Middle Ages—Eleventh Through Fourteenth Centuries

The millennium ushered in the High Middle Ages, a period dominated by the Church in the West. The turn of the millennium brought an expectation of the end of the world. People were convinced that once the thousand year period of the Church was over the end of the world was near. **Joachim of Flore** (1130–1182) divided history into three periods: that of the Father in the Old Testament, that of the Son from Jesus until the millennium, and now in the second millennium that of the Holy Spirit. Joachim's thought was condemned.

The **Crusades** (1096–1270) attempted to regain the Holy Land taken over by Islam. But this was often a pretense for rapine and adventure. And it further drove a wedge in the already festering tensions between the Eastern and Western Churches. Jerusalem fell in 1099 but that did not end the bloodshed.

---

16. Truth 80

The final split between the East and West occurred in 1054 when Pope Leo IX excommunicated the patriarch of Constantinople, **Michael Cerularius**. This was not rescinded until the Second Vatican Council.

Europe itself was enjoying the age of monasticism. The great abbey of **Cluny** in 910 paved the way for monastic reform, but eventually itself was in need of reform. Monastic orders which began here include the Carthusians (1084), an order of hermits, the Cistercians (1098) founded by the great doctor **St. Bernard of Clairvaux** as a recommitment to the original Rule of St. Benedict taken in its purity, and the Carmelites (1156). From this monastic reform sprang a papal reform of the larger Church under Pope Gregory VII (d. 1085), especially aimed at uprooting corruption flowing from political control of the Church.

St. Francis and **St. Dominic** founded a new kind of order. The **mendicant orders** live in common but work for the Church and embrace poverty. St. Francis of Assisi (1182–1226) left his wealthy family to embrace Lady Poverty and to follow Jesus to the letter. He inspired the twelfth century Renaissance. His companion **St. Clare** (1194–1253) founded the Second Order of Franciscans, the Poor Clares. St. Dominic (1170–1221) founded the Order of Preachers who through the promotion of the rosary and through preaching and teaching fought the heresies threatening the Church.

A time of great corruption as well as creative ferment, a number of groups attempted reform but are defeated or cast as heretics. The **Cathars** (1140) attempted to bring the Church back to its roots in the poverty of Jesus. Another group was the **Waldensians** (1176). Individual reformers included **John Wycliffe** in England who translated the Scriptures into English, and **John Hus** (1370–1415) in Central Europe. The Church responded with condemnation, creating the various forms of the **Inquisition**—Church courts which would in time become notorious for their use of torture and bloodshed to "defend the faith."

But the age also flowered with scholarship and mysticism. **St. Anselm** (1033–1109) provided the ontological proof of God's existence.[17] **Abelard** was the greatest dialectician—pure logic applied to theology. He was more famous for his love affair with Heloise which cost him dearly. **Albert the Great** (1193–1280) was great in his own right but eclipsed by his student, **St. Thomas Aquinas** (1224–1302). Aquinas made the thought of Aristotle, until then a threat, a basis for theology.

Aquinas was a Dominican, and his Franciscan counterpart **St. Bonaventure** (1221–1274) charted the path of the soul to God. He was followed by **Duns Scotus** (1256–1308), the theologian of the immaculate

17. Truth 27

conception, who declared that Jesus would have come even if we had no need of a Savior. **William of Ockham** (1280–1349) gave posterity his razor of reason.

Aquinas' baptism of Aristotelian thought gave Scholasticism new life. Unfortunately the followers of Aquinas had neither his genius nor his sanctity, and in lesser hands Scholasticism became a dried-out exercise.

Most of the above theologians were mystics as well. But theology was moving from the monastery to the university becoming an intellectual pursuit divorced from prayer. Another known primarily for her mystical insight was **Hildegard of Bingen** who combined mystical thought with art and was a reformer in her own right. Her thought inspires the Rhineland mystics including **Henry Suso** (1295–1361) and **John Tauler** (1300–1361). **St. Gertrude** (1256–1302) developed nuptial mysticism—the loving union of the person in Christ. And perhaps the greatest of the mystical theologians, although like Origen before him in trouble with the Church, **Meister Eckhart** (1260–1327) finds echoes today in Buddhist and Zen thought.

At this time the different arenas of life were not as separate as they would be later. The mystics were theologians and reformers. Two women deserve special mention. **St. Catherine of Siena** (1347–1380) and **Bridget of Sweden** (1303–1373) both attempted to bring the papacy, at one of its low points in history, back to legitimacy. During the Great Western Schism (1378–1417) two, and at one time even three, rival claimants for the papacy divided the loyalties of Christendom.

34. Reform and Counter-Reform—Fifteenth and Sixteenth Centuries

A continuous call for reform eventually resulted in the Protestant Reformation. Various factors put an end to the old era and inaugurated the new one. Johann Gutenberg (1400–1468) invented the printing press, greatly aiding the Protestant Reform's reliance upon individual reading of the Scriptures. **Girolamo Savonarola** (1439–1498) was one of a succession of voices calling for reform within the Church. Like most he ended in the hands of the Inquisition. Christopher Columbus (1451–1506) made Europe the Old World by discovering the New. Niccolò Machiavelli (1469–1527) was part of the rebirth of classical thinking which led to the post-Christian world. And finally Nicholas Copernicus (1473–1543) put the earth out of the central position in the universe and turned the world from theology to science.

The Reformation officially began when **Martin Luther** (1483–1546) nailed his ninety-five theses to the church door in Wittenberg (1517). The theses were meant to initiate a debate, for Luther was a professor of theology. Rome's intransigence and political entanglements made an effective response to Luther difficult and a division of the Church in Western Europe ensued.

Other key reformers were **Huldreich Zwingli** (1484–1556) and of course **John Calvin** (1509–1564) in Geneva. England's King Henry VIII (1509–1547) broke with Rome and struck a blow for nationalism, and **Thomas Cranmer** engineered the theological side of things. In Scotland **John Knox** (1513–1572) was the key reformer.

The success of the Protestant Reform eventually led Rome to take action. The seeds of the Counter-Reform come however not from Rome but from Spain where Catholicism was flowering. Spanish mysticism reached new heights in **Teresa of Avila** (1515–1582) and **John of the Cross** (1542–1591).[18] And **St. Ignatius Loyola** (1491–1556) founded the Jesuits as key instruments of the Counter-Reformation. Catholic Reform finally achieved its apex in the **Council of Trent** which corrected abuses and set the Church on its course into the modern world, although the course cited was hardly accepting of that world as it emerged.

Catholic theology withdrew into the leftovers of the medieval synthesis, but now dried up in a mechanical scholasticism with little to say either to the modern world or to the faithful. However there were some brilliant Catholic thinkers. Philosopher and mystic **Nicolas of Cusa** defined God as a circle whose center is everywhere and whose circumference is nowhere. The humanist **Erasmus** penned his *Praise of Folly*, but was also a philosopher as well as editor of the Greek New Testament. He criticized the Church vigorously, but unlike Luther refused to rend it assunder. In England **St. Thomas More**, Henry VIII's chancellor, left one of the great visionary works, *Utopia*, and was martyred rather than follow his king against his Church.

The Reform and the new discoveries of the East and the Americas prompted a new missionary drive. The office for the Propagation of the Faith was established in 1622. Illustrious missionaries included **St. Francis Xavier** (1506–1552) in Japan, **Matteo Ricci** (1552–1618) in China and **Robert de Nobili** (1577–1656) in India. These people, finding the first non-Christian cultures in ages, debated whether Christ should not be presented in terms of the culture, and began a creative adaptation unfortunately cut short.

---

18. Life 8

The Reform brought forth new orders in the Church as well. In addition to the Jesuits were the Ursuline sisters (1535), the Capuchins (1528), a branch of the Franciscans, and finally the Oratorians (1564) founded by **St. Philip Neri** (1515–1595), a truly healthy species of saint. **St. Vincent de Paul** (1580–1660) worked with the poor.[19]

35. The Enlightenment—Seventeenth and Eighteenth Centuries

The period from the High Middle Ages to the modern world represented a quite significant change in the Christian Church, moving from a time where it not only dominated but to a significant extent was history to a period where it responded to rather than created history. The Protestant Reformation and the secular Renaissance left the Church behind. It responded by securing itself against future threats. Catholicism for much of modern history was defensive, conservative and hostile toward many of the movements of the time.

The Counter-Reform had two basic thrusts. First was reform of the very abuses that the original Reformers had protested. Had the Church been able to respond to these at the time, the Reformation might have been avoided. Certainly Luther did not set out to establish a new Church. He was pushed by refusal to give him ear and by historical forces which saw an opportunity in breaking up Christendom.

Second, the Counter-Reform tried to win back people to the Church. A key figure was **St. Francis de Sales** (1567–1622), bishop of Geneva, who turned his attention to the Calvinists of his region. Known as the "Gentleman Saint" because of years struggling against his hot temper, he won people through a honeyed style rather than the typical vinegar of religious controversy.

The rise of science was begun and fostered earlier by the Church. **Gregor Mendel**, the father of genetics, was a monk. But science threatened basic medieval assumptions, so the Church was hostile—an attitude which with science's ascendancy left the Church behind. In a major confrontation with **Galileo** (1564–1642) the Church's condemnation forced it into a corner.

The Chinese rites controversy again demonstrated the new attitude. The missionaries sought to adapt the Gospel to the local cultures. But Benedict XIV (1742) condemned the attempt, and from that time Christianity ceased to make significant converts in Asia.

Protestantism's rise was furthered by national rulers. These new

---

19. Life 45

powers threatened the Church's traditional position. And they rightly perceived the Jesuits, concerned with the Church's restoration, as obstacles. Generally this period can be viewed as skirmishes between the Church attempting to secure its traditional power and influence against the rising new movements of thought and power.

This protectionism did not win anything in the world arena but it did preserve the faith. Now the Church realigned with the common people as it lost power and persuasion with secular authorities. The later eighteenth century saw the Church battered by the intellectual assaults of Enlightenment rationalism and by the anti-clericalism of the French Revolution.

The Renaissance of classical knowledge allowed philosophy to throw off its Christian underpinnings, becoming more secular if not anti-religious. Formerly philosophy was the handmaiden of theology. Now it became autonomous. A human-centrism considers the human being as the measure of all things.

The faith survived not on intellectual or political achievements but in the piety of the common people. An age of devotionalism provided solace in the faith. This devotionalism was individual, non-intellectual, pious, emotional and often not concerned with social issues. Yet it nourished a deep trust in the compassion of God.

The major internal heresy was Jansenism, a Catholic variety of Puritanism—excessive concern about purity and an abhorrence of the body. This school developed primarily in France and claimed **Blaise Pascal**, the great philosopher and mystic. Although condemned, its spirit lingered on, adopted by Irish seminarians who studied in France and then imported to America where it flourished alongside Protestant puritanism. **St. Alphonsus Liguori** (1696–1787) crusaded against Jansenist rigidity; he fathered modern Catholic moral theology and founded the Redemptorists who gave popular missions in rural areas.

New religious communities developed along the model of the Jesuits—bound together in prayer but active in the world. Examples were the Sisters of Charity (1629), the Passionists (1725) and the Redemptorists (1732). Monastic communities continued, and some were reformed such as the Trappists who were reformed Cistercians (1664).

36. Into the Modern World—Nineteenth and Twentieth Centuries

Despite a period of restoration and revival in the first half of the nineteenth century, the growth of nationalism and the new states finally deprived the Church of its secular power altogether as Napoleon III seized the Papal States during the First Vatican Council (1869–1870).

The declaration of papal infallibility[20] attempted to insure the papacy's spiritual power at the very time it lost secular power. Faced with these new states the Church was forced for its own well-being to enter into negotiation. The resulting concordats formed a significant part of modern European Church history.

The Church continued under intellectual siege. The Syllabus of Errors (1864) shows a hostile and fearful outlook toward anything in the least sense modern. With the Syllabus came a condemnation of a non-existent heresy—Americanism. The pragmatic American ideals of Isaac Hecker, founder of the Paulists were amplified when translated into French, and were thus seen as a threat to the Church by some.

Having lost out in the political and intellectual arenas, the Church continued to grow strong at the grass roots. The apparitions at Lourdes of the Virgin Mary (1858) strengthened the piety that sustained most Catholics and confirmed in the faithful the recent declaration of the immaculate conception[21]—the first actual announcement using papal infallibility which would only later on be formulated. The saints also came from the common people. **St. John Vianney**, the Curé D'Ars (1786–1859), was thought too dumb to become a priest. But he did so and spent much of his life in the confessional—twelve hours a day—hearing people's problems and giving himself to them.

The hierarchy's finest hour saw a turning toward the plight of the common people. In 1891 Leo XIII began a great strand of modern Catholic thought with his encyclical *Rerum Novarum* on conditions of the working class, inaugurating modern Catholic social teaching.[22] In these documents the Church joined itself with the struggle of peoples oppressed politically, economically and psychologically. To these people has the Gospel been given. The Church acting as spokesperson among the influential found now its new voice in the modern world as advocate of the poor. And it found as well a witness that provides more spiritual power and authority than was possible in the old reliance upon worldly authority. The modern Popes, untrammeled by political concerns, now spoke on behalf of the voiceless—a moral cry against increasing dehumanization.

Although the official Church suspected the modern, people continued to do theology—to understand the unchanging faith in terms of today's best thought. The nineteenth century witnessed the birth of the new liturgical movement, as well as new turns in theology. Often these

---

20. Truth 22
21. Truth 41
22. Life 44

were censured, misunderstood, and even condemned—Pius X condemned modernism in 1907. But these scholars' efforts and agonies eventually paid off, opening the windows at Vatican II.

Key figures in this pre-renaissance are the Oxford movement beginning in the Church of England and leading often to the Roman Catholic Church. Of these **John Henry Cardinal Newman** is of crucial significance today. Often misunderstood in his time, Newman's development of doctrine—a theological parallel to Darwin—laid the basis for much modern theology. Among Germans **Johann Moehler** attempted to reconcile Catholic and Protestant theology.

Joseph Marechal dusted off the scholasticism surrounding Aquinas, and in neo-Thomism allowed St. Thomas to speak again to modern people. **Jacques Maritain** and **Etienne Gilson** continued this work of creating a new Thomism. And **Teilhard de Chardin**, perhaps the most seminal twentieth century Catholic thinker, reconciled faith with evolutionary thought. Although silenced by the Church and unable to have his work published and debated while he was alive, Teilhard's books, issued after his death, have inspired not only theologians and Christians but many unwilling to accept the narrow confines of twentieth century materialism.

When **Pope John XXIII** announced a council, the work of a century of Catholic liturgists and theologians came to fruition. The council was not even a totally radical action from the papal level. For in 1943 Pius XII had given Scripture scholars permission to apply the findings of modern scholarship to the sacred texts.[23] The Church's attitude had begun to change from antagonism to dialogue with the modern world in the hope that the truth would reveal itself anew.

The twentieth century has also seen the dawn of the ecumenical movement—a return to unity among the splintered Churches. The **World Council of Churches** was founded in 1948 as a vehicle for dialogue, communication and cooperation. And although the Catholic Church has not officially joined this body, it works with it and has developed a Secretariat for Christian Unity to continue dialogue and work out agreement preparatory to unity.

This movement toward unity is not limited to the Christian religion. Extensive contact with non-Christian religions and the impact of secularism has brought religious people from all traditions to see themselves as sharers in a heritage that far outweighs the symbols or doctrines which divide. Protest marches against the proliferation of nuclear weapons find Christians and Buddhists on a common mission.

---

23. Way 5

In the twentieth century the Christian axis began to move out of Europe and America and into the third world. Within the near future over half the world's Catholics will live in Latin America. Further, while Europe is filled with empty churches, Christianity flourishes in Africa and Asia.

37. The American Experience

This history has been largely European. But the United States has played a significant role in Christianity since its beginnings little more than two centuries ago. First on the scene were missionaries from France and Spain, working with the Indians. While from our present viewpoint these missionaries may have been chauvinist or even imperialistic, their conversion of the Indians was more civilized than the successful British efforts at genocide. Among these missionaries were **St. Isaac Jogues** among the Huron Indians (1607–1646). In 1700 **Eusebio Kino** founded a Catholic mission in Tucson. And **Junipero Serra**, the Franciscan, opened missions all along the California coast from San Diego to San Rafael.

Many Europeans came to the New World to avoid religious persecution and to find a place where they would be free in their religious expression. **Roger Williams**, the Baptist, established his church in Rhode Island in 1639. He and **William Penn** guaranteed religious freedom to all groups—a now established American principle. Among these groups were Catholics; Maryland was established as a Catholic colony, fleeing the suppression in England.

Colonial Catholics helped shape the new nation. A Catholic was among the signers of the Declaration of Independence. And although America remained a mission territory until fairly recently, the American Church provided courageous and daring thinkers and doers. The first American bishop was **John Carroll** of Baltimore, still the first diocese of the American Church. Other great bishops include **Cardinal Gibbons**, and **John Ireland**.

The nineteenth century immigrant influx brought many more Catholics from Ireland, Italy, Poland and elsewhere. The Church served its people well. America was not always receptive to new peoples. Anti-Catholicism burst forth in the riots of Philadelphia in 1844 and is still a part of certain American life in fundamentalist circles. The evangelist Billy Graham is criticized by some of his own for working with the Catholic Church on his crusades.

Originally American Catholicism participated in the overall confidence and optimism of America itself. Here was the land of opportunity—the great experiment in democracy. **Isaac Hecker** believed that America was at heart Catholic in its confidence in human ability. Democracy is incompatible with a Calvinist belief in innate human depravity. And indeed although America is primarily Protestant, many founding fathers and mothers were only superficially religious. The ideals of American democracy come from the Enlightenment—not from religion.

This American optimism was sorely tested in the Church. Rome met America with suspicion. How could the Church function in a pluralistic society? And were present day Catholics as open to belief in human ability for self-determination as were Americans? The condemnation of **Americanism**,[24] and the debacle of lay trusteeship which gave lay boards control of church properties, ended this Romantic dream.

Nevertheless American Catholicism continued to grow and strengthen. The Church here was of the people, and concerned for their welfare. The Church influenced the growth of the labor movement. Because of this solidarity, the American Church has not experienced the anti-clericalism so endemic, with reason, in much of Europe.

As immigrants were assimilated into the larger culture, the Church moved upward. As late as the 1950's the American Church was still colored by the immigrant experience. No bishop's parents had received more than a high school education. Yet a new age of American Catholic thought was emerging, hesitant in the light of Americanist and Modernist suspicions, but there. And with the Second Vatican Council, the American Church made its first significant contribution to the Church at large in the Document on Religious Freedom, primarily American in history, and largely inspired by **John Courtney Murray**, an American Catholic theologian.

Throughout our history Catholics have stood out and influenced their world and the larger community. The work of **Mother Elizabeth Seton** (1774–1821), the first American saint, began the American experiment in parochial education which assisted thousands of immigrant children where public schools were opposed to the Catholic religion or closed to Catholics altogether. **St. John Neumann**, as bishop of Philadelphia, organized the parochial schools there on a diocesan-wide basis, and increased the number of pupils twenty-fold. **Orestes Brownson**, a convert from the New England transcendentalists, became an American Catholic thinker and a feisty apologist for the Church in a society largely antagonistic and prejudiced against it.

---

24. Life 36

In the present, **Thomas Merton** inspired many, being a secular child of his time, and embracing not only Catholicism, but a Trappist monastery. The 1960's heard Merton's prophetic voice in the civil rights and anti-war movement. The man who had supposedly left the world behind became that world's conscience. Toward the end of his life he initiated dialogue with other religions, and while engaged in such dialogue he met his early death. **Dorothy Day**, a convert from communism, founded the Catholic Worker in New York to minister to the poor of the Bowery. Throughout her life she proved a prophetic voice not always received with sympathy by her Church, for like all prophets she was often embarrassing to those in power and afraid of Christ's truth.

Today the American Catholic Church is one of the most vital and alive in the world. Catholics are assimilated into the American culture. And our voice continues to be heard, and is increasingly respected, when it speaks out concerning the nuclear problem or on behalf of the poor and oppressed who have yet to enter into their inheritance of the American dream. The Church continues to expand. Today immigrants from Latin America are the newest to add their heritage and culture to that of the Irish, Italians, Poles and others who preceded.

TO DEEPEN—

What was the first major crisis for the Christian Church?

Name one important early Church council. What did it do?

Who is the great theologian of the medieval Catholic synthesis?

What are some reasons for the Protestant Reformation? How did the Roman Catholic Church finally respond?

What was the Church's attitude toward the secular world up until Vatican II?

Further Reading:

Bokenkotter, Thomas. *A Concise History of the Catholic Church.* Revised edition. Image, 1979.

Brophy, Don & Westenhaver, Edythe. *Story of Catholics in America.* Paulist Press, 1975.

Buhlmann, Walbert. *The Church of the Future: A Model for the Year 2001.* Orbis, 1986.

Dwyer, John C. *Church History, Twenty Centuries of Catholic Christianity.* Paulist Press, 1985.

Greeley, Andrew. *The American Catholic: A Social Portrait*. Basic Books, 1977.
Marty, Martin. *A Short History of Christianity*. New American Library, 1959.
Marty, Martin. *An Invitation to American Catholic History*. Thomas More, 1986.

The Worship Life of the Church

TO PREPARE—

This material should only be approached after familiarity with the liturgical sections of the Way 8–35. The material from Life 40 on is trivia.

38. THE DAILY PRAYER OF THE CHURCH

The Church continues Christ's prayer to the Father. Mass and the sacraments do not exhaust the Church's worship. The sacraments were originally reserved to special occasions. Its prayer is properly Christ's prayer. Its primary prayerbook is the Book of Psalms[1] prayed in the light of Christ.[2] Vatican II's reforms extended the psalter over a four week cycle, reducing the number of psalms in any one hour. In addition certain psalms not in accord with current attitudes, such as those of cursing, were dropped.

The Church's prayer sanctifies the various times of the day; each service is called an "hour." These are morning (Lauds) and evening (Vespers) prayer, the service of readings (Matins), prayer during the day, and night prayer (Compline). Although the structure of the hours varies slightly, their essence consists of an invitation to prayer (followed by an examination of conscience at night prayer), a hymn, a number of psalms and a canticle (a poem from Scripture) and a Scripture reading followed by prayers of intercession, the Lord's Prayer,[3] and a concluding blessing. The feasts and seasons[4] add color through antiphons (short verses) that precede and conclude the psalms, and through seasonal prayers and hymns.

The morning, evening and night hours are further distinguished by the three Lukan canticles. The Benedictus of Zechariah[5] is prayed at morning prayer, Mary's Magnificat[6] in the evening, and Simeon's Nunc Dimittis[7] at the night hour. The names arise from the Latin first words. These canticles themselves form appropriate morning, evening and night prayers.

Originally celebrated in parishes, the services were sung with

---

1. Truth 20
2. Life 2
3. Way 50
4. Way 28
5. Lk 1:68–79
6. Lk 1:46b–55
7. Lk 2:29–32

processions, candles and incense where appropriate. The hours are central to monasticism, while daily Mass replaced the hours in parishes. Today monks, many nuns and all clerics are obliged to pray the hours joined by many lay people. Often today the "office" is recited privately or in a group.

Vatican II encouraged its reintroduction into the larger Church. And today some parishes celebrate night prayer to conclude meetings or vespers on special occasions.

39. SACRAMENTAL WORSHIP

While the Way[8] covered the essence of Christian worship, this section expands upon the Church's worship, filling in the variety and other acts of worship making up the totality of the Church's worship life.

Kinds of Celebration

The **dominical cycle**[9] comprises the major feasts and seasons celebrating the saving acts of God in Jesus Christ: Sundays and major feasts of the Lord. Weekday Eucharists use a two year **weekday cycle** of readings covering most of the Scriptures. The first reading is taken from everything but the Gospels. The Gospel readings cover a one year cycle. Seasonal readings for Advent-Christmas and the Lent-Easter seasons are special. Weekday readings are used whenever another feast or memorial with its own readings does not supersede.

A Sanctoral Calendar

A third cycle of feasts, the sanctoral, commemorates the saints.[10] Included first are feasts of the Blessed Virgin Mary, then the major saints of the Church. There are many more saints than find a place in the calendar. Only the most important or popular saints are given a memorial in the Roman calendar. Saints' days usually commemorate birthdays or deathdays, but certain feasts christen seasonal events.

These seasonal feasts attune the Christian to the cycles of nature which are given a Christian meaning and celebration. Christians modeled their feast days upon existing Hebrew or pagan festivals.[11] Many

---

8. Way 8ff
9. Way 28ff
10. Life 46
11. Way 28ff

of these seasonal feasts are Marian feasts. Mary symbolizes the redeemed creation.

This cycle begins with the winter solstice (December 21), the
shortest day of the year. It is generally held that Christmas replaced the
ancient Roman saturnalia, celebrating the light coming into our world.
From then on the sun's light grows stronger just as Christ's light grows
stronger from his coming into our world until now. Mid-winter celebrates another feast of light—Candlemas, or the Presentation of the
Lord (February 2).[12] The pagan Groundhog's Day commemorates the
same feeling—a wish for winter to end and the light to triumph. Traditionally Christians brought candles to church for blessing.

The spring equinox is commemorated primarily by Easter.[13] But
another spring feast, the Annunciation (March 25), when Mary received
the good news that she would bear the Savior, replaces the equinox celebration. Mid-spring celebrates the Visitation (May 31) when Mary
greeted her kinswoman Elizabeth whose own son John the Baptist
danced in her womb before the ark of his Lord.[14] Catholics traditionally
dedicated the entire month of May to Mary, with processions replacing
the pagan Maypole dances celebrating spring's flowers and beauty.

John the Baptist commemorates the summer solstice (June 24).
John asked that he might decrease so that Christ might increase,[15] and
now the sun's light decreases toward winter. Mid-summer is the
Assumption[16] of Mary (August 15)—summer is drawing to a close and
Christians remember how Mary, the flower of God's creation, was
taken from us into heaven.

The autumn equinox becomes the Feast of Michael and the Angels
(September 29). Michael fought the great battle against Satan in
heaven.[17] In spite of the dying light, justice and God will in the end
prevail. Mid-fall as the darkness increases turns the Church toward a
consideration of the last things: All Saints (November 1), along with its
companions of Halloween and All Souls (November 2), remember those
who have gone before us.

The Christian feasts are usually a few days off from the equinoxes
and solstices due to calendar modifications. The Christian calendar is
now about five days behind the solar events it commemorates. However in the case of Christmas, five days after the solstice was the amount

12. Lk 2:22–39
13. Way 33
14. Lk 1:44
15. Jn 3:30
16. Truth 41
17. Rev 12:7–12

of time necessary to perceive an increase of daylight and so allow people to rejoice in the returning warmth.

Special Feasts and Celebrations

Certain other feasts do not fall under the rubric of a saint's day and so will be set forth here.

Conversion of St. Paul[18]—
>January 25—culminates a week long prayer for
>Christian Unity marked by ecumenical services
>in different Christian Churches.

Chair of Peter—February 22—celebration of the office
>of the papacy.

St. Joseph the Worker—May 1—a celebration of labor and
>laborers under the patronage of St. Joseph the
>carpenter, the foster-father of Jesus. (Replaces
>communist May Day.)

Beheading of John the Baptist[19]—August 29.

Triumph of the Holy Cross—September 14—commemorates
>finding of the true cross by St. Helena and
>focuses upon the mystery of the cross as the
>instrument of our salvation.

Dedication of St. John Lateran—November 9—the most
>important of a number of feasts which
>commemorate the founding of major Christian
>churches. St. John Lateran is the mother church of
>Christianity and is the Pope's cathedral church.
>(St. Peter's is not the cathedral but one of the
>four basilicas of Rome.)

The figure of Mary is the most important after Jesus and claims a number of feasts under her many aspects.

Solemnity of Mary, Mother of God—January 1—also Day
>of World Peace, and Octave of Christmas, New
>Year's Day and formerly Feast of the Circumcision.

Our Lady of Lourdes—February 11—commemorates the
>Virgin's appearance to Bernadette at

---

18. Acts 6:1–19; Gal 1:12–17
19. Mk 6:17–29

Lourdes, a shrine producing countless
cures and miracles in the modern age.

Visitation[20]—May 31.

Immaculate Heart of Mary—Saturday following the second
Sunday after Pentecost.[21]

Joachim and Ann—July 26—the parents of Mary.

Assumption[22]—August 15.

Queenship of Mary—August 22—octave of Assumption.

Birth of Mary—September 8.

Our Lady of Sorrows—September 15—focuses upon Mary's
suffering at her Son's passion. Celebrated in the
medieval poem "Stabat Mater Dolorosa."

Our Lady of the Rosary—October 7—the entire month of
October is dedicated to the rosary.

Presentation of Mary—November 21—following Jewish
custom Mary (like Jesus, February 2) is dedicated
in the temple.

Immaculate Conception[23]—December 8—
patron feast of the United States.

Our Lady of Guadalupe—December 12—patroness of
Mexico after the appearance of the Virgin to a
Mexican peasant.

Ranking of Celebrations

Church celebrations are ranked according to importance. There
are basically three kinds of observances. The most important are **solemnities**. Only a solemnity can replace the normal Sunday celebration.
These begin with vespers on the evening before, following the Jewish
custom that a day begins at sunset. There may be a vigil Mass such as
the Mass for Christmas Eve or the vigil of Pentecost. The feasts of
Christmas and Easter are so important that they extend throughout the
entire week. Christmas includes an octave (a celebration on the eighth
day) on January 1, and the feast of Easter with Low Sunday following
Easter Sunday.

Next in rank, the **feasts** take place during the limits of the natural
day. Finally **memorials** usually commemorate saints. These are divided
into obligatory (for the whole Church) and optional. Optional memorials

---

20. Lk 1:39–56
21. Way 34
22. Truth 41
23. Truth 41

are kept by communities, countries, or people for whom that celebration or saint is special. For example, St. Patrick's Day (March 17) is an optional memorial kept by the Irish, those of Irish descent, or those heavily influenced by the Irish such as the American Church. If another celebration does not take precedence, Saturdays are optional memorials for the Blessed Virgin Mary.

Kinds of Masses

In addition to weekday Masses and the special feasts and memorials, a number of other optional celebrations may occur. Most important are the various **ritual** Masses celebrated in connection with the stages of the catechumenate[24] or the celebration of the other sacraments. [25]

The rite of **funerals** helps Christians take leave of their dead relative or friend and celebrate that person's entry into the kingdom. Composed of three different stations, the first, a wake service precedes the funeral and includes psalms and prayers, or more traditionally the rosary.

The second station, the Mass of Resurrection, is an Easter celebration. There is grief and sorrow, but, more than that, rejoicing for the Christian now joined to God. Jesus' passage from death into eternal life foreshadows and promises every Christian that same passover. The Eucharist comforts those left behind and celebrates the Christian's passage from death to life, from this foretaste of the heavenly banquet to the banquet itself.

The third station at the cemetery lays the body to rest. A new funeral Mass for non-baptized children presumes that they are gathered to the Lord through the parents' faith.

At various times certain situations call for us to turn to God in prayer and thanksgiving. The Church provides Masses for these special occasions. **Votive Masses** commemorate a special aspect of the faith, or a special devotion. The Church has recently taken account of children and designed special eucharistic prayers and guidelines for celebrations.

TO DEEPEN—

Use the Lukan canticles of Zechariah, Mary and Simeon for your own morning, evening and night prayer.

---

24. Intro 4ff
25. Truth 74ff

Examine the book of the Liturgy of the Hours to see how they are set up.

Attend a celebration of one of the Hours.

What are some of the special Masses apart from the Sunday cycle?

Who is the most honored saint in the Catholic tradition?

What Christian feasts commemorate the changing of the seasons?

Further Reading:

The Liturgy of the Hours. Catholic Book Publishing Co., 1976.

40. OBSERVING THE SEASONS

TO PREPARE—

The Liturgical Year (Way 28ff) should be known. For Lent the Way of Penance (Way 47–49) should be covered.

Christian spirituality is attuned to the different liturgical seasons. Following are some ways Catholics celebrate seasons and feasts. The Lenten season being very special, its discussion is fuller than the others.

Advent

Advent focuses upon expectation and waiting. The Advent wreath displays four candles—three purple, one pink. Kept on the family table, the family gathers before dinner each night for a short prayer as it lights one candle for each week of Advent—the pink candle on the third week. The Advent calendar contains slots for each day. On each day one window is opened until at Christmas the entire calendar with its images are revealed.

The famous Advent song, "O Come, O Come, Emmanuel," points to another feature of Advent. During vespers on the last week before Christmas the Magnificat[1] is introduced by a different antiphon each day. They are the origin of the above hymn. Some commemorate Advent by making the Magnificat their daily prayer and meditating upon the great images and symbols of these antiphons.

---

1. Life 38

Prayer: O Antiphons:

December 17: *O Wisdom, you come forth from the mouth of the Most High. You fill the universe and hold all things together in a strong yet gentle manner. O come to teach us the way of truth.*

December 18: *O Adonai and Leader of Israel, you appeared to Moses in a burning bush and you gave him the Law on Sinai. O come and save us with your mighty power.*

December 19: *O Root of Jesse, you stand as a signal for the nations; kings fall silent before you whom the peoples acclaim. O come to deliver us, and do not delay.*

December 20: *O Key of David and sceptre of israel, what you open no one else can close again; what you close no one can open. O come to lead the captive from prison; free those who sit in darkness and in the shadow of death.*

December 21: *O Rising Sun, you are the splendor of eternal light and the sun of justice. O come and enlighten those who sit in darkness and in the shadow of death.*

December 22: *O King whom all the peoples desire, you are the cornerstone which makes all one. O come and save man whom you made from clay.*

December 23: *O Emmanuel, you are our king and judge, the One whom the people await and their Savior. O come and save us, Lord, our God.*

Christmas

Christmas is kept with many popular customs extending far beyond Christianity's boundaries. Italians celebrate Christmas Eve with a nine course fish dinner which originated when Christmas Eve was a day of abstinence. Many attend Midnight Mass on Christmas Eve. The giving of gifts commemorates the gifts of the magi[2] to the Christ Child. Christmas carols celebrate the sacred story in song and people go caroling to spread the cheer. The crèche or manger scene, invented by St. Francis,[3] has become a feature of almost all churches and communities. Twelfth Night ends the Christmas celebration—the feast of Epiphany[4] in many places is the more popular celebration.

---

2. Mt 2:11–12
3. Life 33
4. Way 30

Lent

The Lenten penance unmasks worldly attitudes which contaminate us. Penance raises conflict in our life. That conflict wakes us up to things previously unconscious. Our ego does not like the conflict and attempts to win us back to its own ways of thinking. But, like Jesus in the wilderness,[5] we can listen to these voices of ego and distance ourselves from them. Instead of allowing the ego to continue to be our all, through the conflict and what we discover we can back off from the ego's tyranny and allow all the different aspects of ourselves to emerge. In addition, the conflict places us in a very difficult situation. We cannot win this conflict on our own. But through the struggle we learn to rely more upon God. We discover God's power to bring us through temptation and make us whole.

There are many possibilities for Lenten penance. The most common practice has been the Lenten fast.[6] In denying our bodies food we are pushed back upon God for sustenance. We learn that physical food does not ultimately sustain us or make our life full.

Fasting makes us share in the experience of the poor and hungry. We come to feel solidarity with them—the poor become a part of our world, our sisters and brothers. We awaken to their needs and join in their struggle for liberation.

For extended Lenten practice we may choose some form of fast. However any prolonged period of rigorous fasting (the Catholic fast[7] is not rigorous) should be supervised by a physician to avoid possible dangers.

But there are other forms of penance as well. Jesus encouraged and practiced almsgiving and the vigil as ways of working upon oneself. The penance should touch some issues in your life which you would like to explore.

Many Christians examine habits which call for attention. Smoking is one of the most popular. Look at your life. Is there some habit you would like to bring under control? Perhaps you drink more than you feel good about. You might abstain from alcohol either with the idea of giving it up altogether or to re-examine its place in your life. Perhaps you might notice that you are stingy with money, time, possessions. You might work on that attitude by choosing to give some money or time each week (whatever will slightly inconvenience you and bring the issue to the fore) to a charity.

---

5. Lk 4:1–13
6. Way 49
7. Intro 18

Other people may be uncomfortable with the negative image of giving up for Lent; instead they develop something missing from their life. Maybe you have been thinking for a long time about meditating, jogging or doing something beneficial. You might visit the sick or do some community volunteer work. Lent is an excellent moment to begin. We have over forty days of discipline in which all Christians strive to come closer to the kingdom. What better opportunity to undertake something new with all this good will, support and community?

Take time before Lent to select a practice. You might discuss it with your confessor or spiritual director, with friends and family. You might undertake a penance in union with others. The group provides support and encouragement to all.

Other Observances

Other popular seasonal customs include **Mardi Gras**—a great blow-out party before Lent. On **Holy Thursday**[8] many visit a number of churches, stopping to pray. Others keep vigil with the reserved sacrament on Holy Thursday night. Some take home the palms from **Passion Sunday**[9] and weave a cross which is then placed behind a crucifix. Polish and Eastern Catholics have many **Easter**[10] customs such as the baking of Easter bread and cakes. Some Catholic communities celebrate the feast of **Corpus Christi**[11] with a public procession.

41. OTHER PUBLIC CEREMONIES

Other public celebrations are conducted. For example, a church must be **consecrated** to God. Other blessings are given and celebrated by certain Catholic communities. Fishing villages bless the fleet. On the feast of **St. Francis** (October 4) many bring animals to be blessed. On the feast of **St. Blaise** (February 3) people have their throats blessed. Polish Catholics bring Easter bread and other food to the Church on Holy Saturday for blessing. And of course ethnic groups have their feasts such as St. Patrick among the Irish, St. Anthony among the Italians, and Our Lady of Guadalupe among the Mexicans.

Certain devotions are sometimes celebrated publicly in church. Catholics may gather to pray the rosary[12] or the stations of the cross.[13]

8. Way 33
9. Way 32
10. Way 33
11. Way 35
12. Life 42
13. Life 42

Benediction is a special devotion to the Blessed Sacrament which is placed in a monstrance to bless the people. The service includes hymns and prayers as well. A **Forty Hour Devotion** exposes the sacrament for that period, initiated and concluded by a special service. During exposition the church is constantly open. **Novenas**[14] may be celebrated in a public manner and may be accompanied by a parish mission—a series of services and homilies delivered by a missionary to renew the people's faith.

Three services are recent innovations. **Scripture services** draw people together to listen to and meditate upon Scripture. **Penance services** enable people at special times and seasons to come together to listen and meditate upon their lives in the light of Scripture, to confess their sins, and to be pardoned and sent to continue their mission. At **charismatic prayer meetings** and healing services people pray using charisms[15] such as prophecy, interpretation of prophecy, speaking in tongues, laying on of hands, and prayer for healing.

42. KEY CATHOLIC PRAYERS

Certain formal prayers are known to every Catholic. These include the **Sign of the Cross**,[16] the **Lord's Prayer**,[17] the **Hail Mary**,[18] the **Apostles' Creed**,[19] the **Doxology**,[20] and the **Act of Contrition**.[21] A **litany** is a group prayer where the leader chants petitions, the group answering with a common response. An example is the prayer of the faithful,[22] but there are a number of special litanies for the saints, the Holy Spirit, the Blessed Virgin, etc.

How To Pray the Rosary

The rosary is a circular string of beads with a short string culminating in a crucifix attached to the circle. The circle has five groups of ten beads each, separated by a band of chain and one large bead.

Begin by taking the crucifix in your hand and recite the Apostles' Creed[23] upon it. Then move up the short string to the first large bead.

---

14. Life 7
15. Truth 42
16. Way 8
17. Way 50
18. Truth 41
19. Truth 25
20. Way 8
21. Way 45
22. Way 22
23. Truth 25

On all large beads recite the Lord's Prayer.[24] Next follow three small beads on which the Hail Mary[25] is recited. At the end of the sequence the Doxology[26] is prayed. The small chain introduces and centers the prayer before the meditations.

The meditations focus upon key events in the life of Jesus and Mary. This prayer places one in the position of Mary contemplating the mysteries of salvation. There are three sets of five mysteries each. The joyful mysteries center upon Jesus' birth, the sorrowful around his passion and death, the glorious around his resurrection and our salvation.

JOYFUL MYSTERIES
1. The Annunciation (Lk 1:26–38)
2. The Visitation (Lk 1:39–56)
3. The Nativity (Lk 2:1–20)
4. The Presentation in the Temple (Lk 1:22–40)
5. The Finding in the Temple (Lk 2:41–52)

SORROWFUL MYSTERIES
1. The Agony in the Garden (Lk 29:39–53)
2. The Scourging at the Pillar (Mk 15:15)
3. The Crowning with Thorns (Jn 19:1–2)
4. The Carrying of the Cross (Mt 27:31)
5. The Crucifixion (Lk 23:33–49)

GLORIOUS MYSTERIES
1. The Resurrection (Lk 24:1–11)
2. The Ascension (Acts 1:6–11)
3. The Descent of the Holy Spirit on Pentecost (Acts 2:1–47)
4. The Assumption (Sir 24:9–10)
5. The Coronation of Mary (Rev 12:1–5)

Usually the person or group prays one series of mysteries at a given time. Upon reaching the medal joining the short string to the circle announce the series of mysteries you intend to pray. Then begin with the Lord's Prayer on the first large bead, having announced the first mystery. Then in praying the Hail Mary ten times let your imagination create the scene of the mystery. At the end of the decade pray the Doxology. Continue through the series until the medal. Some end the rosary with a prayer to Mary such as the Salve Regina.

---

24. Way 50
25. Truth 41
26. Way 8

How To Pray the Stations of the Cross

The stations have no fixed formula beyond the set of stations. They may be prayed as a group using one of the many different formulae, or by an individual either in church walking the stations or in meditation. In church walk to the station and spend some time in meditation upon that event, then move to the next. The last station is usually next to the altar and many conclude with a prayer at the altar.

Here is a list of the stations with a biblical reference (and where necessary an explanation). Following that is a sample formula suitable for group prayer.

1. Jesus is condemned to death by Pilate. (Mk 15:15–18)
2. Jesus is made to carry the cross. (Mk 15:20)
3. Jesus falls for the first time. (Mk 14:35–36)
4. Jesus meets his mother. (Lk 2:34–35)
5. Simon of Cyrene carries Jesus' cross. (Lk 23:26)
6. Veronica wipes the face of Jesus. (Is 53:2)[27]
7. Jesus falls for the second time. (Mk 14:37–38)
8. Jesus speaks to the women of Jerusalem. (Lk 23:27–31)
9. Jesus falls for the third time. (Jn 12:23–26)
10. Jesus is stripped of his garments and given gall to drink. (Mk 15:22–24)
11. Jesus is nailed to the cross. (Lk 23:32–35)
12. Jesus dies on the cross. (Lk 23:44–46)
13. Jesus is taken down from the cross. (Jn 19:25–27, 32–34, 38)
14. Jesus is laid in the sepulcher. (Jn 19:39–42)
15. Jesus rises from the dead. (Mk 16:5–6)[28]

Prayer for Each Station:
We adore You, O Christ,
and we praise you
because by your holy cross
you have redeemed the world.

---

27. This refers to an extra-biblical story which says that on the way of the cross Veronica wiped the face of Jesus with her veil. The veil was then said to miraculously show the image of Jesus' face and was regarded as a relic in the Middle Ages.

28. This station does not belong to the original devotion but is often added today to complete the story of our salvation.

43. LITURGICAL OBJECTS AND FURNISHINGS

The Church uses a number of objects and furnishings in its worship. This section is best studied in a church. Here is a short description of the most common objects.

The **baptistry**, a pool or font, is usually near the church entrance. Baptism[29] is the means by which one enters the Christian community. In some churches the baptistry is found at the front or on the side.

The **holy water font** reminds us of baptism. On entering a church Catholics dip their hand in the holy water (or the baptistry) and make the sign of the cross[30] to symbolize entering the house of God and the beginning of prayer and worship.

The benches in most American churches are "pews," adopted by Catholics from Protestantism. European churches generally either do not have seats—Christians originally stood for prayer, signifying the resurrection—or have individual, movable chairs. Catholics added kneelers to the back of pews for kneeling. Before sitting a Catholic genuflects (kneels down on the right knee in the direction of the tabernacle and makes the sign of the cross) acknowledging Christ's presence in the reserved sacrament.

A number of prominent objects dominate the front of the church known as the **sanctuary**. First is the **altar-table** where the liturgy of the Eucharist is celebrated. As altar it symbolizes the Mass as sacrifice, and as table it symbolizes the eucharistic meal.[31]

Above the altar or in a prominent place is the **crucifix**—the cross with a corpus (the body of Jesus) upon it. It may represent the suffering Christ, or Christ in glory. It symbolizes our salvation accomplished through Jesus' death on the cross which the Mass makes present throughout time and space. Older churches have a canopy over the altar, a **baldachino**, which prevents debris falling from lofty church ceilings onto the altar.

The altar is decorated with **altar cloths** whose color is appropriate to the season or feast. The church may also be decorated with **banners** or hangings in the liturgical color or with a symbol. **Candles** on the altar or standing next to it signify the light of Christ.

To the left of the altar a **lectern** is central to the liturgy of the word. From it the word of God is proclaimed. Also known as the table of the word, catechumens are invited to learn the Gospel and the faith.

---

29. Truth 76
30. Way 8
31. Older churches may have two altars. The original altar is against the wall. A free-standing altar faces the people—a Vatican II reform reverting to earlier days.

The prominent chair in the sanctuary is the **presidential seat**. From here the presbyter leads the community in prayer and worship. In a cathedral (bishop's church) the place of honor is given to the bishop's seat, from which the word "cathedral" derives. Another seat to the side is used for other presiders. Other seats accommodate acolytes or lectors.

Finally to the side, in a side chapel, or on the old altar, the **tabernacle** reserves the Eucharist for Communion to the sick and private devotion. To the side in the sanctuary or in the back of the church is the **choir** as well as an organ or other instruments. Either behind the sanctuary in another room or perhaps at the back of the church is the **sacristy** where the vestments and other worship materials are kept and where the ministers vest and prepare for worship.

Moving from the key objects to those which may or may not be present, first is the **confessional** or **reconciliation** room—a small room or box where the sacrament of penance[32] is celebrated. Older confessionals usually have a box for the priest flanked by two for penitents. A light above each box tells whether it is occupied. To go to confession, one goes to a box where the middle light is on and one of the side lights shows that confessional vacant. Inside is a prie-dieu (a kneeler with a hand ledge for one person) in front a screen to the priest's box. When ready to hear a confession the priest slides the window open and asks the person to begin. Reconciliation rooms are larger than confessionals and offer the option of anonymity behind a screen, or face to face sitting in a chair opposite the priest. A small table with a Bible and a candle as well as a crucifix on the wall completes the set-up.

A church may have a number of small **side altars** to the left and right of the main altar or along the sides. These are dedicated to a particular saint or devotion and have a statue or picture over it. In the past side altars were used for private Masses. Today they honor the saint. Small candles burning and available nearby are **votive lights**. A person makes a small donation to the church and lights a candle. The candle is a sacramental of the person's prayer—in this case a prayer of action and symbol as well as words. The side walls display the stations of the cross.[33]

Five primary liturgical books are used in the Church's worship. Scripture readings for sacraments and rituals are collected in the **lectionary** placed upon the lectern. The Gospels may also be in a separate book. The **sacramentary** contains the prayers for celebration of Mass.[34]

---

32. Truth 80
33. Way 42
34. Way 19ff

The book of **rites** includes the celebration of the other sacraments.[35] The **pontifical** includes celebrations proper to a bishop such as ordination[36] or consecration of churches.[37] The daily prayer[38] of the Church is contained in a set of books, the **breviary**. Hymnals or service books used by the people are found in the pews.

Vestments

For official worship the celebrants wear **vestments**, modifications of the Roman garb of the earliest Christians. The **stole** is the sign of priestly office. The priest wears it draped around the neck and shoulders hanging down the front. The deacon drapes his over the left shoulder, slanting across the chest and back and pinned together on the right side. This stole signifies the sacramental office and is always worn for the celebration of the sacraments as well as for other worship.

The foundation garment is an **alb** (Latin for white). Over this is worn a garment like a poncho, called a **chasuble**. The stole is worn under or outside the chasuble. Special ceremonies such as Benediction require a **cope** (a kind of cape).

Other ministers of the Eucharist may also wear vestments. Altar servers are dressed in **cassocks** (a black clerical robe) with a **surplice** (a white blouse) over it, or in an alb. Eucharistic ministers may wear a special robe or a cross.

A bishop has two special signs of his office: the **mitre** or peaked hat, and the **staff** or crosier (symbolic of the shepherd's staff). He also wears a skull cap known as a zuchetta (purple for bishops, red for cardinals, white for the Pope). Otherwise he vests just as a priest does.

Liturgical Objects

Besides the people, certain objects are needed to celebrate Mass. The **chalice** holds the wine and a vessel for the bread. The wine must be free from additives.

When incense is used it is placed, at the proper time, in a **censer** or **thurible**—a bowl attached to a chain which is then swung. An **aspergellum** sprinkles the people with holy water at the entrance rite or to renew baptismal promises.

Benediction employs a **monstrance**—a windowed stand for show-

---

35. Truth 74ff
36. Truth 84
37. Life 41
38. Life 38

ing the host. **Bells** announce the hours and call the people to Mass. On Good Friday a **clapper**—two pieces of wood struck together—substitutes for the bells. **Palm branches**[39] are distributed on Passion Sunday. Saved through the next year they are then burned before Lent to become **ashes**, a sign of repentance on Ash Wednesday.[40]

These objects are called **sacramentals**, for they aid us in opening to God. They may be used in public worship and private devotion. Catholics often have holy water and a crucifix or holy pictures in their homes to remind them of God and aid prayer. Crucifixes or **medals** and **scapulars** are worn as signs of devotion. The rosary is another key sacramental.

TO DEEPEN—

Identify the various objects in your local church.

Take a tour of the church and sacristy.

How do sacramentals help us to pray and worship?

Further Reading:

Chilson, Richard W. *A Lenten Pilgrimage—Dying and Rising in the Lord.* Paulist Press, 1983.

McCarroll, Tolbert. *A Way of the Cross.* Paulist Press, 1985.

O'Dea, Barbara. *Of Fast and Festival: Celebrating Lent and Easter.* Paulist Press, 1982.

---

39. Way 32
40. Way 32

The Life of the Church in the World

What does the Church have to offer our contemporary world? The Catholic Church has reflected upon modern situations and difficulties in the social sphere. Official pronouncements discern the situation and trends. But the Church does not restrict itself to theory; it promotes organizations which interact with the modern world apostolically—putting theory into practice.

44. THE CHURCH IN THE MODERN WORLD

Vatican II's "Church in the Modern World" is the watershed of Catholic social teaching: the capstone toward which papal teaching in the last century led and from which other documents expand and delineate this new attitude. This brief section can not hope to present these social teachings in their completeness. It cites major documents and refers the reader there to their rich analyses and insights.

Rerum Novarum by Pope Leo XIII begins the movement. On the eightieth anniversary of that document Pope Paul VI issued A Call to Action in which he stated:

> The Church, in fact, travels forward with humanity and shares its lot in the setting of history. At the same time that it announces to men the good news of God's love and of salvation in Christ, it clarifies their activity in the light of the Gospel and in this way helps them to correspond to God's plan of love and to realize the fullness of their aspirations.[1]

There is no way in which the Gospel does not have an impact upon human life and history or politics. The Gospel is concerned with this life—not simply with another life or sphere.

Other roadmarks on the way to Vatican Council II are the two encyclicals of Pope John XXIII—**Mater et Magistra** (1960) and **Pacem in Terris** (1963). The first was well received by people both within and outside the Church, but the second with its concern for peace has become a symbol in our world of this quest.

> Men are becoming more and more convinced that disputes which arise between states should not be resolved by recourse to arms, but rather by negotiation.

---

1. A Call to Action, p. 1

We grant indeed that this conviction is chiefly based on the terrible destructive force of modern weapons and a fear of the calamities and frightful destruction which such weapons would cause. Therefore, in an age such as ours which prides itself on its atomic energy it is contrary to reason to hold that war is now a suitable way to restore rights which have been violated.[2]

Here is the beginning of the current Catholic reassessment of the traditional doctrine of just war (that war is justified to protect one's country). In the light of nuclear proliferation this issue was discussed throughout succeeding years by the council, by Popes, and most recently by the American bishops' pastoral letter on the arms race.

The Church in the Modern World (1965) articulates the Church's vision of how it is to relate to the world.

Christ, to be sure, gave his Church no proper mission in the political, economic, or social order. The purpose which he set before it is a religious one. But out of this religious mission itself come a function, a light, and an energy which can serve to structure and consolidate the human community according to the divine law. As a matter of fact, when circumstances of time and place create the need, it can and indeed should initiate activities on behalf of all men. This is particularly true of activities designed for the needy, such as the works of mercy and similar undertakings.

The Church further recognizes that worthy elements are found in today's social movements, especially an evolution toward unity, a process of wholesome socialization and association in civic and economic realms. . . .

Thus it shows the world that an authentic union, social and external, results from a union of minds and hearts, namely, from that faith and charity by which its own unity is firmly rooted in the Holy Spirit. For the force which the Church can inject into the modern society of man consists in that faith and charity put into vital practice, not in any external dominion exercised by merely human means.[3]

---

2. Pacem in Terris, pp. 126–27
3. The Church in the Modern World, p. 42

Pope Paul VI continued the tradition of social teachings, most significantly in his encyclical **Progressio Populorum** (1967). Here he provides the correct Catholic understanding of peace as development:

> Excessive economic, social and cultural inequalities among peoples arouse tensions and conflicts, and are a danger to peace. As we said to the fathers of the council when we returned from our journey of peace to the United Nations: "The condition of the peoples in process of development ought to be the object of our consideration; or better: our charity for the poor in the world—and there are multitudes of them—must become more considerate, more active, more generous." To wage war on misery and to struggle against injustice is to promote, along with improved conditions, the human and spiritual progress of all men, and therefore the common good of humanity. Peace cannot be limited to a mere absence of war, the result of an ever precarious balance of forces. No, peace is something that is built up day after day, in the pursuit of an order intended by God, which implies a more perfect form of justice among men.
> . . . Some would consider such hope utopian. It may be that these persons are not realistic enough, and that they have not perceived the dynamism of a world which desires to live more fraternally—a world which, in spite of its ignorance, its mistakes and even its sins, its relapses into barbarism and its wanderings far from the road of salvation, is, even unawares, taking slow but sure steps toward its Creator. This road toward a greater humanity requires effort and sacrifice, but suffering itself, accepted for the love of our brethren, favors the progress of the entire human family. Christians know that union with the sacrifice of our Savior contributes to the building up of the body of Christ in its plenitude, the assembled people of God.[4]

Pope John Paul II has continued and is deepening this strand of social teaching. He has issued two encyclicals which address this area. **Redemptor Hominis** is rather general in tone and sets up the Catholic understanding of human nature and of our task in this world.

---

4. Progressio Populorum, pp. 76, 79

We all know well that the areas of misery and hunger on our globe could have been made fertile in a short time, if the gigantic investments for armaments at the service of war and destruction had been changed into investments for food at the service of life.[5]

Laborem Exercens addresses the problems of workers. The Pope takes a stance between capitalism which values property primarily and communism which values the state or group primarily. Catholicism instead places primary value upon the individual and seeks that each person attain the rights and opportunities granted because of our basic humanity.

The U.S. bishops have also considered current social problems. The Appalachian bishops issued a beautiful-poetic, yet forceful letter on the economic and social problems of their area brought on by the corporations, entitled **This Land Is Home to Me**. More recently the American bishops have issued two pastoral letters, on the nuclear arms race and on the American economy, inviting Catholics and other people to consider these issues in dialogue and to work for solutions that are humane and in the light of Christ.

Why do we address these matters fraught with such complexity, controversy and passion? We speak as pastors, not politicians. We are teachers, not technicians. We cannot avoid our responsibility to lift up the moral dimensions of the choices before our world and nation. The nuclear age is an era of moral as well as physical danger. We are the first generation since Genesis with the power to threaten the created order. We cannot remain silent in the face of such danger. Why do we address these issues? We are simply trying to live up to the call of Jesus to be peacemakers in our own time and situation. What are we saying? Fundamentally, we are saying that the decisions about nuclear weapons are among the most pressing moral questions of our age. While these decisions have obvious military and political aspects, they involve fundamental moral choices. In simple terms, we are saying that good ends (defending one's country, protecting freedom, etc) cannot justify immoral means (the use of weapons which kill indiscri-

---

5. Redemptor Hominis

minately and threaten whole societies). We fear that our world
and nation are headed in the wrong direction. More weapons
with greater destructive potential are produced every day.
More and more nations are seeking to become nuclear powers. In our quest for more and more security we fear that we
are actually becoming less and less secure.[6]

The Latin American bishops spearhead the Church's social teachings today. One of the most economically and socially depressed in the
world, the Church is finding a new voice in solidarity with the poor.
The bishops statements at **Puebla** and **Medellín** spurred the growth of
Liberation thought and action not only in Latin America but elsewhere.
Pope John Paul II is considered to have deepened his own thought as
themes discovered on his trip to the bishops' conference in Mexico surface in his teachings.

For our authentic liberation, all of us need a profound conversion so that "the kingdom of justice, love and peace" might
come to us. The origin of all disdain for mankind, of all injustice, should be sought in the internal imbalance of human liberty, which will always need to be rectified in history. The
uniqueness of the Christian message does not so much consist
in the affirmation of the necessity for structural change, as it
does in the insistence on the conversion of men which will in
turn bring about this change. We will not have a new continent without new and reformed structures, but, above all,
there will be no new continent without new men, who know
how to be truly free and responsible according to light of the
Gospel.[7]

Some theologians of liberation have been questioned by Rome.
However, it is not liberation itself which is controversial. The concepts
of revolution or ideas borrowed from Marxism are what the Church criticizes.

Christ Jesus, although he was rich, became poor in order to
make us rich by means of his poverty. St. Paul is speaking here
of the mystery of the incarnation of the eternal Son, who came

---

6. The Challenge of Peace
7. Medellín Conference—Justice, p. 3

to take on mortal human nature in order to save man from the misery into which sin had plunged him. Christ chose a state of poverty and deprivation in order to show in what consists the true wealth which ought to be sought, that of communion of life with God. He taught detachment from earthly riches so that we might desire the riches of heaven. The apostles whom he chose also had to leave all things and share his deprivation. . . .

It is this sort of poverty, made up of detachment, trust in God, sobriety and a readiness to share, that Jesus declared blessed. But Jesus not only brought the grace and peace of God; he also healed innumerable sick people; he had compassion on the crowd who had nothing to eat and he fed them; with the disciples who followed him he practiced almsgiving. Therefore the beatitude of poverty which he proclaimed can never signify that Christians are permitted to ignore the poor, who lack what is necessary for human life in this world. This poverty is the result and consequence of people's sin and natural frailty, and it is an evil from which human beings must be freed as completely as possible.

In its various forms—material deprivation, unjust oppression, physical and psychological illnesses, and finally death—human misery is the obvious sign of the natural condition of weakness in which man finds himself since original sin and the sign of his need for salvation. Hence it drew the compassion of Christ the Savior to take it upon himself and to be identified with the least of his brethren. Hence also those who are oppressed by poverty are the object of a love of preference on the part of the Church, which, since its origin and in spite of the failings of many of its members, has not ceased to work for their relief, defense and liberation. It has done this through numberless works of charity which remain always and everywhere indispensable. In addition, through its social doctrine which it strives to apply, it has sought to promote structural changes in society so as to secure conditions of life worthy of the human person. . . .

In loving the poor, the Church also witnesses to man's dignity. It clearly affirms that man is worth more for what he is than for what he has. It bears witness to the fact that this dignity cannot be destroyed, whatever the situation of poverty, scorn, rejection or powerlessness to which a human being has been reduced. It shows its solidarity with those who do not count in a society by which they are rejected spiritually and sometimes even physically. . . .

The special option for the poor, far from being a sign of particularism or sectarianism, manifests the universality of the Church's being and mission. This option excludes no one.[8]

45. CATHOLIC SOCIAL ACTION

A great number of Catholic institutions and individuals are involved in the social ministries. **Religious communities** are committed to apostolates to the poor, the imprisoned, the sick. They are significantly involved in education. When white Catholics left the inner city, the churches often remained behind to provide education and services for the urban poor.

The **Catholic Worker**, founded by Dorothy Day[9] and Peter Maurin, deserves special mention for its presence in the Bowery and elsewhere, feeding and caring for the outcast. In India Mother Teresa and her **Missioners of Charity** are only one of many groups which work with the abandoned and untouchable.

Some communities have lay people such as the **Jesuit** and **Maryknoll Volunteers** who give a few years of their life to the poor. Finally, Church agencies such as **Catholic Charities**, and **Catholic Relief Services** channel money and service to the local and world community.

Many Catholics engage in their own apostolate to their sisters and brothers through community action and Church organizations such as the **Vincent de Paul Society**[10] or larger organizations such as Oxfam and Bread for the World. We cannot consider ourselves to be fully Christian if our lives do not in some way reach out to those who are poor and in need.

TO DEEPEN—

Study one of the Church's social documents in detail to see how the social teachings flow from Christ.

What is the apex of modern Catholic social teaching?

Should the Church be concerned about liberation of peoples? Why or why not?

---

8. Instruction on Christian Freedom and Liberation, pp. 66–68
9. Life 13
10. Life 34

Talk to Catholics involved in social action. How do they see their role? What do they do?

Join in some social justice activity. How does this activity deepen your understanding and appreciation for Jesus and his message?

Further reading:

American Bishops. *The Challenge of Peace.* USCC, 1983.

American Bishops. *Catholic Social Teaching and the U.S. Economy.* USCC, 1986.

Baum, Gregory. *The Priority of Labor: A Commentary on "Laborem Exercens" of John Paul II.* Paulist Press, 1983.

Hanks, Thomas. *Oppression, Poverty and Liberation: Biblical Reflections.* Orbis, 1983.

Haughey, John C. ed. *Faith That Does Justice: Examining the Christian Sources for Social Change.* Paulist Press, 1977.

Hollenbach, David. *Claims in Conflict: Retrieving and Renewing the Catholic Human Rights Tradition.* Paulist Press, 1979.

McGinnis, James B. *Bread and Justice.* Paulist Press, 1979.

O'Brien, David & Shannon, Thomas, eds. *Renewing the Earth—Catholic Documents on Peace, Justice and Liberation.* Doubleday, 1977.

Simon, Arthur. *Bread for the World.* Paulist Press, 1984.

Treacy, William. *Biblical Meditations on Peace.* Sheed & Ward, 1985.

◊

Life in the Kingdom

With this section we reach the ultimate: life in the kingdom of God. First the saints show forth Christ's kingdom. Then, the beatitudes are keys opening onto the kingdom. And finally the kingdom is built through our love and service of God and neighbor.

46. The Saints

The Cult of the Saints

Aspects of the kingdom are revealed through people who shine Christ's light upon their age, Church and world. The Church declares such people saints, offering them as models for Christian living.

Devotion to the saints begins in the age of martyrdom.[1] The martyrs were regarded differently from other deceased Christians. While the faithful prayed for the deceased, they venerated and rejoiced in the martyrs. Their tombs, the bodies and bones (called relics) became altars upon which Mass was celebrated.

Later other Christian exemplars were honored by a public cult within the Church. The lives of holy men and women inspired the faithful who honored them by asking for their prayers and venerated their relics praying for healing and intercession.

As these exemplars multiplied, the Church came to rely upon the Pope to determine whether a person was worthy of being honored as a saint. The Pope proclaims a person a saint—part of God's kingdom—and worthy of imitation and honor. With time a process developed to investigate the person's words and works, advancing their cause toward canonization (the declaration that the person is a saint). In addition, the process demands miracles attributed to the person as signs of God's favor. This procedure is argued in court where a prosecutor, the devil's advocate, attempts to discredit the person.

In a favorable outcome the person is first declared "venerable," allowing veneration by a certain group. The next step is "blessed": the person is allowed veneration by the Church, but the cult is restricted to a city, diocese, region, or religious family. Only these are allowed to use the special prayer, Mass and divine office.

Finally if signs (including more miracles) show the person's influence and inspiration extending to the entire Church, the person is canonized, again by the Pope. At this point the person is designated a saint: the Church declares this person worthy of imitation and honor, an exemplary Christian, and in God's company. Relics may be venerated, a Mass and office is instituted, and prayers may be addressed to the saint asking his or her intercession with God.

---

1. Life 29–30

Place of the Saints

Canonized saints are placed before the entire Church as worthy of emulation and veneration. The saints are invoked and asked to intercede with Christ both privately and publicly in the Church. While this is Catholic teaching, the practical place of the saints in a Catholic's life depends upon the piety of the age and individual. While all Catholics acknowledge the saints as models of Christian excellence and believe in their intercessions, the degree to which saints play a significant part in one's spiritual life may vary. Today devotion to the saints is not as prevalent as before Vatican II.

Catholics do not worship saints—only God is deserving of worship. Further the saints do not in any way detract from Christ's saving work. Their glory is Christ's. "It is not I who live, but Christ who lives in me."[2] The saint incarnates that glory in a particular life which inspires others. Asking the saints to intercede does not imply that they have any blessing of their own to bestow, but only that their life displayed an eagerness for the kingdom which well disposes them to aid our cause with God. The saint also manifests some particular aspect of grace. Other settings shine with other facets. Only Jesus Christ manifests the full glory.

Catholics are encouraged to adopt as patrons saints who appeal to and inspire them. Practices include asking the saint for prayers, veneration of the saint's relics, keeping the saint's feast day, bringing flowers to his or her statue, and engaging in prayers and devotions centered upon the saint and his or her cause.

Catholics customarily name their children after saints. This custom at one time became law to insure that children were not named after pagan gods or irreverent names. Adults becoming Christians choose a new, Christian name honoring a saint who manifests qualities that have drawn them to Christ.

Saints are also patrons of people and places. Churches are named after a saint who is the patron of that parish. Countries have patron saints; the United States is under the patronage of the immaculate conception[3] of Mary, Ireland under Patrick, Italy under Joseph. There are patrons of special groups: Joseph for laborers, Thomas Aquinas for students, the Curé d'Ars (John Vianney) for pastors, and patrons of particular predicaments such as Jude for lost causes.

---

2. Gal 2:20
3. Truth 41

The Communion of the Church's Saints:
Biblical Saints

The earliest saints are found in Scripture. The Church does not customarily address Old Testament figures as saints, although popular piety has done so: thus St. David[4] was popular in the Middle Ages.

Mary, Jesus' Mother, is unique among the saints. While the other saints deserve dulia or veneration, Mary alone deserves hyperdulia in the light of her pre-eminent position as the Mother of God.[5] Other saints in Jesus' immediate family are Joseph, patron of the Universal Church (March 19 and May 1), and Joachim and Anne (July 26), Mary's father and mother (known by tradition). Other New Testament figures include John the Baptist (June 24[6] and August 29, his beheading[7]), Mary Magdalene[8] (July 22) and Martha[9] (July 29).

The four evangelists and the apostles comprise special groups:

Evangelists[10]
    Mark (April 25)
    Matthew (September 21)
    Luke (October 18)
    John (December 27)
Apostles[11]
    Phillip and James (May 3)[12]
    Matthias (May 14)[13]
    Barnabas (June 11)[14]
    Peter and Paul (June 29)
        Conversion of Paul (January 25)[15]
        Chair of Peter (February 22)
    Thomas (July 3)[16]
    James (July 25)[17]

---

4. Truth 11
5. Truth 31, 41
6. Mt 3:1–12; Truth 16
7. Mt 14:3–12
8. Lk 8:2; Mt 28:9
9. Jn 11:5
10. Truth 14
11. Truth 22
12. Mt 10:3; Jn 14:8
13. Acts 1:26
14. Acts 9:26–27; 13:1—14:28
15. Acts 9:1–19
16. Jn 20:24–29
17. Mt 4:21; 17:1; Acts 12:2

Bartholomew (August 24)[18]
Simon and Jude (October 28)[19]
Andrew (November 30)[20]

Martyrs

Beginning in the New Testament martyrs comprise the primary category in the early Church, and possibly the largest group in general. They witness to Christ by shedding their blood. Martyrdom itself is sufficient for sanctification.

The Church has had to downplay the quest for martyrdom. The Church turned from fleeing the world to redeeming the world. The first martyr is Stephen (December 26).[21] The Holy Innocents (December 28)[22] are martyrs because of their role in Christ's life. The Church does not regard other baptized children who die as saints, for although they are assuredly with God they did not have the opportunity to exhibit sanctity and so are not models of Christian living.

Other martyrs include Lawrence (August 10) who when roasted over a fire joked with his tormentors, saying that he was done on one side. Lucy (December 13) was blinded and may be legendary since her name means "light." Modern witnesses include Thomas More (June 22), Henry VIII's chancellor who honored his king, but honored God first. Thomas Becket (December 29) shed his blood to uphold the separation of Church and state in an earlier England. And Charles Lwanga (June 3) was one of twenty-two Ugandan youths who refused to give in to the sexual demands of the Bagandan ruler.

Bishops

Later New Testament writings speak of bishops. Timothy[23] and Titus[24] (January 26—the feast next to Paul's conversion) were placed over communities that Paul had established. Only those taught and sent by Jesus were apostles (again with the exception of Paul). Bishops succeeded the apostles, and prominent among these were:

Justin Martyr (June 1)
Irenaeus of Lyons (June 28)

---

18. Mt 10:3
19. Mt 13:55
20. Mt 4:18; Way 29
21. Acts 6:5—7:59
22. Mt 2:16–18
23. Acts 16:1–4; 1 Tim 4:14
24. Tit 1:4

Ignatius of Antioch (October 17)
Clement I (November 23)

Missionaries

As the Church moved into the Roman empire and beyond, missionaries carried the faith, beginning with Paul. Others included Augustine of Canterbury (May 27) to England, Boniface (June 5) to Germany, Stanislaus (April 11) to Poland, Francis Xavier (December 3) to Japan, and Isaac Jogues (October 19) and others (including Junipero Serra in California whose cause is being advanced in Rome) to America.

Doctors

Others are teachers and honored as doctors of the Church. Until recently this group included only men, but Paul VI elevated a number of women to the rank of doctor, including Teresa of Avila and Catherine of Siena.

Basil the Great and Gregory Nazianzen (January 2)[25]
Francis de Sales (January 24)[26]
Thomas Aquinas (January 28)[27]
Anselm (April 21)[28]
Catherine of Siena (April 29)[29]
Athanasius (May 2)[30]
Venerable Bede (May 25)
Anthony of Padua (June 13)
Bonaventure (July 15)[31]
Cyril of Alexandria (June 27)
Alphonsus Liguori (August 1)[32]
Bernard (August 20)[33]
Augustine (August 28)[34]
Gregory the Great (September 3)[35]

---

25. Life 31
26. Life 35
27. Life 33
28. Life 33
29. Life 33
30. Life 30
31. Life 33
32. Life 35
33. Life 33
34. Life 31
35. Life 31

John Chrysostom (September 13)[36]
Jerome (September 30)[37]
Teresa of Avila (October 15)[38]
Leo the Great (November 10)
Albert the Great (November 15)[39]
Ambrose (December 7)[40]
John of the Cross (December 14)[41]

Religious and Clerics

The Church honors saints who were abbots such as Antony (January 17)[42] and Benedict (July 11),[43] as well as bishops such as Nicolas (December 6—the original Santa Claus) and Martin of Tours (November 11). Priests include Philip Neri (May 26),[44] Ignatius of Loyola (July 31),[45] Dominic (August 8)[46] and Vincent de Paul (September 27). Among religious are Bridget (July 23), Elizabeth of Hungary (November 17) who although the daughter of a king became a nun and served the poor in a hospital she founded, and Jane Frances de Chantal (December 12) who with Francis de Sales[47] founded the Visitation Sisters.

Virgins

Religious women also are known as virgins. St. Clare (August 11), the friend of Francis of Assisi, founded the Second Order of Franciscans—the Poor Clares. Rose of Lima (August 23) was the first canonized saint of the Americas and through her work with the homeless poor instituted the first social services in Peru. Theresa of the Child Jesus—the Little Flower (October 1)—is the patroness of missions because although she never left the convent her prayer and suffering were offered up for those who might be converted.

---

36. Life 31
37. Life 31
38. Life 34
39. Life 33
40. Life 31
41. Life 34
42. Life 31
43. Life 31
44. Life 34
45. Life 34
46. Life 33
47. Life 35

Angels

Although technically not saints since they are not human, the angels are honored like saints in the Catholic tradition. Catholics honor guardian angels (October 2) who watch over and protect us. Michael[48] the archangel led the victorious war in heaven against Satan. Gabriel[49] announced the good news to Mary that she would bear Jesus. And Raphael[50] accompanied Tobias on his journeys.[51] These three are commemorated on September 29.[52]

American Saints

Although relatively new, our country has produced saints. John Neumann (January 5) coming from Czechoslovakia became the bishop of Philadelphia where he reorganized the parochial school system and increased the students twenty-fold. A native of Spain, the Jesuit Peter Clavier (September 9) devoted himself to work among the slaves of America. As soon as a boat arrived from Africa he went aboard with medicine and food and he instructed and baptized over 300,000 slaves. Frances Cabrini (November 13), the first U.S. citizen to be canonized, came here to work with Italian immigrants and founded sixty-seven institutions caring for the poor. Mother Elizabeth Seton (June 4), the first natural-born U.S. citizen canonized, was a widow who founded a religious order to teach Catholic children and pioneered the revolutionary idea of a totally free school for the poor.

TO DEEPEN—

Pick one of the saints and read his or her life. How does that life reflect the glory of Christ?

Does a Catholic have to pray to the saints?

How does Mary differ from the other saints?

Perhaps you bear a saint's name. If so, look up the saint and find out who he or she was and what day he or she is celebrated?

---

48. Rev 12:7–9
49. Truth 15
50. Truth 20
51. Tob 5:5ff
52. Life 39

Further Reading:

Butler. *Lives of the Saints*. Christian Classics, 1962. This is the classic reference in four volumes.

Delaney, John J. *Pocket Dictionary of the Saints*. Doubleday, 1983.

McGinley, Phyllis. *Saint Watching*. Thomas More, 1982. A wonderful book by a modern poet.

Penguin Dictionary of Saints. Penguin Books, 1965.

Walsh, Michael, ed. *Butler's Lives of the Saints*, concise edition. Harper and Row, 1985.

TO CONTINUE—

Many of the saints are described in the history of the Church (Life 29ff)

47. The Beatitudes

Seeing the crowds, Jesus went up on the mountain, and when he sat down his disciples came to him. And he opened his mouth and taught them, saying:

Blessed are the poor in spirit, for theirs is the kingdom of heaven.

Blessed are those who mourn, for they shall be comforted.

Blessed are the meek, for they shall inherit the earth.

Blessed are those who hunger and thirst for righteousness, for they shall be satisfied.

Blessed are the merciful, for they shall obtain mercy.

Blessed are the pure in heart, for they shall see God.

Blessed are the peacemakers, for they shall be called sons of God.

Blessed are those who are persecuted for righteousness' sake, for theirs is the kingdom of heaven.

Blessed are you when men revile you and persecute you and utter all kinds of evil against you falsely on my account. Rejoice and be glad, for your reward is great in heaven, for so men persecuted the prophets who were before you.

The beatitudes describe life lived in and for God's kingdom. They are cherished by all Christians, but they reveal their depth only to those capable of appreciating them.

The beatitudes are not easy to understand. They do not reveal themselves at first glance. Some may remain hidden mysteries no matter how hard we try. Yet if we wrestle with them, seeking to understand them, if we use them to cast a light in our life and point us toward the kingdom, they become immensely valuable keys which transform us so that the kingdom becomes known. Although they are the common treasure of the entire Christian community, they only open fully to those few ready to receive their message, which goes quite contrary to the world and its ways.

Seeing the crowds, he went up on the mountain, and when he sat down his disciples came to him. And he opened his mouth and taught them, saying:

In this introduction Matthew is ambivalent about the audience addressed. Jesus seems to address the crowd. But he gathers his disciples around him and then teaches. Could not this intimate that the teaching was only for the disciples, for those committed to the kingdom way? Indeed these high teachings do not primarily apply to the average person, but more to the disciple willing to risk all for the kingdom.

Blessed are the poor in spirit, for theirs is the kingdom of heaven.

This beatitude differs from its equivalent in Luke's Gospel.[1] Luke says baldly: "Blessed are the poor." Luke's version may be closer to the original. Perhaps Matthew's community was no longer composed primarily of the poor. Thus it was necessary to view this beatitude in a new light: blessed are the poor in spirit.

But this phrase "the poor in spirit" is purposely ambiguous. Just what does it mean? Throughout Christian history people have argued its meaning, from the original of being physically impoverished, to an impoverishment (loss) of self.

Furthermore, its present context sets it off from the other beatitudes. This first, and the last Beatitude, alone promise a present outcome. "Blessed are the poor in spirit, for theirs *is* the kingdom of heaven." The others offer a future beatitude: "they shall be comforted," "they shall see God," etc. These two might be overall descriptions of beatitude whereas those in between describe the various components which make up the "poor in spirit." Being poor in spirit might mean to be mournful, meek, hungry for righteousness' sake, etc.

Blessed are those who mourn, for they shall be comforted.

The second beatitude addresses our emotional nature. Emotion forms a part of our true wholeness. The perfect person is not without emotions. Rather the full person's emotional life is in balance. The emotions serve their proper function.

For most people, emotion is warped. It may be suppressed altogether as in many males, since the society does not allow men to display emotion. Or it may be inappropriate, out of proportion to what evokes it. Hatred is much greater and more consuming than the anger which triggered it.

Ideally emotion moves things; the word comes from the idea of motion. If something or someone is aggravating, anger alerts the other to the irritation and hopefully corrects the situation. If the emotion fails to do this or if it results in overkill, it is out of alignment and needs healing.

1. Lk 6:20

This beatitude also points out the need to deal with and to confront sorrow in our life. Many if not most would love to have an emotional life restricted to "positive" emotions. However emotions cannot be separated in this way. To be able to rejoice, one must be able to mourn. And it is precisely mourning that most would avoid. Yet one cannot experience true happiness without going into mourning and finding there comfort.

To experience life in any real depth entails encountering sorrow. The Greeks and Romans characterized life as "lacrimae rerum"—the tears of things. Buddhism's first noble truth claims that existence inevitably leads to suffering—one cannot avoid the insufficiency of existence that leads to mourning. Jesus confronts such sorrow not by avoiding it, or by running away, or by pretending that it does not exist. Such joy bought by denying the intrinsic sorrow in existence is cheap and shallow. True beatitude enters into the sorrow. Only then can one be comforted and move out of the tomb and into the light.

Finally, some mystics speak of the gift of tears. The more we enter into communion with God and realize how God loves us and what God does for us, the more moved we become. Our response to such gracious love is tears—tears of sorrow for the selfishness and sin that we have committed, and tears of joy for the forgiveness that Christ grants us.

Blessed are the meek, for they shall inherit the earth.

Meekness is hardly a virtue that most seek. Indeed many give Christianity a bad name for promoting meekness. But false meekness is not in keeping with this beatitude. Such false meekness is akin to passive-aggressive behavior. The person acts as though meek and without power, but all the while he or she manipulates behind the scenes.

To understand true meekness, consider the result of this beatitude. The meek shall inherit the earth. Now to inherit something there is nothing one has done to achieve the goal. One simply is an heir— born into the right family. And here the inheritance is the earth itself.

In the world, the earth is not actually inherited. First, property, the basis for worldly wealth, must be gained and secured. Thus mankind's industry since the discovery of the notion of property. And this acquisitiveness and cunning used to acquire property has divided up most of the earth today.

But this acquisitiveness extends far beyond accumulation of possessions. It dominates our entire life. In almost all areas we attempt to secure our "illusory" control whether it be over our wealth and property, health, prestige, fame, or loved ones. Our nature is primarily "grasping." And this seems to work—at least to a limited extent, which we in our daydreaming would prefer to see effective over all we wish to control.

But do we have any real control over our lives? Does grasping provide real happiness? The meek are those with no power. They have nothing to grasp, nothing to control. Yet in their powerlessness, in their control over nothing, they are in a position to truly inherit the earth. Are not those who attempt to possess what they in truth cannot possess indeed possessed by their possessiveness. They live a delusion, and beatitude cannot be theirs. Real happiness is a gift, an inheritance. In Jesus Christ we are heirs of the kingdom.

This beatitude is an antidote to our worldly attitude of possessiveness and control. While such tactics may be all right for the game of business, politics and the marketplace, they are disastrous when applied to life itself. Jesus teaches a path which practices surrender, giving up, letting go—in other words, meekness. Only then can one be given all that God wishes to give his heirs.

Blessed are those who hunger and thirst for righteousness, for they shall be satisfied.

This beatitude addresses our appetites, hungers and thirsts. Again these appetites are not evil or sinful, but they are often misdirected. If allowed their true aim, they lead toward satisfaction.

Hungers are misdirected when they aim toward a secondary good in place of the primary good which alone can satisfy. We may come to see our happiness in food, drink, sex, power, or any number of secondary goods. Yet if these drives are successful they do not bring deep satisfaction. Instead they may simply change their object to other secondary goods.

Jesus' path involves rectifying our hungers and thirsts. The Christian fasts not because food is wrong or evil. Rather our appetite for food and drink can easily become all-consuming so that we eat much more than we need (and pick up weight on the side). Or we may hunger and thirst for food which is not beneficial and nurturing—an addiction to junk food. Fasting purifies our hunger. We realize that we do not live for bread alone. Our fast allows our body to train its desires, redirecting them toward nourishing food and away from addictive junk food. In hunger we find solidarity with the poor and find our true hunger in seeking righteousness—justice and equality of the earth's abundance with all God's people.

Only our thirst for God can find true satisfaction. Other thirsts are at best substitutes. The woman at the well[2] seeks love in her many husbands. And she is constantly disappointed, never satisfied. Jesus gives her the living water which quenches all thirst: God and God's justice.

Blessed are the merciful, for they shall obtain mercy.

The previous beatitudes open our eyes to the sinful condition. A natural human response to this sin is indignation, anger, and thoughts of vengeance. In every revolution people rise up in anger toward oppression and wrongs. If successful they rise to the top of the new society, and they quickly secure their position by reimposing the same oppressive conditions on those below. The world can not heal the human condition, for its ways create and maintain that condition.

This beatitude reveals the kingdom response to sin and hurt: not vengeance but mercy. Healing arises through compassion. Jesus heals out of compassion upon the suffering people.[3] He does not look down from some superior position. He enters into their condition, just as he entered into our human condition. Compassion is not pity.

We are called to act from compassion. Jesus asks us to meet hurt and wrong with forgiveness and healing. As God has been merciful to us, he calls us in turn to extend mercy to others. In this way the kingdom enters our sinful world, breaking the chain of oppression.

But if we do not show mercy, mercy cannot be shown us. Our anger breeds more violence which eventually redounds upon us. There is no way out of this vicious circle on the world's terms. Only compassion breaks the circle and allows new life in. Jesus is the sign of God's compassion upon all creation. We who live in Christ are in turn signs of compassion which heals, forgives and allows the kingdom to break into the midst of sin and violence.

Blessed are the pure in heart, for they shall see God.

So far the beatitudes have addressed our emotions, our grasping for power and security, our appetites, our response to others and world. This beatitude focuses upon the inner self, calling us to be pure in heart.

Our hearts are not pure; our loyalties are divided. We have many gods, conflicting interests. Jesus' path journeys toward purity. We seek to make our will God's will. We try to desire only what God desires for us. Soren Kierkegaard says, "Purity of heart is to will one thing": to make our will consonant with God.

---

2. Jn 4:15–19
3. Mk 1:41

Only in such purity will we actually see God. Our divided loyalties do not allow us to see at all. Instead we look in various ways, tinged and distorted by our worldly minds. We do not see God, only the world.

Our seeing may be controlled by the "curious look." Our looking remains on the surface of life. Not seeing deeply, we settle for surface satisfactions and solutions. We fall prey to those who control the curious look—namely advertisers and the media.

Our seeing may be distorted by the "look of pleasure." When this look of pleasure is sexual we view women or men not as persons but as sexual objects to be exploited. When it is focused upon the marketplace we enter the consumer mentality and see only what will supposedly make us happy rather than the price of such luxuries in terms of the third world and the poor.

Our seeing may be distorted by the "ideal look." We see things only in terms of our ideal about them. We are always comparing ourselves to others. We see only in terms of standards and comparisons. We view life exclusively in terms of "more or less," "better or worse." We do not see God's creation, only the rat race in which we compete as we scramble to our ideals. Jesus counsels us to give up judgment. We are incapable of judging well. Simply see and accept what is seen. To compare it to more or less accomplishes nothing and distorts vision.

Surrendering these various looks, we are then able simply to see. And then we perceive not the world, but instead God. When we are caught in the looks, other people may become our enemies, adversaries, competitors, whatever. But when we simply see, then we see in each person Christ's light and encounter Christ in each.

Blessed are the peacemakers, for they shall be called sons of God.

It is not enough to simply see God. Once our hearts are pure, we are ready to undertake Jesus' mission—bringing peace into this troubled, war-torn world.

But this peace must be real. Often what passes for peace is institutionalized violence. Peace maintains the status quo. Such a peace buys rest for the establishment and the wealthy, but at the price of continued oppression and poverty for the lower classes. Pope Paul VI in Progressio Populorum supplied the working Catholic definition: peace is development. It is the opposite of stasis or maintaining the present sinful situation through suppression of any struggle to make things equal.

Only the continuing development of peoples fosters real peace. This development is economic, religious, political, social, and cultural.

And development is hardly a peaceful situation from the worldly point of view since it involves risk, change, newness, and uncertainty. But only in development are people assured a progression toward their true inheritance. As peacemakers Christians are to foster just such development among this world's peoples.

However even defined as development peace is not quite the peace which is of God. Human peace is always a matter of negotiation and compromise. Peace is worked out among the various parties. But God's peace is not negotiated or bargained. God gives peace as a gift. God's word creates peace. "Peace be with you," Jesus tells the disciples.[4]

Christians enjoy God's peace as a gift from Jesus. We have the peace of God now, even though we may not experience its peacefulness in the midst of the world. As peacemakers we are given that peace to in turn offer as a gift that establishes peace. We make peace not with our own notions of peace no matter how spiritual. The only true peace is God's gift to us.

Making peace, we become known as children of God. Carrying out Jesus' mission we share in his relation to God as Son. St. Athanasius said, "In Jesus God became man, so that through Jesus man might become God." This divinization is worked out by entering into God's peacemaking within our interior selves, family, community, society, nation, world. And being called children of God we see how this world shows forth the kingdom where God's children have their dwelling.

Blessed are those who are persecuted for righteousness' sake, for theirs is the kingdom of heaven.

Where does the path of Jesus lead us in this life? What is our lot? Should we become mourners, meek, hungry for righteousness, pure in heart, and peacemakers? There is no question but that such action leads in this world to the same fate Jesus found—persecution.

There can be no accommodation between the kingdom and this world. The Christian Church may and often has accommodated itself to the world. But the world by its very nature is antagonistic toward the kingdom, and therefore toward all true citizens of the kingdom.

In this world the Christian's final destination will always be the cross. At times and places Christians can exist in a relatively secure and comfortable relationship toward the world. But in those situations such as present day America, Christians should also question their involve-

4. Jn 14:27

ment in the world's sin and miseries. To what extent is our ease at the expense of others' suffering and disease? And what would happen should we dissociate from those structures? What happens to those Christians today who speak out against the military-industrial establishment?

> Blessed are you when men revile you and persecute you and utter all kinds of evil against you falsely on my account. Rejoice and be glad, for your reward is great in heaven, for so men persecuted the prophets who were before you.

This final beatitude, which most prefer not to think about, needs no explanation. Finding ourselves in such a situation, the beatitude opens itself to us, providing the comfort and assurance that in spite of our suffering and pain, and in spite of any possible future, we are indeed in God's care, and we are indeed on the very path of Jesus—a path that does not skirt suffering and rejection, but which dares plunge through these worldly realities into the kingdom of heaven where we find our true reward.

TO DEEPEN—

Select a beatitude that particularly speaks or appeals to you or even confuses you. Meditate upon it. Does it reveal itself more deeply? Does it become even more puzzling? How might you put this beatitude into practice in your life?

How do these beatitudes describe the Christian's life?

Read the rest of the Sermon on the Mount which the beatitudes open. How does the sermon throw light on the beatitudes? Do passages in the sermon help you understand the beatitudes?

Do you know of any saints or holy people who show a way to live one or more of the beatitudes concretely? For example, which beatitude would St. Francis of Assisi exemplify?

Further Reading:

Augustine. *On the Beatitudes.* St. Paul Editions, 1961.

Crosby, Michael H. *Spirituality of the Beatitudes—Matthew's Challenge for First World Christians.* Orbis, 1981.

Tugwell, Simon. *The Beatitudes: Soundings in Christian Traditions.* Templegate, 1980.

The Kingdom in the World

Christians, when all is said and done, live their lives for the sake of the kingdom's advent. Augustine sums it up: love God and do what you will. But how that kingdom comes is best described by Jesus in a teaching grounding much of our exploration: love God and love your neighbor. To conclude we examine three texts illuminating Jesus' injunction. The first comes from the liturgy where the praise and love of God is cultivated and celebrated among Christians. The others are from Scripture. However here our usual process is inverted. Whereas before the traditions led the way in our exploration and exposition of Christianity, here these traditions are themselves the end. To comment on them adequately takes us beyond this introductory guide. Meditation upon them sustains the journey beyond in a Christian life.

48. THE LOVE OF GOD

The Te Deum (You, God) is an ancient Latin hymn prayed and usually sung on festive occasions. It is simple praise of God which forms the very foundation for Christian life.

You are God: we praise you;
you are the Lord: we acclaim you;
you are the eternal Father:
all creation worships you.

To you all angels, all the powers of heaven,
Cherubim and Seraphim, sing in endless praise:
Holy, holy, holy, Lord, God of power and might,
heaven and earth are full of your glory.

The glorious company of apostles praise you.
The noble fellowship of prophets praise you.
The white-robed army of martyrs praise you.

Throughout the world the holy Church acclaims you:
Father, of majesty unbounded,
your true and only Son, worthy of all worship,
and the Holy Spirit, advocate and guide.

You, Christ, are the King of glory,
the eternal Son of the Father.

When you became man to set us free
you did not spurn the Virgin's womb.

You overcame the sting of death,
and opened the kingdom of heaven to all believers.

You are seated at God's right hand in glory.
We believe that you will come, and be our judge.

Come then, Lord, and help your people,
bought with the price of your own blood,
and bring us with your saints
to glory everlasting.

49. THE LIFE OF SERVICE

The Christian ideal of service is rooted in Jesus' life. He teaches his disciples to be servants to one another.[1] He himself, the night before his death, acts the role of servant, washing their feet.[2] And one of the earliest Christian descriptions of Jesus, a hymn, speaks of him primarily as servant. Jesus does not call us to become anything other than what he has become for us.

Your attitude must be that of Christ:
Though he was in the form of God,
he did not count equality with God
a thing to be grasped,
but emptied himself, taking the form of a servant,
being born in the likeness of men.
And being found in human form
he humbled himself
and became obedient unto death,
even death on a cross.
Therefore God has highly exalted him
and has bestowed on him the name
which is above every name,
that at the name of Jesus
every knee should bow,
in heaven and on earth and under the earth
and every tongue confess
that Jesus Christ is Lord,
to the glory of God the Father.[3]

---

1. Lk 22:26
2. Jn 13:1–17
3. Phil 2:5–11

50. THE LIFE OF LOVE

The motivation for Christian service is love itself. As John teaches, this love is none other than God.[4] But what is the meaning of love in a world where its definition can range from sex to a soft drink? Again John qualifies the kind of love he means when he says: Greater love than this has no one but that he lay down his life for his friends.[5] And Paul provides a veritable hymn on love which has become the standard Christian definition.

As an introduction to Paul's hymn this passage from Vatican II places love in its Christian context:

> While every activity of the apostolate should find in charity its origin and driving force, certain works are of their nature a most eloquent expression of this charity; and Christ has willed that these should be signs of his messianic mission. . . . [6]
> Today these activities and works of charity have become much more urgent and worldwide, now that means of communication are more rapid, distance between people has been more or less conquered, people in every part of the globe have become as members of a single family. Charitable action today can and should reach all people and all needs. Wherever people are to be found who are in want of food and drink, of clothing, housing, medicine, work, education, the means necessary for leading a truly human life, wherever there are people racked by misfortune or illness, suffering exile or imprisonment, Christian charity should go in search of them and find them out, comfort them with devoted care and give them the helps that will relieve their needs. This obligation binds first and foremost the more affluent individuals and nations.
> If this exercise of charity is to be above all criticism, and seen to be so, one should see in one's neighbor the image of God to which he has been created, and Christ the Lord to whom is really offered all that is given to the needy. The liberty and dignity of the person helped must be respected with the greatest sensitivity. Purity of intention should not be stained by any self-seeking or desire to dominate. The demands of justice must first of all be satisfied; that which is already due in justice

4. 1 Jn 4:16
5. Jn 15:13
6. Cf Mt 11:4–5

is not to be offered as a gift of charity. The cause of evils, and not merely their effects, ought to disappear. The aid contributed should be organized in such a way that beneficiaries are gradually freed from their dependence on others and become self-supporting.[7]

If I speak in the tongues of men and of angels,
but have not love,
I am a noisy gong or a clanging cymbal.
And if I have prophetic powers,
and understand all mysteries and all knowledge,
and if I have all faith, so as to remove mountains,
but have not love,
I am nothing.
If I give away all I have,
and if I deliver my body to be burned,
but have not love,
I gain nothing.
Love is patient and kind;
love is not jealous or boastful;
it is not arrogant or rude.
Love does not insist on its own way;
it is not irritable or resentful;
it does not rejoice at wrong,
but rejoices in the right.
Love bears all things,
believes all things,
hopes all things,
endures all things.
Love never ends;
as for prophecies, they will pass away;
as for tongues, they will cease;
as for knowledge, it will pass away.
For our knowledge is imperfect
and our prophecy is imperfect;
but when the perfect comes,
the imperfect will pass away.

7. Decree on the Apostolate of Lay People, p. 8

When I was a child,
I spoke like a child,
I thought like a child,
I reasoned like a child;
when I became a man,
I gave up childish ways.
For now we see in a mirror dimly,
but then face to face.
Now I know in part;
then I shall understand fully,
even as I have been fully understood.
So faith, hope, love abide,
these three;
but the greatest of these is love.[8]

Charles de Foucauld is an inspiration of service and charity in modern Catholicism. He went to live among the Muslims of North Africa, not to preach or to attempt to convert them, although he saw himself as a missionary. Rather he lived a simple, unassuming life of charity and service to these people. He made not one convert, but who knows how many lives he lit up by God's love? Christians do not take success or failure seriously. It is enough that we are servants of God.[9] We do what we can, hoping that our efforts further rather than impede the coming reign.

Further Reading:

De Sales, Francis. *Treatise on the Love of God.* Greenwood, 1942.
Lewis, C. S. *The Four Loves.* Harcourt Brace Jovanovich, 1960.
Muggeridge, Malcolm. *Something Beautiful for God.* Doubleday, 1977. The story of Mother Teresa of India and her work with the outcast.

---

8. 1 Cor 13:1–12
9. Lk 17:10

EPILOGUE

While Paul might wish the last word, that honor, like the first word, is reserved to John. This book merely gives a roadmap of the Christian tradition—Catholic style. It indicates directions where one's understanding can be further nurtured. It began with an introduction to the good news from John. It ends like that Gospel:

> But there are also many other things which Jesus did; were every one of them to be written, I suppose that the world itself could not contain the books that would be written.[10]

---

10. Jn 21:25

Scripture Index

Subject Index